T0213975

Refinement

John Derrick · Eerke Boiten

Refinement

Semantics, Languages and Applications

 Springer

John Derrick
Department of Computer Science
University of Sheffield
Sheffield, UK

Eerke Boiten
School of Computer Science
  and Informatics
De Montfort University
Leicester, Leicestershire, UK

ISBN 978-3-030-06497-6   ISBN 978-3-319-92711-4   (eBook)
https://doi.org/10.1007/978-3-319-92711-4

This Springer imprint is published by the registered company Springer Nature Switzerland AG
The registered company address is: Gewerbestrasse 11, 6330 Cham, Switzerland

To our families:
  Michelle and Bea;
  Gwen, Sara, Ivor, Rowan and Sam.

Contents

Part I Semantics

1 Labeled Transition Systems and Their Refinement 3
   1.1   Introduction 3
   1.2   Labelled Transition Systems – A Simple Model
        of Computation. 4
   1.3   Trace Refinement 7
   1.4   Completed Trace Refinement. 11
   1.5   Failures Refinement 12
   1.6   Readiness Refinement 16
   1.7   Failure Trace Refinement 17
   1.8   Ready Trace Refinement 18
   1.9   Conformance and Extension 18
   1.10 Data and Infinite Traces 21
        1.10.1   Adding Data 21
        1.10.2   Infinite Trace Refinement 22
        1.10.3   Infinite Completed Trace Refinement. 23
   1.11 Summary 23
   1.12 Bibliographical Notes 24
   References 26

2 Automata - Introducing Simulations 27
   2.1   Introduction 27
   2.2   Refinement and Simulations 29
        2.2.1   Forward and Backward Simulations. 30
        2.2.2   Completeness Results 34
   2.3   Bisimulation 36
   2.4   Bibliographical Notes 37
   References 38

3   Simple State-Based Refinement   39
   3.1   Introduction   39
   3.2   A Basic Model with Refinement   40
   3.3   Termination and Refinement   41
   3.4   More than One Observation.   42
   3.5   Towards Total Correctness   43
   3.6   Observations Including Initial States   44
   3.7   State Abstraction.   45
   3.8   State Variables and Observation   47
   3.9   Programs and Labeled Transitions   48
   3.10   Bibliographical Notes   49
   References   49

4   A Relational View of Refinement   51
   4.1   Introduction   52
   4.2   Relational Data Types   53
   4.3   Relational Refinement   55
   4.4   From a Theory of Total Relational Refinement to Partial
       Relational Refinement   59
       4.4.1   Partial Relations and Their Totalisation   59
       4.4.2   Simulation Rules   62
       4.4.3   Completeness of Partial Relational Simulations   63
       4.4.4   A Fully Partial Relational Theory   65
   4.5   Bibliographical Notes   66
   References   67

5   Perspicuity, Divergence, and Internal Operations   69
   5.1   Perspicuous Operations   70
   5.2   Error Behaviour: Catastrophic or Not?   72
   5.3   Divergence   73
   5.4   Internal Operations   75
       5.4.1   Internal Operations and Choice in LTS   76
       5.4.2   Internal Actions in a Relational Context   78
       5.4.3   Divergence from Internal Operations   79
   5.5   Bibliographical Notes   80
   References   80

Part II   Refinement in Specification Languages

6   Process Algebra   85
   6.1   CSP - The Language.   85
       6.1.1   Sequential Operators.   86
       6.1.2   Building Concurrent Specifications   89

6.2 CSP - The Semantics 93
  6.2.1 The CSP Failures Model 96
  6.2.2 The CSP Failures, Divergences and Infinite
      Traces Semantics 100
6.3 CSP - Refinement 104
  6.3.1 Trace Refinement 105
  6.3.2 Stable Failures Refinement 106
  6.3.3 FDI Refinement 107
6.4 LOTOS - Language, Semantics and Refinement 108
  6.4.1 The LOTOS Language 108
  6.4.2 LOTOS Semantics and Refinement 110
6.5 CCS - Language, Semantics and Refinement 114
  6.5.1 The CCS Language 114
  6.5.2 CCS Semantics and Refinement 116
6.6 Bibliographical Notes 119
References 120

7 State-Based Languages: Z and B 121
7.1 Z - The Language 121
  7.1.1 Using Schemas 122
  7.1.2 The Z Schema Calculus 124
7.2 Z – Refinement 126
  7.2.1 The Relational Semantics of a Z Specification 126
  7.2.2 Data Refinement and Simulations for Z 127
  7.2.3 Z Refinement in Practice 130
7.3 The B-Method 135
  7.3.1 Machine Consistency 137
7.4 Refinement in the B-Method 139
  7.4.1 Proof Obligations for Refinement 141
  7.4.2 Implementation Machines 143
7.5 Bibliographical Notes 144
References 145

8 State-Based Languages: Event-B and ASM 149
8.1 Event-B 149
  8.1.1 Specifying Machines in Event-B 150
  8.1.2 Proof Obligations for Event-B Machines 151
8.2 Refinement in Event-B 152
  8.2.1 A Relational Semantics for Event-B 154
  8.2.2 Data Refinement and Simulations for Event-B 158
8.3 ASM 168
  8.3.1 ASM Semantics and ASM Refinement 169
8.4 Bibliographical Notes 174
References 176

Part III   Relating Notions of Refinement

9   Relational Concurrent Refinement 179
   9.1   Introduction 179
   9.2   Background 180
   9.3   Relating Process Algebraic and Relational Refinement 181
         9.3.1   Trace Refinement 183
         9.3.2   Completed Trace Refinement 185
         9.3.3   Failure Refinement 188
         9.3.4   Failure Trace Refinement 189
         9.3.5   Extension and Conformance 190
   9.4   Relating Data Refinement to Process Algebraic Refinement.... 192
         9.4.1   Non-blocking Data Refinement and the
                 Traces-Divergences Semantics.................. 194
         9.4.2   Blocking Data Refinement and the Singleton
                 Failures Semantics 195
   9.5   Relating Automata and Relational Refinement 196
         9.5.1   IO Automata 197
   9.6   Internal Events and Divergence 201
   9.7   Bibliographical Notes 202
   References 204

**10   Relating Data Refinement and Failures-Divergences
     Refinement** 207
   10.1   Introduction 207
   10.2   The Basic Relational Embedding 207
   10.3   Dealing with Input and Output 211
          10.3.1   Defining the Extended Finalisation 212
          10.3.2   Deriving the New Simulation Rules............... 214
          10.3.3   An Example................................ 223
   10.4   Summary of Simulation Conditions 226
          10.4.1   Discussion 228
   10.5   Bibliographical Notes 231
   References 232

**11   Process Data Types - A Fully General Model of Concurrent
     Refinement** 235
   11.1   Introduction 235
   11.2   A Relational ADT with Divergence and Blocking 237
          11.2.1   Forward Simulation for Process Data Types........ 239
          11.2.2   Backward Simulation for Process Data Types 241
          11.2.3   Simulations on Process Data Types and Basic
                   Data Types 243

11.3   Using Process Data Types – Failures-Divergences
        Refinement with Internal Operations and Divergence   243
        11.3.1 Embedding a Basic Data Type with Internal
                Operations into a Process Data Type   243
        11.3.2 Correctness of the Embedding: Blocking
                Approach.   246
        11.3.3 Simulations in the Blocking Approach.   248
        11.3.4 The Non-blocking Approach   251
11.4   Adding in a Consideration of Outputs   254
        11.4.1 Refinement Conditions for Output Embeddings   254
        11.4.2 Outputs in the Blocking Approach   255
        11.4.3 Outputs in the Non-blocking Approach   258
11.5   Summary   261
11.6   Bibliographical Notes   261
References   261

12 Conclusions   263
    References   267

Motivation

Part I

Refinement is the process of moving from an abstract description to one that is more concrete. The fact that we start with an *abstract* description leads to two central aspects of refinement. Firstly, being abstract often means that not all the implementation details are pinned down, and we will be able to make some specific choices as part of the refinement process. This is known as the *reduction of non-determinism.*

Example 0.1. For example, suppose you were told to draw a Queen of Hearts playing card, then this description leaves you quite a lot of leeway in what you draw. An *implementation* of this specification would allow you to choose just about any picture to actually draw. This is perfectly acceptable, the specification contains a lot of *non-determinism* in its description, and as part of the implementation process you are allowed to reduce this non-determinism. This is a key tenet of refinement—the reduction of non-determinism. We will meet it in many guises in this book. □

Secondly, being abstract often means that there are internal details that are just not visible, such as mechanisms that are more concerned with *how* a goal is to be achieved than with *what* is to be achieved. These details are not necessary in order to understand the abstract functioning of the system, and one can change them in a refinement as long as the *observable behaviour is consistent.*

Example 0.2. For example, suppose you were told to implement a program to add two numbers together. Such a description tells you nothing about how this should be done—merely that the observable behaviour at the interface performs the required sum. You are then free to implement this in any number of ways—as long as the observable behaviour of the implementation does the addition correctly. This is another key tenet of refinement—the consistency of observable behaviour on the system's interface. Again, we will meet it in many guises in this book. □

Example 0.3. Let us consider a slightly more realistic example—a frequency server for a mobile phone network [1]. Such a server is responsible for managing frequencies that mobile phones use, and a phone requests a frequency in order to connect a call and releases the frequency for other phones to use it when a call terminates.

At an abstract level, one can consider this as a system with two operations (or events): *allocate* and *deallocate*. Calling the allocation operation on the server will return one of two things: either a frequency if there is one available or an error message if they are all in use. Deallocate is slightly simpler, deallocating a frequency will allow that frequency to be used by another phone.

To achieve either of these, the phone will be identified by its unique identifier, which it will pass as a parameter.   □

Already contained in this, small description are several key components of a specification. There is a notion of *state*—the set of frequencies that are available or unavailable for allocation. There are *operations* or *events* such as *allocate* and *deallocate* which change the state. Then there are notions of *input* and *output* from these operations, such as the phone identifier (an input in both operations) and the frequency allocated (output in *allocate* and input in *deallocate*).

Already in this description, there is a lot of non-determinism. For example, we are not told how the system is initialised. We are not told what frequency is returned as output (if any) all the frequencies are in use. We are not told how frequencies are allocated.

Then there are a vast array of internal details that are simply (and correctly) hidden at this level of abstraction. How are the frequencies represented internally as a data structure (list, set, ⋯), and so forth?

A refinement could correctly reduce any of this non-determinism as long as the observable behaviour was consistent with the abstract description.

Although one can think of refinement as being a process that takes a set of requirements and turns them into code, here we will start exploring our understanding of what refinement is on a very simple model of computation—that provided by *labelled transition systems*, or LTS as they are known. Here, and throughout this book, the abstract and concrete specification will be written in the same model of computation, but at different levels of abstraction. A labelled transition system represents computations as events (or operations) causing a system's state to change. Although such a model of computation looks very simple, labelled transition systems can already code up some very interesting questions about refinement.

As commented above, refinement can be viewed in terms of a system's input and output, and more generally, its observable behaviour, and we will compare abstract and concrete specifications to see if their observable behaviour is consistent. Now, "seeing if their observable behaviour is consistent" is close (if not identical) to the activity that is known as testing, and thus unsurprisingly there is a strong relationship between testing and refinement. That relationship is a generalisation of the idea that, in the V-model of software engineering [2], what is tested in acceptance testing follows directly from what is specified by requirements engineering. However, our interest here will be in how to verify a refinement (and in general, how to determine such verification conditions), rather than how to generate tests. Crucially, what you can test, or what you can observe is not fixed for most computational models, and varying what you think of as observable varies the associated notion of refinement. Thus instead of there being just one notion of refinement, we end up with a whole collection of different refinement relations each dependant on some notion of observation. Chapter 1 in this book is devoted to exploring this rich and fascinating aspect of the subject.

However, labelled transition systems are not the only model of computation, there are others and each has a theory of refinement. What is the relationship between them, and how do they compare? After gaining the basic understanding of refinement, this is the central question of this book, and in answering it, we will start to understand the different nature of different refinement relations.

So, in Chaps. 1–4 we introduce different models of computation and look at their refinement relations. There are a large number of languages, models and semantics for expressing computation, and it is not possible to survey all of them here. Instead we try to be representative of some of the major trends, so we can illustrate the different approaches and draw comparisons and parallels between them. One distinction that we make is between *languages* and underlying *models*. By the former, we mean notations used for describing or specifying a system, whereas the latter is used to assign meanings to specifications and reason about their behaviour. Part II of this book considers refinement in particular languages, whereas Part I considers fundamental models of computation, and what refinement means in them.

Having looked at labelled transition systems in Chap. 1, in Chap. 2, we look at the related model of *automata*. The differences in mathematical models and approach between LTS and automata are not large, but the purpose of making the distinction here is not because of their different approach to modelling a system, but because of their different approach to refinement of those models. Specifically, we introduce the idea of *simulations* in Chap. 2 – a notion that is crucial to the material we cover in this book.

Simulations, as the name suggests, compare two specifications by seeing if one can simulate the other in the sense that for every step in the first one can do a corresponding step in the second. A "step" in this context will be an operation or event (in the same sense as a LTS), and "corresponding" will mean that we will link states in the two systems, and one pair of linked states must lead to another pair of linked states. Such simulations can themselves come in different forms, and we will make a distinction between bisimulations and simulations. In the case of the latter, there are two differing forms: forward and backward simulations, and these are central to this book. They are central to our work because simulations can serve not only as a means of refining a system, they can also serve (if correctly formulated) to verify different types of refinement relations—and we will use them in such a way in Part III.

The refinement notions for LTS and automata are entirely based on the events (or operations). States, for example when they are linked in a simulation relation, serve only as a vehicle for recording the behaviour possible from that point.

In Chap. 3, we introduce a model that is in some sense dual to that, where what is observable is not determined by "what happens" but by "what is"—i.e., the value of the state; there are transitions from one state to another, but if we assign names to these at all, that has no impact on what is observable. Refinement can be defined on such systems as well, including via notions of simulation. Ultimately, this model can be viewed as a relational one, where state is observable and there is only a single operation.

Most state-based formal methods such as Z, B, and VDM are based on hybrids and generalisations of these basic models. A relational setting places emphasis on the state of a system, and this is described here using simple notions from set theory and logic. In Chap. 4, we discuss refinement in a relational framework of abstract data types including how forward and backward simulations are defined and how *partiality* is dealt with.

Partiality is something we have not really met yet—it is the notion that initially not everything may be defined. For example, in Example 0.3 we are not told how *allocate* behaves if the phone identifier is not one the system knows about. What does such an undefined description mean? There are a number of different aspects of how a system might be undefined. A key one being what happens if an operation is called outside of its defined area (i.e., outside of its *precondition*).

There are a number of ways to deal with that, and a relational setting has two principle ones—blocking and non-blocking—and each gives a slightly different refinement relation, and thus each notion has a different simulation rule associated with it. Chapter 4 will introduce and discuss the consequences of these ideas.

Finally, we discuss, in Chap. 5, the role of divergence in refinement at a semantic level, both in an LTS model where we may have divergence due to some internal, unobservable, activity, but also in a relational model where divergence can represent undefined behaviour.

Part II

All of this discussion has been undertaken at the semantic level. The purpose of Part II is to show how refinement is defined in a particular formal notation. We survey the major (types of) notations, and for each we define refinement as it is typically used in that notation, before linking it to its semantic model introduced in Part I.

Chapter 6 looks at these issues in a process algebra. As a canonical example we look at CSP, but we also discuss the process algebras CCS and LOTOS which allows us to discuss differing process algebraic styles and thus covering the major branches in the subject. For each, we describe the basic components of the language, its semantics (which links into Chap. 1) and how, from this semantics, notions of refinement are defined in the language.

Chapter 7 is the first of two chapters on state-based notations. This chapter defines refinement in Z and B and shows how it derives from the relational model in Chap. 4. The approach taken in state-based languages is different from that in a process algebra. Specifically, the emphasis in a process algebra is on the events that take place—and state is very much implicit in any process algebraic description. The opposite is true in a state-based language, where the states are explicitly defined and operations concern themselves with how this state is altered. In this chapter, we illustrate the approach to state-based specification by introducing the Z and B notations, and showing how we can apply our theory of refinement to it by using the models described in Chap. 4. The second chapter on state-based systems introduces Event-B and ASM (standing for abstract state machines) and shows how the theory of refinement developed so far applies in their context. They represent an evolution of the languages discussed in Chap. 7 in that they contain a flavour of event-based description as well as state-based description.

Part III

By this point in the book, we should be in a position to understand how various refinement relations are defined on different semantic models, and how those impact on refinement as defined in a specific specification notion.

The natural question in a reader's mind should now be: "Why all these different ones?" Some of these differences are due to different notions of observation—and this is covered in Part I—but not all, and this part describes the relationship between notions of refinement across the different languages and semantics.

We do this by defining a relational framework that is sufficiently rich to enable us to embed the different models we have looked at into it. Once we have done so we can start to compare refinement relations, and in particular use simulations to verify specific refinement relations. In Chap. 9, we describe the basic relational framework, and in doing so we derive simulation rules for some of the refinement relations introduced in earlier chapters, such as trace refinement and failures refinement. We do this in a simple model where events do not have input or output. The subsequent chapter looks at failures–divergences refinement in more depth. This is necessary because the inclusion of inputs and (in particular) outputs adds considerable subtly to the calculation of a refinement relation such as failures-divergences, as one needs to consider when an output might be refused by the environment. Finally, in Chap. 11 we introduce something we term *process data types*, which enhances the relational framework introduced in Chap. 9 to allow the full range of behaviours such as deadlock and divergence to be incorporated, and hence considered in a general refinement framework.

Readership

The book is intended primarily as a monograph aimed at researchers in the field of formal methods, academics, industrialists using formal methods, and postgraduate researchers. By including an introduction to the languages and notations used, the book is self-contained and should appeal to all those with an interest in formal methods and formal development.

The book is also relevant to a number of courses, particularly at postgraduate level, on software engineering, formal methods, semantics and refinement.

Acknowledgements

Fragments of Chap. 4 including Figs. 4.5 and 4.6 were republished with permission of Elsevier Science and Technology Journals, from "Incompleteness of relational simulations in the blocking paradigm", Eerke Boiten and John Derrick, Science of Computer Programming Volume 5 Issue 12, 2010; permission conveyed through Copyright Clearance Center, Inc.

Fragments of Chaps. 9–11 were reprinted from *Formal Aspects of Computing*: Volume 15, J. Derrick and E.A. Boiten, "Relational concurrent refinement"; Volume 21, E.A. Boiten, J. Derrick and G. Schellhorn, "Relational concurrent refinement part II: Internal operations and output"; Volume 26, J. Derrick and E.A. Boiten, "Relational concurrent refinement part III: traces, partial relations and automata"; copyright (2003, 2008, 2012), with permission from Springer Nature.

Many people have contributed to this book in a variety of ways. We have had numerous discussions on aspects of specification and refinement and benefited from related work in this area with other researchers including: Alasdair Armstrong, Ralph Back, Richard Banach, Mark Batty, Behzad Bordbar, Howard Bowman, Michael Butler, Jim Davies, Steve Dunne, Lindsay Groves, Ian Hayes, Martin Henson, Rob Hierons, Cliff Jones, Christie Marr (née Bolton), Ralph Miarka, Carroll Morgan, Siobhan North, Ernst-Rüdiger Olderog, Scott Owens, Steve Reeves, Steve Schneider, Kaisa Sere, Tony Simons, Maarten Steen, Susan Stepney, Ketil Stølen, David Streader, Georg Struth, Ramsay Taylor, Helen Treharne, Marina Waldén, Neil Walkinshaw, and Kirsten Winter.

Thanks are especially due to Simon Doherty, Brijesh Dongol, Gerhard Schellhorn, Graeme Smith, and Heike Wehrheim, for our joint work on refinement over the years.

We also wish to thank staff at Springer UK for their help and guidance in preparing this book: Beverley Ford and Nancy Wade-Jones.

Finally, thanks to our friends and families who have provided love and support throughout this project. We would not have completed this book without them.

References

1. Cesarini F, Thompson S (2009) Erlang programming. O'Reilly series. O'Reilly Media, Sebastopol
2. Forsberg K, Mooz H (1991) The relationship of system engineering to the project cycle. In: Proceedings of the first annual symposium of national council on system engineering, pp 57–65

References

Part I
Semantics

The purpose of this part is to give the reader a grounding in what refinement means semantically, that is in simple models of computation without clutter of a particular design syntax. The aim is to show where the differences between notions of refinement really lie. We begin by discussing labeled transition systems as a simple model of computation that gives rise to several notions of refinement based upon different observations one could make. This is followed by a closely related semantic model, namely that given by automata. This is where we first introduce the idea of a *simulation* between two systems–an idea that is central to the much of the material in the book. In Chaps. 3 and 4 we discuss an alternative model of computation and refinement–that given by state-based or relational models. Finally, we end this part with a discussion on divergence and erroneous behaviour, and the effect that it has on the model of computation.

Chapter 1
Labeled Transition Systems and Their Refinement

On purpose we start with one of the simplest models of computation, that given by labeled transition systems. After introducing the reader to this simple set up we start to explore what refinement might mean, beginning with trace refinement, then adding in various notions such as refusals, so that each refinement relation we introduce is more discriminating than the last. The most discriminating of all, bisimulation, will then be introduced in Chap. 2. The material in this chapter serves as the foundation of refinement in process algebras such as CSP, CCS and LOTOS which we consider in Chap. 6.

1.1 Introduction

We have discussed the idea that refinement is about *comparing the behaviour of systems*, and if C refines A then the behaviours of C are consistent with those of A. We will measure behaviours in terms of what we can *observe*, and thus ask that every observation of C is also an observation of A. If we let $\mathscr{O}(A)$ stand for the set of observations of A, then this amounts to requiring that

$$\mathscr{O}(C) \subseteq \mathscr{O}(A)$$

and when this happens we write

$$A \sqsubseteq_{\mathscr{O}} C$$

to denote the refinement of A by C (we sometimes drop the subscript $\mathscr{O}$). To get much further we need to fix a notation to describe our systems and their observations. The very simple model of computation we shall begin with is that of *Labelled Transition Systems*, abbreviated to LTS, which describe a system in terms of the

© Springer International Publishing AG, part of Springer Nature 2018
J. Derrick and E. Boiten, *Refinement*, https://doi.org/10.1007/978-3-319-92711-4_1

events (transitions) it can perform. Events take the system from one *state* of the system to another, and another perspective is that states are essentially equivalent to all the event behaviour that can follow from that point. Such a system is often called a *process*, and indeed labelled transition systems are often used as the semantic model for *process algebra* (more on this later). Although this looks almost too simple to be of use, in fact it turns out to be the ideal model to discuss the basics of refinement, and illustrate the variety of ways one can think about observing a system.

1.2   Labelled Transition Systems – A Simple Model of Computation

Let us begin with a definition:

Definition 1.1 (*Labelled Transition System (LTS)*)
A labelled transition system is a tuple $L = (States, Act, T, Init)$ where *States* is a non-empty set of states, $Init \subseteq States$ is the initial state (a set of size one), *Act* is a set of actions (or events), and $T \subseteq States \times Act \times States$ is a transition relation. The components of L are also accessed as $states(L) = States$ and $init(L) = Init$.   □

The usual notation for transitions is

$$p \xrightarrow{a} q$$

in place of $(p, a, q) \in T$, and we say that the process or system p can evolve into q while performing the event or action a. In our use each LTS has a unique initial state (this is relaxed in the next chapter when we discuss automata). We frequently represent LTS by diagrams without losing any formality, like in the following examples.

Example 1.1 We can define a labelled transition system $L = (States, Act, T, Init)$ for a simple vending machine as follows. Let $States = \{s_0, s_1, s_2, s_3, s_4, s_5\}$, $Init = \{s_0\}$, $Act = \{pound, coffee\_button, tea\_button, coffee, tea\}$,   and $T = \{\langle s_0, pound, s_1 \rangle,$ $\langle s_1, coffee\_button, s_2 \rangle, \langle s_1, tea\_button, s_3 \rangle, \langle s_2, coffee, s_4 \rangle, \langle s_3, tea, s_5 \rangle\}$.

This LTS specifies the first action of inserting a coin (a *pound*) after which the systems state changes to s_1. In this state there is a choice between the two actions *coffee_button* and *tea_button*. These change the state to s_2 and s_3 respectively, and in those states the actions *coffee* and *tea* are available.

Precise though this is, it quickly becomes clear that representing LTS as a diagram is more instructive, the obvious rendering of the above is as Fig. 1.1.

As you can see we elide the names on the states, actions are represented as named arrows between states, and the initial state is indicated by a short arrow into it.   □

We might represent the frequency server (see Example 0.3) abstractly without any data (frequencies) as follows:

Fig. 1.1 An LTS of a simple
vending machine

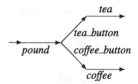

Example 1.2 A simple frequency server which had just two frequencies to allocate
might be specified as the LTS $L = (States, Act, T, Init)$, where $States = \{s_0, s_1, s_2\}$,
$Init = \{s_0\}$, $Act = \{allocate, deallocate\}$, and $T = \{\langle s_0, allocate, s_1 \rangle, \langle s_1, allocate,$
$s_2 \rangle, \langle s_2, deallocate, s_1 \rangle, \langle s_1, deallocate, s_0 \rangle\}$.

Again this is easier to see as a diagram (where this time, just for a change, we
explicitly represent state and state names):

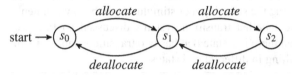

Note that we have not represented any data here – we have abstracted away from
that level of detail initially. Note also that although this LTS is finite state, the system
can perform an unbounded number of *allocate* and *deallocate* actions. □

So far we have not said what is observable, that comes when we define the refinement relations. Our observations will mainly be concerned with observing the actions
or events, rather than the state. The idea of observing something leads to the idea
of an *environment* of a system - the entity that sees the observations, and sometimes
controls the system under consideration. The idea of an environment is central to how
refinement is viewed in a concurrent system, and gives rise to the testing scenarios
that we detail for each refinement relation in this chapter.

The set *Act* in an LTS is the set of events that a process may engage in. We
shall think of the environment (e.g., a user) controlling a process, indeed it is the
environment that will observe the behaviour of the process, and thus a transition
$p \xrightarrow{a} q$ occurs if the environment cooperates, or synchronises, with the process.

Notation for sequences: The notation we use for sequences is standard, and in
particular we need the following usual definitions.

1. For any alphabet Σ, let Σ^* be the set of finite sequences over Σ, similarly Σ^∞
   is the set of infinite sequences over Σ, and Σ^ω the union of Σ^* and Σ^∞.
2. The empty sequence is denoted ε or $\langle \rangle$.
3. Concatenation of τ and σ is written as $\tau \frown \sigma$ or simply $\tau\sigma$.
4. We write $\sigma_1 \leq \sigma_2$ when σ_1 is a prefix of σ_2. We write $\sigma_1 < \sigma_2$ when σ_1 is a strict
   prefix of σ_2 (i.e., a prefix but with $\sigma_1 \neq \sigma_2$). □

Notation for LTS: We will need some additional notation and definitions, most of
which we give informally.

1. The set of enabled actions of a process (i.e., a state) is defined as:

$$next(p) = \{a \in Act \mid \exists q \bullet p \xrightarrow{a} q\}$$

2. We extend $p \xrightarrow{a} q$ as a notation for individual transitions to $p \overset{a_1 a_2 ..., a_n}{\Longrightarrow} q$ as a notation for possibly multiple transitions in the obvious way, that is $p \overset{a_1 a_2 ..., a_n}{\Longrightarrow} q$ whenever there exists $p_0, \ldots, p_n \bullet p = p_0 \xrightarrow{a_1} p_1 \xrightarrow{a_2} \ldots \xrightarrow{a_n} p_n = q$.

3. We say that a system is *deadlocked* in a state if no event is possible. That is, p is deadlocked if $next(p) = \emptyset$. ☐

Non-determinism

Non-determinism is central to our discussion of refinement. Non-determinism refers to a system behaving differently on different runs when run under the same conditions (e.g., when using the same input or stimulus from the environment.)

In the context of the labelled transition systems discussed so far, non-determinism occurs when there is a state that has two transitions labelled with the same action but resulting in different end states.

Example 1.3 In Example 1.2 we have $next(s_0) = \{allocate\}$ and $next(s_1) = \{allocate, deallocate\}$. There are no deadlocked states in that LTS. However, in Example 1.1 we have $next(s_4) = \emptyset$ since no action is possible from that state - the LTS deadlocks when it reaches the final state of each branch. ☐

Neither Example 1.1 or Example 1.2 have any non-determinism within the system. However, the following system is non-deterministic, as it has two different branches labelled with the same action in the initial state - thus performing this action will non-deterministically move you to one of the two subsequent states. This has the effect of not being in control of whether the machine dispenses tea or coffee.

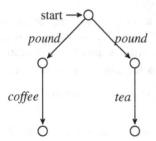

Subsequently, where it is unambiguous, we will not explicitly label the initial states.

To begin our account of refinement we will limit ourselves to this simple class of labelled transition systems. Specifically, we will only consider LTS with visible or external actions, and thus for the moment have no internal actions. In addition, we shall assume here that all our LTS are *finitely branching*, that is, in each state only a finite number of actions are enabled. We relax these conditions later, specifically we deal with infinitely branching systems in Sect. 1.10 and with internal actions when we also consider divergence in Chap. 5.

In the remainder of this chapter we detail differing refinement relations, for each we will give its definition, its characterisation as a testing scenario, and some examples to illustrate how it behaves. We begin with the simplest of all refinement relations: *trace refinement*.

To motivate why it might be an appropriate refinement relation, consider the simple LTS given in Example 1.1. Faced with this, what are acceptable implementations? One answer might be the only acceptable implementation is that described in the original LTS. However, one might also consider any of the following systems in Fig. 1.2 as valid alternatives (in this figure the start states are implicit but obvious).

These have viewed refinement in different ways – and this will be reflected in different refinement relations that we will define. C_1 is identical to the original system, whereas both C_2 and C_3 have added behaviour with an event or action not mentioned in the abstract specification. The remaining six possible refinements have altered the behaviour in different ways: C_4 has introduced some non-determinism, whereas the others have reduced the allowed behaviours in different ways. Trace refinement, the simplest relation other than equality, allows one to refine a system as long as no new traces are introduced in the implementation.

1.3 Trace Refinement

The simplest observations we can make are to observe the sequence of events that a process undergoes as it evolves. Such a sequence is called a *trace*. Trace refinement then looks to see if the traces are consistent between the abstract and concrete system. In what follows we will use the terms system, process and LTS interchangeably. We make the following definition.

Definition 1.2 (*Traces and trace refinement*)
A finite sequence of events $\sigma \in Act^*$ is a trace of a process p if $\exists q \bullet p \stackrel{\sigma}{\Longrightarrow} q$.
We let $\mathcal{T}(p)$ denote the set of traces of p, which we also write as *traces(p)*.
Trace refinement is defined by $p \sqsubseteq_{tr} q$ iff $\mathcal{T}(q) \subseteq \mathcal{T}(p)$. □

Example 1.4 Systems C_1, C_5, C_6, C_7, C_8 and C_9 in Fig. 1.2 are all trace refinements of the LTS given in Example 1.1. For example, the traces of C_5 are

$$traces(C_5) = \{\langle\rangle, \langle pound\rangle, \langle pound, coffee\_button\rangle, \langle pound, coffee\_button, coffee\rangle\}$$

and each of these traces is in the trace set of the abstract description. This set is $\{\langle\rangle, \langle pound\rangle, \langle pound, coffee\_button\rangle, \langle pound, coffee\_button, coffee\rangle, \langle pound, tea\_button\rangle, \langle pound, tea\_button, tea\rangle\}$.

What about C_9? This is a system that does nothing, it is deadlocked in its initial state. Its traces are just $\{\langle\rangle\}$. Now the empty trace is in the trace set of every system, thus according to trace refinement, C_9 is an acceptable refinement of *any* system.

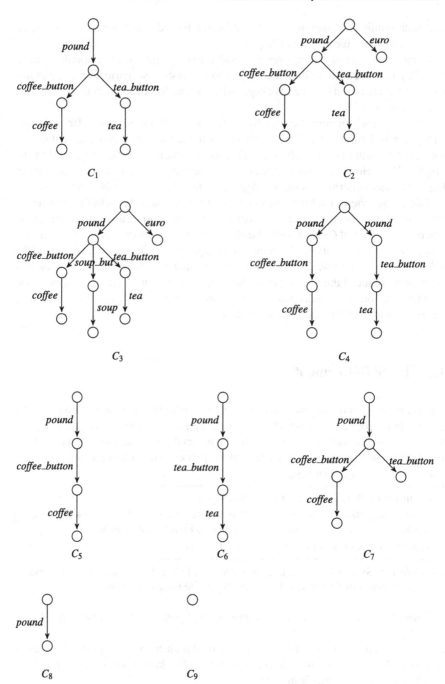

Fig. 1.2 Different possible refinements of Example 1.1

What about C_4? Although this system looks similar to C_1 it contains some non-determinism. However, when we calculate the trace sets we find that

$$traces(C_4) \subseteq traces(C_1)$$

So according to trace refinement we have $C_1 \sqsubseteq_{tr} C_4$ that is, we have been able to introduce (rather than remove) some non-determinism with trace refinement.   □

Preorders and equivalences

Refinement relations have a number of desirable characteristics. One of them is that they are *preorders*, that is a refinement relation is reflexive and transitive: a system can be refined by itself, and it can be refined in a series of refinement steps. Then, as preorders, they give rise to an associated equivalence relation, defined by:

$$P \equiv Q \qquad \text{if and only if} \qquad P \sqsubseteq Q \text{ and } Q \sqsubseteq P$$

for any preorder $\sqsubseteq$.

A refinement relation based on inclusion of observations inherits the property of being a preorder from set inclusion, and the corresponding equivalence becomes equality of observation sets.

One way of interpreting systems and their possible observations is to see them as a "testing scenario". This involves an imaginary observer with a display that changes over time as the system evolves, and possibly some "buttons" that allow them to interact with the evolution at some points.

The following scenario envisages what sort of display and observation one would make to characterise the trace refinement relation.

Testing scenario: Observations consist of a sequence of actions performed by the process in succession, that is, the interface is just a display which shows the name of the action that is currently carried out by the process, and the name remains visible in the display if deadlock occurs (unless deadlock occurs initially). The observer watches the process evolve.   □

Although this may seem an adequate refinement relation, the following example should strike a note of caution.

Example 1.5 Returning to the issue of a system that does nothing, if we write *stop* for a process that does nothing, i.e., its transition relation is empty, then we have for every process p: $p \sqsubseteq_{tr} stop$. A particular example of this was the specification C_9 in the example above.   □

Thus the system that does nothing is a valid refinement according to the trace refinement relation. This is because trace refinement preserves *safety properties* but not *liveness properties*.

Safety and liveness properties.

Two classes of properties important in concurrent or distributed systems are safety and liveness properties. Safety properties informally require that "something bad does not happen". Such a property can obviously be satisfied by a system that does nothing. Therefore safety properties are often accompanied by liveness properties, which informally require that "something good eventually happens". Unlike liveness properties, safety properties can be violated by a finite execution of a system, whereas liveness properties require the consideration of infinite runs. (When expressed in an appropriate formal framework) all properties can be expressed as the intersection of safety and liveness properties.

Even taking account of the nature of checking safety and not liveness properties, trace refinement is very weak. That is, it does not discriminate some processes one might naturally think of as being different.

Example 1.6 Consider the following two systems:

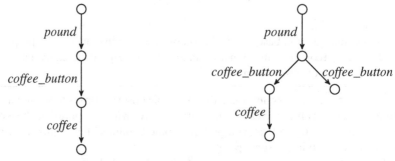

As we can see these two processes are considered as equivalent according to their trace semantics: they have exactly the same traces. However, after a *pound* action if an observer performed a *coffee_button* action, then in the second system it could move into a state where it was deadlocked. This behaviour is not possible in the first system.   □

Surely one would therefore argue that an observer could tell them apart. However, in this model, the two different states after pressing the coffee button cannot be distinguished: in one, coffee can arrive at any point in the (distant) future, in the other, it never does. To distinguish them, we need the observer to see more of the process' behaviour than simply its traces. One simple way of doing this is to observe when the process has finished, i.e., reached a deadlock state. This leads us to the following.

1.4 Completed Trace Refinement

Completed traces record the traces which are maximal, i.e., cannot be extended
further. The refinement relation based on it uses both traces and completed traces,
and is enough to discriminate between the two processes in Example 1.6.

Definition 1.3 (*Completed trace refinement*)
A sequence $\sigma \in Act^*$ is a completed trace of a process p if $\exists q \bullet p \overset{\sigma}{\Longrightarrow} q$ and
$next(q) = \emptyset$. $\mathscr{C}T(p)$ denotes the set of completed traces of p. The completed
trace refinement relation, $\sqsubseteq_{ctr}$, is defined by $p \sqsubseteq_{ctr} q$ iff $\mathscr{T}(q) \subseteq \mathscr{T}(p)$ and
$\mathscr{C}T(q) \subseteq \mathscr{C}T(p)$.   □

That is, to be a refinement under the completed trace relation both the observed
traces *and* the completed traces of the concrete system must be consistent with those
of the abstract system.

Example 1.7 Consider the following two systems we introduced above (let's call
them P, on the left, and Q, on the right):

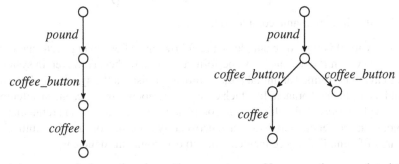

As we argued above they have the same traces. However, the completed trace
semantics can distinguish between them, since $\langle pound, coffee\_button\rangle$ is a completed
trace of Q but not of P. In fact all the completed traces of P are also completed traces
of Q, so $Q \sqsubseteq_{ctr} P$.   □

Obviously, completed trace refinement is stronger than trace refinement. By that
we mean the following holds.

Proposition 1.1 *For all processes P and Q, if $P \sqsubseteq_{ctr} Q$ then $P \sqsubseteq_{tr} Q$.*   □

Note that the inclusion of traces, in addition to completed traces, is necessary as
the following example shows.

Example 1.8 Let p be the LTS that just does an a then deadlocks. Let q be the system
that in the initial state either does an a then deadlocks or can do an arbitrary number
of b's. Then $\mathscr{C}\mathscr{T}(q) \subseteq \mathscr{C}\mathscr{T}(p)$ but we do not have $\mathscr{T}(q) \subseteq \mathscr{T}(p)$.   □

Again we can think of a testing scenario that would distinguish processes on the
basis of their completed traces. This might be described as follows.

Testing scenario: Observations consist of a sequence of actions performed by the process in succession, that is, the interface is just a display which shows the name of the action that is currently carried out by the process, where the display becomes empty if deadlock occurs. The observer watches the display and records the sequence of actions.   □

Although completed traces record more information than just traces alone, the refinement relation is still weak in that it cannot distinguish between the following processes.

Example 1.9 Consider the following two systems given as LTS:

$$P \qquad\qquad\qquad\qquad\qquad Q$$

Then P and Q have the same completed traces.   □

The issue with this type of example is the following. After having performed an initial a, in system P one can always perform a c if one wishes. However, in system Q after having performed an initial a the non-determinism in the system might have selected the right hand branch. In which case one cannot perform a c, and an attempt to do so will be *refused*. For this reason, completed trace semantics (and refinement) does not seem rich enough to distinguish between systems that one might intuitively think are different. Failures refinement aims to overcome this deficiency.

1.5   Failures Refinement

A *failures* semantics is one way to distinguish between processes such as these, and can be thought of as the result of an experiment by the environment (i.e., a test) that determines when an action or event can occur, and when it cannot.

So the failures semantics records both the traces that a process can do, and also sets of actions which it can *refuse*, that is, actions which are not enabled. These are recorded as failures of a process, consisting of a trace σ and a *refusal set X*. This corresponds to the experiment which records the evolution of the process, doing all the events in the trace σ, after which it reaches a state which has no transitions from the set X. See Fig. 1.3.

Fig. 1.3 The refusals of a
process P after a trace tr

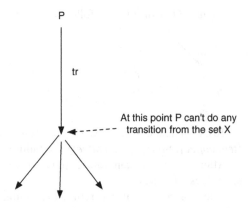

P

tr

At this point P can't do any
transition from the set X

Definition 1.4 (*Failures and failures refinement*)
The pair $(\sigma, X) \in Act^* \times \mathbb{P}(Act)$ is a failure of a process p if there is a process q
such that $p \overset{\sigma}{\Longrightarrow} q$, and $next(q) \cap X = \emptyset$. We let $\mathscr{F}(p)$ denote the set of failures
of p. This is also denoted *failures*(p). The failures refinement relation, $\sqsubseteq_f$, is
defined by $p \sqsubseteq_f q$ iff $\mathscr{F}(q) \subseteq \mathscr{F}(p)$. $\qquad\Box$

Example 1.10 (*Calculating refusals*)
Consider the very simple system given as follows:

To calculate the refusals one needs to know: what can P refuse to do initially? What
can P refuse to do after it's done an a? What can P refuse to do after it's done a b?
Looking at these we find that:

- After the empty trace it can refuse nothing. So $(\langle\rangle, \emptyset)$ is one failure.
- After it's done an a it can refuse $\{a, b\}$. So $(\langle a\rangle, \{a, b\})$ is another failure.
- After it's done an b it can refuse $\{a, b\}$. So $(\langle b\rangle, \{a, b\})$ is another failure.

The *failures* are the set of all of these, plus the downward closure of the refusals. This
means, for each failure, e.g., $(\langle a\rangle, \{a, b\})$, you include all $(\langle a\rangle, X)$ where $X \subseteq \{a, b\}$:
if all events in the larger set can be refused, then so can all events in the subset. So
in this case we get:

$(\langle\rangle, \emptyset)$,

$(\langle a\rangle, \{a, b\})$, $(\langle a\rangle, \{a\})$, $(\langle a\rangle, \{b\})$, $(\langle a\rangle, \emptyset)$

$(\langle b\rangle, \{a, b\})$, $(\langle b\rangle, \{a\})$, $(\langle b\rangle, \{b\})$, $(\langle b\rangle, \emptyset)$

The failures consist of all the above pairs. $\qquad\Box$

Example 1.11 Consider the following system:

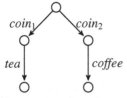

To calculate the refusals we proceed as follows: After the empty trace it can refuse {*tea, coffee*}. So ($\langle\rangle$, {*tea, coffee*}) is a failure.

After a *coin*$_1$ it can refuse {*coin*$_1$, *coin*$_2$, *coffee*}. So ($\langle coin_1 \rangle$, {*coin*$_1$, *coin*$_2$, *coffee*}) is a failure.

After $\langle coin_1, tea \rangle$ it can refuse everything. So ($\langle coin_1, tea \rangle$, {*coin*$_1$, *coin*$_2$, *tea*, *coffee*}) is a failure.

After *coin*$_2$ it can refuse {*coin*$_1$, *coin*$_2$, *tea*}. So ($\langle coin_2 \rangle$, {*coin*$_1$, *coin*$_2$, *tea*}) is a failure.

After $\langle coin_2, coffee \rangle$ it can refuse everything. So ($\langle coin_2, coffee \rangle$, {*coin*$_1$, *coin*$_2$, *tea*, *coffee*}) is a failure.

Then, as above, the failures of this process are the set of all of these, plus the downward closure of the refusals.   □

Observing failures is enough to detect non-determinism, which cannot be detected by observing traces alone. For example, for some process P suppose one possible observation is ($\langle a \rangle$, $\emptyset$), and another is ($\langle\rangle$, {a}). This means that if a is offered to the process, it might be accepted, or it might be refused. These two observations provide evidence that the process P is non-deterministic.

In fact a process P is deterministic if:

$$\forall tr \in traces(P) \bullet (tr, X) \in failures(P) \land a \in X \implies tr \frown \langle a \rangle \notin traces(P)$$

That is, if a could be refused after tr, then the trace $tr \frown \langle a \rangle$ is not possible. Put differently, a deterministic process is defined by its traces: it can refuse precisely those events that cannot extend the trace.

We mentioned refusals and failures being a product of an experiment on a process, we can rephrase this as a testing scenario in a manner similar to traces and completed traces. This time the interface records when the action will be blocked.

Testing scenario: The machine for testing failures has, in addition to the interface of the completed trace machine, a switch for each action in *Act* which will indicate whether that action is enabled or blocked. By this means we can then observe which actions are blocked. If the process reaches a state where all actions are blocked, then this can be observed by an empty display. Observations are thus the failures of a process.

We would hope that failures refinement is stronger than completed trace refinement, and indeed it is:

Proposition 1.2 (Failures refinement is stronger than completed trace refinement)
For all processes P and Q, if P $\sqsubseteq_f$ Q then P $\sqsubseteq_{ctr}$ Q.   □

Example 1.12 Consider the following two systems given as LTS:

$$P \qquad\qquad\qquad\qquad Q$$

As we noted above P and Q have the same completed traces. However they are
not equivalent in the failures semantics. To see this the refusals after a in P are $\{a\}$
whereas in Q they include $\{a, c\}$. However, every failure of P is also a failure of Q
so that $Q \sqsubseteq_f P$, but not $P \sqsubseteq_f Q$.   □

Remember from our discussion above that in the trace semantics we had $P \sqsubseteq_{tr}$ *stop*
for any process P. The natural question to ask is whether this is true under the failures
semantics? That is, do we have: $P \sqsubseteq_f$ *stop* for every process P?

In fact, failures refinement, unlike trace refinement, has an element of ensuring
liveness properties hold (see above). Specifically, the restriction that $P \sqsubseteq_{tr} Q$ limits
what Q can do, but does not require it to do anything. In that sense it preserves safety
properties rather than liveness properties. On the other hand $P \sqsubseteq_f Q$ not only limits
what Q can do (in the sense that its traces must also be traces of P), it also cannot
introduce refusals and thus forces Q to offer certain events.

An alternative to failures and failures refinement is a semantics and refinement
relation where we record individual single failures rather than a complete failures
set. This is called singleton failures, since the failures sets are now singletons. The
definitions are as follows.

Definition 1.5 (*Singleton failures and singleton failures refinement*)
The pair $(\sigma, X) \in Act^* \times \mathbb{P}(Act)$ is a singleton failure of a process p if there is
a process q such that $p \overset{\sigma}{\Longrightarrow} q$, and $next(q) \cap X = \emptyset$ and X is a singleton. We let
$\mathscr{F}^1(p)$ denote the set of singleton failures of p. The singleton failures refinement
relation, $\sqsubseteq_{f^1}$, is defined by $p \sqsubseteq_{f^1} q$ iff $\mathscr{T}(q) \subseteq \mathscr{T}(p)$ and $\mathscr{F}^1(q) \subseteq \mathscr{F}^1(p)$. □

Notice that, unlike for failures, we have required that the traces are included
in addition to the singleton failures. We need this here because the inclusion
$\mathscr{F}^1(q) \subseteq \mathscr{F}^1(p)$ doesn't guarantee $\mathscr{T}(q) \subseteq \mathscr{T}(p)$ unlike the corresponding inclusion for failures.

The following example shows that singleton failures is distinct from completed
trace or failures.

Example 1.13 Consider the following two systems given as LTS:

Then both P and Q have identical singleton failures, since the singleton refusals after the trace $\langle a \rangle$ are $\{a\}$, $\{b\}$ and $\{c\}$ in both systems, However, the failures are different after the trace $\langle a \rangle$. □

In a failures refinement one records which events are *refused* at the end of a trace, surely this is a little convoluted, why don't we just record which events are *enabled* instead? The answer is that we can, but perhaps a bit surprisingly this doesn't yield the same refinement relation or semantics.

1.6   Readiness Refinement

In readiness refinement we record a pair (σ, X) where this time X is the set of events enabled after the trace σ.

Definition 1.6 (*Readiness and readiness refinement*)
The pair $(\sigma, X) \in Act^* \times \mathbb{P}(Act)$ is a ready pair of a process p if there is a process q such that $p \stackrel{\sigma}{\Longrightarrow} q$, and $next(q) = X$. We let $\mathscr{R}(p)$ denote the set of ready pairs of p. The readiness refinement relation, $\sqsubseteq_r$, is defined by $p \sqsubseteq_r q$ iff $\mathscr{R}(q) \subseteq \mathscr{R}(p)$. □

Example 1.14   Consider the following two systems given as LTS:

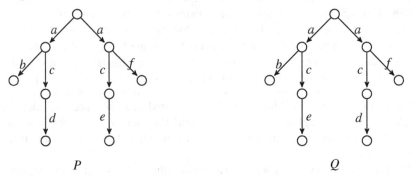

Then both P and Q have identical failures and ready sets, and are thus equivalent in both semantics, and hence are refinements of each other. □

However, the following example shows that the two semantics, and refinement relations do not coincide.

Example 1.15 Consider the following two systems given as LTS:

P Q

Then both P and Q have identical failures. However, they are distinguished in the readiness semantics. To see this, note that every ready set of P is included in that of Q. However, $(\langle a \rangle, \{b, c\})$ is a ready set of Q which is not a ready set of P. □

Testing scenario: The machine for testing readiness has, in addition to switches for all the actions, a lamp for each action which is alight when that action is enabled and the process has completed its evolution. The observer can see which actions were enabled at the end of each trace, that is he / she can record the ready set.

Proposition 1.3 (Readiness refinement is stronger than failures refinement) *For all processes P and Q, if $P \sqsubseteq_r Q$ then $P \sqsubseteq_f Q$.* □

So far we have been recording the sets of actions which are enabled / refused at the end of a process's execution. The alternative is to record this sequence as we proceed. And there are two refinement relations corresponding to readiness / failures that do this. Again it might be surprising that these give refinement relations that are different from when we just record this information at the end of a trace. We begin with *failure trace refinement*.

1.7 Failure Trace Refinement

The failure trace semantics considers refusal sets not only at the end of a trace, but also between each action in a trace.

Definition 1.7 (*Failure traces and failure trace refinement*)
The sequence $\sigma \in (Act \cup \mathbb{P} Act)^*$ is a failure trace of a process p if $\sigma = X_1 a_1 X_2 a_2 \ldots X_n a_n X_{n+1}$ where $\langle a_1, a_2, \ldots, a_n \rangle$ is a trace of p and each $(\langle a_1 \ldots a_i \rangle, X_{i+1})$ is a failure of p. We let $\mathscr{F}\mathscr{T}(p)$ denote the set of failure traces of p. The failures traces preorder, $\sqsubseteq_{ftr}$, is defined by $p \sqsubseteq_{ftr} q$ iff $\mathscr{F}\mathscr{T}(q) \subseteq \mathscr{F}\mathscr{T}(p)$. □

Example 1.16 The two systems in Example 1.14 are equivalent in the failures and readiness semantics. However, they have different failure traces, and are not failure trace refinements of each other.   □

Proposition 1.4 (Failure trace refinement is stronger than failures refinement) *For all processes P and Q, if P $\sqsubseteq_{ftr}$ Q then P $\sqsubseteq_f$ Q.*   □

Testing scenario: The display in the machine for testing failure traces is the same as that for failures. However, it does not halt if the process cannot proceed, rather it idles until the observer allows one of the actions the process is ready to perform. The observations are traces with idle periods in between, and for each idle period the set of actions that are not blocked by the observer.

It has been argued that this is a better notion for testing than simply observing failures of a process, and is appropriate when one can detect that a process refuses an action, and if this is the case, one has the ability to try another action.

1.8 Ready Trace Refinement

In a similar way to failure trace refinement, one can define a variant of readiness refinement called ready trace refinement (and semantics). We don't give all the details here, but the construction should be clear: a ready trace will be an alternating sequence of sets and actions, where the sets are the ready set at that point in the evolution.

We just give a simple example to show the difference to the refinement relations we have defined above.

Example 1.17 The two systems in Example 1.14 also serve to show the difference between failures or readiness semantics and the ready trace semantics.   □

1.9 Conformance and Extension

Failure trace refinement was motivated by considerations from testing, and in this section we introduce two further relations that were motivated by testing, specifically test generation from the process algebra LOTOS. These are called *conformance*, denoted *conf*, and *extension*, denoted *ext*. See also Chap. 6.

The idea behind their introduction was that one can distinguish different classes of implementation, which include:

• implementation as a real/physical system;
• implementation as a (deterministic) reduction of a given specification;
• implementation as a (conforming) extension of a given specification;

We've already met the second of these, which is essentially the failures refinement relation. Why do we need two more based around the same idea? Well the issue with the failures refinement relation (which in the context of LOTOS was called *reduction* or *red*) is that to verify it by testing more tests are needed than one would really like. To make this idea precise, and to define these refinement relations formally, we need the following notation which defines refusals sets after a particular trace (i.e., a failure in Definition 1.4).

Definition 1.8 (*Refusals after a trace*)
Let p be a LTS, σ a trace of p, and $X \subseteq Act$. Then p **after** σ **ref** X iff

$$\exists q \bullet p \overset{\sigma}{\Longrightarrow} q \text{ and } next(q) \cap X = \emptyset$$

That is, after process p does the events in the trace σ it can refuse all the events in the set X.   □

Failures refinement can then be characterised as follows: $p \sqsubseteq_f q$ iff

$$\forall \sigma : Act^*; X \subseteq Act \bullet (q \text{ after } \sigma \text{ ref } X) \text{ implies } (p \text{ after } \sigma \text{ ref } X) \tag{1.1}$$

Now in conformance testing terms this involves a quantification of all traces $\sigma : Act^*$, not just quantification over traces that were in the specification to start with. This has led to the definition of an alternative refinement relation that doesn't have that weakness.

Definition 1.9 (*Conformance*)
Let p, q be LTS. Then $p \sqsubseteq_{conf} q$ whenever

$$\forall \sigma : \mathscr{T}(p); X \subseteq Act \bullet (q \text{ after } \sigma \text{ ref } X) \text{ implies } (p \text{ after } \sigma \text{ ref } X) \qquad □$$

The difference between failures and conformance can be seen in the quantification over the traces: $\forall \sigma : Act^*$ in the definition of failures refinement verses $\forall \sigma : \mathscr{T}(p)$ in the definition of conformance. That is, one has to check the particular refusals implication for fewer traces in conformance.

   Conformance also has the following characteristics: if $p \sqsubseteq_{conf} q$ then q deadlocks less often than p in any environment whose traces are limited to those of p. Thus conformance restricts the quantification (of traces one must check refusals about) to be over the abstract specification, and this restriction gives rise to efficient test generation algorithms. However, this means it is not verified whether q has additional traces, thus extensions in the functionality of an implementation over the specification remain undetected.

Example 1.18 Consider the example systems given in Fig. 1.2. Some of these are related by trace refinement. For example, we have $C_i \sqsubseteq_{tr} C_9$ for all i. We also have

$$C_2 \sqsubseteq_{tr} C_1, C_4, C_5, C_6, C_7, C_8$$
$$C_3 \sqsubseteq_{tr} C_1, C_2, C_4, C_5, C_6, C_7, C_8$$

However, the reverse don't necessarily hold, so that $\neg C_2 \sqsubseteq_{tr} C_3$.

Some of the systems are also related by failures refinement. So $C_4 \equiv_{tr} C_1$ and $C_4 \sqsubseteq_f C_1$, but $\neg C_1 \sqsubseteq_f C_4$ as C_4 can refuse *tea_button* after *pound*.

We know that failures refinement is stronger than trace refinement, and specifically we cannot refine to deadlock. That is, $\neg C_i \sqsubseteq_f C_9$ for all $i \le 8$. In addition, $\neg C_1 \sqsubseteq_f C_2$ and similarly, $\neg C_2 \sqsubseteq_f C_3$. Indeed, in general failures refinement places the constraint that if $P \sqsubseteq_f Q$ then all traces not in P are also not in Q – thus we cannot add traces in a failures refinement.

Conformance, on the other hand, allows one to add traces that weren't in the abstract process in an implementation step. So, for example,

$$C_1, C_2, C_3 \sqsubseteq_{conf} C_3$$

However, branches cannot be added arbitrarily. Thus if C_{10} is the following system

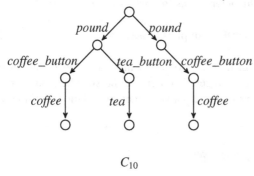

$$C_{10}$$

we have

$$C_5 \sqsubseteq_{conf} C_{10}$$

however, arbitrary introduction of new branches is not allowed as

$$\neg C_1 \sqsubseteq_{conf} C_{10}$$

as C_{10} allows *tea_button* to be refused afer *pound*, which was not possible for that particular existing trace of C_1.   □

There are two points worth noting now. Firstly, failures refinement can be characterised as a conformance check together with a check for trace inclusion. Second, although conformance looks well motivated, it is not a preorder because it is not transitive.

Proposition 1.5 (Properties of conformance)

1. $\sqsubseteq_f = \sqsubseteq_{tr} \cap \sqsubseteq_{conf}$.
2. $\sqsubseteq_{conf}$ is *reflexive but not transitive*.[1]   □

---

[1] See Example 6.22.

This last point really makes conformance suitable for an idea of implementation as a real/physical system, but not as a refinement relation in a whole chain of developments. However, it does have one interesting characteristic that leads us to the next relation we look at, namely that this is the only relation so far that allows additional traces in the implementation.

The *extension* refinement relation exploits this idea, and can be defined as conformance together with the additional property that traces can be extended. Thus, if $p \sqsubseteq_{ext} q$ then q has at least the same traces as p, but in an environment whose traces are limited to those of p, it deadlocks no more often. So, like conformance, extension allows some additional functionality, but now it is a preorder, that is, it is reflexive and transitive. It can be defined as follows.

Definition 1.10 (*Extension*)
Let p, q be LTS. Then q is an extension of p, written $p \sqsubseteq_{ext} q$, whenever

$$\mathcal{T}(p) \subseteq \mathcal{T}(q) \text{ and}$$

$$\forall \sigma : \mathcal{T}(p); X \subseteq Act \bullet (q \textbf{ after } \sigma \textbf{ ref } X) \text{ implies } (p \textbf{ after } \sigma \textbf{ ref } X) \qquad \square$$

Example 1.19 Referring to the example above, we now have $C_1 \sqsubseteq_{ext} C_2$ and $C_2 \sqsubseteq_{ext} C_3$. $\qquad \square$

The equivalence induced by extension, denoted $\equiv_{ext}$, is the same as that by failures refinement.

Proposition 1.6 (Properties of extension)

1. $\equiv_{ext} = \equiv_f$.
2. $\sqsubseteq_{ext}$ *is a preorder.* $\qquad \square$

1.10 Data and Infinite Traces

So far our discussion has concentrated on LTSs without data and which were finitely branching, however, many real systems we would want to model might well contain both.

1.10.1 Adding Data

The set up and examples we have looked at so far have simple events as transitions, and there has been no notion of *data* associated with events. Thus in the frequency server example our transitions abstracted away from the specific frequencies. If we wanted to include data such as this in our LTS there are a number of ways to do it, and we shall see how specific specification notations achieve this later in the book.

The most obvious way is to use a unique label for each data value one needs, often associated with a particular event.

Example 1.20 Suppose we wanted to specify a system that inputted a number then doubled it and passed that value out as output. For this we might use the following events: *in*.0, *in*.1, *in*.2, . . . , *out*.0, *out*.1, *out*2, . . . and a simple version of the system might be:

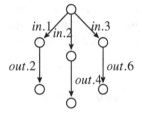

1.10.2 Infinite Trace Refinement

So far the semantics we have considered have been concerned with finite behaviour in that we, for example, considered trace refinement to be defined by the inclusion of the finite traces. In addition, we have assumed our systems are *image finite*, that is, are finitely branching (there are only a finite number of transitions from each state). Clearly many systems one might wish to specify are naturally not image finite. So in Example 1.20 a full description might have an infinite number of transitions in the initial state: *in*.0, *in*.1, *in*.2, . . . and would thus not be image finite.

To reason about systems with infinite behaviour where the behaviour in the limit is important one can use the infinite trace semantics and infinite trace refinement. These are defined as follows.

Definition 1.11 (*Infinite traces and infinite trace refinement*)
A sequence of events $\langle a_0, a_1, \ldots \rangle \in Act^\infty$ is an infinite trace of a process p if there exists $p_0, p_1, \ldots \bullet p = p_0 \xrightarrow{a_0} p_1 \xrightarrow{a_1} \ldots$. We let $\mathcal{T}^\infty(p)$ denote the set of infinite traces of p, which we also write as $traces^\infty(p)$.

Infinite trace refinement is defined by $p \sqsubseteq_{tr}^\infty q$ iff $\mathcal{T}(q) \subseteq \mathcal{T}(p)$ and $\mathcal{T}^\infty(q) \subseteq \mathcal{T}^\infty(p)$. □

It is obvious that if $p \sqsubseteq_{tr}^\infty q$ then $p \sqsubseteq_{tr} q$, but the reverse doesn't hold, the following is the standard counter-example.

Example 1.21 Consider the following system A which is infinitely branching in the initial state, but each trace is finite.

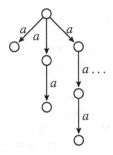

If we extend this system to a system B which in addition has an infinite trace $\langle a, a, \ldots \rangle$ from the initial state, then $A \sqsubseteq_{tr} B$ but one does not have $A \sqsubseteq_{tr}^{\infty} B$. □

However, with the use of what is known as *König's lemma* the converse does hold for image finite systems (that is, systems with a finite number of initial states where no state has infinite branches).

Proposition 1.7 *Let p and q be image finite LTSs. If $p \sqsubseteq_{tr} q$ then $p \sqsubseteq_{tr}^{\infty} q$.* □

1.10.3 Infinite Completed Trace Refinement

As for trace refinement, an infinitary version of completed trace refinement can be given, but obviously completed traces themselves must be finite. This gives us the following definition.

> **Definition 1.12** (*Infinite completed trace refinement*)
> The infinite completed trace refinement relation, $\sqsubseteq_{ctr}^{\infty}$, is defined by $p \sqsubseteq_{ctr}^{\infty} q$ iff $\mathscr{T}^{\infty}(q) \subseteq \mathscr{T}^{\infty}(p)$ and $\mathscr{CT}(q) \subseteq \mathscr{CT}(p)$. □

From Proposition 1.7 it follows that for image finite systems, completed trace refinement and infinite completed trace refinement coincide. The example above also shows that in general completed trace refinement and infinite completed trace refinement are distinct.

1.11 Summary

We began this chapter with a model of computation, labelled transition systems, which looked so simple that it was doubtful there would be much to say in terms of refinement. We have ended with a variety of refinement relations, and their associated equivalences. The complexity arises because in this simple model of computation and refinement we have embedded the possibility to vary the observations made - and it is the different observations alone that give rise to different refinement relations.

Which one is appropriate for any particular circumstance is a design choice as much as any design choice made within an actual specification.

However, that said, by far the most important relations used in the literature are *trace refinement, failures refinement* and *bisimulation* (which we will meet in the next chapter). And each of these forms the basis of refinement relations used in particular specification notations as we shall see later in this book. Trace refinement offers the basic relation, requiring that a concrete system's behaviour is a behaviour of the abstract when judged in very simple terms of "can I do this trace of events". However, it does not, as we discussed, offer any guarantees on preserving liveness, and failures refinement (or related) offers the next step up whereby we add in consideration that we can't refuse to do events or actions when they weren't refused in the original, abstract, specification. Bisimulation goes the full way to looking at structural equivalence of the two specifications (in terms of simulating one event by another).

Finally, we note that because each refinement relation is linked to notions of observation, they are linked to notions of testing. Specifically each refinement relation had an associated testing scenario which detailed the observations and the sequences of tests that would characterise that refinement relation.

1.12   Bibliographical Notes

This chapter draws heavily on the excellent survey by van Glabbeek detailed in [1]. There different refinement relations are defined, the relationships between them articulated and a testing scenario for each given. The diagram given in Fig. 1.4, again taken from [1], details the relationship between the semantics, and hence the refinement relations (and includes some further refinement relations defined in [1]).

Some additional points are worth noting. For example, sometimes the same relation has a different name in a different context. So *reduction* as defined for use in the LOTOS specification language (see [2]) is in our context (of no divergence) identical to the failures preorder. It is also called the testing preorder in [3]. Testing equivalence is the equivalence induced by that preorder (see also *may* and *must testing* [4, 5]).

Reduction was defined and motivated by testing and test generation from LOTOS specifications, along with *extension* and *conformance* [6]. The equivalence induced by extension is the same as that by reduction (that is, testing equivalence). Leduc [7] documents the relationship between these relations in some detail. Langerak in [8, 9] discusses failure trace semantics and testing in some detail.

Failures refinement and reduction, and other relations based on the idea of a process refusing events set adopt the same definition of a refusal set. By duality one would be tempted to conclude that the idea of a ready set (or acceptance set) was similarly invariant under different refinement relations based on the notion of accepting events. As we have noted, this rather surprisingly isn't the case though, and [7] details the different refinement relations that arise by using slightly different variants of acceptance / ready sets.

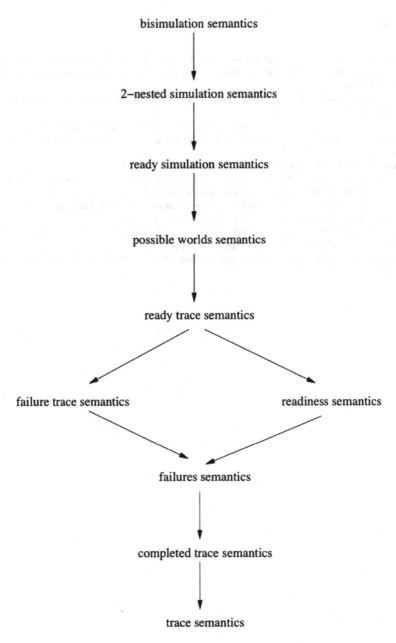

Fig. 1.4 Relating basic notions of refinement, taken from [1]

References

1. van Glabbeek RJ (2001) The linear time - branching time spectrum I. the semantics of concrete sequential processes. In: Bergstra JA, Ponse A, Smolka SA (eds) Handbook of process algebra. North-Holland, pp 3–99
2. Bolognesi T, Brinksma E (1988) Introduction to the ISO specification language LOTOS. Comput Netw ISDN Syst 14(1):25–59
3. de Nicola R (1987) Extensional equivalences for transition systems. Acta Inform 24(2):211–237
4. de Nicola R, Hennessy MCB (1984) Testing equivalences for processes. Theor Comput Sci 34(1):83–133
5. Hennessy M (1988) Algebraic theory of processes. MIT Press, USA
6. Brinksma E, Scollo G (1986) Formal notions of implementation and conformance in LOTOS. Technical Report INF-86-13, Dept of Informatics, Twente University of Technology
7. Leduc G (1991) On the role of implementation relations in the design of distributed systems using LOTOS. Ph.D. thesis, University of Liège, Liège, Belgium
8. Langerak R (1989) A testing theory for LOTOS using deadlock detection. In: Protocol specification testing and verification IX. North-Holland, pp 87–98
9. Langerak R (1992) Transformations and semantics for LOTOS. Ph.D. thesis, University of Twente, The Netherlands

Chapter 2
Automata - Introducing Simulations

An alternative semantic model is that provided by automata, and here we explore how refinement is defined in that setting, introducing the idea of forward and backward simulations. This causes us to consider the role of infinite behaviour in more depth. We discuss completeness results, that is whether the use of simulations is sufficient to verify a refinement. Finally, we introduce the important concept of bisimulation.

2.1 Introduction

Automata are an alternative semantic model that has been used as a vehicle to explore some of the definitions of refinement. The definition is usually given as follows:

Definition 2.1 (*Automata*)
An automaton is a tuple $A = (States, Act, T, Start)$ where *States* is a non-empty set of states, $Start \subseteq States$ is the set of initial states, *Act* is a set of actions which includes a special element τ, and $T \subseteq States \times Act \times States$ is a transition relation. The components of A are also accessed as $states(A) = States$ and $start(A) = Start$. $\qquad \square$

A cursory glance at Definition 1.1 shows that these definitions are almost identical. There are just two differences. First, automata can have a set of initial states, instead of just one. Second, we have included a silent, or unobservable, action τ in the definition of an automaton. Actions apart from τ are then called *external actions*, and τ is called an *internal action*. We use the same notation for writing transitions in an automaton as we did in a LTS. Because we have the additional internal action τ we define $\hat{\rho}$ to be the sequence of actions obtained from a trace ρ by deleting all the internal actions.

One can define traces and trace refinement in an almost identical way as to the definition in Chap. 1, the only caveat being that we now extend these definitions to the case when we might have infinite behaviour. First let us give the definitions.

© Springer International Publishing AG, part of Springer Nature 2018

J. Derrick and E. Boiten, *Refinement*, https://doi.org/10.1007/978-3-319-92711-4_2

> **Definition 2.2** (*Traces and trace refinement in automata*)
>
> A finite sequence of events $\sigma \in (Act \setminus \tau)^*$ is a trace of a process p if $\exists q \bullet p \overset{\sigma}{\Longrightarrow} q$. We let $\mathscr{T}^*(p)$, $\mathscr{T}^\omega(p)$ and $\mathscr{T}(p)$ denote the sets of finite, infinite and all traces of p respectively, these are also written as $traces^*(p)$, $traces^\omega(p)$ and $traces(p)$.
>
> Trace refinement is defined by $p \sqsubseteq_{tr*} q$ iff $\mathscr{T}^*(q) \subseteq \mathscr{T}^*(p)$, $p \sqsubseteq_{tr\omega} q$ iff $\mathscr{T}^\omega(q) \subseteq \mathscr{T}^\omega(p)$, and $p \sqsubseteq_{tr} q$ iff $\mathscr{T}(q) \subseteq \mathscr{T}(p)$. $\square$

So what we have done with this definition is extend the notion of traces and trace refinement to explicitly cover (i) finite traces, (ii) infinite traces, or (iii) both finite and infinite traces. Beware the abuse of notation here. In Chap. 1 we were considering only finite traces, and thus $\mathscr{T}(p)$ and *traces(p)* denoted all finite traces - here this means all finite and infinite traces. We will make clear which definition we are using in each context.

> **The naming of parts**
>
> There is an alternative way of writing the refinement relation $\sqsubseteq$ which can be confusing. Specifically, it is sometimes written $C \leq A$ to mean $A \sqsubseteq C$, i.e., C is a refinement of A. You will find both uses in the literature.

The following example nicely illustrates the difference between finite and infinite traces and their preorders.

Example 2.1 The start states are denoted by the short incoming arrows in the two specifications in Fig. 2.1. The traces of C are all finite sequences of a's, whereas the traces of A are those but in addition the infinite sequence of a's. This means that we have: $A \sqsubseteq_{tr*} C$, $C \sqsubseteq_{tr*} A$ and $A \sqsubseteq_{tr\omega} C$ but not $C \sqsubseteq_{tr\omega} A$. $\square$

Before we introduce *simulations* for automata we define some additional notation that will be used in their description.

Definition 2.3 (*Finite invisible non-determinism (fin)*)

An automaton A has *finite invisible non-determinism* (*fin* for short) if $start(A)$ is finite, and every state is finitely branching (i.e., only has finitely many transitions leading from it).

A is a *forest* if all states of A are reachable, start states have no incoming transitions and every other state has exactly one incoming transition. $\square$

The issue of finite branching (alternatively called being *image finite*) is to do with when results from finite traces can be lifted to the corresponding ones for infinite traces in the manner of the following result:

$$a \qquad a \qquad a \qquad\qquad a \qquad a \qquad a$$
$$A \qquad\qquad\qquad\qquad\qquad C$$

Fig. 2.1 Finite versus infinite traces in automata

Proposition 2.1 *If A has fin then A $\sqsubseteq_{tr*} C$ iff A $\sqsubseteq_{tr} C$.* □

This result is consistent with the example above, since C does not have fin: its start states are not finite.

2.2 Refinement and Simulations

We can now introduce another notion of refinement on automata, which is the simplest form of *simulation* - one of the principle means by which one can verify refinements. We shall then introduce the substantive notions of *forward* and *backward simulations*, and explore their properties. Key amongst these is the idea of *completeness*, that is, that every refinement can be verified by use of forward and backward simulations. This is a central theme in the use of simulations, and important because by themselves neither forward or backward simulations are complete.

We begin with the definition of what is called *refinement* in the automata literature. To avoid overloading that term (which we reserve for the generic concept), we will call this notion a *simple simulation*. It works by defining a function from concrete to abstract states (in time we will call this the retrieve relation and generalise it from a function to an arbitrary relation), and then asks that using this mapping every step of the concrete state can be simulated by one of the abstract state.

This fits with our basic tenet of refinement that the refined specification should exhibit behaviour that was allowed by the original abstract specification. In this incarnation it takes the form of saying if C can do a transition it should have been allowed by A in any *corresponding* state - where corresponding states are those that are linked by the function.

In the following definition $\longrightarrow_X$ denotes the transition relation in system X.

Definition 2.4 (*Simple simulation*)
A simple simulation is a function R from $states(C)$ to $states(A)$ such that

1. If $s \in start(C)$ then $R(s) \in start(A)$
2. For all actions $a \in Act$, if $s \xrightarrow{a}_C s'$ then $R(s) \xRightarrow{a}_A R(s')$

We will write $A \sqsubseteq_{SS} C$ when there exists a simple simulation from C to A. □

Lurking in this definition is the implicit assumption that the two automata A and C are *conformal*, that is, have the same sets of external actions. This assumption will hold unless we make it explicit to the contrary.

At first glance it would seem that simple simulations are all that is needed to show that trace refinement holds. However, this is not the case as the following example illustrates.

Example 2.2 The two automata in Fig. 2.2 have identical (finite and infinite) traces. However, whilst we have $A \sqsubseteq_{SS} C$ we do not have $C \sqsubseteq_{SS} A$. □

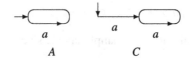

Fig. 2.2 Traces and simple simulations

Simple simulations are preorders, and they are *sound* with respect to trace refinement. Soundness here means that any simple simulation is also a trace refinement, and along with completeness is the most important property that we require of simulations. That is, we have:

$$A \sqsubseteq_{SS} C \implies A \sqsubseteq_{tr} C$$

2.2.1 Forward and Backward Simulations

Closely related to simple simulations are forward and backward simulations - one of the key concepts in refinement theory. These simulations enable a proper step by step comparison to be made between two specifications. Their name arises because of a pictorial representation whereby one either steps forwards through the simulation, or steps backwards.

So, suppose schematically we want to compare two systems represented in Fig. 2.3. Ideally, we would like to make the comparison inductively, by considering a limited number of base cases, and then by a finite number of compositions of such results obtain the result for any finite sequence of operations. To do so we use this idea of linking up corresponding states as in Fig. 2.4, which naturally lends itself to being decomposed into (semi-)commuting squares plus an additional 'triangle' to start with. Indeed these two conditions will be at the heart of the requirements of a simulation.

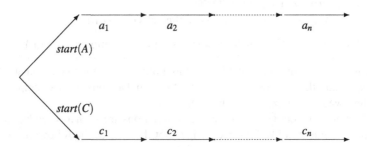

Fig. 2.3 Comparing two systems....

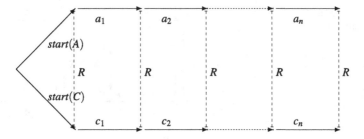

Fig. 2.4 ... which are verified by a simulation

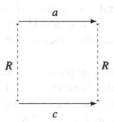

Fig. 2.5 The simulation condition for a single event

Simulations are also known as *retrieve relations, abstraction relations,* or *coupling invariants.* Apart from triangles at the beginning and at the end, we get instances of the commuting square pictured in Fig. 2.5. This leads to the following definition. In this definition $R(\!|\{s\}|\!)$ denotes the relational image of set $\{s\}$ under relation R (see formal definition in Sect. 4.1).

Definition 2.5 (*Forward simulation*)
A forward simulation is a relation R over $states(C)$ and $states(A)$ such that

1. If $s \in start(C)$ then $R(\!|\{s\}|\!) \cap start(A) \neq \varnothing$
2. For all actions $a \in Act$, if $s \xrightarrow{a}_C s'$ and $t \in R(\!|\{s\}|\!)$ then there exists $t' \in R(\!|\{s'\}|\!)$ such that $t \xRightarrow{a}_A t'$

We will write $A \sqsubseteq_{fs} C$ when there exists a forward simulation from C to A.   □

Example 2.3 Given the automata in Fig. 2.2, we have $A \sqsubseteq_{fs} C$.   □

Obviously a simple simulation is a forward simulation, but not necessarily vice versa in general. Forward simulations are also preorders as one would expect. They are also sound, and we have a partial completeness result:

Theorem 2.1 (Soundness and partial completeness of forward simulations)

1. *If $A \sqsubseteq_{fs} C$ then $A \sqsubseteq_{tr} C$.*
2. *If A is deterministic and $A \sqsubseteq_{tr*} C$ then $A \sqsubseteq_{fs} C$.*   □

Fig. 2.6 Forward and
backward simulations

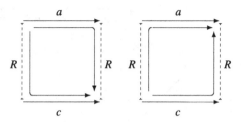

With a square depicted in Fig. 2.5, there are of course four ways of "going around the square". De Roever and Engelhardt [1] name them after the shapes of the paths. U-simulation (the top line versus the rest) and U^{-1}-simulation (the bottom line versus the rest) are not compositional since they do not guarantee that squares can be concatenated.

Starting at the top-left has given us forward simulations (which De Roever and Engelhardt call L-simulations), the alternative is to start at the bottom left. This will give us another type of simulation, called a *backward simulation* (which De Roever and Engelhardt call L^{-1}-simulations), see Fig. 2.6.

Note that since we do not need to establish equality in Fig. 2.4 but only the inclusion of the "concrete" path in the "abstract" path, we will need "semi-commutativity" of the squares, with the path involving c *included* in, rather than equal to, the other path.

Finally, there are also two possible ways for the initialisation triangle to semi-commute, the particular choices for forward and backward simulation are dictated by the need for the diagrams to be concatenated, and again to have the concrete component on the smaller side of the inclusion.

Although there is symmetry in their definition, one should note that forward and backward simulations are different not just in definition but they verify different refinements, in that there are valid refinements that one type of simulation can verify but that the other cannot.

The naming of parts

Forward and backward simulations are also often called downward and upward simulations respectively. This is due to the 'direction' of the relation R, for example, in Fig. 2.6 the relation R can be seen to be going 'down' and 'up' in the respective diagrams. However, in the rest of this book we will use the terms *forward* and *backward* simulation.

A forward simulation is so called because one starts with two pre-states $(t, s) \in R$ and steps forward one transition, and requires the post-states are also linked up. Backward simulations are the dual to this in the sense that one begins with two post-states and steps backwards one transition, requiring that these pre-states are also related by R. The definition is as follows.

Definition 2.6 (*Backward simulation*)
A backward simulation is a relation R over *states*(C) and *states*(A) such that

1. If $s \in start(C)$ then $R(|\{s\}|) \subseteq start(A)$
2. For all actions $a \in Act$, if $s \overset{a}{\longrightarrow}_C s'$ and $t' \in R(|\{s'\}|)$ then there exists $t \in$ $R(|\{s\}|)$ such that $t \overset{a}{\Longrightarrow}_A t'$
3. R is total on *states*(C).

We will write $A \sqsubseteq_{bs} C$ when there exists a backward simulation from C to A. In addition, we write $A \sqsubseteq_{ibs} C$ if there is an *image finite* backward simulation from C to A. $\square$

One striking difference in this definition is the requirement of totality of R for backwards simulations. This is necessary for soundness – and if we didn't have it an empty retrieve relation would verify simulations that were not refinements. Stressing image finite backward simulations is also necessary for soundness. This is due to an asymmetry between the future and the past – and hence between forward and backward simulations. In the former a future execution can be infinite, whereas if we consider backward simulations we will only ever have explored finite executions – lifting those finite executions to infinite ones requires that we have image finiteness. Before we give these results, some examples.

Example 2.4 For A and C in Fig. 2.1 we have $C \sqsubseteq_{bs} A$. For A and C in Fig. 2.2, we have $C \not\sqsubseteq_{bs} A$. $\square$

Like forward simulations, backward simulations are preorders. A simple simulation is also an image finite backward simulation. Backward simulations are also sound, and we have a partial completeness result:

Theorem 2.2 (Soundness of backward simulations)

1. *If $A \sqsubseteq_{bs} C$ then $A \sqsubseteq_{tr*} C$.*
2. *If $A \sqsubseteq_{ibs} C$ then $A \sqsubseteq_{tr} C$.* $\square$

Theorem 2.3 (Partial completeness of backward simulations) *Let C be a forest and $A \sqsubseteq_{tr*} C$. Then*

1. *$A \sqsubseteq_{bs} C$.*
2. *If additionally A is fin, then $A \sqsubseteq_{ibs} C$.* $\square$

Looking at this last result, it might be tempting to conclude that under the assumption of *fin* backward and image backward simulations were the same. But no! We need an additional assumption of reachability, as the following result and example shows.

Proposition 2.2 *Suppose that all states of C are reachable, A has fin, and that $A \sqsubseteq_{bs} C$. Then $A \sqsubseteq_{ibs} C$.*

Example 2.5 Given A and C as in Fig. 2.7, we have $C \sqsubseteq_{bs} A$ but $C \not\sqsubseteq_{ibs} A$ - there is no image finite backward simulation. $\square$

Fig. 2.7 Reachability is
needed to relate $\sqsubseteq_{bs}$ and $\sqsubseteq_{ibs}$

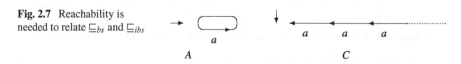

A C

2.2.2 Completeness Results

One natural question to ask at this stage is: why are neither forward nor backward
simulations complete in themselves. The following example suffices.

Example 2.6 Consider A and C in Fig. 2.8. The possible traces of A are 1 or more
a's followed by a b or c, plus their prefixes. The possible traces of C are 2 or more
a's followed by b or c, plus their prefixes. Every trace of C is a valid trace of A, so
C is a refinement of A (but not the other way round).

However, the refinement cannot be verified by using a forward or backward simulation on its own, and to verify the refinement we have to proceed in two steps: using
one simulation to an intermediate specification, then another simulation to make the
refinement to C.   □

So are simulations in any sense complete? Well the answer (in the finite world)
is yes, they are jointly complete, and further you just need one forward and one
backward simulation together which link up a canonical specification. We have the
following.

Theorem 2.4 (Joint completeness of simulations)
Suppose $A \sqsubseteq_{tr*} C$. Then

1. *There exists an intermediate specification B such that $A \sqsubseteq_{bs} B \sqsubseteq_{fs} C$.*
2. *If A has fin, then $A \sqsubseteq_{ibs} B \sqsubseteq_{fs} C$.*   □

From this observation it is not far to the thought that one could combine forwards
and backwards simulations to produce a single type of simulation which is complete.
Indeed, this is the case, and there are a number of ways of doing it (in the following
definition $\mathbb{P}_1$ are sets of size at most 1).

Fig. 2.8 The incompleteness
of simulations

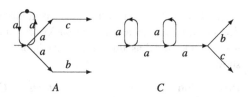

A C

Definition 2.7 (*Forward-backward simulation*)
A forward simulation is a relation R over $\mathbb{P}_1(states(A))$ and $states(C)$ such that

1. If $s \in start(C)$ then there exists $S \in R(\{s\})$ such that $S \subseteq start(A)$.
2. For all actions $a \in Act$, if $s \xrightarrow{a}_C s'$ and $T \in R(\{s\})$ then there exists a set $T' \in R(\{s'\})$ such that for every $t' \in T'$ there exists $t \in T$ with $t \overset{a}{\Longrightarrow}_A t'$.

We will write $A \sqsubseteq_{fb} C$ when there exists a forward-backward simulation from C to A, and write $\sqsubseteq_{ifb}$ if it is image finite. □

These simulations are preorders. A forward simulation is an image finite forward-backward simulation, as is an image finite backward simulation. A backward simulation (whether image finite or not) is a forward-backward simulation.

They are sound, as one would hope, but also complete - as was our aim.

Theorem 2.5 (Soundness of forward-backward simulations)

1. *If $A \sqsubseteq_{fb} C$ then $A \sqsubseteq_{tr*} C$.*
2. *If $A \sqsubseteq_{ifb} C$ then $A \sqsubseteq_{tr} C$.* □

Theorem 2.6 (Completeness of forward-backward simulations)
Suppose $A \sqsubseteq_{tr*} C$. Then

1. *$A \sqsubseteq_{fb} C$.*
2. *If additionally A is fin, then $A \sqsubseteq_{ifb} C$.* □

Of course forward-backward simulations can be decomposed into one forward and one backward simulation in the manner of the joint completeness result. The following classic example shows why the requirement of *fin* is necessary in Theorem 2.6.

Example 2.7 In the example in Fig. 2.9 we have $A \sqsubseteq_{tr} C$ but not $A \sqsubseteq_{ifb} C$ and this can arise because A does not have *fin* as $start(A)$ is not finite. □

Fig. 2.9 Relating $\sqsubseteq_{tr}$ and $\sqsubseteq_{ifb}$

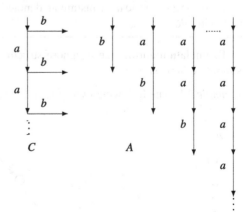

There is an obvious dual to forward-backward simulations, namely, backward-forward simulations. However, they are not central to the remainder of our discussion, and details are in [2] for the interested reader.

2.3 Bisimulation

The simulations we have considered so far in this chapter have been defined with respect to trace refinement, and can thus principally be thought of as a methodology by which to verify such refinements. The final relation we consider in this chapter, *bisimulation*, is a refinement relation in its own right, and provides another link to the work discussed in Chap. 1. Indeed it is the finest of the relations defined on LTS - in that it distinguishes more processes than any of the others we have considered.

It is phrased differently from the other refinement relations considered in Chap. 1, in that it is defined not in terms of observations of traces, failures etc, but in terms of simulations. However, it differs from the simulations in this chapter, and indeed is called a *bi*simulation, as we ask for both LTS to simulate each other with the same relation R, and for that reason defines an equivalence rather than a preorder. However, it has been so important in the literature (and is the equivalence most used with the process algebra CCS, see Chap. 6) it deserves mention here.

The definition we give is phrased in terms of the relation R being defined on processes in a manner similar to those given in Chap. 1, rephrasing it in terms of the context of this chapter is straightforward. (In the definition we write pRq for $(p, q) \in R$ to be consistent with the usual presentation of bisimulations.)

Definition 2.8 (*Bisimulation*)
A bisimulation is a relation R on processes such that, for $a \in Act$:

1. if pRq and $p \xrightarrow{a} p'$ then $\exists q' \bullet q \xrightarrow{a} q'$ with $p'Rq'$
2. if pRq and $q \xrightarrow{a} q'$ then $\exists p' \bullet p \xrightarrow{a} p'$ with $p'Rq'$

Two processes p and q are bisimular, denoted $p \equiv q$ if there exists a bisimulation R with pRq. $\square$

Bisimulation allows one to ignore structural differences, as the following very simple example shows.

Example 2.8 The following two systems are bisimular.

$\square$

Proposition 2.3
Bisimulation is stronger than the refinement relations defined in Chap. 1. □

For example, for all processes P and Q, if P and Q are bisimular then $P \sqsubseteq_{tr} Q$. The converse doesn't hold, as the following example shows for trace refinement.

Example 2.9 The following two systems are trace equivalent but there is no bisimulation between them.

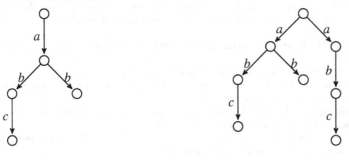

□

We will discuss bisimulation more in Sect. 6.5 when we look at refinement in the process algebra CCS.

2.4 Bibliographical Notes

The results in this chapter appear in the excellent survey paper by Lynch and Vaandrager [2], and most examples in this chapter appear in [2]. The work in [2] is extended to timed systems in [3]. Both are required reading for those interested in refinement in an automata setting and the use of simulations. Bisimulations were introduced by Park [4] as a small variant of a behavioural equivalence defined by Hennessy and Milner [5]. A fuller explanation of bisimulation, together with more examples, is given in both [6, 7].

As mentioned in the text, De Roever and Engelhardt also discuss the use of simulations in [1], this time in a relational context (a related approach is detailed in Chap. 4).

Single complete simulations have been introduced by a number of different authors in different guises. The ones discussed above appear in [2]. They appear in [8, 9] by Klarlund and Schneider, where they are called *invariants* and *ND measures*. In the work of Jonsson [10] they are called *subset simulations* and *power simulations* in [11].

References

1. de Roever W-P, Engelhardt K (1998) Data refinement: model-oriented proof methods and their comparison. CUP
2. Lynch N, Vaandrager FW (1995) Forward and backward simulations I: untimed systems. Inf Comput 121(2):214–233
3. Lynch N, Vaandrager FW (1996) Forward and backward simulations part II: timing-based systems. Inf Comput 128:1–25
4. Park D (1981) Concurrency and automata on infinite sequences. In: Deussen P (ed) Theoretical computer science. Lecture notes in computer science, vol 104. Springer, Heidelberg, pp 167–183
5. Hennessy M, Milner R (1985) Algebraic laws for nondeterminism and concurrency. J. ACM 32(1):137–161
6. Milner R (1989) Communication and concurrency. Prentice-Hall
7. Bowman H, Gomez R (2005) Concurrency theory: calculi an automata for modelling untimed and timed concurrent systems. Springer, USA
8. Klarlund N, Schneider FB (1989) Verifying safety properties using non-deterministic infinite-state automata. Technical report, Cornell University, USA
9. Klarlund N, Schneider FB (1993) Proving nondeterministically specified safety properties using progress measures. Inf Comput 107(1):151–170
10. Jonsson B (1991) Simulations between specifications of distributed systems. In: Baeten JCM, Groote JF (eds) CONCUR '91: 2nd international conference on concurrency theory. Lecture notes in computer science, vol 527. Springer, Heidelberg, pp 346–360
11. Derrick J, Boiten EA (2014) Refinement in Z and Object-Z, 2nd edn. Springer, Berlin

Chapter 3
Simple State-Based Refinement

3.1 Introduction

One central distinction in formal methods is between those based on state, and those based on behaviour. In most applications it is essential or at least practical to have both. State based systems need behavioural elements in order to consider aspects of interaction with an environment, for example to record which changes of state are due to the system's ongoing execution and which are in response to an externally provided stimulus. Behaviour based systems can use state and data for abstraction, for example recording the number of free spaces as a number instead of a behaviour that encodes directly how many allocation operations will still succeed. The rich research field of "integrated formal methods" [1] considers formalisms that have both, through extensions or integration of different formalisms. We will return in detail to these issues in Chap. 9 and on.

The models we have looked at so far concentrate on behaviour, and states are fully characterised by the behaviour that will be possible from that point on. Observing only the (possible) behaviour tells us everything there is to know in a LTS. In this chapter we will look at a different class of elementary models that take the complementary view. What we will be observing is states rather than behaviours; and behaviour will be implicit, in the sense that we have to draw the conclusion that "something must have happened" if we can observe that the state has changed. We observe what "is", not directly what "happens".

Elementary models like this are central to some common notions of refinement, including Lamport's refinement relations such as that underlying TLA, and also aspects of action systems and sequential program refinement.

© Springer International Publishing AG, part of Springer Nature 2018
J. Derrick and E. Boiten, *Refinement*, https://doi.org/10.1007/978-3-319-92711-4_3

3.2   A Basic Model with Refinement

The simplest state based model is one where we have states, initial states, and computations which relate states. As we do not observe anything of the computations, the transition relation is no more complicated than just a relation between states, which records only that one state may occur sometime before the other.

It may be odd for us to give this simple model such a complicated name; however, the name reflects how it relates to standard models for refinement as covered in other chapters.

Definition 3.1 (*Concrete State Machine with Anonymous Transitions (CSMAT)*)
A concrete state machine with anonymous transitions is a tuple (*State*, *Init*, *T*) where *State* is a non-empty set of states, *Init* $\subseteq$ *State* is the set of initial states, and $T \subseteq$ *State* $\times$ *State* is a reflexive and transitive transition relation. $\square$

We also write $p \longrightarrow_T q$ for $(p, q) \in T$, possibly leaving out T when it is clear from the context. This is in close analogy with $\longrightarrow$ in LTS and automata, and at the same time also with $\Longrightarrow$ because T is reflexive and transitive, and thus equal to T^*.

It is a *state machine* because it describes transitions between states; but those transitions are *anonymous*, omitting the labels that are included in the LTS transition relation. As we observe no information on transitions (not even how many there are), we cannot observe individual steps, and hence we only look at the outcomes before and after a possibly empty sequence of state changes, which we might also call a *computation*. Reflexivity of T is also known as *stuttering*.

So far this only looks like a simplification (abstraction) of LTS that removes all the observations we might make of an LTS. However, we called it a *concrete* state machine – the reason for this comes to light in the notions of observation we define for CSMATs. The most elementary of these simply characterises the states that are reachable in M, starting from a state in *Init* and following T.

Definition 3.2 (*CSMAT observations*)
For a CSMAT $M = ($*State*, *Init*, *T*$)$ its observations are a set of states defined by

$$\mathcal{O}(M) = \{s : State \mid \exists\, init : Init \bullet (init, s) \in T\}$$

$\square$

This allows a first definition of refinement for CSMATs.

Definition 3.3 (*CSMAT safety refinement*)
For CSMATs $C = (S, CI, CT)$ and $A = (S, AI, AT)$, C is a safety refinement of A, denoted $A \sqsubseteq_S C$, iff $\mathcal{O}(C) \subseteq \mathcal{O}(A)$. $\square$

This is called "safety refinement" because, just like trace refinement for LTS, it prevents a concrete system from doing anything "bad", i.e. the concrete system cannot end up in states that the abstract system disallows. Like in trace refinement, doing nothing is always safe, for example if either *CI* or *CT* is empty then (S, CI, CT)

refines any CSMAT on the same state space S. For now we have to restrict our definition of refinement to CSMATs on the same state space, as comparisons only make sense when the observations live in the same universe – this is the same issue which led to choosing the action alphabets in two LTS identical or at least from the same superset.

3.3   Termination and Refinement

Trace refinement on LTS reflected a notion of observation that is not aware of whether a behaviour has "finished", which we then addressed by considering completed trace refinement. We do something similar here. One way would have been through the *explicit* characterisation of "final" or accepting states, as is normally done for finite state machines. However, we will choose an *implicit* notion of termination that lies closer to the idea of deadlock in LTS. There, a deadlock means that no further behaviour is possible. Here, the presence of stuttering in the model means that there is *always* a possibility of "further" computation – however, in some states stuttering may be the *only* possibility, and we will consider those as "terminating" states. Intuitively, nothing significant or "interesting" can happen anymore once we have ended up in such a state, in particular we cannot escape from them.

Definition 3.4 (*CSMAT terminating states and observations*)
The terminating states and terminating observations of a CSMAT $M = (S, Init, T)$ are defined by

$$term(M) = \{s \in S \mid \forall t \in S \bullet (s, t) \in T \Rightarrow s = t\}$$
$$\mathscr{O}_t(M) = \mathscr{O}(M) \cap term(M)$$

As should have been expected, set inclusion on these observations can be viewed as a refinement relation. We will call it "partial correctness" as it is very close to that traditional correctness relation for programs: if the computation terminates, it delivers the correct results; and when it does not, we impose no constraints.

Definition 3.5 (*CSMAT partial correctness refinement*)
For CSMATs $C = (S, CI, CT)$ and $A = (S, AI, AT)$, C is a partial correctness refinement of A, denoted $A \sqsubseteq_{PC} C$, iff $\mathscr{O}_T(C) \subseteq \mathscr{O}_T(A)$.

In some contexts, a system's failure to terminate is a problem – for example, when we are modelling traditional sequential programs. As we have chosen for non-termination to be implicitly characterised, the definition of those sets of states is also in terms of CSMATs states and behaviour.

Definition 3.6 (*Nonterminating states in a CSMAT*)
For a CSMAT $C = (S, CI, CT)$ the set of states from where the system cannot terminate, i.e. cannot reach a terminating state,

$$mustnotterm(M) = \{s \in S \mid \forall t \in S \bullet (s, t) \in T \Rightarrow t \notin term(M)\}$$

and the set of states from where it may end up not terminating contains all those which may evolve to such states, i.e.

$$mayfailtoterm(M) = \{s \in S \mid \exists t \in S \bullet (s, t) \in T \wedge t \in mustnotterm(M)\} \qquad \square$$

Reflexivity of T implies that $term(M)$ and $mustnotterm(M)$ are disjoint, and that $mustnotterm(M) \subseteq mayfailtoterm(M)$; the definition of $term(M)$ then implies that $mayfailtoterm(M)$ is also disjoint from $term(M)$.

3.4 More than One Observation

The CSMAT semantics we have looked at so far recorded only a single observation. In safety refinement, the system is stopped at some point, and the resulting state recorded; for partial correctness refinement, we only make that observation once the system stops by itself. This may be an acceptable model for batch computing, but not for systems that can be observed all the time – for example, a traffic light. (See [2, Chapter 9] for how we addressed this as an extension to Z refinement.)

A single control sequence of a Dutch traffic light displays amber before red, and then goes straight to green. This is characterised in the first system below; the second one switches the order of lights. (Note that for the described CSMAT, its transition relation T is the transitive and reflexive closure of the arrows included in the diagrams.)

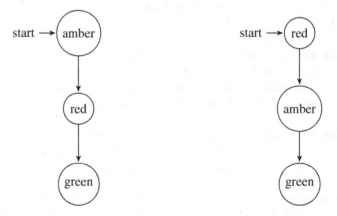

In both cases, the observations $\mathscr{O}$ are the three possible colours. The single terminating observation is "green" in either case.

Making multiple observations on a CSMAT can be modelled directly as follows.

Definition 3.7 (*State trace semantics of CSMAT*)
For a CSMAT $M = (State, Init, T)$, its state traces $\mathscr{ST}(M)$ are the smallest set of sequences over *State* satisfying the following properties:

- the singleton trace $\langle s \rangle$ is in $\mathscr{ST}(M)$ iff s is a state reachable from *Init*, i.e. $s \in \mathcal{O}(M)$;
- for trace t, states $s, s' \in State$, whenever $t \frown \langle s \rangle \in \mathscr{ST}(M)$ and $(s, s') \in T$ then also $t \frown \langle s, s' \rangle \in \mathscr{ST}(M)$.

The terminating state traces of M are the subset of these which end in a state $s \in term(M)$. For either of these notions, we could also consider the stutter-free subset, which avoids repetitions (by taking $s \neq s'$ in the second condition). $\qquad \square$

Refinement relations can be defined as set inclusions in the obvious way.

For the example above, the sequence $\langle amber, red \rangle$ is a state trace of the left system, but not of the right, and conversely for the reverse sequence. If we added realism to the example by also modelling the loop back from green to amber, the systems would become equivalent. This is because we are unable to guarantee that every state change will actually be observed – informally, each traffic light system can look like the other one if we "blink" long enough at the right times.

State trace semantics of machines like this, more precisely the extension of CSMATs that also contains abstract state (see Sect. 3.8), comes close to the model for the refinement theories of Abadi and Lamport [3, 4].

3.5   Towards Total Correctness

Calling our earlier refinement relation "partial correctness" invites the question: can we define total correctness as well? The answer to that is positive, but it needs a change of perspective to get a non-trivial definition.

Partial and total correctness
Partial correctness and total correctness of a system, notions typically used for sequential programs, are concerned with both systems terminating and delivering the correct outcome. In relation to a given specification, an implementation is *partially correct* if it delivers an outcome consistent with the specification whenever it terminates; *total correctness* is when in addition to that, the implementation also terminates whenever the specification does.

What we would normally have to add is that the concrete computation is only allowed to not terminate whenever that is also allowed by the abstract one. As we have it now, that would be the simple all-or-nothing conjunct to partial correctness that $\mathcal{O}_T(C) = \varnothing \Rightarrow \mathcal{O}_T(A) = \varnothing$. This relates closely to ideas of termination and refinement in action systems and Event-B. The most generous interpretation of "whenever", namely that a state must be a terminating one in the concrete system whenever the same state is terminating in the abstract system, trivialises the refinement relation by forcing equality instead of $\subseteq$ in Definition 3.5, as we restrict making observations to terminal states, and observe those states themselves.

A different way of looking at it is that "whenever" implies a quantification over all initial states – and this invites a different view of what the different initial states represent.

3.6 Observations Including Initial States

Our definition of observations above only considers whether states (or terminating states) can be reached from *some* initial state. This implies that, when there are multiple initial states, we do not know or we do not care in which of these the computation started. Effectively, the CSMAT starts its operation by a nondeterministic choice of one of the possible initial states. The CSMAT operates in a vacuum, it takes in no information from outside.

Having possibly multiple initial states in the machine also allows another interpretation. We could imagine that the different initial states represent a variable input to the system. This would make observations a relation between the initial state chosen and the final state observed – in other words, we get *relational* observations. This would even allow sequential (and other) composition of CSMATs.

Thus, we can define relational observations that connect an initial state to another (final) state as follows.

Definition 3.8 (*Relational observations of a CSMAT*)
For a CSMAT $M = (State, Init, T)$ its relational observations and terminating relational observations are relations defined as

$$\mathscr{R}(M) = (Init \times State) \cap T$$
$$\mathscr{R}_T(M) = (Init \times term(M)) \cap T$$

$\square$

A particular consequence (using reflexivity of T) is that $id_{Init} \subseteq \mathscr{R}(M)$ – initial states can be observed to evolve to themselves. Similarly, $id_{Init \cap term(M)} \subseteq \mathscr{R}_T(M)$. From the definitions it is clear that dom $\mathscr{R}(M) = Init$, and $\mathscr{R}_T(M) \subseteq Init \times term(M)$, and hence states in those sets are indeed the *only* ones that can be observed to evolve to themselves.

Analogous refinement relations can be defined using these observations.

Definition 3.9 (*Relational refinements for CSMATs*)
For CSMATs C and A,

- C is a (relational) trace refinement of A, denoted $A \sqsubseteq_{RT} C$, iff $\mathscr{R}(C) \subseteq \mathscr{R}(A)$;
- C is a relational partial correctness refinement of A, denoted $A \sqsubseteq_R C$, iff $\mathscr{R}_T(C) \subseteq \mathscr{R}_T(A)$.

$\square$

Relational refinement has an implication for the initialisations of the respective CSMATs, given the properties we observed above. Namely, for $(S, AI, AT) \sqsubseteq_{RT}$ (S, CI, CT) to hold, it needs to be the case that $CI \subseteq AI$. For partial correctness refinement, the same condition restricted to terminating initial states needs to hold.

We can now extend partial correctness meaningfully to total correctness. A first formulation is that, if the abstract system can terminate when started in a certain initial state, then the concrete system can also terminate from that same initial state. A small calculation allows to reformulate that in a more natural way:

$s \in Init \wedge s \notin mustnottterm(M)$

$\equiv \{$ definition of $mustnotterm \}$

$s \in Init \wedge s \notin \{s' \in S \mid \forall t \in S \bullet (s', t) \in T \Rightarrow t \notin term(M)\}$

$\equiv \{$ set comprehension, predicate calculus$\}$

$s \in Init \wedge \exists t \in S \bullet (s, t) \in T \wedge t \in term(M)$

$\equiv \{$ definition of $\mathscr{R}_T(M) \}$

$s \in \operatorname{dom} \mathscr{R}_T(M)$

Hence we have:

Definition 3.10   (*Total correctness refinement for CSMATs*)
For CSMATs C and A, C is a total correctness refinement of A, denoted $A \sqsubseteq_R C$, iff $\mathscr{R}_T(C) \subseteq \mathscr{R}_T(A)$ and $\operatorname{dom} \mathscr{R}_T(A) \subseteq \operatorname{dom} \mathscr{R}_T(C)$.   □

This interpretation assumes that only *certain* non-termination is a problem. An alternative view would be that *possible* non-termination is already to be avoided, and hence we need to limit the total correctness condition to states where termination is guaranteed. The complement of *mayfailtoterm(M)* does not simplify to something as simple as the domain of the observations. Different methods of implicitly and explicitly modelling such non-termination issues will be addressed in Chap. 11.

These are still concrete states, i.e. the values of the states become directly observable. As a consequence, we have no use for simulations yet, as the only states these could meaningfully relate would be identical ones.

3.7   State Abstraction

We have so far only described (refinement) relations between CSMATs using the same state space – this was essential in order to be able to compare observations. On the way to machines with abstract state, we will consider a mechanism that allows different state spaces to be compared. In a context of states being visible, a change of state representation can only happen if we can link it to the observable state that it is meant to represent. Having general relations between abstract and concrete states does not allow for that connection to be made unambiguously and for every state. Thus, rather than considering simulations as in the previous chapter, we only look at total functions from "concrete" to "abstract" state, in essence the notion of a "simple simulation" as in Definition 2.4. Here they have the dual role of relating states, and recovering observations – whereas in the models considered in other chapters these two roles can be separated.

Definition 3.11 (*State abstraction on CSMATs*)
Given a (total) function $f : S \to S'$, the state abstraction of a CSMAT $M = (S, Init, T)$ under f is the state machine $f(M) = (S', Init', T')$ defined by

$$Init' = \{f(s) \mid s \in Init\}$$
$$T' = \{(f(s), f(s')) \mid (s, s') \in T\}$$

$\square$

Observe that the resulting machine is not necessarily a CSMAT, as its transition relation may not be transitive: if states s_1 and s_2 have the same image under f, a path ending in s_1 may join up with a path beginning in s_2, creating a connection that may not have existed in the original CSMAT. However, none of the observation sets defined in this chapter depend essentially on transitivity of the transition relation, though state traces as defined would move through such new connections.

State abstraction does preserve reflexivity of the transition relation, or in other words it preserves "stuttering steps". Moreover, it can introduce stuttering steps in the abstraction that were actual changes of state in the original: when both the before state and the after state of a step are abstracted to the same state. Such a step, where a concrete change of state corresponds to a step that preserves the abstract state value, is called a *perspicuous* step [5] – we will return to these in Chap. 5. Abstraction can introduce additional stuttering; as a consequence, it also has the potential of mapping states that had further non-trivial behaviour to states that only exhibit stuttering. For example, a concrete system that loops endlessly between two states may be abstracted to a single stuttering state. This does not sit well with the implicit definition of termination that we have been using in this chapter, as we would end up with abstract systems that terminate more often than concrete ones – the opposite of what we would normally require.

A state abstraction based on $f : S \to S'$ allows us to compare refinement relations in terms of S and S', respectively, by considering images under f in the observation space. Abstraction in formal specification normally means the removal of implementation detail, and as such it tends to be the converse of refinement. This determines the direction of the implication in definitions like the following.

Definition 3.12 (*Relational abstraction trace refinement*)
For CSMATs $C = (S, CI, CT)$ and $A = (S', AI, AT)$ and a function $f : S \to S'$, C is a relational abstraction trace refinement of A for abstraction function f, denoted $A \sqsubseteq_{RT_f} C$, if $A \sqsubseteq_{RT} f(C)$, i.e.,

$$\forall c, c' \in S \bullet c \in CI \wedge (c, c') \in CT \Rightarrow f(c) \in AI \wedge (f(c), f(c')) \in AT \quad \square$$

The implication here could be split in two, one for initialisation and one for the transition relation. The inclusion of initialisations (under abstraction) is already implied by the above implication, using reflexivity of the transition relation. Inclusion of the transition relations would be a strict strengthening, as it also imposes conditions on parts of the state space that may not be reachable from initial states.

3.8 State Variables and Observation

So far we have not assumed any structure on the state space. In models of sequential programming, the state space is typically composed of the values of all the variables. This is also the model that underlies Hoare and He's Unifying Theories of Programming [6]. Refinement relations in this world operate on the same basis as the ones in this chapter, but with extra complications arising from the direct encoding of termination, deadlock, and other paradigm-specific concepts as auxiliary variables that receive special treatment.

If we view the state as made up of variables, we can consider a special type of state abstraction, namely projection on a particular subset of the variables. As these are the variables that occur in the semantics of our "abstract" specification, we could call them "observable" variables. De Roever and Engelhardt [7] call them "normal" variables. Any additional variables that might occur in the "concrete" machine could be viewed as "local" or "auxiliary" variables, whose values are only relevant while the computation runs, but get discarded at the end.

With this particular type of abstraction function in mind, we revisit the ideas of the previous section. Initialisation gives us some flexibility in the concrete system, as only the values of the observable variables are viewed as input values provided by the environment. The values of local variables are initially unconstrained. We may give them useful values, for example derived from observable variables' values, immediately – in the abstract system, such an initialisation would appear as a stuttering step as no observable variable changes value, and hence it would be an acceptable refinement. Any atomic assignment of a variable value at the abstract level could be split into multiple steps at the concrete level, only one of which (the one which actually makes the assignment to the observable variable) does not correspond to an abstract stuttering. Hence we can increase the granularity of operations at the concrete level.

At the point at which the concrete counterpart of the intended abstract computation is completed, we could execute more concrete steps that correspond to abstract stuttering – but none that make a difference in the abstract view. At this point, we might as well stop the concrete computation. All that remains is that the state contains local variables that are not observable. We could apply the abstraction function at this point, to remove the excess information and achieve a result at our abstract specification level. This will turn out to be a special case of the *finalisation* operation that we will encounter for abstract data types in the next chapter.

Transitivity of the transition relation in this chapter represented the idea that we cannot distinguish individual steps of a system. Conceptually, this idea is undermined at this point in our theory development by some concrete steps being identifiable as abstract stutterings, but not some other concrete steps. The formal level counterpart to this is that even this particular type of abstraction function does not necessarily preserve transitivity of the transition relation, as the existence of a particular transition on observable variables may depend on the value of a local variable.

The other semantic difficulty that arises with abstraction functions is that stuttering at the abstract level can be connected to infinite behaviour at the concrete level. This will be addressed in detail in Chap. 5.

3.9 Programs and Labeled Transitions

The model we have been using in this chapter has been useful to illustrate a number of concepts at the most basic level – in particular, an implicit notion of *termination*, the role of *stuttering*, and a first step towards abstract state. However, it is also somewhat problematic in practice in a number of ways.

- The model essentially describes a *single* computation (with inputs provided only at initialisation). This is respectable practice in theoretical computer science (e.g. Turing machines are essentially in the same family) but less adequate for software development. It does not match the interaction model of a module or object which offers functionality at an interface. It is even less suitable for reactive systems which actively engage with an environment, for example by offering a choice of behaviour.
- We argued above that transitivity of the relation becomes problematic when semantic sophistications begin to discern boundaries between steps. Similar issues arise for reflexivity, including the need for a distinction between making a (possibly unbounded) sequence of transitions all of which change nothing, and not making a transition at all.
- There is a single transition relation, which means that any verification of refinement will be essentially between one relation at the abstract level and another at the concrete level, with few opportunities to use compositional reasoning on simpler components.
- Related to that, specifying complex behaviour as a single relation is unwieldy. If we decompose the abstract behaviour using relational operators like composition, union, and transitive closure, not all implementing concrete systems are guaranteed to match that same structure.

All these issues can be addressed in one go by essentially merging this computational model with the labeled transition systems model of Chap. 1, leading to the relational models discussed in the next chapter. This involves three steps:

- We identify a number of elementary transitions, we call these the repertoire, or if we focus on their names: the *alphabet* of the system.
- We put the CSMAT transition relation under a magnifying glass and discover that it is the union of all possible finite sequences of elementary transitions just

defined. We identify any such sequence by the sequence of labels of the constituent elementary operations, and call this a "program".

- Rather than defining and verifying refinement for the single computation of the CSMAT, we define a (normally formally stronger) refinement relation by verifying refinement for every single program separately, i.e. using a universal quantification over all programs.

Simulations as described in Chap. 2 will of course be the tool that ensures the latter step becomes a simplification rather than a complication.

3.10 Bibliographical Notes

The CSMAT model is conceptually close to standard models in theoretical computer science, such as state machines without labels, or Turing machines where the system state then consists of a control state and the contents of the tape(s).

The standard theory of refinement on the basis of sequences of machine states is due to Abadi and Lamport [3], and forms essentially the programming model assumed by temporal logic based specification methods like Lamport's TLA [8]. The corresponding refinement theory was further developed by Hesselink [4].

This chapter identified some links with action systems [9] and Event-B [10] and defined essentially the model for ASM [11]. All of this will be explored in more detail in later chapters.

References

1. Araki K, Galloway A, Taguchi K (eds) (1999) International conference on integrated formal methods 1999 (IFM'99). Springer, New York
2. Derrick J, Boiten EA (2014) Refinement in Z and object-Z, 2nd edn. Springer, London
3. Abadi M, Lamport L (1991) The existence of refinement mappings. Theor Comput Sci 2(82):253–284
4. Hesselink WH (2005) Eternity variables to prove simulation of specifications. ACM Trans Comput Log 6(1):175–201
5. Boiten EA (2011) Perspicuity and granularity in refinement. In: Proceedings 15th international refinement workshop, vol 55 of EPTCS, pp 155–165
6. Hoare CAR, He Jifeng (1998) Unifying theories of programming. Prentice Hall, London
7. de Roever W-P, Engelhardt K (1998) Data refinement: model-oriented proof methods and their comparison. CUP, Cambridge
8. Lamport L (1994) The temporal logic of actions. ACM Trans Program Lang Syst 16(3):872–923
9. Back RJR (1993) Refinement of parallel and reactive programs. In: Broy M (ed) Program design calculi. Springer, Berlin, pp 73–92
10. Abrial J-R (2010) Modeling in event-B: system and software engineering, 1st edn. Cambridge University Press, New York
11. Schellhorn G (2005) ASM refinement and generalizations of forward simulation in data refinement: a comparison. Theor Comput Sci 336(2–3):403–436

Chapter 4
A Relational View of Refinement

In Chap. 1 we introduced differing notions of refinement in the LTS setting - each one based upon a different notion of observation. In Chap. 2 we focused on simulations as a means to verify trace refinements in an Automata context, and we discussed both finite trace refinement as well as trace refinement in the presence of infinite traces. In Chap. 3 we developed a basic refinement model that looked at states in the first place, and constructed a relational semantics for it. We ended with sketching how labels on transitions could be added to that and how we could apply abstraction to state spaces, in preparation for the model in the current chapter.

In this chapter we will look at a semantic model that is entirely based on relations and abstract state as a model of computation. In this context programs will be finite relational compositions of operations together with a *finalisation* which makes explicit the observations made of that program. As in Chap. 1 and ever since refinement will be the consistency of observations. We will then explore, without fixing the exact observations to be made, how *simulations* can be used to verify the refinement in a way similar to that found in Chap. 2.

This theory of relational refinement was initially formulated for abstract data types (ADTs) whose operations are total relations. In order to apply this theory to a particular specification language such as Z, we consider the application of the simulation rules to a partial relational framework.

Not only are there different observations to be made of a system, there are also different ways of interpreting partial relations as total relations on an extended domain; the standard theory is equally valid for partial relations, and thus can be applied directly as well - leading to a total of at least three different notions of refinement. This chapter will explore some of the consequent issues.

We begin by recalling some of the relational notation we will use.

© Springer International Publishing AG, part of Springer Nature 2018   51
J. Derrick and E. Boiten, *Refinement*, https://doi.org/10.1007/978-3-319-92711-4_4

4.1   Introduction

A relation is a set of ordered pairs, and for sets X and Y, the set of all relations between X and Y is denoted $X \leftrightarrow Y$. Thus $X \leftrightarrow Y$ is just an abbreviation for $\mathbb{P}(X \times Y)$. When defining relations the so-called maplet notation $x \mapsto y$ is often used as an alternative to (x, y).

The simplest relation is the *identity relation*, defined (using set comprehension) by

$$id \ X == \{x : X \bullet x \mapsto x\}$$

This is sometimes also denoted by id_X.

First and second *component projections* are provided. For any ordered pair p, *first p* and *second p* are the first and second components of the pair respectively. As an alternative, numeric selectors can also be used, as in $p.1$ and $p.2$. These generalise to allow an arbitrary selection from an n-tuple.

The *domain* of a relation $R : X \leftrightarrow Y$ is the set of elements in X related to something in Y. Similarly the *range* of R is the set of elements of Y to which some element of X is related.

$$\mathrm{dom}\, R = \{p : R \bullet \textit{first } p\}$$
$$\mathrm{ran}\, R = \{p : R \bullet \textit{second } p\}$$

Instead of considering the whole of the domain and range we will frequently need to consider restrictions of these sets. The *domain restriction* of a relation $R : X \leftrightarrow Y$ by a set $S \subseteq X$ is the subset of R whose first components are in S. Similarly the *range restriction* of R by a set $T \subseteq Y$ is the set of pairs whose second components are in T.

$$S \lhd R = \{p : R \mid \textit{first } p \in S\}$$
$$R \rhd T = \{p : R \mid \textit{second } p \in T\}$$

In a similar fashion we also often need subtractions from the domain and range. The *domain subtraction* of a relation $R : X \leftrightarrow Y$ by a set $S \subseteq X$ is the subset of R whose first components are not in S. Similarly the *range subtraction* of R by a set $T \subseteq Y$ is the set of pairs whose second components are not in T.

$$S \ntriangleleft R = \{p : R \mid \textit{first } p \notin S\}$$
$$R \ntriangleright T = \{p : R \mid \textit{second } p \notin T\}$$

In Chap. 2 we needed to determine the effect of a relation on a particular subset of elements, and for this we used the *relational image*. Formally, the relational image of a set $S \subseteq X$ through $R : X \leftrightarrow Y$ is the subset of Y whose elements are related by R to S:

$$R(\!| S |\!) = \{p : R \mid first\ p \in S \bullet second\ p\} = ran(S \lhd R)$$

We will use a relational model as the basis for state-based descriptions written in, e.g., Z. In that context we shall sometimes want to specify that a new state is the same as the old except for a small alteration. For a relation this will involve changing some of the pairs in a relation to new ones, and to do this we use *overriding*. If R and Q are relations between X and Y the relational overriding, $Q \oplus R$, of Q by R is Q outside the domain of R but is R wherever R is defined:

$$Q \oplus R = ((\text{dom}\ R) \lhd\!\!\!- Q) \cup R$$

The *inverse* of a relation R, denoted $R^\sim$ or R^{-1}, is the relation obtained by reversing every ordered pair in the relation.

Perhaps the most important operator on relations is *relational composition*. If $R_1 : X \leftrightarrow Y$ and $R_2 : Y \leftrightarrow Z$ then $R_1 \,\mathring{,}\, R_2$ denotes their composition, and $(x, z) \in R_1 \,\mathring{,}\, R_2$ whenever there exists y with $(x, y) \in R_1$ and $(y, z) \in R_2$:

$$R_1 \,\mathring{,}\, R_2 = \{q : R_1, r : R_2 \mid (second\ q = first\ r) \bullet (first\ q) \mapsto (second\ r)\}$$

The *transitive closure* R^+ of a relation R is the union of all finite compositions of R with itself:

$$R^+ = R \cup (R \,\mathring{,}\, R) \cup (R \,\mathring{,}\, R \,\mathring{,}\, R) \cup \cdots$$

The *reflexive and transitive closure* R^* of a relation R of type $T \leftrightarrow T$ adds the identity relation on T to the transitive closure:

$$R^* = R^+ \cup id_T$$

Finally, a pair of relations can be combined using parallel composition $\|$. If we have $R : X \leftrightarrow Y$ and $S : U \leftrightarrow V$ then $R\|S : X \times U \leftrightarrow Y \times V$ is defined by

$$\forall x : X;\ y : Y;\ u : U;\ v : V \bullet (x, u) \mapsto (y, v) \in R\|S \Leftrightarrow (x, y) \in R \land (u, v) \in S.$$

4.2 Relational Data Types

To define refinement in our relational model, we need to define programs, and indeed what a "user" is allowed to do, and what the observations are. As in Chap. 1 (but not in Chap. 2 where we fixed the notion of refinement as trace refinement), these are all questions with different possible answers, and they will lead to different formal definitions of refinement later on. In the models in the first two chapters we have not had an explicit notion of state, and 'programs' were sequences of events or actions. In contrast in our relational context:

- a *program* is a finite sequence of *operations*, interpreted as their *sequential composition*;
- an *operation* is a binary relation over the state space of interest, taken from a fixed collection (indexed set) of such operations.
- an *observation* is a pair of states: the state before execution of a program, and a state after.

Thus in this model, a program is given a semantics as a relation over a global state G. The global state G is defined such that values in G, or more generally: relations on G form the observations that we wish to make of programs. The operations of the ADT, however, are concerned with a *local* state State. In order to make observations on global states from these, any sequence of operations is bracketed between an *initialisation* and a *finalisation* which translate between global and local state.

The following defines our notion of relational abstract data type.

Definition 4.1 (*Data type*)
A (partial) *data type* is a tuple (State, Init, $\{Op_i\}_{i \in I}$, Fin). In this tuple, State is its local state, and operations $\{Op_i\}$, indexed by $i \in I$, are relations on this local state. The initialisation Init is a total relation from G to State, and the finalisation Fin is a total relation from State to G.   □

For now we require that Init and Fin are total; this is not a significant restriction of expressiveness, and it could be relaxed if needed.

Insisting that Init and Fin be total merely records the facts that we can always start a program sequence (the extension to partial initialisations is trivial) and that we can always make an observation afterwards.

Particular classes of data types are those which have only total or functional operations.

Definition 4.2 (*Total and canonical data type*)
A data type (State, Init, $\{Op_i\}_{i \in I}$, Fin) is *total* if Op_i are all *total*, and *canonical* if Init, and Op_i are all *functions*.   □

As was implicit in Chaps. 1 and 2, we only consider refinement between conformal data types.

Definition 4.3 (*Conformal data types*)
Two data types are *conformal* if their global data space G and the indexing sets of their operations are equal.   □

For the rest of this chapter, assume that all data types considered are conformal, using some fixed index set I. In later chapters we will consider more liberal notions of conformity where in some notations operations can be split or merged in refinement steps.

We can then define programs as follows:

Definition 4.4 (*Program*)

Given a data type $D = (\mathsf{State}, \mathsf{Init}, \{\mathsf{Op_i}\}_{i \in I}, \mathsf{Fin})$ a *program* is a sequence over I. For a program $\mathsf{p} = \langle \mathsf{p_1}, ..., \mathsf{p_n} \rangle$ over D, its meaning is defined as $\mathsf{p_D} = \mathsf{Init} \, \mathring{,} \, \mathsf{Op_{p_1}} \, \mathring{,} \, ... \, \mathring{,} \, \mathsf{Op_{p_n}} \, \mathring{,} \, \mathsf{Fin}$. □

Our programs are simple sequential compositions of operations, however, additional choices could be made as to which constructors can be used for programs. In the literature, one often finds Dijkstra's guarded command language as the programming language for ADTs. The key point to note here is that we include only *finite* sequences of operations, as this will be sufficient for the required notions of refinement in languages such as Z. This is in contrast to some of the discussion in Chap. 2. Any program in Dijkstra's language would represent a collection of such straight line programs. However, the combination of recursion (or while-loops) and unbounded non-determinism that is offered in such a language presents an extra level of complication (some of which we discussed in the last chapter), which we will not go into in this chapter.

4.3 Relational Refinement

Having defined our notion of program in our relational world, we are now in a position to define *relational refinement*, or *data refinement* as it is usually known. The starting point here is exactly the same as in our previous models - we want the behaviour (that is, observations) of a concrete system C to be consistent with those of an abstract system A. In our relational models we determine the observations by comparing the concrete and abstract programs since each program contains a finalisation which records the observations. We are led naturally to the following definition:

Definition 4.5 (*Data refinement*)
For data types A and C, C *refines* A, denoted $A \sqsubseteq_{data} C$ (dropping the subscript if the context is clear), iff for each program p over I, $p_C \subseteq p_A$. □

We can represent this pictorially as in Fig. 4.1 - which should be compared to Fig. 2.3. We execute the same program on concrete and abstract data types, and check that the result of the concrete is a possible result of the abstract. Here 'result' means the observations that we make when the program is executed, and in our relational set-up these observations are determined in the finalisations of the program. We thus end up comparing abstract and concrete programs in a way typified by Fig. 4.1. Once that comparison is made it should be obvious that one can define simulations in an analogous manner to the definition we provided for automata. The only difference now is that we have an explicit finalisation which wasn't present in the simulations we defined earlier. However, it acts as, essentially, the dual to the initialisation.

Before we do this we observe that data refinement is defined here in terms of inclusion of *total* relations, and is thus only concerned with what is called the *reduction of non-determinism*. This term is used if one thinks of relations as determining

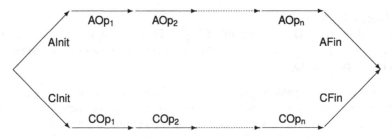

Fig. 4.1 Data refinement ...

the possible after-states of an operation - multiple after-states (i.e., a relation which isn't functional) then indicates a non-deterministic specification. Data refinement will allow for the reduction of that non-determinism.

Example 4.1 Let $G = \mathbb{N}$, and two data types be defined by $A = (\mathbb{N}, id_\mathbb{N}, \{AOp\}, id_\mathbb{N})$, $C = (\mathbb{N}, id_\mathbb{N}, \{COp\}, id_\mathbb{N})$ where the single operation in each are given by

$$AOp = \{x, y : \mathbb{N} \mid x < y \bullet (x, y)\},$$
$$COp = \{x : \mathbb{N} \bullet (x, x + 1)\}.$$

It can then be proved that for any sequence p (as there is only one operation, only its length is relevant):

$$p_A = \{x, y : \mathbb{N} \mid x + \#p \le y \bullet (x, y)\}, \quad \text{whereas}$$
$$p_C = \{x : \mathbb{N} \bullet (x, x + \#p)\}.$$

Clearly $p_C \subseteq p_A$, and therefore C refines A.   □

As with our previous notions of refinement we have the following:

Theorem 4.1 (Data refinement is a preorder)
Data refinement is transitive and reflexive, i.e., it is a preorder.   □

Returning to the idea of defining simulations as a means to verify data refinement, we first add in a correspondence between states of the system as in Fig. 4.2. We then need to determine the conditions necessary to make the diagram commute.

This time the diagram is decomposed into commuting squares plus *two* additional triangles - one for the initialisation, and one (which we didn't have before) for the finalisation. And because of that we will end up with three conditions in our relational simulations. In the same way that there are two ways to make the squares commute in a simulation-type diagram, there are also two possible ways for the initialisation/finalisation triangles to semi-commute, the particular choices are dictated by the need for the diagrams to be concatenated, and again to have the concrete component on the smaller side of the inclusion. We thus end up with the following two definitions.

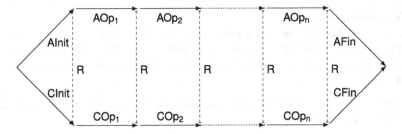

Fig. 4.2 ... which can verified by a simulation

Definition 4.6 (*Forward simulation*)
Let $A = (\text{AState}, \text{AInit}, \{\text{AOp}_i\}_{i \in I}, \text{AFin})$ and $C = (\text{CState}, \text{CInit}, \{\text{COp}_i\}_{i \in I}, \text{CFin})$ be data types. A *forward* simulation is a relation $R \subseteq \text{AState} \times \text{CState}$ satisfying

$$\text{CInit} \subseteq \text{AInit} \,\substack{\circ \\ 9}\, R \tag{4.1}$$

$$R \,\substack{\circ \\ 9}\, \text{CFin} \subseteq \text{AFin} \tag{4.2}$$

$$\forall i : I \bullet R \,\substack{\circ \\ 9}\, \text{COp}_i \subseteq \text{AOp}_i \,\substack{\circ \\ 9}\, R \tag{4.3}$$

If such a simulation exists, we also say that C is a forward simulation of A, also denoted $A \sqsubseteq_{\text{FS}} C$, and similarly for corresponding operations of A and C.   □

Definition 4.7 (*Backward simulation*)
For data types A and C as above, a *backward* simulation is a relation $T \subseteq \text{CState} \times \text{AState}$ satisfying

$$\text{CInit} \,\substack{\circ \\ 9}\, T \subseteq \text{AInit} \tag{4.4}$$

$$\text{CFin} \subseteq T \,\substack{\circ \\ 9}\, \text{AFin} \tag{4.5}$$

$$\forall i : I \bullet \text{COp}_i \,\substack{\circ \\ 9}\, T \subseteq T \,\substack{\circ \\ 9}\, \text{AOp}_i \tag{4.6}$$

If such a simulation exists, we also say that C is a backward simulation of A, also denoted $A \sqsubseteq_{\text{BS}} C$, and similarly for corresponding operations of A and C.   □

The naming of parts

As we remarked in Chap. 2, forward and backward simulations are also often called downward and upward simulations respectively. The simulations themselves are also known as *retrieve relations*, *abstraction relations*, or *coupling invariants*.

The two types of simulations coincide when the simulation is a function, as the following result tells us.

Theorem 4.2 (Functional simulations)
For data types A *and* C *as above, and a relation* T *between* CState *and* AState *such that* T *is total and functional, then* T *is a backward simulation between* A *and* C *if and only if* T^{-1} *is a forward simulation between* A *and* C. □

As with the simulations we discussed in the previous chapter, they are sound (i.e., every simulation establishes data refinement).

Theorem 4.3 (Soundness of simulations)
If a forward or backward simulation exists between conformal data types A *and* C, *then* C *is a data refinement of* A.

Proof
The proof works by induction on the (complete) programs.

The induction step involves establishing that the sub-diagrams of Fig. 4.2 can be combined in the appropriate way. If we put two diagrams together which semi-commute according to forward / backward simulation rules, the outer paths of the combined diagram should semi-commute in the same way.

The base case of the soundness proofs is the soundness of simulations between empty programs. □

However, neither forward or backward simulations are *complete* by themselves. Indeed there are data refinements which require *both* forward and backward simulations for their proof. We leave it as an exercise for the reader to translate the example in Fig. 2.8 into a relational setting to prove that completeness fails.

Of course, as in Chap. 2, forward and backward simulations are jointly complete for our definition of data refinement.

Theorem 4.4 (Joint completeness of simulations)
Forward and backward simulations are jointly complete, i.e., any data refinement can be proved by a combination of simulations.

Proof
In fact, any data refinement can be proved by an backward simulation, followed by a forward simulation. The backward simulation constructs a canonical ADT, i.e., a deterministic equivalent of the "abstract" type, using the familiar powerset construction or using a construction where states are characterised as traces (sequences of operations). A forward simulation can then always be found to the "concrete" type. □

4.4 From a Theory of Total Relational Refinement to Partial Relational Refinement

In the simulations developed above we have not been explicit about whether the data types are *total* or whether the operations in the data type are *partial relations*. First let us assume that all operations must be total for the refinement theory to apply, so in Sect. 4.4.1 we describe how to turn a partial data type into a total one in one of two ways. We then relax this restriction and describe refinement for a partial relational model in Sect. 4.4.4.

4.4.1 Partial Relations and Their Totalisation

Suppose we are given a data type in which one or more operations are partial. How should we interpret these as total relations? To understand this we need to look forward to how this theory will be applied to a particular specification language. For example, when we apply such a theory to the Z notation (see Chap. 7) an operation in the specification will be interpreted as a relation. If the operation is partial, i.e., not defined for all elements in its domain, what does it mean to apply it outside the domain?

There are a number of answers to this question, but initially we will focus on two. The first says: partiality means underspecification, so that outside the domain *anything may happen*, including non-termination. The second says: partiality means the operation is simply not possible outside the domain, so that *nothing may happen*. These two views give us two ways to totalise a partial relation, that is, turn a partial relation into a total relation on an extended domain that preserves the appropriate interpretation.

4.4.1.1 The Non-blocking Interpretation

The first interpretation is called the *non-blocking* model - since operations are always possible (they are never blocked). To make a partial operation total, each element outside the domain is mapped to an arbitrary element in the range. To represent non-termination we will also add in a distinguished state $\bot$, which is also a possible outcome of the total operation - of course, this means we will also add this to the potential before-states.

Figure 4.3 illustrates augmenting a partial operation with these undefined outcomes. In the figure a partial operation $Op = \{(0, 0), (0, 1), (1, 2)\}$ over the state $\{0, 1, 2\}$ is turned into a total operation by augmenting it with elements represented by the dotted lines.

This non-blocking interpretation is also known as the *contract* interpretation, as it takes the specification of the operation as a contract that prescribes an outcome

Fig. 4.3 The non-blocking
totalisation of an operation
$Op = \{(0, 0), (0, 1), (1, 2)\}$

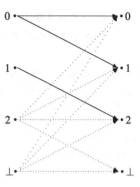

in specific circumstances only. We will use it to derive simulation rules in the Z
specification notation. In both this approach as well as the alternative interpretation
the simulation rules for partial operations are derived from those for total operations.
So partial relations on a set S are modelled as total relations on a set $S_\perp$, which is S
extended with a distinguished value $\perp$ not in S.

Definition 4.8 (*Totalisation - non-blocking*)

For a partial relation Op on $State$, its totalisation is a total relation $\widehat{Op}$ on $State_\perp$,
defined in the non-blocking approach to ADTs by

$$\widehat{Op} == Op \cup \{x, y : State_\perp \mid x \notin dom\ Op \bullet (x, y)\} \qquad \square$$

We will not consider partial initialisations or finalisations. However, if we did
their totalisations could be defined analogously, and no generality of the theory is
lost by making this assumption.

To preserve undefinedness, simulation relations of particular forms only are considered, *viz.* those which relate $\perp$ to every other value, or $\perp$ to $\perp$, depending on
the ADT interpretation. We thus need the following definition for the non-blocking
approach.

Definition 4.9 (*Extension - non-blocking*)

A relation R between $AState$ and $CState$ is extended to a relation $\widetilde{R}$ between
$AState_\perp$ and $CState_\perp$, defined in the non-blocking approach by

$$\widetilde{R} == R \cup (\{\perp_{AState}\} \times CState_\perp) \qquad \square$$

4.4.1.2   The Blocking Interpretation

The alternative interpretation is the *behavioural* or *blocking* approach to ADTs: operations may not be applied outside their precondition; doing so anyway leads to an
"error" result. The precondition is often called the *guard* in this context. This represents the situation where operations of the ADT correspond to possible interactions
between the system and its environment. A number of specification notations use
this interpretation, e.g., Object-Z, the object-oriented variant of Z, or Event-B (see
Chap. 8), and this links to the ideas of refusal which we discussed in Chap. 1.

Explicit guards

Several notations specify operations as a combination of a *guard*: a predicate or set indicating its domain, and an *effect*: a relation connecting before and after state. When the effect relation is partial, this introduces a risk of operations becoming infeasible or "magic": when the guard holds in a before state, but there is no after state related to it by the effect relation. Some notations such as the refinement calculus embrace this as an opportunity; others like Event-B impose "feasibility" well-formedness conditions to avoid it. When such a feasibility condition holds, the guard correctly represents the operation's domain in a relational interpretation.

Definition 4.10 (*Totalisation - blocking*)

For a partial relation Op on State, its totalisation is a total relation $\widehat{\mathsf{Op}}$ on $\mathsf{State}_\perp$, defined in the blocking approach to ADTs by

$$\widehat{\mathsf{Op}} == \mathsf{Op} \cup \{x : \mathsf{State}_\perp \mid x \notin \mathrm{dom}\,\mathsf{Op} \bullet (x, \perp)\}$$

Again, totalisations of initialisation and finalisation are defined analogously. □

The non-blocking totalisation of the operation $\{(0, 0), (0, 1), (1, 2)\}$ over the state $\{0, 1, 2\}$ was illustrated in Fig. 4.3. The blocking totalisation of the same example is given in Fig. 4.4 where values outside the domain are linked to $\perp$ only.

In order to take account of the extended domain for the relations, we also need to extend the retrieve relation accordingly.

Definition 4.11 (*Extension - blocking*)

A relation R between AState and CState is extended to a relation $\widetilde{\mathsf{R}}$ between $\mathsf{AState}_\perp$ and $\mathsf{CState}_\perp$, defined in the blocking approach by

$$\widetilde{\mathsf{R}} == \mathsf{R} \cup \{(\perp_{\mathsf{AState}}, \perp_{\mathsf{CState}})\}$$

□

Fig. 4.4 The blocking totalisation of an operation $Op = \{(0, 0), (0, 1), (1, 2)\}$

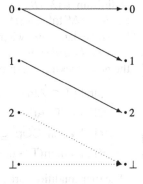

4.4.2 Simulation Rules

The resulting simulation rules for totalised relations can then be simplified to remove any reference to $\perp$. The aim is to apply the simulation rules to the totalised versions of these data types, and then to remove all occurrences of $\sim$, $\frown$ and $\perp$ in the rules. After doing these calculations we are left with the following requirements.

Definition 4.12 (*Forward simulation for partial relations*)
Let $A = (\mathsf{AState}, \mathsf{AInit}, \{\mathsf{AOp}_i\}_{i \in I}, \mathsf{AFin})$ and $C = (\mathsf{CState}, \mathsf{CInit}, \{\mathsf{COp}_i\}_{i \in I}, \mathsf{CFin})$ be data types where the operations may be partial.

A *forward* simulation is a relation R from AState to CState satisfying, in the non-blocking interpretation

$$\mathsf{CInit} \subseteq \mathsf{AInit} \, \mathbin{_9^o} \, R$$

$$R \, \mathbin{_9^o} \, \mathsf{CFin} \subseteq \mathsf{AFin}$$

$$\forall i : I \bullet \mathrm{ran}(\mathrm{dom}\,\mathsf{AOp}_i \lhd R) \subseteq \mathrm{dom}\,\mathsf{COp}_i$$

$$\forall i : I \bullet (\mathrm{dom}\,\mathsf{AOp}_i \lhd R) \, \mathbin{_9^o} \, \mathsf{COp}_i \subseteq \mathsf{AOp}_i \, \mathbin{_9^o} \, R$$

The four conditions are commonly referred to as "initialisation", "finalisation", "applicability" and "correctness". In the blocking interpretation, correctness is strengthened to:

$$\forall i : I \bullet R \, \mathbin{_9^o} \, \mathsf{COp}_i \subseteq \mathsf{AOp}_i \, \mathbin{_9^o} \, R \qquad\qquad \square$$

In the blocking approach when R is the identity relation, correctness reduces to $\mathsf{COp} \subseteq \mathsf{AOp}$ and applicability to $\mathrm{dom}\,\mathsf{AOp} \subseteq \mathrm{dom}\,\mathsf{COp}$. As a consequence, we obtain $\mathrm{dom}\,\mathsf{AOp} = \mathrm{dom}\,\mathsf{COp}$ as expected: the precondition may not be widened in refinement.

We can make an analogous derivation for backward simulations which results in the following conditions.

Definition 4.13 (*Backward simulation for partial relations*)
Let $A = (\mathsf{AState}, \mathsf{AInit}, \{\mathsf{AOp}_i\}_{i \in I}, \mathsf{AFin})$ and $C = (\mathsf{CState}, \mathsf{CInit}, \{\mathsf{COp}_i\}_{i \in I}, \mathsf{CFin})$ be data types where the operations may be partial.

A *backward* simulation is a relation T from CState to AState satisfying, in the non-blocking interpretation

$$\mathsf{CInit} \, \mathbin{_9^o} \, T \subseteq \mathsf{AInit}$$

$$\mathsf{CFin} \subseteq T \, \mathbin{_9^o} \, \mathsf{AFin}$$

$$\forall i : I \bullet \overline{\mathrm{dom}\,\mathsf{COp}_i} \subseteq \mathrm{dom}(T \rhd \mathrm{dom}\,\mathsf{AOp}_i)$$

$$\forall i : I \bullet \mathrm{dom}(T \rhd \mathrm{dom}\,\mathsf{AOp}_i) \lhd \mathsf{COp}_i \, \mathbin{_9^o} \, T \subseteq T \, \mathbin{_9^o} \, \mathsf{AOp}_i$$

The four conditions are commonly referred to as "initialisation", "finalisation", "applicability" and "correctness". In the blocking interpretation, correctness is strengthened to:

$$\forall i : I \bullet \mathsf{COp}_i \, \mathbin{_9^o} \, T \subseteq T \, \mathbin{_9^o} \, \mathsf{AOp}_i \qquad\qquad \square$$

An important consequence of this definition is the following (see also the definition of backward simulations in Chap. 2).

Theorem 4.5   (Backward simulations are total)
When the concrete finalisation is total, the backward simulation T *from* CState *to* AState *is* total *on* CState.   □

Example 4.2   Let $G = 0..4$. Let $AS = 0..4$, and $BS = \{0, 1, 3, 4\}$ be the local states. The two data types have the same initialisation: $A = (AS, \text{Init}, \{AOp_1, AOp_2\}, AFin)$, $B = (BS, \text{Init}, \{BOp_1, BOp_2, \}, BFin)$, where

> $\text{Init} = \{x : G \bullet (x, 0)\}$,
>
> $AOp_1 = \{(0, 1), (0, 2)\}$,
>
> $AOp_2 = \{(1, 3), (2, 4)\}$,
>
> $AFin = id_{AS} \cup \{(1, 2), (2, 1)\}$,
>
> $BOp_1 = \{(0, 1)\}$,
>
> $BOp_2 = \{(1, 3), (1, 4)\}$,
>
> $BFin = id_{BS} \cup \{(1, 2))\}$.

B is a data refinement of A. To verify this one needs to use a backward simulation from B to A defined by $T = \{(0, 0), (1, 1), (1, 2), (3, 3), (4, 4)\}$. This can be verified as follows:

- $\text{Init} \,{}_9^\circ\, T = \text{Init} \subseteq \text{Init}$;
- $BFin = T \subseteq T \,{}_9^\circ\, AFin$;
- $\text{dom } BOp_1 = \{1, 3, 4\}$; $\text{dom}(T \rhd \text{dom } AOp_1) = \{1, 3, 4\}$.
- $\{1, 3, 4\} \lhd BOp_1 = BOp_1$; $BOp_1 \,{}_9^\circ\, T = \{(0, 1), (0, 2)\} = AOp_1 \subseteq T \,{}_9^\circ\, AOp_1$.
- $\text{dom } BOp_2 = \{0, 3, 4\}$; $\text{dom}(T \rhd \text{dom } AOp_2) = \{0, 3, 4\}$.
- $\{0, 3, 4\} \lhd BOp_2 = BOp_2$; $BOp_2 \,{}_9^\circ\, T = \{(1, 3), (1, 4)\}$;
  $T \,{}_9^\circ\, AOp_2 = \{(1, 2), (1, 1)\} \,{}_9^\circ\, \{(1, 3), (2, 4)\} = \{(1, 3), (1, 4)\}$.

In addition, A is a data refinement of B, but this can only be proved using a *forward* simulation. The derivation of this is left as an exercise to the reader.   □

4.4.3   Completeness of Partial Relational Simulations

To recap we started with a theory of refinement for data types that were total in Sect. 4.3, and Theorem 4.4 tells us that the simulations are jointly complete. This mirrors the result in Chap. 2 (see Sect. 2.2.2). We then investigated a partial framework, where partial data types were totalised, so that the simulation relations for the total framework could be applied to them. These simulation rules can be simplified to avoid any reference to the augmented element of the state, $\bot$. These rules were presented in Definitions 4.12 and 4.13.

So, of course, it follows that these rules are jointly complete - doesn't it?

The slightly surprising answer is - no!

Or to be more accurate, the simulation rules for the blocking interpretation are not jointly complete - and in this section we discuss why.

For a specification C which is a refinement of A, the original joint completeness proof constructs an intermediate specification B and a simulation from A to B and another from B to C. For total relations clearly B is also a total relational specification. For a partial relational specification the proof is adapted so that C and A are *totalised*, that is turned into total relations via the addition of the error state as we have discussed in this section. One then finds, since they are now all total relations, a specification B as before. However, one must now also check that this B could have arisen as the totalisation of an underlying partial specification. In the non-blocking approach this is indeed the case - which is why the joint completeness result still holds. However, in the blocking approach this does not hold, as we discuss here.

Figure 4.5 represents the situation that might arise, where circles represent partial data types. These are then totalised, leading to an embedding of a partial data type as a total data type. This embedding is depicted as the circle being part of the large oval - the space of total specifications. To attempt to prove completeness, take A and C and consider their totalisation - the standard theory constructs an intermediate *total* data type in some normal form, here called A_{nf}, and simulations from it to the totalised A and C.

The question now is whether there are simulations from the partial A and C to some intermediate B - which is also a *partial* data type. For this to be the case, A_{nf} needs to be derivable as a totalised partial data type - in terms of the picture it must lie within the circle, not just the oval. This is not always the case, and is why joint completeness for the blocking simulation rules does not hold.

Fig. 4.5 Joint completeness of simulation rules in a partial framework

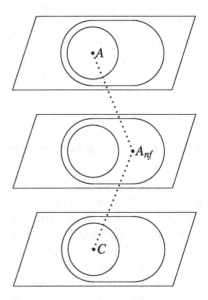

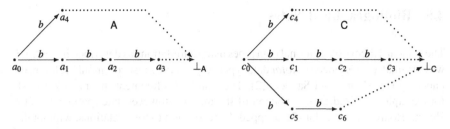

Fig. 4.6 Partial data types A and C

First, however, the positive result:

Theorem 4.6 (Joint completeness of simulations in the non-blocking interpretation)
The non-blocking simulation rules are jointly complete for partial data types in the non-blocking interpretation.   □

Now the counter-example for the blocking interpretation. The two relevant data types are given in Fig. 4.6, each has a single operation b. They are totalised in the blocking model, where transitions added by totalisation are indicated with dotted arrows but we have omitted the b transition from $\perp$ to itself. When totalised in the blocking intepretation, C is a relational refinement of A.

However, we have the following two facts:

1. There is no blocking forward simulation from A to C.
2. There is no blocking backward simulation from C to A, even though a simulation exists between their embeddings.

So far this construction looks at one simulation - it might be argued that a sequence of simulations would suffice. However, a proof can be given that this is not the case (for details see [1]).

4.4.4 A Fully Partial Relational Theory

The rules derived in this section start with a partial data type and totalise it to apply a theory of simulations for total data types. However, this theory is also applicable to partial data types directly. Thus a theory of partial simulations can be derived more directly. This has found application in work relating process algebraic refinement and relational models, and we will return to this in Part III when we explore the differences between the models.

4.5   Bibliographical Notes

The standard theory of relational data types using simulations as described in Sect. 4.3 was originally developed for *total* data types, e.g., in the most commonly referenced paper by He, Hoare, and Sanders [2]. The standard refinement theory of Z [3, 4], for example, is based on this version of the theory. However, later publications by He and Hoare, in particular [5], dropped the restriction to total relations, without the authors emphasizing this relaxation, and proved soundness and joint completeness of the same set of simulation rules in the more general case. De Roever and Engelhardt [6] also present the partial relations theory, without putting much emphasis on this aspect.

Later on (in Part III) we will discuss application of this theory to derive notions of refinement in Z that correspond to definitions of refinement we discussed in Chap. 1. Most of the early literature on the foundations of relational refinement did not recognise the possibility to use the theory of partial relations directly, thus, refinement notions for Z (which allows partiality in its specification of operations) were based on embeddings of partial relations into total relations (as is discussed in Sect. 4.4) and then using the He/Hoare/Sanders simulation theory.

The simplification ("relaxing") of the simulation rules for partial relations is given in detail for the non-blocking approach in [3], and for the blocking approach in [4].

The complete derivation of the non-blocking theory was (to our knowledge) first published by Woodcock and Davies [3]. The blocking theory with its embedding was described by Bolton et al [7], without details of the derivation. Our monograph [4] contains full details of both; Deutsch and Henson [8] have investigated the design choices for totalisations in the blocking theory. We will use variants of embeddings in Part III, culminating in a relational framework which contains the ability to reason about both divergence and blocking (see Chap. 11).

For details of the proof of Theorem 4.4, see the literature, e.g., [2, 6, 9]. The joint completeness of simulations in the non-blocking interpretation (Theorem 4.6) is not directly proved in the literature. However, De Roever and Engelhardt [6, pp. 187-188] prove a closely related theorem. Their non-blocking rules are derived from the *partial* relations simulations of He and Hoare, so their formalism observes both (certain) blocking and (possible) divergence using possibly partial relations on $S_\perp$; see [10] for a discussion. Their theorem does not imply Theorem 4.6 (as they operate in a larger domain of relations), but its proof carries over successfully. The proof inherits the construction of the proof of joint completeness in the total framework and incorporates the additional proof obligation: that the intermediate datatype is in the image of the embedding,[1] avoiding the situation in Fig. 4.5.

---

[1] Their embedding is not explicit, instead they characterise relations in its image axiomatically.

References

1. Boiten EA, Derrick J (2010) Incompleteness of relational simulations in the blocking paradigm. Sci Comput Program 75(12):1262–1269
2. He Jifeng, Hoare CAR, Sanders JW (1986) Data refinement refined. In: Robinet B, Wilhelm R (eds) Proceedings of the ESOP 86. Lecture notes in computer science, vol 213. Springer, Berlin, pp 187–196
3. Woodcock JCP, Davies J (1996) Using Z: specification, refinement, and proof. Prentice Hall, Upper Saddle River
4. Derrick J, Boiten EA (2014) Refinement in Z and object-Z, 2nd edn. Springer, Berlin
5. He Jifeng, Hoare CAR (1990) Prespecification and data refinement. Data refinement in a categorical setting, Technical monograph, number PRG-90. Oxford University Computing Laboratory, Oxford
6. de Roever W-P, Engelhardt K (1998) Data refinement: model-oriented proof methods and their comparison. CUP, London
7. Bolton C, Davies J, Woodcock JCP On the refinement and simulation of data types and processes. In Araki et al. [9], pp 273–292
8. Deutsch M, Henson MC (2006) An analysis of refinement in an abortive paradigm. Form Asp Comput 18(3):329–363
9. Josephs MB (1988) A state-based approach to communicating processes. Distrib Comput 3:9–18
10. Boiten EA, de Roever W-P (2003) Getting to the bottom of relational refinement: relations and correctness, partial and total. In: Berghammer R, Möller B (eds) 7th International seminar on relational methods in computer science (RelMiCS 7). University of Kiel, Kiel, pp 82–88

Chapter 5
Perspicuity, Divergence, and Internal Operations

In going from the relational semantics of CSMATs in Chap. 3 to the abstract data types of Chap. 4 we made a number of radical changes. We labelled individual transitions with the name of an operation, much as we had been doing in LTS and automata in Chaps. 1 and 2, and removed transitivity from the transition relation as we were now able to observe individual steps. We also created a separation between local (abstract) state and global (concrete) state that extended the idea of state abstraction in Chap. 3.

One aspect of CSMATs that has not been fully reflected in the relational data types yet is reflexivity of the transition relation, or "stuttering": an unchanged state *could* be the outcome of a labelled transition, but not every occurrence of "nothing has changed" is worth recording explicitly as a transition. This chapter will look more closely at this – leading to the concept of "perspicuous" operations in refinement. CSMATs allowed us to remain agnostic about having potentially infinite traces in the model; uncovering perspicuous operations forces us to worry about invisible things happening infinitely often ("livelock"). Thus, *divergence* needs to be addressed now.

Finally, we look at a particular view of operations that can occur in a system without interacting with the environment: so-called *internal* actions that represent independent action of the system. They had a brief mention in the context of automata already (see τ in Definition 2.1) but they are an important specification mechanism with semantic consequences that need more detailed discussion. In particular, unbounded sequences of internal operations are also an issue of divergence, with infinite behaviour occurring without any interaction with the environment.

5.1   Perspicuous Operations

In moving from CSMATs to abstract data types between Chaps. 3 and 4 we assigned labels to transitions. The transitivity of the transition relation was factored out by considering elementary transitions as "operations" or "events", and transitions that could potentially be further decomposed as "programs". Establishing a refinement relation meant quantification over all programs – and making that practically veri-fiable meant reducing it to a quantification over all operations instead, and letting induction sort out the rest.

Reflexivity of the transition relation was introduced purposefully in Chap. 3. It was foundationally unavoidable, as we could not guarantee that the system whose state we were observing had actually done anything between two observations. It was also relevant for the theory development, as many refinement theories consider so-called stuttering steps, and we wanted the mechanism for this to be visible at the simplest possible level. The role of reflexivity or "stuttering" has not come to the surface in Chap. 4, so we complete that aspect of the theory development in this chapter.

Essentially we end up with a characterisation of "transitions" along two dimen-sions, characterised by the questions:

- Has the (abstract) state changed?
- Has an observable event taken place?

In the previous chapter we have concentrated on the situation where the answers to both these two questions is "yes". When both answers are "no", we are looking at the trivial case of the empty program having a null effect. It remains to fill the square, and this will work out in the rest of this chapter as follows:

Obs event? State change?	Yes	No
Yes	Operation (Chap. 4)	Internal operation (Sect. 5.4)
No	Perspicuous operation (This section)	The empty program (Chap. 4)

For each of the three non-trivial sectors of this square, it is also worthwhile consid-ering what happens when such transitions happen infinitely often. We have already encountered infinite traces, for the situation of normal operations with associated state transitions happening infinitely often. For the other two corners of the square, infinite behaviour is somewhat degenerate: either an infinite sequence of observable events that does not progress the evolution of the system's state, or an infinite evolu-tion of the state that remains outside the scope of the environment's observation and interaction. This is why the topic of divergence arises also in this chapter.

Perspicuity of operations refers to the situation where we have *not* observed a state change between two observations, but we nevertheless want to consider this as an event. We call it perspicuous because like a perspicuous material, it is there but you

Fig. 5.1 A perspicuous event COp_{persp} with simulation R

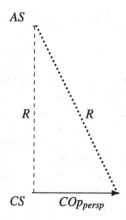

may not be able to see it. It may not be immediately obvious, but an operation which has no effect is not just semantically meaningful but also practical – for example as "skip" or the empty statement in a programming language, or "NOP" in assembly languages. Programs that need to wait for a collaborating program to be ready have "active waiting" loops containing these – effectively, such a "skip" is an abstraction of time passing. More generally, in a refinement context, a perspicuous operation is one that comes with no change of state *at the given level of abstraction*. Data refinement steps can then refine this to a concrete operation that does effect some change to a state component that was not abstractly visible.

In a relational model, the introduction of perspicuous operations is intimately tied to simulations: whether a concrete action "leaves the abstract state unchanged" can only be decided in relation to a specific retrieve relation between abstract and concrete states. It then generalises the refinement situation of Fig. 4.2 by not just having semi-commuting squares for each occurrence of an operation, but additionally allowing triangles as depicted in Fig. 5.1 for any perspicuous operation COp_{persp}.

The overall generalisation of Definition 4.5 achieved by such a simulation is then the following.

Definition 5.1 (*Data refinement with perspicuous operations*)
For data types $A = (AS, AInit, \{AOp_i\}_{i \in I}, AFin)$ and $C = (CS, CInit, \{COp_i\}_{i \in I \cup J}, CFin)$, C *refines* A, denoted $A \sqsubseteq_{perspic} C$ iff for each program p over $I \cup J$, $p_C \subseteq (p \restriction I)_A$. □

That is, every concrete program (with normal operations in I and perspicuous ones in J) is consistent with the corresponding abstract program, which is obtained by dropping all perspicuous operations wherever they occur in the program sequence. Taking J to be empty, it reduces to Definition 4.5.

This semantic definition makes no reference to any given simulation R, and hence makes no direct requirements on any individual perspicuous operation. Simulations introducing perspicuous operations are therefore unlikely to form a complete method for this notion of refinement.

The coverage of perspicuous operations we give here chimes with the introduction of new events in Event-B, which in turn is analogous to how this is done in action systems [1]. We will describe this in more detail in Chap. 8. In the words of Abrial [2], it is "observing our discrete system in the refinement with a finer grain than in the abstraction". Typically, a more finely described state will also allow the operations to be described at a finer granularity: an effect achieved in a single step at the abstract level takes several steps at the concrete level, some of these steps modelled as perspicuous operations refining abstract skips, and one as refining the abstract step. This is a common form of *action refinement* which is compatible with some basic refinement relations but not all [3]. Essentially, in a refinement model where all further developments are (indirectly) tied to the initial specification, the introduction of perspicuous steps is less useful. If a concrete operation has no abstractly visible effect, it may not do any harm, but it also will not be able to make any useful progress. In such a context, the model for action refinement is necessarily more complex, and closer to the ideas in ASM refinement as described in Chap. 8. Further coverage of this topic is beyond the scope of this book – we refer to our monograph [4] for a detailed discussion of how action refinement can work in Z and similar formalisms.

5.2   Error Behaviour: Catastrophic or Not?

The semantic models we considered in Chaps. 1 and 3 both allowed types of observations that were based on a notion of termination. Termination was observed in states where there was no subsequent (non-trivial) evolution possible. Non-termination might occur because there is some infinite path, and it might even be unavoidable in some evolutions, but that did not impact on the observations of terminating behaviour. This "problematic" part of systems' behaviour was simply ignored.

We have encountered one further treatment of "problematic" behaviour so far. The different totalisations of partial relations in Chap. 4 encode different ways of looking at what an operation "means" outside its domain. In the partial relations model, the existence of a path that leads to an operation being blocked only comes to light if that sequence of operations is *always* blocked – so we only record *certain* error. The blocking totalisation only records an error value ⊥, and this means that any sequence of operations which may lead to an operation applied outside its domain will add ⊥ to its regular outcomes, and no more – we record *possible* error as well. In the non-blocking totalisation, however, the mere possibility of an operation being applied outside its domain for a given sequence means that the sequence will lead to the full set of all possible outcomes. The version of this theory described by De Roever and Engelhardt [5] identifies ⊥ explicitly as "non-termination" or the value of an unguarded recursive definition.

The latter type of interpretation of an error is called a *catastrophic* or *chaotic* interpretation. It is *catastrophic* because the mere possibility of error is taken to be as bad as the certainty of error. It is called *chaotic* because "chaos" is the system which has every possible outcome, including ones worse than anything else. In the relational model, this is mathematically encoded as follows: non-deterministic choice ("possibility") is union of relations, and "error" relates to the full set of outcomes, so a genuine normal outcome added to such a set is not distinguishable. A catastrophic error, in other words, is a zero in the algebra of behaviours with non-deterministic choice as the binary operator.

Consider again the system C of Fig. 4.6. In the blocking totalisation of C, as given in the figure, the program bb takes us from starting state c_0 to c_2 or c_6 as well as to $\perp_C$. So after executing bb, we may be able to execute another b, we may be finished, or we may have reached an error state. The non-blocking totalisation on the other hand would add paths labeled bb from c_0 to *any* state including $\perp_C$, due to the top branch, making the second and third branches essentially invisible.

For every problematic behaviour we come across, we can construct semantic models and observations that interpret it as a chaotic error, or not. It should be clear from the description above that, so far, only the non-blocking semantics of partial relations included a chaotic error situation.

Having identified error situations, refinement based methods have three options. They can take a "partial correctness" approach, which acknowledges that problems may occur, but simply stops providing any correctness guarantees in those situations. This is how the partial correctness semantics of Chap. 3 operates with respect to the problem of non-termination. They can also ensure that initial specifications do not contain problematic situations, and include proof obligations that ensure no problems arise in individual refinement steps either. For relational specifications as in Chap. 4, the potential problem of the initialisation being unsatisfiable (which trivialises the entire ADT) is often dealt with in this way. Finally, they can model the problematic outcomes explicitly, and ensure that refinement steps do not make things worse in that respect – this is the approach we have taken in the totalised relational semantics in Chap. 4. More instances of each of these three approaches will occur later in this book.

5.3   Divergence

A particular class of problematic behaviour arises when we consider perspicuous, and later also internal operations. From a mathematical point of view, we have so far been skirting the edge when considering potentially infinite behaviours and observations. In the CSMAT model of Chap. 3 we did not count the transition steps, and as a consequence we had no issue of infinite series of transitions by definition. The LTS of Chap. 1 potentially contain loops, and as a consequence their observations may include infinite traces. In a few places, the consideration of infinite traces was shown to have profound semantic implications. However, the existence of an infinite trace by itself was not considered a degenerate situation. It merely indicates a modelling framework in which we do not assume that a correct system eventually stops operating – for example, a door that always alternates between opening and closing, with the model abstracting from the eventual failure of its hinges. More importantly, an infinite LTS trace can "only" arise in interaction with an environment that is engaging with it infinitely often anyway – it is not something that a modelled system embarks on by itself.

Both perspicuous and internal operations introduce a risk of moving out of this safety zone. To see this we stay with the simplest model which contains this issue, the CSMATs of Chap. 3. The state traces we can observe there (Definition 3.7) contain repeated occurrences of the same state, as a consequence of reflexivity of the transition relation ("stuttering"). These could either represent that nothing had happened, or that the system had moved in a cycle, coincidentally ending up at the same state as "when" we last observed it. (Like when we were blinking at the traffic lights in Sect. 3.4.) In Definition 3.4 we suggested we might just record the *non*-stuttering steps in such traces, which seems like a convenient way of keeping these traces no more infinite than the number of actual changes of the state.

However, refinements that introduce perspicuous operations break that idea. To match a concrete state trace of a CSMAT against a corresponding abstract one, we would need to record a stuttering step in the abstract system for every perspicuous step in the concrete one. And here is where a potentially degenerate situation arises. As we have described it so far, there is no guarantee that the perspicuous concrete operations occur only a finite number of times during an abstract stuttering period. Hence, a finite abstract state trace (possibly obtained by avoiding the recording of any stuttering) could correspond with an infinite concrete one. At the very least this is semantically hairy; depending on the interpretation of the models, it could indeed represent an error situation.

A mathematical definition of divergence is only possible in the context of a fixed model with its notion of observation. We attempt a somewhat less formal one first for the general case.

Definition 5.2 (*Divergence*)
A *divergent state* is a state from which a system can perform infinite behaviour that is not observable.
A *strictly divergent trace* is a trace of a system that may end in a divergent state. □

We used "strictly" to reflect that some theories define "divergent traces" as any trace with a strictly divergent prefix.

Thus, if from a state in a CSMAT, an infinite (non-stuttering) trace consisting of just perspicuous behaviour is possible, such a state is divergent. (Recall that the mere use of "perspicuous" implies the existence of an abstraction of the system in which the corresponding behaviour is stuttering.) The refinement relations we have considered for CSMATs so far have treated divergence (if considered an error at all) as a non-catastrophic error. Refinement relations that actively prevent the introduction of divergence in refinement of CSMAT-like models will be covered in Sect. 8.3, where ASM refinement includes classic reasoning for termination of programs to bound the introduction of triangles like the one pictured in Fig. 5.1.

In the next section, we will cover internal operations, like τ in automata as briefly discussed in Chap. 2. These are not included in the observations via traces, and thus any state from which an infinite sequence of τ steps is possible is a divergent state according to the above informal definition.

5.4 Internal Operations

An internal operation is an operation with a special status: it is assumed to be invisible to the environment, and under internal control of the system only. Thus, the introduction of internal operations does *not* extend the alphabet of available actions that a client could use. The special action τ in Chap. 2 which was not included in automata traces was the first time we encountered internal operations in this book. As it is not externally visible anyway, it is often customary to include only a single internal operation, whose behaviour is the disjunction (union, non-deterministic choice) of all internal operations.

In process algebras, internal operations naturally occur in a number of ways, as we will see in Chap. 6. In CSP [6] they arise from channels being hidden, for example encapsulating an internal communication channel when considering a system of communicating subsystems, or from the combination of successful termination and sequential composition (not discussed in this book). They may also be used, for example in LOTOS [7], to encode internal choice when only external choice is available as a basic operator. The representation of CSP using LTS in Sect. 6.1 will also use internal events in that way.

Definitions of observations (and from that, or directly, definitions of refinement) can be given straightforwardly in a context with internal operations once we take into account that internal operations should not be observable. For example, trace semantics of a LTS with internal operation τ can be constructed by first taking all traces as if τ is a normal event, and then erasing all occurrences of τ from each trace. This takes into account that we have silent evolution before and after external events.

Definitions that ask whether there is a transition labelled a from state p to q are normally given in terms of $p \xrightarrow{a} q$; this can be generalised using the normal notation to $p \xRightarrow{a} q$ which still means that p and q are connected via a trace a, but in a context of internal actions this implies a trace containing a single event a as well as possibly an arbitrary number of internal actions before and/or after it. We say "arbitrary" here but we usually mean "finite", to avoid divergence issues – more on that later.

For LTS and automata, we end up with an entire new collection of refinement relations which generalise the ones from the first two chapters of this book to the inclusion of an internal operation. Some of these are traditionally named as the "weak" variants, the most commonly mentioned one of these may well be weak bisimulation, a generalisation of Definition 2.8.

Definition 5.3 (*Weak bisimulation*)
A weak bisimulation is a relation R on processes such that, for $a \in Act$:

1. if pRq and $p \overset{a}{\Longrightarrow} p'$ then $\exists q' \bullet q \overset{a}{\Longrightarrow} q'$ with $p'Rq'$
2. if pRq and $q \overset{a}{\Longrightarrow} q'$ then $\exists p' \bullet p \overset{a}{\Longrightarrow} p'$ with $p'Rq'$
3. if pRq and $p \overset{\varepsilon}{\Longrightarrow} p'$ then $\exists q' \bullet q \overset{\varepsilon}{\Longrightarrow} q'$ with $p'Rq'$
4. if pRq and $q \overset{\varepsilon}{\Longrightarrow} q'$ then $\exists p' \bullet p \overset{\varepsilon}{\Longrightarrow} p'$ with $p'Rq'$

Two processes p and q are weakly bisimilar, denoted $p \equiv q$ if there exists a weak bisimulation R with pRq.   □

5.4.1 Internal Operations and Choice in LTS

Adding internal operations to LTS increases the ways in which choice between alternative behaviours can be expressed. In Fig. 5.2 we show three ways in which choice between a and b can be represented.

All three versions have the same set of traces: $\{\varepsilon, \langle a \rangle, \langle b \rangle\}$, and the same set of completed traces: $\{\langle a \rangle, \langle b \rangle\}$, as the internal actions do not get recorded in traces. However, they represent fundamentally different behaviours, as recognised by more detailed semantics.

Version (i) is the normal choice between alternatives as we have already seen in LTS. The choice between a and b is left to the environment choosing to engage with either of them – in the initial state, both a and b are possible, and neither can be refused.

We had seen examples of where the environment could lack control over availability of choices, but they needed to be preceded by a non-deterministic action. (For example, the drinks machine that allows a coin initially, and on that action already chooses whether to go down the "tea" or "coffee" branch.) Version (iii) in Fig. 5.2 represents that same lack of external control in choice, without requiring a non-deterministic visible action first. (It will come as no surprise that the link between these kinds of situations can be made explicit in particular specification notations,

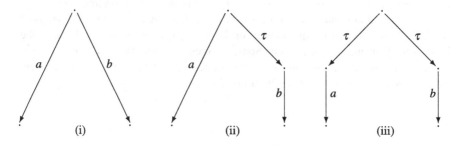

Fig. 5.2 Internal actions providing different ways of expressing choice in LTSs

namely through "hiding" the initial action – see Chap. 6.) In version (iii), *before* any visible action takes place, we may be in a situation where action a is enabled, or we may be in one where a is refused! Thus, if we ask whether (iii) can refuse the action a after the empty trace, the answer is "yes" – even though a may also be enabled after the empty trace. Plain LTS without internal actions would not be able to represent this kind of refusal behaviour where something is both enabled and refused.

Version (ii) is an asymmetric oddity. For action a, it can both allow it and refuse it initially, but action b is allowed initially and not refused. This weird system has both events enabled initially, but "at any time" may decide to withdraw the offer of a. We do not cover timed calculi in this book, but note that this one causes particular difficulty in combination with the common assumption that internal actions are "urgent", i.e. happen as soon as they are enabled.

In the non-timed world, version (ii), or to be more precise: the difference between version (ii) and the others, is also important as a "pathological" example in another context. A desirable property for a refinement relation to have is that of being a pre-congruence. That is, if specification S is refined by S', then for a specification T' obtained from T by replacing all occurrences of S by S', we have that T is also refined by T'. This might also be called compositionality or part-wise refinement: we may refine a system by refining a part of it.

However, this example shows that weak bisimulation is not a pre-congruence (despite it being an equivalence). If we look at the branches of the three systems in Fig. 5.2 individually, the branches with the same action in are all weakly bisimilar. Whether the single action is preceded by an internal operation or not makes no difference – the states before the visible action, and the states after, can be linked across the systems. However, when we consider the systems in full, none of them are weakly bisimilar. This is because weak bisimulation wants to put the initial state and the state after an internal action in the same equivalence class – but they have different sets of refusals. As a consequence, weak bisimulation and many other plausible refinement relations formed in this sphere are less ideal for refinement, as to establish that refinement holds we will have to make "global" refinement checks in response to "local" changes in the specification.

In this whole discussion, we have mostly and purposefully avoided talking about actions being enabled or refused in a particular *state*. Rather, we have talked about refusals after a certain trace. For the systems (ii) and (iii) in Fig. 5.2 it is ambiguous in which state it is after executing the empty trace: it could be before, or after τ. Observation functions have (at least) two choices here: they can explicitly consider all such states, or they can constrain observations to so-called *stable* states.[1]

Definition 5.4 (*Stable state*)
A state in a LTS with internal operation τ is *stable* if there is no τ transition out of that state.   □

In version (iii), the initial state is not stable – so the stable states to be considered after the empty trace are the two intermediate states. Version (ii) is the one most

---

[1] See also Chap. 6.

affected by this distinction on states: in a semantics considering only stable states, the fact that a is 'briefly" enabled initially is no longer observable from that state.

5.4.2 Internal Actions in a Relational Context

In the relational world, we can add the internal operation as a separate component to ADTs, so we get the following definition.

Definition 5.5 (τ-*Data type*)
A τ-*data type* is a tuple $(\mathsf{State}, \mathsf{Init}, \{\mathsf{Op}_k\}_{k\in I}, \tau, \mathsf{Fin})$ such that $(\mathsf{State}, \mathsf{Init}, \{\mathsf{Op}_k\}_{k\in I}, \mathsf{Fin})$ is a partial data type as in Definition 4.1, and τ is a relation on State. $\qquad\square$

The generalisation of data refinement is the following.

Definition 5.6 (*Weak data refinement*)
Define *programs* over τ-data types $\mathsf{D} = (\mathsf{State}, \mathsf{Init}, \{\mathsf{Op}_k\}_{k\in I}, \tau, \mathsf{Fin})$ as sequences over $I \cup \{i\}$ with $i\notin I$, with the convention that $Op_i = \tau$, using the meanings of programs as in Definition 4.4. The set of meanings of a program over I in D is then given by

$$\hat{\mathsf{p}}_{\mathsf{D}} = \{\mathsf{q}_{\mathsf{D}} \mid \mathsf{q} \in \mathrm{seq}(I \cup \{i\}) \wedge \mathsf{q} \restriction I = \mathsf{p}\}$$

Now a τ-data type C refines a τ-data type A iff for each finite sequence p over I we have:

$$\bigcup \hat{\mathsf{p}}_{\mathsf{C}} \subseteq \bigcup \hat{\mathsf{p}}_{\mathsf{A}}$$

$\qquad\square$

The union over all possible programs with τ actions interspersed is necessary to allow a non-deterministic internal action in the abstract system to be implemented by a deterministic internal action that may or may not occur in the concrete system, so we cannot insist on a one-to-one matching of traces over $I \cup \{i\}$.

The definition for weak refinement looks similar to the one for perspicuous operations (Definition 5.1). We already noted at that point that it was a more general definition, with perspicuous operations refining *skip* a sufficient but not generally necessary condition. Weak refinement generalises it further, by also considering internal operations in the *abstract* specification. For practical examples of specifications, internal operations being refinements of *skip* may not be the correct answer in any case.

Foreshadowing discussion of divergence, it makes sense for internal operations to be applicable only in limited circumstances – which means their preconditions are stronger than that of *skip*, which would not be allowed for all refinement relations. Moreover, in a state based system it is acceptable for an event to change (abstract) state without it being available for interaction. The modelling of a web browser session, for example, might be done as an interspersion of commands (HTTP requests) with internal actions that model webpages being gradually loaded and displayed.

One method of obtaining refinement relations for systems with internal operations is to define an embedding of τ-data types into regular data types, and then to consider the normal refinement relation in the embedded types. The general technique of embedding a more complicated semantics into an existing model for which we can then apply the refinement rules will be covered at length in Chaps. 9 to 11. The following is only a basic example.

Definition 5.7 (*Embedding τ-data types*)

A τ-data type $D = (\text{State}, \text{Init}, \{Op_k\}_{k \in I}, \tau, \text{Fin})$ is embedded as the data type $\widehat{D} = (\text{State}, \widehat{\text{Init}}, \{\widehat{Op_k}\}_{k \in I}, \text{Fin})$ where $\widehat{Op} = Op \, \S \, i^*$ and $\widehat{\text{Init}} = \text{Init} \, \S \, i^*$. $\qquad \Box$

Refinement relations for τ-data types can then be obtained by substituting their embeddings as data types into the normal refinement conditions. The simulation rules deriving from this are those of Definitions 4.6 and 4.7 with internal behaviour inserted after all occurrences of operations and initialisation. A more elaborate version of this type of embedding will be central to Chap. 11.

5.4.3 Divergence from Internal Operations

The refinement models with internal operations discussed in this section so far have ignored divergence. For example, the traces with interspersed internal operations in Definition 5.6 might be an infinite set for a given "normal" trace, with an unbounded number of internal operations occurring in one particular position in the trace. That particular position would then likely[2] indicate a divergent state.

In LTS we encountered the idea of "deadlock", when no further actions are possible – or, as we will see in the next chapter, when two communicating systems insist on different actions to synchronise on next. Divergence through internal actions is sometimes called *livelock*, as it might be semantically interpreted as internal actions potentially always taking precedence over external actions, with as a consequence no opportunity for external actions to occur, much like in deadlock.

Given a specific model, we can define precisely what divergence means in a LTS, as an instance of Definition 5.2.

Definition 5.8 (*Divergence in LTS*)

A state p is divergent in a given LTS, denoted $p \uparrow$, if an infinite sequence of τ actions is possible starting from p, i.e. p is contained in the largest fixed point of $\lambda S. \text{dom}(\tau \rhd S)$.

A trace t is strictly divergent in the LTS with initial state p if there is a divergent state q such that $p \overset{t}{\Longrightarrow} q$. $\qquad \Box$

---

[2]That is, if it is not a situation of infinite branching like in Example 1.21.

Divergent states are not stable, but unstable states do not need to be divergent, see for example the initial states in systems (ii) and (iii) in Fig. 5.2.

In later chapters, we will discuss refinement semantics for specific notations that explicitly model divergences as observations, alongside previously discussed observations such as traces and failures.

5.5 Bibliographical Notes

The concept of a perspicuous operation was first identified in [3, 8], and these papers also analyse their relation to internal operations in detail. It captures the justification for adding new events in action systems [1], in particular "auxiliary actions" in superposition refinement [9] and in Event-B [2, 10].

The explicit modelling of catastrophic and non-catastrophic notions of error is described by Boiten and De Roever [11] in order to combine the blocking and non-blocking relational models. We have explored the issue more generally in [12], in the context of the relational concurrent refinement method that will be described further in Chaps. 9–11.

Refinement with internal operations is discussed in more detail in [4, Chapter 11], building on earlier work by Butler [13]. A detailed analysis and comparison of this to ASM refinement was done by Schellhorn [14].

The literature on Event-B is ambiguous on the extent to which perspicuous operations should be interpreted as internal ones: Butler's non-divergence criterion in [15] implies that they are, whereas Abrial [2, p. 414] only selectively applies such an interpretation ("it corresponds to a "daemon" acting").

References

1. Back RJR (1993) Refinement of parallel and reactive programs. In: Broy M (ed) Program design calculi. Springer, Berlin, pp 73–92
2. Abrial J-R (2010) Modeling in Event-B: system and software engineering, 1st edn. Cambridge University Press, New York
3. Boiten EA (2014) Introducing extra operations in refinement. Form Asp Comput 26(2):305–317
4. Derrick J, Boiten EA (2014) Refinement in Z and Object-Z, 2nd edn. Springer, Berlin
5. de Roever W-P, Engelhardt K (1998) Data refinement: model-oriented proof methods and their comparison. Cambridge University Press, Cambridge
6. Hoare CAR (1985) Communicating sequential processes. Prentice Hall, Upper Saddle River
7. Bolognesi T, Brinksma E (1988) Introduction to the ISO specification language LOTOS. Comput Netw ISDN Syst 14(1):25–59
8. Boiten EA (2011) Perspicuity and granularity in refinement. In: Proceedings 15th international refinement workshop. EPTCS, vol 55, pp 155–165
9. Back R, Sere K (1996) Superposition refinement of reactive systems. Form Asp Comput 8(3):324–346

10. Abrial JR, Cansell D, Méry D Refinement and reachability in Event-B. In: Treharne et al [16], pp 222–241
11. Boiten, EA, de Roever W-P (2003) Getting to the bottom of relational refinement: relations and correctness, partial and total. In: Berghammer R, Möller B (eds) 7th international seminar on relational methods in computer science (RelMiCS 7). University of Kiel, pp 82–88
12. Boiten EA, Derrick J (2009) Modelling divergence in relational concurrent refinement. In: Leuschel M, Wehrheim H (eds) IFM 2009: Integrated formal methods. Lecture notes in computer science, vol 5423. Springer, Berlin, pp 183–199
13. Butler M An approach to the design of distributed systems with B AMN. In: Bowen et al [17], pp 223–241
14. Schellhorn G (2005) ASM refinement and generalizations of forward simulation in data refinement: a comparison. Theor Comput Sci 336(2–3):403–436
15. Butler M (2009) Decomposition structures for Event-B. In: Leuschel M, Wehrheim H (eds) IFM. Lecture notes in computer science, vol 5423. Springer, Berlin, pp 20–38
16. Treharne H, King S, Henson MC, Schneider SA (eds) (2005) ZB 2005: formal specification and development in Z and B, 4th international conference of B and Z users, Guildford, UK, 13–15 April 2005, proceedings. Lecture notes in computer science, vol 3455. Springer, Berlin
17. Bowen JP, Hinchey MG, Till D (eds) (1997) ZUM'97: The Z formal specification notation. Lecture notes in computer science, vol 1212. Springer, Berlin

Part II
Refinement in Specification Languages

The purpose of this part is to show how refinement is defined in particular formal notations. We survey some of the major (types of) notations, and for each we define refinement as it is typically used in that language, before linking it to its semantic model introduced in Part I. The aim is to give the reader

1. an understanding of how refinement is defined in a particular notation,
2. understanding of where the definition of refinement came from,
3. a collection of examples so they can appreciate its characteristics.

We begin with a discussion of process algebras, followed by the introduction of two state-based languages Z and B. Finally, we look at Event-B and ASM.

Part II
Refinement and Specification Languages

Chapter 6
Process Algebra

This chapter looks at these issues in process algebras. As a canonical example we look at CSP, but we also discuss CCS and LOTOS. The link to the semantics is made to Chap. 1 as well as elements of Chap. 5.

Process algebras describe a system in terms of interacting components which evolve concurrently. The components are called processes. The use of the word algebra refers to the fact that these languages are often equipped with a rich algebraic theory in terms of laws giving equivalence of processes. The alternative term of "process calculi" is sometimes used.

6.1 CSP - The Language

CSP (for Communicating Sequential Processes) describes a system as a collection of interacting communicating components running concurrently. The components are called processes, and the interaction between them is in terms of the synchronisation on events. We will think of a process as a self-contained component with an *interface*, through which it interacts with the environment, and the interface is described as a set of *events*. Events are instantaneous and atomic, just as the actions in a labelled transition system.

Notation: We will use the following notation. Σ is the set of all possible events. $\checkmark$ will be a termination event, not in Σ. We define the set $\Sigma^{\checkmark}$ to be $\Sigma \cup \{\checkmark\}$ (and similarly for $A^{\checkmark}$). *TRACE* is the set of all traces over $\Sigma^{\checkmark}$. As usual *traces(P)* is the set of all finite traces of a process P. $\qquad\qquad\Box$

Processes are described by guarded equations as in the following small example (c.f. Fig. 1.1 in Chap. 1):

$$VM = pound \to ((coffee\_button \to coffee \to stop)$$
$$\Box$$
$$(tea\_button \to tea \to stop))$$

© Springer International Publishing AG, part of Springer Nature 2018
J. Derrick and E. Boiten, *Refinement*, https://doi.org/10.1007/978-3-319-92711-4_6

Here, the process, called *VM*, first can do a *pound* event, and subsequently offers the environment (i.e., user) a choice of performing either the *coffee_button* or the *tea_button* event. Depending upon which was chosen the process can either do a *coffee* event or a *tea* event, it then deadlocks, that is, it can do no further events.

We describe here a fragment of the CSP language, and we begin with a description of operators that build sequential specifications.

6.1.1 Sequential Operators

The two key building blocks in the language are the processes *stop* and *skip*.

6.1.1.1 Stop and Skip

The process *stop* is never prepared to engage in any activity, nor does it successfully terminate. Such a process deadlocks, and is not able to perform any activity nor terminate successfully.

The process *skip*[1] similarly is never prepared to engage in any activity, however, instead it terminates successfully, and thus allows control to pass to another process.

6.1.1.2 Event Prefix

Event prefix, as in the process specification

$$a \rightarrow P$$

describes a process which is initially able to perform only *a*, and after performing *a* it behaves like *P*. For example,

$$P = coffee\_button \rightarrow coffee \rightarrow stop$$

describes a process which can initially perform a *coffee_button* event, then subsequently a *coffee*, and then deadlocks.

We think of these events as being *offered* to the environment, which can choose to perform them if it wishes. We can think of the environment as modelling a user of the system.

---

[1] The relation with "skip" as stuttering in Chap. 3 is that both do nothing, doing so successfully. However, the respective semantic models will turn out rather different.

6.1.1.3 Input and Output

In order that CSP can describe real systems, it is necessary to be able to specify the input and output of a process. For this reason, events in CSP can be structured and, in particular, can consist of a *channel* which can carry a *value*. If values v of type T are being communicated along channel c, the set of events associated with this communication is $\{c.v \mid v \in T\}$.

If c is a channel and v a value, then output is modelled by the CSP expression

$$c!v \to P$$

which describes a process that is initially willing to output v along channel c and subsequently behaves like P. The only event that this process is able to perform initially is $c.v$.

In a similar way we can describe input by the CSP expression

$$c?v : T \to P$$

which describes a process that is initially willing to accept any value v of type T along c and subsequently behaves like P. This process can therefore perform a number of events, i.e., any event of the form $c.v$ for $v \in T$.

We will omit the typing information on the inputs where this is clear from the context, and simply write $c?v \to P$.

Any input can be subsequently used in the process expression. As a simple example, the following process inputs a natural number then outputs twice that value.

$$P = in?x : \mathbb{N} \to double!(2 * x) \to skip$$

6.1.1.4 External and Internal Choice

External choice, in which control over the choice is external to the process, is described by

$$P_1 \square P_2$$

This process is initially ready to perform the events that either process can engage in, and the choice is resolved by the first event in favour of the process that performs it. The choice is external because events of both P_1 and P_2 are initially available. For example, in

$$P = (coffee\_button \to coffee \to stop)$$
$$\square$$
$$(tea\_button \to tea \to stop)$$

both events *coffee_button* and *tea_button* are enabled, however once the environment engages on one of these, say *coffee_button*, then subsequently the process behaves like *coffee* → *stop*.

Internal choice, on the other hand, describes a process in which the choice is resolved by the process itself, and is written

$$P_1 \sqcap P_2$$

For example, consider the following process:

$$Q = (coffee\_button \rightarrow coffee \rightarrow stop)$$
$$\sqcap$$
$$(tea\_button \rightarrow tea \rightarrow stop)$$

This process will non-deterministically choose which branch of the choice to offer to the environment, and thus its behaviour will be very different from P described above.

To understand the difference between internal and external choice, and thus P and Q, consider an environment which is initially only willing to perform a *coffee_button*. In such an environment process P can always proceed since it is willing to perform either a *coffee_button* or a *tea_button* initially. However, process Q may deadlock since the process itself makes the non-deterministic choice as to which event is initially enabled.

Thinking ahead to the semantics of such a construct, it should be clear that labelled transition systems alone, e.g., as presented in Sect. 1.2, are not sufficient to represent a construct such as internal choice, and we will need internal actions as discussed in Sect. 5.4 to model it.

6.1.1.5 Recursion

Process definitions can be recursive or mutually recursive. This allows one to specify systems with unbounded behaviour. For example,

$$FS = allocate \rightarrow deallocate \rightarrow FS$$

describes a process that can perform an *allocate* followed by a *deallocate*, and do this repeatedly. Mutual recursion, as in

$$FS = allocate \rightarrow S1$$
$$S1 = allocate \rightarrow deallocate \rightarrow S1$$
$$\square$$
$$deallocate \rightarrow FS$$

is frequently used in process definitions. In recursive definitions, processes are often parameterised by values such as sets or sequences. For example, the following process definition specifies a one place buffer holding values of type M:

$$Buf(\langle\rangle) = put?x : M \rightarrow Buf(\langle x \rangle)$$
$$Buf(\langle x \rangle) = get!x \rightarrow Buf(\langle\rangle)$$

Example 6.1 A frequency server might be specified in CSP as follows, where the frequencies are taken from some (here unspecified) set that includes a null value *no_freq*:

$$FreqServer(\varnothing) = allocate!error!no\_freq \rightarrow FreqServer(\varnothing)$$
$$\square$$
$$deallocate?freq \rightarrow FreqServer(\{freq\})$$
$$FreqServer(F) = (\square_{f \in F} \ allocate!ok!f \rightarrow FreqServer(F \setminus \{f\}))$$
$$\square$$
$$deallocate?freq \rightarrow FreqServer(F \cup \{freq\}) \quad \text{for non-empty } F$$

Here, the frequency server can always free up a frequency via a *deallocate* event, but can only allocate a frequency if they are not all in use. $\square$

6.1.1.6   Renaming

Events (or channels) can be renamed using a substitution notation $P[\![a/b]\!]$ which means that the event or channel b has been replaced by a throughout the process definition. For example, $Buf[\![mid/put]\!]$ is a buffer with channel name *put* renamed to *mid*.

6.1.2   Building Concurrent Specifications

The motivation behind process algebra was the description of interacting concurrent processes. However, so far the process definitions we have described only allow for sequential execution of events. These essentially correspond to the description of simple labelled transition systems. We now expand the fragment of CSP to include a description of how processes can be combined together in forms of parallel execution.

6.1.2.1   The Interface of a Process

In our definition of parallel composition below we will need the idea of an *interface* of a process. This is necessary because when we compose processes, we need to specify how they will interact. We do this by giving an explicit description of the interface of a process, which is the set of all events that the process can engage in. Often the interface of a process will simply be the set of events named in its definition, and unless told otherwise we will assume that is the case here. For example, the interface of

$$FS = allocate \rightarrow deallocate \rightarrow FS$$

would be {*allocate*, *deallocate*} unless defined otherwise. An interface can, however, be larger than the set of events named in its definition. For example, one could *define* the interface of *FS* to be any set larger than {*allocate*, *deallocate*}. This isn't often needed, but occasionally one does need to take such an approach.

6.1.2.2 Interleaving

The simplest way of combining components is to do so by allowing the *interleaving* of their behaviour. Interleaving is the concurrent execution of two processes where no synchronisation is required between the components. It is described by the process

$$P_1 \| P_2$$

in which processes P_1 and P_2 execute completely independently of each other (and do not synchronise even on events in common). For example, given

$$P = coffee \rightarrow P$$
$$Q = tea \rightarrow Q$$

the process $P \| Q$ can initially perform either a *coffee* or *tea* and also subsequently perform either a *tea* or *coffee*. Interleaving is sometimes used to describe replication of a resource or process, e.g., a pool of two independent frequency servers can be specified as

$$FS \| FS$$

where there is no communication or interaction between the two component processes. More interesting are the ways to describe processes that interact with each other. In CSP this is done by specifying their parallel composition.

6.1.2.3 Parallel Composition

CSP has a number of different operators to describe the parallel composition of processes, and in which the processes selectively synchronise on events. In our fragment of CSP, we consider just the *interface parallel* operator ‖.

A

The process

$$P_1 \parallel_A P_2$$

synchronises on events in the set A but all other events are interleaved. Thus P_1 and P_2 evolve separately, but events in A are enabled only when they are enabled in *both* P_1 and P_2.

When the required synchronisation set is the intersection of the interfaces of the two processes we omit explicit reference to the synchronisation set and simply write $P \parallel Q$.

For a description of the other parallel composition operators, such as the alphabetised parallel operator $P_A\|_B Q$, see [1].

Synchronous and asynchronous communication

In CSP components (i.e., processes) interact by *synchronising* on events in the interface of the participating components. By synchronising on an event a we mean that the event a occurs in both processes simultaneously. Such synchronisation is symmetric and instantaneous, and only occurs when both processes undertake it simultaneously. The semantics we give for CSP below will make this precise.

In general, there are two forms of interaction, or communication: synchronous and asynchronous communication. In synchronous communication all participants interact at the same time, synchronising on events in the manner just described. On the other hand in asynchronous communication the communication is not symmetric, one participant sends data and the other receives it, not necessarily at the same time. An example of synchronous communication is a 'phone call, whereas email is an example of asynchronous communication.

Example 6.2 Consider the vending machine:

$$VM = pound \rightarrow ((coffee\_button \rightarrow coffee \rightarrow stop)$$
$$\square$$
$$(tea\_button \rightarrow tea \rightarrow stop))$$

together with a customer who wants coffee, which might be specified by:

$$Cust = pound \rightarrow coffee\_button \rightarrow coffee \rightarrow stop$$

Their interaction could be described by the process $VM \parallel Cust$. Because we are synchronising on the events in the intersection of the interfaces of both processes,[2] VM and $Cust$ must synchronise initially on the *pound* event, after this both processes evolve, so that the subsequent behaviour is given by

---

[2]Remember that unless we give an explicit definition, the interface is simply the set of events listed in the process definition.

$$((\textit{coffee\_button} \rightarrow \textit{coffee} \rightarrow \textit{stop}) \square (\textit{tea\_button} \rightarrow \textit{tea} \rightarrow \textit{stop}))$$

$$\|$$

$$(\textit{coffee\_button} \rightarrow \textit{coffee} \rightarrow \textit{stop})$$

If this process synchronises on the *coffee_button* event, then after its occurrence the system overall evolves to:

$$(\textit{coffee} \rightarrow \textit{stop})$$

$$\|$$

$$(\textit{coffee} \rightarrow \textit{stop})$$

This, finally, can synchronise on the *coffee* event, and then deadlock.

However, because the events *tea_button* and *tea* aren't in the synchronisation set then another possible evolution of the system after a *pound* event is to perform the *tea_button* event and evolve to:

$$(\textit{tea} \rightarrow \textit{stop})$$

$$\|$$

$$(\textit{coffee\_button} \rightarrow \textit{coffee} \rightarrow \textit{stop})$$

and this can perform a *tea* event, and then deadlock.

To enforce synchronisation on all events one would have to write:

$$VM \quad\underset{\{\textit{pound},\textit{coffee\_button},\textit{coffee},\textit{tea\_button},\textit{tea}\}}{\|}\quad Cust$$

in which the only possible behaviour is that components VM and $Cust$ synchronise on the events *pound*, *coffee_button* and *coffee* in turn, and then deadlock.

Communication

The synchronisation that is required in a parallel composition allows communication between processes to be specified, achieved by the synchronisation of input and output values in events.

Example 6.3 A simple specification of a lift and a user of that lift might be as follows:

$$Lift = target?x : \mathbb{N} \rightarrow floor!x \rightarrow Lift$$
$$Person = target!7 \rightarrow request \rightarrow Con$$

Then the process $Lift \parallel Person$ synchronises on the *target* channel. The effect of this process is to first communicate the value 7 to $Lift$ and then to interleave the *floor.7* and *request* events.

Example 6.4 Given the frequency server process *FreqServer* from Example 6.1 we might specify mobile phones as follows:

$$Phone_i = allocate?reply?freq \rightarrow call_i \rightarrow deallocate!freq \rightarrow Phone_i \text{ if } reply = ok$$
$$\square$$
$$allocate?reply?no\_freq \rightarrow Phone_i \qquad\qquad \text{if } reply = error$$

The interaction between phone and server is then given by the process *FreqServer(F)* || *Phone_i*. This can be generalised to an arbitrary number of phones, as in:

$$FreqServer \parallel (\parallel^{i \in I} Phone_i)$$

with the obvious interpretation. $\square$

6.1.2.4 Hiding

Hiding encapsulates an event within a process and removes it from its interface. In

$$P \backslash L$$

the process behaves as P except that events in L are hidden from the environment and the process P has complete control over its hidden (or internal) events.

We can use hiding (together with composition and renaming) to specify a two place buffer by using two copies of the one place buffer.

$$Buf_2 = (Buf \llbracket mid/get \rrbracket \parallel Buf \llbracket mid/put \rrbracket) \backslash \{mid.x \mid x \in M\}$$

6.1.2.5 Further CSP Operators

There are further CSP operators, such as chaining $\gg$, sequential composition; and interrupt Δ which we do not detail here. Full details of their definition and use can be found in [2] or [1].

6.2 CSP - The Semantics

There are a number of different semantic models for CSP which are used to capture various aspects of a process and its interaction with its environment. We consider here the standard failures-divergences semantics, first detailing how the *traces* of a process are derived.

The traces of a process can be derived from a labelled transition system representation of its behaviour. However, it is more convenient to calculate them directly. Some small examples illustrate the basic principles, remembering that as in Chap. 1, *traces(P)* will denote the set of all traces of a process *P*.

Example 6.5 The set of all traces associated with the process

$$Cust = pound \rightarrow coffee\_button \rightarrow coffee \rightarrow stop$$

will be the set $\{\langle \rangle, \langle pound \rangle, \langle pound, coffee\_button \rangle, \langle pound, coffee\_button, coffee \rangle\}$. Similarly, the set of all traces associated with the process

$$VM = pound \rightarrow ((coffee\_button \rightarrow coffee \rightarrow stop)$$
$$\square$$
$$(tea\_button \rightarrow tea \rightarrow skip))$$

is the set $\{\langle \rangle, \langle pound \rangle, \langle pound, coffee\_button \rangle, \langle pound, coffee\_button, coffee \rangle, \langle pound, tea\_b$
The presence of $\checkmark$ in the last trace in this set is due to the *skip* action, and denotes successful termination at the semantic level. It is needed to distinguish *skip* from *stop*.

Finally consider

$$VM2 = pound \rightarrow ((coffee\_button \rightarrow coffee \rightarrow stop)$$
$$\sqcap$$
$$(tea\_button \rightarrow tea \rightarrow skip))$$

Although we have replaced external choice with internal choice, the set of traces of *VM*2 is exactly the same as the set of traces of *VM*. This means that traces alone do not have the power to discriminate between internal and external choice. $\square$

Using this example as a guide, we can calculate the traces of a process in a compositional manner in the following way:

$$traces(stop) = \{\langle \rangle\}$$

$$traces(skip) = \{\langle \rangle, \langle \checkmark \rangle\}$$

$$traces(a \rightarrow P) = \{\langle \rangle\} \cup \{\langle a \rangle \frown tr \mid tr \in traces(P)\}$$

$$traces(a!v \rightarrow P) = \{\langle \rangle\} \cup \{\langle a.v \rangle \frown tr \mid tr \in traces(P)\}$$

$$traces(a?x : T \rightarrow P(x)) = \{\langle \rangle\} \cup \{\langle a.v \rangle \frown tr \mid v \in T \wedge tr \in traces(P(v))\}$$

Note that the traces associated with input and output constructors include components associated with the values communicated.

Example 6.6 The traces of the process *Lift* = *target?x* : $\mathbb{N} \to$ *floor!x* $\to$ *stop* are described by the following set: $\{\langle\rangle\} \cup \{\langle target.v\rangle \mid v \in \mathbb{N}\} \cup \{\langle target.v, floor.v\rangle \mid v \in \mathbb{N}\}$.   □

In a similar fashion we can calculate the traces for choice and hiding as follows:

$$traces(P \setminus A) = \{tr \setminus A \mid tr \in traces(P)\}$$

$$traces(P \Box Q) = traces(P) \cup traces(Q)$$

$$traces(P \sqcap Q) = traces(P) \cup traces(Q)$$

Note that because traces are only concerned with the visible events of a process, events which are hidden do not appear in the traces of a process.

Example 6.7 The traces of the process $(a \to b \to a \to c \to stop)\backslash\{a\}$ are described by the following set: $\{\langle\rangle, \langle b\rangle, \langle b, c\rangle\}$.   □

Although in the examples we have looked at so far, the set of traces is finite, this is not always so. For example, recursion typically produces an infinite set of (finite) traces.

Example 6.8 Given definitions of P and Q below, we can calculate the traces of $P \underset{\{pound\}}{\|} Q$.

$$P = pound \to coffee \to P$$

$$Q = pound \to tea \to Q$$

These will consist of the collection:
$\langle\rangle, \langle pound\rangle, \langle pound, coffee\rangle, \langle pound, tea\rangle, \langle pound, tea, coffee\rangle, \langle pound, coffee, tea\rangle$, $\langle pound, coffee, tea, pound\rangle, \langle pound, tea, coffee, pound\rangle$, and so forth.   □

However, note that although the number of traces is infinite, the traces themselves consist of finite sequences of events, and the semantics assumes that the infinite traces can be extrapolated from the finite ones. This, in general, is true except in the presence of unbounded non-determinism.

Unbounded non-determinism

Unbounded non-determinism refers to the situation when a process can choose from an infinite set of options. For example, a process which non-deterministically selects *any* natural number n and performs an event n times contains unbounded non-determinism.

We have already commented in Chap. 1 that the trace model is not very discriminating, since it fails to distinguish between internal and external choice. This is because traces tell us what a process *can* do but nothing about what it *must* do. That is, it doesn't consider liveness but just the preservation of safety. Another example, not involving internal choice, appeared in Example 1.6 of two systems that the traces semantics could not discriminate between, yet were intuitively different.

We need therefore to consider a stronger semantic model that can make such distinctions. The usual semantic model that is used in CSP is derived from the failures semantics, which we discussed in Sect. 1.5.

6.2.1 The CSP Failures Model

In this semantics each process is now modelled by a pair (T, F) where T are its traces and F its failures - that is a pair consisting of trace and refusal set. More specifically, we will consider *stable failures* here, that is failures at points where the system cannot do any internal evolution. We return to this point in Sect. 6.2.2 below. When we speak of failures in this section we are strictly speaking restricting ourselves to stable failures.

The traces and failures of a process will satisfy certain conditions that guarantee they are well-formed. In particular the set of traces T of a process will contain the empty trace, it will also be prefix-closed. This is captured by the following:

T1 $\langle\rangle \in T$
T2 $t_1 \leq t_2 \wedge t_2 \in T \Rightarrow t_1 \in T$

If, in addition to the traces, we consider the failures F, we need the following well-formedness conditions to hold.

F1 $(t, X) \in F \Rightarrow t \in T$
F2 $(t, X) \in F \wedge Y \subseteq X \Rightarrow (t, Y) \in F$
F3 $(t, X) \in F \wedge (\forall e \in Y \bullet t ^\frown \langle e \rangle \notin T) \Rightarrow (t, X \cup Y) \in F$
F4 $t ^\frown \langle \checkmark \rangle \in T \Rightarrow (t ^\frown \langle \checkmark \rangle, X) \in F$

The first is a consistency property between traces and failures, and the second requires subset closure of the refusals. The third requires that a process can refuse any event which cannot occur as the next event. Finally, after a terminating event no further events are possible (and thus all are refused). Before we give the derivation of the failures for a general process, some examples illustrate their calculation.

Example 6.9 In this example we assume that the alphabet of each process is restricted to consist of only those events mentioned in their definition.

We have given the traces associated with the process

$Cust = pound \rightarrow coffee\_button \rightarrow coffee \rightarrow stop$

above. Each trace gives rise to a refusal set, resulting in the following failures:

$(\langle\,\rangle, \{coffee\_button, coffee, \checkmark\})$

$(\langle pound \rangle, \{pound, coffee, \checkmark\})$

$(\langle pound, coffee\_button \rangle, \{pound, coffee\_button, \checkmark\})$

$(\langle pound, coffee\_button, coffee \rangle, \{pound, coffee\_button, coffee, \checkmark\})$

Note, that these are not the only failures, but ones based on the maximal refusal sets. Additional failures are given by the downward closure of the refusal sets (condition F2), so, for example $(\langle\,\rangle, \{coffee\_button\})$ is also a failure of this process. Similarly, we can calculate the refusals associated with each trace of the process

$$VM = pound \rightarrow ((coffee\_button \rightarrow coffee \rightarrow stop)$$
$$\square$$
$$(tea\_button \rightarrow tea \rightarrow skip))$$

to include the following (plus the obvious downward closures of these):

$(\langle\,\rangle, \{coffee\_button, coffee, tea\_button, tea\})$

$(\langle pound \rangle, \{pound, coffee, tea\})$

$(\langle pound, coffee\_button \rangle, \{pound, coffee\_button, tea\_button, tea\})$

$(\langle pound, coffee\_button, coffee \rangle, \{pound, coffee\_button, coffee, tea\_button, tea\})$

$(\langle pound, tea\_button \rangle, \{pound, coffee\_button, coffee, tea\_button\})$

$(\langle pound, tea\_button, tea \rangle, \{pound, coffee\_button, coffee, tea\_button, tea\})$

$(\langle pound, tea\_button, tea, \checkmark \rangle, \{pound, coffee\_button, coffee, tea\_button, tea\})$ $\square$

Having seen this illustration of how to calculate the failures on these examples we can define the general calculation compositionally as follows, where we denote the stable failures of a process by $SF(P)$.

$$SF(stop) = \{(\langle\,\rangle, X) \mid X \subseteq \Sigma^{\checkmark}\}$$

$$SF(skip) = \{(\langle\,\rangle, X) \mid \checkmark \notin X\} \cup \{(\langle\checkmark\rangle, X) \mid X \subseteq \Sigma^{\checkmark}\}$$

$$SF(a \rightarrow P) = \{(\langle\,\rangle, X) \mid a \notin X\} \cup \{(\langle a\rangle \frown tr, X) \mid (tr, X) \in SF(P)\}$$

$$SF(P \square Q) = \{(\langle\,\rangle, X) \mid (\langle\,\rangle, X) \in SF(P) \cap SF(Q)\}$$
$$\cup$$
$$\{(tr, X) \mid tr \neq \langle\,\rangle \wedge (tr, X) \in SF(P) \cup SF(Q)\}$$

$$SF(P \sqcap Q) = SF(P) \cup SF(Q)$$

Note the difference between the failures of internal and external choice. The trace semantics wasn't powerful enough to show a difference between them, but the failures semantics is. So, for example, $(\langle\,\rangle, \{coffee\_button\})$ is a failure of

$(coffee\_button \rightarrow coffee \rightarrow stop)$

$\sqcap$

$(tea\_button \rightarrow tea \rightarrow skip)$

but not of

$(coffee\_button \rightarrow coffee \rightarrow stop)$

$\square$

$(tea\_button \rightarrow tea \rightarrow skip)$

The remaining three operators we introduced above were interleaving, parallel composition and hiding.

In the interleaving of two processes there is no synchronisation between the components, thus an event will be refused only when it is refused by both components. One can calculate the failures therefore as follows:

$$SF(P \| Q) = \{(tr, X \cup Y) \mid (\exists tr_1, tr_2 \bullet tr \; interleaves \; tr_1, tr_2) \wedge (X \upharpoonright \Sigma = Y \upharpoonright \Sigma) \wedge$$

$$(tr, X) \in SF(P) \wedge (tr, Y) \in SF(Q)\}$$

Here *interleaves* determines if a trace is an interleaving of two others. It is defined by structural induction, we don't give the full definition here but note, for example, that $\langle x, z, y \rangle$ *interleaves* $\langle x, y \rangle \; \langle z \rangle$. So events in tr where $tr \; interleaves \; tr_1, tr_2$ occur in the same order as

events in tr_1, tr_2, and each event from tr_1 and tr_2 occurs once in tr, and no other event does.

In a similar way, the failures of the parallel composition

$$P \parallel_A Q$$

which synchronises on events in the set A but all other events are interleaved, can be calculated as follows.

$$SF(P \parallel_A Q) = \{(tr, X \cup Y) \mid (\exists tr_1, tr_2 \bullet tr \; synch_A \; tr_1, tr_2) \wedge (X \setminus A^{\checkmark} = Y \setminus A^{\checkmark}) \wedge$$

$$(tr, X) \in SF(P) \wedge (tr, Y) \in SF(Q)\}$$

Again, this uses an auxiliary function *synch* which describes the synchronisation of traces. For a full definition see [1]. Finally, the failures of a process that involves hiding.

$$SF(P \setminus A) = \{(tr \setminus A, X) \mid (tr, X \cup A) \in SF(P)\}$$

where $tr \setminus A$ removes elements of A from tr in a manner one would expect.

After all those definitions, some examples are overdue.

Example 6.10 Again in this example we assume that the alphabet of each process is restricted to consist of only those events mentioned in their definition. Then the process $P = pound \rightarrow stop$ has associated failures: $(\langle \rangle, \varnothing)$, $(\langle pound \rangle, \varnothing)$ and $(\langle pound \rangle, \{pound\})$. The failures of Q, where Q is defined as

$$Q = a \rightarrow b \rightarrow stop$$
$$\square$$
$$b \rightarrow a \rightarrow stop$$

include $(\langle \rangle, \varnothing)$, $(\langle a \rangle, \{a\})$, $(\langle b \rangle, \{b\})$, $(\langle a, b \rangle, \{a, b\})$, and $(\langle b, a \rangle, \{a, b\})$, plus their downward closure.

In a similar way, the failures of

$$R = ((b \rightarrow c \rightarrow stop)$$
$$\square$$
$$(c \rightarrow a \rightarrow stop))\setminus\{c\}$$

are $\{(\langle \rangle, X) \mid X \subseteq \{b, c\}\} \cup \{(\langle a \rangle, X), (\langle b \rangle, X) \mid X \subseteq \{a, b, c\}\}$. Note here that b can be refused initially, despite it being available initially. This is because the hiding of c allows R to non-deterministically and silently evolve to a state where b is not enabled (cf. system (ii) in Fig. 5.2). Finally consider

$$S = (a \rightarrow stop)$$
$$\sqcap$$
$$(b \rightarrow stop)$$

This has failures $\{(\langle \rangle, X) \mid \{a, b\} \nsubseteq X\} \cup \{(\langle a \rangle, X), (\langle b \rangle, X) \mid X \subseteq \{a, b\}\}$. Notice that, for a larger alphabet, the failures of each process would include additional elements due to the refusal of events from the enlarged alphabet. $\square$

Example 6.11 We had seen above that given P and Q as follows

$$P = pound \rightarrow coffee \rightarrow P$$
$$Q = pound \rightarrow tea \rightarrow Q$$

the traces of their composition $P \parallel Q$ consisted of the collection:
$\langle \rangle$, $\langle pound \rangle$, $\langle pound, coffee \rangle$, $\langle pound, tea \rangle$, $\langle pound, coffee, tea \rangle$, $\langle pound, tea, coffee \rangle$, $\langle pound, coffee, tea, pound \rangle$, $\langle pound, tea, coffee, pound \rangle$, and so forth.

We can calculate some of the refusals associated with each trace to give the failures of $P \parallel Q$ as follows:

$(\langle\rangle, \{coffee, tea\}), (\langle pound \rangle, \{pound\}), (\langle pound, coffee \rangle, \{pound, coffee\}),$
$(\langle pound, tea \rangle, \{pound, tea\}), (\langle pound, coffee, tea \rangle, \{coffee, tea\}),$
$(\langle pound, tea, coffee \rangle, \{coffee, tea\}), (\langle pound, coffee, tea, pound \rangle, \{pound\}),$
$(\langle pound, tea, coffee, pound \rangle, \{pound\}),$ etc.   □

6.2.2 The CSP Failures, Divergences and Infinite Traces Semantics

The model we have described so far for CSP has defined traces and failures for processes. We haven't yet, however, discussed how it treats any divergence that might arise in the model, and whether it is discriminating enough in the presence of divergence.

The source of divergence in CSP is *livelock* – and this often occurs when events have been hidden. Consider, for example, the following process:

$P = (a \rightarrow P) \setminus \{a\}$

In this case P never performs any visible event, nor reaches any stable state. P is therefore divergent, and this is denoted by writing $P \uparrow$.

Probably the easiest way to think about divergence, and indeed states that are *stable* is to think about the *transitions* that a process can undergo - in the manner described in Chap. 1. We don't give such a full *operational semantics* here beyond noting here that the occurrence of events gives rise to the corresponding transition in the obvious way. The key point with respect to divergence is to note that, in addition to observable transitions, an operational semantics also records internal evolution that might arise (e.g., from the type of hiding illustrated above).

As is standard (e.g., Definition 2.1) we denote internal events by τ and thus internal transitions by $P \xrightarrow{\tau} Q$. In terms of the fragment of CSP introduced so far there are two key points whereby internal evolution can occur. Firstly in hiding. So if P can undergo an a event and evolve to Q, ie $P \xrightarrow{a} Q$, then $P \setminus A \xrightarrow{\tau} Q \setminus A$ if $a \in A$. Secondly, in the semantics of an internal choice the system $P \sqcap Q$ can silently evolve to either P or Q, and this is represented by an internal τ transition as in Fig. 5.2 (iii).

Applying these ideas to the example above, we see that P can undergo an unbounded number of τ transitions, so P really is divergent.

Two types of arrow

We now have two types of arrow, and we need to be careful not to confuse the two. One arrow, prefixing, is part of the language of CSP, as in $P = a \rightarrow stop$. The other arrow, a transition, is part of the semantics of CSP, as in $P \xrightarrow{a} stop$. They are different, but related - the arrow in the language generating a transition in the semantics.

In the failures, divergences and infinite traces (*FDI*) semantic model we use here, the divergences (*D*) record the divergent traces of a system, the infinite traces (*I*) the possible infinite evolutions of the system, and the failures (*F*) the finite traces with their associated refusals. A catastrophic view of divergence is taken (cf. Chap. 5), in that after a strictly divergent trace, all subsequent traces are divergent – it is not possible to subsequently escape from divergence in this view. The set of all infinite traces is denoted *IT* or *itraces*.

In the failures we will now record the stable failures as before, but also refusals of its divergent traces. Here again we take the most pessimistic view, and thus a divergent process can refuse any set. Because we record both the stable and unstable failures, we can dispense with recording the traces as a separate component. In this semantic model, therefore, we do not need to worry about the conditions T1 and T2 above. Specifically, in the stable failures model, not all traces appeared in the failures. However, in the FDI model a trace will either be divergent, or lead to a stable state. In either case $(tr, \varnothing)$ will be in the failures set.

As in the stable failures or traces semantic model, this model has a number of conditions on its failures, divergences and infinite traces as follows. The conditions on the failures require:

F1 $(\langle \rangle, \varnothing) \in F$
F2 $(tr, X) \in F \wedge tr' \leq tr \Rightarrow (tr', \varnothing) \in F$
F3 $(tr, X) \in F \wedge Y \subseteq X \Rightarrow (tr, Y) \in F$
F4 $(tr, X) \in F \wedge (\forall e \in Y \bullet (tr \frown \langle e \rangle, \langle \rangle) \notin F) \Rightarrow (tr, X \cup Y) \in F$

The first of these says that *F* is non-empty and will contain at minimum the failure $(\langle \rangle, \varnothing)$. The second condition is the prefix closure of traces. The third is the subset closure of the refusal sets. The final one is the relationship between not being able to extend a trace with a particular event and that event being in the refusal set. The conditions on the divergences are as follows:

D1 $tr_1 \in D \wedge tr_1 \leq tr_2 \Rightarrow tr_2 \in D$
D2 $tr \in D \wedge X \subseteq \Sigma^\checkmark \Rightarrow (tr, X) \in F$
D3 $tr_1 \in D \wedge tr_2 \in \Sigma^\omega \Rightarrow tr_1 \frown tr_2 \in I$
D4 $tr \frown \langle \checkmark \rangle \in D \Rightarrow tr \in D$

The first property simply states that you can never escape divergence – all extensions of (strictly) divergent traces are divergent too. The second that a divergence trace can refuse anything, the third that once a process has diverged then any infinite behaviour is possible, the final one says successful termination cannot be the cause of divergence. Finally the infinite traces have two properties:

I1 $tr_2 \in I \wedge tr_1 < tr_2 \Rightarrow (tr_1, \varnothing) \in F$
I2 $\forall (tr, X) \in F \bullet \exists T \bullet \{(tr \frown tr', Y) \mid (tr', Y) \in F_T\} \subseteq F \wedge \{tr \frown tr' \mid tr' \in I_T\} \subseteq I$

The first says that finite prefixes of infinite traces must be possible behaviours (and thus appear in *F*). The second says which infinite traces must be in *I* given knowledge about the finite traces that are in the system. This condition uses two sets

F_T and I_T, which are the failures and infinite traces of a deterministic process whose traces are T. These are defined by:

$$F_T = \{(tr, X) \mid tr \in T \land \forall e \in X \bullet tr \,^\frown \langle e \rangle \notin T\}$$

$$I_T = \{tr' \mid \forall tr \le tr' \bullet tr \text{ finite} \Rightarrow tr \in T\}$$

Having defined the semantics we are to use, we are now in a position to define the semantics for a specific process in a compositional fashion as we did for the stable failures model. The aim of the FDI model is to incorporate additional information about the divergences of a system, it should then in some sense be consistent with the stable failures model. Indeed it is, in the sense that when the divergences are empty, the failures and stable failures coincide, and the traces of a system in the stable failures semantics are those recorded in the failures in the FDI model. That is, when the divergences are empty we have:

$$traces(P) = \{tr \mid (tr, \varnothing) \in F(P)\}$$

$$SF(P) = F(P)$$

For each process construct we define three sets, F, D and I, recording their failures, divergences and infinite traces. Most of the definitions are straightforward now we have seen the calculation for stable failures.

Stop

$$F(stop) = \{(\langle \rangle, X) \mid X \subseteq \Sigma^\checkmark\}$$

$$D(stop) = \varnothing$$

$$I(stop) = \varnothing$$

Skip

$$F(skip) = \{(\langle \rangle, X) \mid \checkmark \notin X\} \cup \{(\langle \checkmark \rangle, X) \mid X \subseteq \Sigma^\checkmark\}$$

$$D(skip) = \varnothing$$

$$I(skip) = \varnothing$$

Prefixing

$$F(a \to P) = \{(\langle \rangle, X) \mid a \notin X\} \cup \{(\langle a \rangle \,^\frown tr, X) \mid (tr, X) \in F(P)\}$$

$$D(a \to P) = \{\langle a \rangle \,^\frown tr \mid tr \in D(P)\}$$

$$I(a \to P) = \{\langle a \rangle \,^\frown tr \mid tr \in I(P)\}$$

External Choice

$$F(P \square Q) = \{(\langle \rangle, X) \mid ((\langle \rangle, X) \in F(P) \cap F(Q)) \vee \langle \rangle \in D(P \square Q)\}$$
$$\cup \{(tr, X) \mid tr \neq \langle \rangle \wedge (tr, X) \in F(P) \cup F(Q)\}$$
$$D(P \square Q) = D(P) \cup D(Q)$$
$$I(P \square Q) = I(P) \cup I(Q)$$

Internal Choice

$$F(P \sqcap Q) = F(P) \cup F(Q)$$
$$D(P \sqcap Q) = D(P) \cup D(Q)$$
$$I(P \sqcap Q) = I(P) \cup I(Q)$$

****

Interleaving

$$F(P \| Q) = \{(tr, X \cup Y) \mid \exists tr_1, tr_2 \bullet tr \text{ interleaves } tr_1, tr_2 \wedge X \upharpoonright \Sigma = Y \upharpoonright \Sigma \wedge$$
$$(tr_1, X) \in F(P) \wedge (tr_2, Y) \in F(Q)\}$$
$$\cup \{(tr, X) \mid tr \in D(P \| Q)\}$$
$$D(P \| Q) = \{tr \frown tr' \mid \exists tr_1, tr_2 \bullet tr \text{ interleaves } tr_1, tr_2 \wedge$$
$$((tr_1 \in D(P) \wedge (tr_2, \varnothing) \in F(Q))$$
$$\vee ((tr_2 \in D(Q) \wedge (tr_1, \varnothing) \in F(P)))\}$$
$$I(P \| Q) = \{tr \mid \exists tr_1, tr_2 \bullet tr \text{ interleaves } tr_1, tr_2 \wedge tr_1 \in I(P) \wedge tr_2 \in I(Q)\}$$
$$\cup \{tr \mid \exists tr_1, tr_2 \bullet tr \text{ interleaves } tr_1, tr_2 \wedge tr_1 \in I(P) \wedge (tr_2, \varnothing) \in F(Q)\}$$
$$\cup \{tr \mid \exists tr_1, tr_2 \bullet tr \text{ interleaves } tr_1, tr_2 \wedge tr_2 \in I(Q) \wedge (tr_1, \varnothing) \in F(P)\}$$
$$\cup \{tr \frown tr' \mid tr \in D(P \| Q)\}$$

The latter two conditions are just saying that as soon as one component diverges, the whole system does, and that the infinite traces are just the infinite interleavings of finite or infinite traces.

Parallel Composition

In a similar vein, the definitions for parallel composition for the failures are analogous to those for stable failures, and the divergences and infinite traces just obtained from those of the components. The full definitions are:

$$F(P \parallel_A Q) = \{(tr, X \cup Y) \mid \exists tr_1, tr_2 \bullet tr \ synch_A \ tr_1, tr_2 \wedge (X \setminus A^{\checkmark} = Y \setminus A^{\checkmark}) \wedge$$

$$(tr, X) \in F(P) \wedge (tr, Y) \in F(Q)\}$$

$$\cup \ \{(tr, X) \mid tr \in D(P \parallel_A Q)\}$$

$$D(P \parallel_A Q) = \{tr \frown tr' \mid \exists tr_1, tr_2 \bullet tr \ synch_A \ tr_1, tr_2 \wedge$$

$$((tr_1 \in D(P) \wedge (tr_2, \varnothing) \in F(Q))$$

$$\vee ((tr_2 \in D(Q) \wedge (tr_1, \varnothing) \in F(P))))\}$$

$$I(P \parallel_A Q) = \{tr \mid \exists tr_1, tr_2 \bullet tr \ synch_A \ tr_1, tr_2 \wedge tr_1 \in I(P) \wedge tr_2 \in I(Q)\}$$

$$\cup \{tr \mid \exists tr_1, tr_2 \bullet tr \ synch_A \ tr_1, tr_2 \wedge tr_1 \in I(P) \wedge (tr_2, \varnothing) \in F(Q)\}$$

$$\cup \{tr \mid \exists tr_1, tr_2 \bullet tr \ synch_A \ tr_1, tr_2 \wedge tr_2 \in I(Q) \wedge (tr_1, \varnothing) \in F(P)\}$$

$$\cup \{tr \frown tr' \mid tr \in D(P \parallel Q)\}$$

Finally, the FDI semantics of a process that involves hiding.

Hiding

$$F(P \setminus A) = \{(tr \setminus A, X) \mid (tr, X \cup A) \in F(P)\} \cup \{(tr, X) \mid tr \in D(P \setminus A)\}$$

$$D(P \setminus A) = \{(tr \setminus A) \frown tr' \mid tr \in D(P)\} \cup \{(tr \setminus A) \frown tr' \mid tr \in I(P) \wedge (tr \setminus A) \text{ is finite}\}$$

$$I(P \setminus A) = \{(tr \setminus A) \mid tr \in I(P) \wedge (tr \setminus A) \text{ is infinite}\}$$

Example 6.12 The process $P = stop \sqcap (a \to P)$ can deadlock at every point, or (non-deterministically) undergo an a event and recurse. Calculation can show that it has no divergences, its infinite traces consist of $\langle a \rangle^{\omega}$ and its failures all the elements $(\langle a \rangle^n, X)$ for every $n \in \mathbb{N}$ and all refusal sets X.   □

6.3 CSP - Refinement

The hard work in defining refinement in a language is, if we have set things up correctly, the definition of the semantics. The semantics will tell us what observations there are, and then, as we discussed in Sect. 1.1, refinement amounts to checking that $\mathcal{O}(C) \subseteq \mathcal{O}(A)$ and when this happens we write $A \sqsubseteq_{\mathcal{O}} C$ to denote the refinement of A by C under the observation $\mathcal{O}$.

The last section has defined three possible semantics for us to use, each one with a different observational power: the trace semantics, the stable failures semantics, and lastly the FDI semantics. These generate, therefore, three refinement relations, which we denote: $A \sqsubseteq_{tr} C$, $A \sqsubseteq_{sf} C$, and $A \sqsubseteq_{fdi} C$. So, for example, $P \sqsubseteq_{fdi} Q$ means that $F(Q) \subseteq F(P)$, $D(Q) \subseteq D(P)$, and $I(Q) \subseteq I(P)$.

Definition 6.1 (*Refinement in CSP*)

$P \sqsubseteq_{tr} Q$ whenever the traces of Q are included in those of P.

$P \sqsubseteq_{sf} Q$ whenever the stable failures of Q are included in those of P.

$P \sqsubseteq_{fdi} Q$ whenever $F(Q) \subseteq F(P)$, $D(Q) \subseteq D(P)$, and $I(Q) \subseteq I(P)$.   □

6.3.1 Trace Refinement

We discussed the basics of trace refinement in Sect. 1.3. We can now see the effect of this refinement relation in CSP.

Example 6.13 We saw that the set of all traces of the process

$Cust = pound \rightarrow coffee\_button \rightarrow coffee \rightarrow stop$

was $\{\langle\rangle, \langle pound\rangle, \langle pound, coffee\_button\rangle, \langle pound, coffee\_button, coffee\rangle\}$. The trace subsetting requirement of trace refinement means that the following processes all refine *Cust*.

$pound \rightarrow coffee\_button \rightarrow coffee \rightarrow stop$
$pound \rightarrow coffee\_button \rightarrow stop$
$pound \rightarrow stop$
$stop$

but that neither, for example, $coffee\_button \rightarrow stop$ nor $coffee \rightarrow coffee \rightarrow stop$ are trace refinements of *Cust*.   □

Example 6.14 We saw that the set of all traces of the process

$VM = pound \rightarrow ((coffee\_button \rightarrow coffee \rightarrow stop)$
$$\square$$
$(tea\_button \rightarrow tea \rightarrow skip))$

was $\{\langle\rangle, \langle pound\rangle, \langle pound, coffee\_button\rangle, \langle pound, coffee\_button, coffee\rangle,$
$\langle pound, tea\_button\rangle, \langle pound, tea\_button, tea\rangle, \langle pound, tea\_button, tea, \checkmark\rangle\}$.
This means that, for example, $VM \sqsubseteq_{tr} Cust$ since every trace of *Cust* is also a trace of *VM*. Trace semantics also allows us to replace the *stop* by *skip* in the abstract specification, so that if

$$VM' = pound \rightarrow ((coffee\_button \rightarrow coffee \rightarrow skip)$$

$$\Box$$

$$(tea\_button \rightarrow tea \rightarrow skip))$$

then $VM' \sqsubseteq_{tr} VM$ since all traces of VM are also traces of VM'.   □

Example 6.15 Finally if we have

$$VM2 = pound \rightarrow ((coffee\_button \rightarrow coffee \rightarrow stop)$$

$$\sqcap$$

$$(tea\_button \rightarrow tea \rightarrow skip))$$

then since the traces of $VM2$ are the same as the traces of VM we have both $VM2 \sqsubseteq_{tr} VM$ and $VM \sqsubseteq_{tr} VM2$ □

6.3.2 Stable Failures Refinement

With the stable failures semantics, refinement can now distinguish between internal and external choice.

Example 6.16 Consider VM and $VM2$ defined above. The failures semantics distinguishes between the two processes. Every stable failure of VM is a stable failure of $VM2$, but there are failures in $VM2$ not in VM. Thus we have: $VM2 \sqsubseteq_{sf} VM$, but not the converse $VM \sqsubseteq_{sf} VM2$.   □

Example 6.17 Consider *Cust* and VM defined above. The failures of the two processes are not comparable, thus neither is a failures refinement of the other.   □

It is easy to write CSP descriptions of the LTS specifications that we considered in Chap. 1 to generate more examples of systems that are related by failures refinement. For example, we can write CSP descriptions for the LTSs in Example 1.6:

$$P = pound \rightarrow coffee\_button \rightarrow coffee \rightarrow stop$$
$$Q = pound \rightarrow ((coffee\_button \rightarrow coffee \rightarrow stop)$$

$$\Box$$

$$(coffee\_button \rightarrow stop))$$

And as discussed in that example, $P \equiv_{tr} Q$ and $Q \sqsubseteq_{sf} P$ but it is not the case that $P \sqsubseteq_{sf} Q$.

Stable failures refinement preserves liveness as well as safety - we can't refine away the behaviour to *stop* as we can with traces refinement. It does, however, allow the reduction of non-determinism in a fashion which should be familiar by now.

Example 6.18 Consider the processes P_1, P_2 and P_3:

$$P_1 = (a \rightarrow stop) \square (b \rightarrow stop)$$
$$P_2 = (a \rightarrow stop) \sqcap (b \rightarrow stop)$$
$$P_3 = stop \sqcap ((a \rightarrow stop) \square (b \rightarrow stop))$$

Then $P_3 \sqsubseteq_{sf} P_2 \sqsubseteq_{sf} P_1$. To see this, note that the key trace to consider is the empty trace, since the refusals after $\langle a \rangle$ or $\langle b \rangle$ are identical for all three processes.

However, after $\langle \rangle$ the refusals of P_1 are $\varnothing$, those of P_2 are $\varnothing$, $\{a\}$, $\{b\}$ but crucially not $\{a, b\}$, whereas the refusals of P_3 are any $X \subseteq \{a, b\}$. Hence $failures(P_1) \subseteq failures(P_2) \subseteq failures(P_3)$. Hence $P_3 \sqsubseteq_{sf} P_2 \sqsubseteq_{sf} P_1$. $\square$

6.3.3 FDI Refinement

FDI refinement adds in the consideration of divergences and infinite traces. We know that when the divergences are empty, then the failures and stable failures coincide. So, for example, in Example 6.17, the divergences of all three process are empty, and thus we can deduce that $P_3 \sqsubseteq_{fdi} P_2 \sqsubseteq_{fdi} P_1$.

So examples that show the difference between failures refinement and FDI refinement are centred around either infinite traces or divergences. An example of the difference between systems with finite and infinite traces was given in Example 2.1. In that example $A \sqsubseteq_{fdi} C$ since the failures are identical, there are no divergences, and the infinite traces of C (there aren't any!) are included in those of A (which has an infinite trace $\langle a \rangle^\omega$).

Example 6.19 Consider the process P, defined in terms of a (divergent) process Q:

$$P =(a \rightarrow b \rightarrow P)$$
$$\square$$
$$(c \rightarrow Q)$$
$$\square$$
$$(c \rightarrow d \rightarrow stop)$$
$$Q =(e \rightarrow Q) \setminus \{e\}$$

P has both infinite and divergent traces. It has $\langle a, b, a, b, \ldots \rangle$ as an infinite trace. Traces that end up at Q will be divergent, e.g., $\langle c \rangle$ or $\langle a, b, c \ldots \rangle$. Since $\langle c \rangle$ is a divergent trace, any set is refused after it, thus $(\langle c \rangle, \{a, b, c, d, e\})$ is a failure of the system (among many others).

Any refinement of P has to make sure its failures, divergences and infinite traces are included in those of P. For example, we could simply remove the divergence at Q and the following is an FDI refinement of P:

$R = (a \rightarrow b \rightarrow R)$

$\Box$

$(c \rightarrow skip)$

$\Box$

$(c \rightarrow d \rightarrow stop)$

$\Box$

6.4   LOTOS - Language, Semantics and Refinement

LOTOS (Language Of Temporal Ordering Specification) is another process algebra, bearing similarities to CSP and CCS, although taking a different approach to divergence and refinement. A LOTOS specification consists of two parts: a behavioural part (i.e., the process algebraic part) and a data part. The process algebraic part specifies the behaviour of a system in the same manner as we have seen in CSP, the data part (which is not present in CSP or CCS) allows one to specify data types (numbers, queues etc) that can be used in the behavioural part. The terms *full LOTOS* and *basic LOTOS* are often used to refer to the complete language and just the behavioural part respectively.

6.4.1   The LOTOS Language

The language and style of specification in LOTOS is similar to that in CSP. As in CSP, the process

   stop

deadlocks and performs no actions. Prefixing is similar to CSP, but described with the syntax:

   $a; P$

The difference to CSP here is that a can be a visible action but also an explicit internal action. Internal actions are denoted i in LOTOS. Thus if Σ is the set of external actions, then a can range over $\Sigma \cup \{i\}$ in an action prefix definition. The effect of

   $i; P$

is that the system unobservably performs i and evolves to P.

> **Events and actions**: there are some terminological differences between process algebras. One of those is the term for the basic atomic actions. These are known as *events* in CSP, but *actions* in CCS and LOTOS.

Input and output are represented in the same way as in CSP. Thus in LOTOS we would write expressions such as

$$c!v; P \quad \text{or} \quad c?v : T; P$$

to represent outputting and inputting values respectively.

There is only one choice construct in LOTOS, which is denoted

$$P[]Q$$

which could, for example, be used as follows

$$P = (coffee\_button; coffee; stop)$$
$$[]$$
$$(tea\_button; tea; stop)$$

We do not need a definition of internal choice since this can be modelled using explicit internal actions. For example, instead of writing the CSP expression

$$Q = (coffee\_button \rightarrow coffee \rightarrow stop)$$
$$\sqcap$$
$$(tea\_button \rightarrow tea \rightarrow stop)$$

in LOTOS one would write

$$Q = (i; coffee\_button; coffee; stop)$$
$$[]$$
$$(i; tea\_button; tea; stop)$$

which has the same effect. The syntax of LOTOS then also allows us to write explicit expressions such as

$$(i; P)[]Q \quad \text{or} \quad P[](i; Q)$$

with the obvious interpretation.

Recursion is supported in exactly the same way as in CSP, and renaming is denoted $P[a/b]$. As in CSP there are a number of operators that allow one to build concurrent behaviour. Interleaving, or independent parallelism, is supported in the same fashion, writing

$$P_1 \| P_2$$

Fig. 6.1 The behaviour of P

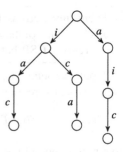

to mean processes P_1 and P_2 execute completely independently of each other (and do not synchronise even on events in common).

The general form of parallelism in LOTOS is written

$$P_1 \ |[x_1, \ldots, x_n]| \ P_2$$

which defines a behaviour where P_1 and P_2 evolve independently subject to synchronisation on external actions $x_1, \ldots, x_n$. With this definition, it is easy to see that $P_1 \| P_2$ is the same as $P_1 \ |[]| \ P_2$. We also define

$$P_1 \ \| \ P_2$$

to be $P_1 \ |[x_1, \ldots, x_n]| \ P_2$ where $x_1, \ldots, x_n$ range over all the actions of P_1 and P_2. Internal actions cannot synchronise, thus the behaviour of

$$P = a; b; stop \ |[b]| \ i; c; stop$$

can be thought of as defining the LTS in Fig. 6.1.

Synchronisation in LOTOS is synchronous as in CSP, and multi-way, so that in

$$P \ |[a]| \ Q \ |[a]| \ R$$

all three processes perform the action a together. Finally, hiding is written

$$\text{hide } x_1, \ldots, x_n \text{ in } P$$

having the obvious, and same, meaning as hiding in CSP.

6.4.2   LOTOS Semantics and Refinement

The standard semantics for LOTOS is given using LTS, where the basic approach is to give a LTS for each process definition. The derivations are straightforward for the fragment of LOTOS we have presented. For example, the LTS of a; b; $stop$ $|[b]|$ i; c; $stop$ was already given in Fig. 6.1, and we do not give further details here.

The semantics then allows one, as in CSP, to define a number of refinement relations for the language. For example, trace refinement has the same definition as in CSP or LTSs:

Definition 6.2 *(Trace refinement in LOTOS)*
$P \sqsubseteq_{tr} Q$ whenever the traces of Q are included in those of P. □

The traces of a LOTOS specification can be derived in an obvious fashion from its LTS semantics. For example, the traces of a; b; $stop$ $|[b]|$ i; c; $stop$ are

$$\{\langle\,\rangle, \langle a\rangle, \langle c\rangle, \langle a, c\rangle, \langle c, a\rangle\}.$$

Example 6.20 If we define

$$P_1 = x; stop$$
$$P_2 = \text{hide } y, z \text{ in } (y; x; z; stop[]z; x; stop)$$
$$P_3 = x; y; stop\|z; stop$$

then we have

$$P_3 \sqsubseteq_{tr} P_2 \sqsubseteq_{tr} P_1 \qquad\qquad □$$

However, as we have discussed already several times, trace refinement is not very discriminating, and more powerful notions of refinement are used in practice. Central to the definition of more powerful refinement relations in LOTOS is the notion of a *refusal*, see Sects. 1.5 and 1.9. In general, the refusals in a language can be derived in a number of ways. For example, for CSP one can derive them from the CSP failures semantics, or directly from an LTS semantics. In fact Definition 1.8 does the latter and defines the refusals of a process from its LTS representation.

To ease the presentation one often writes the refusals as

$$Ref_P(\sigma)$$

for the set of refusals X in the refusals definition as given in Definition 1.8, i.e.,

P **after** σ **ref** X.

Example 6.21 If we define $\Sigma = \{x, y, z\}$ and

$$P = x; (y; stop[]z; stop)$$

then the traces of P are:

$$\{\langle\,\rangle, \langle x\rangle, \langle x, y\rangle, \langle x, z\rangle\}$$

and its refusals after these traces are:

$Ref_P(\langle\rangle) = \{\varnothing, \{y\}, \{z\}, \{y, z\}\}$

$Ref_P(\langle x\rangle) = \{\varnothing, \{x\}\}$

$Ref_P(\langle x, y\rangle) = \mathbb{P}\Sigma$

$Ref_P(\langle x, z\rangle) = \mathbb{P}\Sigma$ $\square$

Using this definition we can define (as we did in Sect. 1.9) a number of refinement relations for use in LOTOS. The three principal ones are *reduction*, *conformance*, and *extension*, and these give rise to associated equivalence relations. We give their definitions in turn, and they are direct reformulations of the definitions given in Chap. newexlinkch:LTSrefinement11.

Definition 6.3 (*Conformance in LOTOS*)
Let P, Q be LOTOS process definitions. Then $P \sqsubseteq_{conf} Q$ whenever:
$\forall\sigma : traces(P) \bullet Ref_Q(\sigma) \subseteq Ref_P(\sigma).$ $\square$

Conformance received attention in LOTOS as it was proposed as a refinement relation that corresponded to a feasible notion of testing. However, from our point of view, as a refinement relation it has deficiencies - it is not a preorder for example. In its mitigation it has been argued that it isn't a development relation in the sense that refinement is, but a one-time check between specification and implementation. For that reason it is not necessary for it to be transitive. The following example shows why it is not transitive.

Example 6.22 If we define

$P_1 = x; stop[]i; y; stop$

$P_2 = i; y; stop$

$P_3 = x; z; stop[]i; y; stop$

then $P_3 \sqsubseteq_{conf} P_2$ and $P_2 \sqsubseteq_{conf} P_1$, but not $P_3 \sqsubseteq_{conf} P_1$. $\square$

With this weakness in mind, *reduction* has been defined which overcomes the problem of transitivity. In the absence of divergence, it is the same as failures refinement in CSP, and *must testing*. It is usually formulated as follows.

Definition 6.4 (*Reduction in LOTOS*).
Let P, Q be LOTOS process definitions. Then Q is an reduction of P, written $P \sqsubseteq_{red} Q$, whenever $traces(Q) \subseteq traces(P)$ and $P \sqsubseteq_{conf} Q$. $\square$

Reduction (which is the same as failures refinement in the absence of divergence) requires that no new traces are added, and that no new deadlocks are added, and so once again can be thought of as the reduction of non-determinism in a refinement.

Example 6.23 If we define

$P_1 = x; stop$

$P_2 = x; stop[]x; y; stop$

$P_3 = i; x; stop[]y; stop$

$P_4 = x; stop[]y; stop$

$P_5 = i; x; stop[]i; y; stop$

$P_6 = y; stop$

then $P_2 \sqsubseteq_{red} P_1$, $P_3 \sqsubseteq_{red} P_1$, $P_3 \sqsubseteq_{red} P_4$, $P_5 \sqsubseteq_{red} P_4$, and $P_5 \sqsubseteq_{red} P_3$ but, for example, neither $P_4 \sqsubseteq_{red} P_1$ nor $P_3 \sqsubseteq_{red} P_6$ hold.   □

The LOTOS extension refinement relation also doesn't allow new deadlocks to be added (that is, for traces of the abstract system the concrete system must not add deadlocks), but also allows new behaviour to be added in terms of new traces. Its definition is as follows, identical to that of reduction except for the addition of new traces.

Definition 6.5 *(Extension in LOTOS).*
Let P, Q be LOTOS process definitions. Then Q is an extension of P, written $P \sqsubseteq_{ext} Q$, whenever $\mathscr{T}(P) \subseteq \mathscr{T}(Q)$ and $P \sqsubseteq_{conf} Q$.   □

Example 6.24 If we define

$P_1 = x; y; stop$

$P_2 = x; stop[]x; y; stop$

$P_3 = x; y; stop[]x; stop$

$P_4 = x; y; stop[]i; z; stop$

then $P_1 \sqsubseteq_{ext} P_2$, $P_4 \sqsubseteq_{ext} P_2$, but, for example, neither $P_1 \sqsubseteq_{ext} P_3$ nor $P_1 \sqsubseteq_{ext} P_4$ hold.   □

Finally, the same equivalence is induced by both reduction and extension. This is know as *testing equivalence* and defined as follows:

Definition 6.6 *(Testing equivalence)*
Let P, Q be LOTOS process definitions. Then P and Q are testing equivalent, written P *te* Q, or $P \equiv_{te} Q$, whenever the traces and refusals of P and Q are equal.   □

6.5   CCS - Language, Semantics and Refinement

The Calculus of Communicating Systems (CCS) is another process calculus that
was hugely influential. The constructs and operators to build a description in the
language are similar to CSP and LOTOS, although there are some key differences
in the language as well as its approach to refinement. The core of CCS is small by
design, and is extensible with further operators if needed.

6.5.1   The CCS Language

In CSP and LOTOS inaction, that is the process *stop*, was one of the building blocks
in the language. In CCS it is actually defined in terms of an empty choice. However,
it is used in the same way as *stop* in CSP and LOTOS, and in CCS is denoted **0**.
   Prefixing is again similar to CSP and LOTOS, but is denoted in CCS by

$$a.P$$

As in LOTOS there is an explicit internal action, denoted τ in CCS.
   The specification of input and output is different in CCS to CSP or LOTOS. In
CCS communication takes place through *ports*, and a distinction is made in actions
as to whether they will accept input or output. So in CCS we write

$$c(v).P(v) \quad \text{and} \quad \overline{c}(v).P$$

for the description of input and output respectively. Thus a one-place buffer would
be written

$$P = in(x).\overline{out}(x).P$$

As in CSP and LOTOS, any input can be subsequently used in the process expression,
as in:

$$P = in(x).\overline{double}(2*x).\mathbf{0}$$

Choice, or *summation*, in CCS is written

$$P_1 + P_2$$

with the obvious interpretation. As in LOTOS there is no separation into internal
and external choice, since the use of the silent action τ allows internal choice to
be modelled in the same way we did in LOTOS. As with CSP and LOTOS we can
specify process definitions using recursion. Again, processes can be parameterised
by values such as sets or sequences. For example, the one place buffer could be
rewritten as:

$Buf(\langle\rangle) = put(x). \, Buf(\langle x\rangle)$

$Buf(\langle x\rangle) = \overline{get}(x). \, Buf(\langle\rangle)$

This fragment of CCS is very similar to CSP and LOTOS. There are more differences, however, in its approach to concurrency and specifically synchronisation. Composition in CCS is written

$P \mid Q$

There are perhaps two key differences in how this composition works however when compared to composition in LOTOS. The first is that in CCS composed processes may interact whenever one process is prepared to perform some action a and the other is prepared to perform its *complementary action*, that is, perform $\overline{a}$. The second difference is that in CCS interactions between two processes are immediately hidden from the environment. Thus CCS uses a *bi-party* synchronous communication mechanism whiles CSP and LOTOS use *multi-party* synchronous communication (which is more awkward to express in CCS).

To illustrate the difference, consider the following process definition in LOTOS:

$P = (x; Q) \mid[x]\mid (x; R) \mid[x]\mid (x; T)$

Because of the multi-party synchronisation on x, this is capable of performing the single action x and evolving to $Q \mid[x]\mid R \mid[x]\mid T$. However, the similar process definition in CCS:

$P = x.Q \mid \overline{x}.R \mid \overline{x}.T$

can perform the following behaviours:

$P = x; Q \mid \overline{x}; R \mid \overline{x}; T \quad \xrightarrow{x} \quad Q \mid \overline{x}.R \mid \overline{x}.T$

$P = x; Q \mid \overline{x}; R \mid \overline{x}; T \quad \xrightarrow{\tau} \quad Q \mid R \mid \overline{x}.T$

$P = x; Q \mid \overline{x}; R \mid \overline{x}; T \quad \xrightarrow{\overline{x}} \quad x.Q \mid R \mid \overline{x}.T$

$P = x; Q \mid \overline{x}; R \mid \overline{x}; T \quad \xrightarrow{\tau} \quad Q \mid \overline{x}.R \mid T$

$P = x; Q \mid \overline{x}; R \mid \overline{x}; T \quad \xrightarrow{\overline{x}} \quad x.Q \mid \overline{x}.R \mid T$

In this we can see that the composition allows any of the actions that are initially offered by the three components to be offered by the composite behaviour. In addition, the action x can synchronise with either of the two complement actions $\overline{x}$. And when it does so the synchronisation is hidden and not available for further synchronisation. It is in this sense that the synchronisation is bi-party rather than multi-party.

Related to this issue is the use in CCS of *restriction* as opposed to *hiding*. This operator removes actions altogether rather than generating internal actions. So in

$P \setminus \{a_1, \ldots, a_n\}$, if P is ready to perform some restricted action a_i then that action cannot occur at all (the complementary action $\overline{a_i}$ is also restricted).

In general, if P was prepared to perform an action a and the environment is ready to perform the complementary action $\overline{a}$ then two things may occur: (i) the two processes interact, without the knowledge of the environment, or (ii) they visibly perform a and $\overline{a}$ independently. If, however, a or $\overline{a}$ is restricted, then that action cannot visibly occur at all; only the interaction between the two processes can take place.

This allows one to use restriction to limit the evolution of a process to just the internal actions. Thus in

$$(x.Q \mid \overline{x}.R \mid \overline{x}.T) \setminus \{x\}$$

only the two internal evolutions happen due to the direct synchronisation between x and $\overline{x}$.

Communication. In addition to the difference between bi and multi-party synchronisation, there are differences in the three languages as to how communication is dealt with.

CSP and CCS assume that value-passing interactions take place only between two processes. On the other hand LOTOS allows any number of processes to participate in a value-passing interaction, as long as all participants agree on the type of the data value. All the participating input actions receive the value sent. Likewise, all the participating output actions must be attempting to send the same value, otherwise interaction cannot take place.

This means that where CSP and CCS only allow a single output to interact with a single input, in LOTOS there are three possibilities: (i) in value passing an output expression is matched with an input variable. The variable is assigned the value of expression. (ii) in value matching one output expression $!e$ matches with another $!f$. Both expressions must return the same value (and be of the same type), otherwise interaction is not possible. (iii) in value generation an input variable $?u : t$ matches with another input variable $?v : t$. In this case both u and v receive the same value. If there is no corresponding output event then the value is created nondeterministically.

6.5.2 CCS Semantics and Refinement

The standard semantics of CCS defines a *derivation tree* for each process, which in turn defines a LTS in a fashion similar to LOTOS. Derivation trees define the complete behaviour of a process, however, for our purposes we can think of a CCS process defining a LTS directly in the obvious manner. Such derivations are straightforward, and we do not give further details here.

The semantics, as before, allows one to define refinement over it. In CCS the emphasis has always been on *equivalences* between processes, as opposed to pre-orders. Specifically, strong and observational equivalence are defined for use with the language based on the notion of *bisimulation* that we discussed in Sect. 2.3.

In Definition 2.8 we did not consider the role of the internal action τ in a bisimulation, however we do so now. And this gives rise to two definitions for use within CCS: strong equivalence and observational equivalence.

6.5.2.1   Strong Bisimulation and Strong Equivalence

In a strong bisimulation the internal action τ is not treated as special. Thus, for two processes to be strongly equivalent, they must be capable of performing exactly the same sequences of actions, including internal ones.

For the definition of a strong bisimulation in CCS we will use the basic definition given in Definition 2.8, where *Act* ranges over all visible and internal actions. For two CCS processes P and Q to be strongly equivalent whenever P can perform some action a (which may be τ), then Q can perform the same action, and the two resulting processes are also strongly bisimilar; and similarly for any actions Q can perform.

Example 6.25   For example, the two processes $a.b.0$ and $a.(b.0 + b.0)$ are strongly equivalent, where the relation $\{(a.b.0, a.(b.0 + b.0)), (b.0, b.0 + b.0), (0, 0)\}$ defines the bisimulation. □

We write $P \sim Q$ when P and Q are strongly bisimilar. We give some more examples.

Example 6.26   Let

$$P_1 = a.b.0 + c.0$$
$$P_2 = c.0 + a.b.0$$
$$P_3 = a.b.0$$

Then $P_1 \sim P_2$ but $P_1 \nsim P_3$ and $P_2 \nsim P_3$. □

6.5.2.2   Weak Bisimulation: Observational Equivalence

Whilst strong bisimulation gives a perfectly well-defined way of comparing two specifications, it does not fit very well with a key idea when we motivated refinement, specifically that internal actions should not be observable in defining refinement or equivalence, and that we should only consider observable behaviour. To remedy this CCS uses weak bisimulation as given in Definition 5.3. As described previously, for P and Q to be weakly bisimilar, whenever P can perform some action a, then Q must be able to perform the same action, possibly preceded and succeeded by some internal actions which are ignored, and the two resulting agents are also bisimilar. Similarly for any actions Q can perform. If action a is the internal action τ then the other process must be able to make a transition without performing any visible actions.

We call two processes *observationally equivalent* when they are weakly bisimilar.

Example 6.27 For example, the two processes $a.b.0$ and $a.\tau.b.0$ are observationally equivalent (and not strongly equivalent), where the relation

$$\{(a.b.0,\ a.\tau.b.0),\ (b.0,\ \tau.b.0),\ (b.0,\ b.0),\ (0, 0)\}$$

defines the weak bisimulation.   □

None of the following can be related by a weak bisimulation.

$a.0 + b.0$

$a.0 + \tau.b.0$

$\tau.a.0 + \tau.b.0$

Despite this weakness, bisimulations do possess some pleasing algebraic properties. For example, we have (for all processes P and Q):

$P + Q \sim Q + P$

$P + P \sim P$

$P + 0 \sim P$

$P \mid Q \sim Q \mid P$

$P \mid 0 \sim P$

amongst many others.

Strong bisimulation is also strongly congruent in CCS, that is, is substitutive under all the CCS operators. So, for example, if P_1 and P_2 are processes with $P_1 \sim P_2$ then

$a.P_1 \sim a.P_2$

$P_1 + Q \sim P_2 + Q$

$P_1 \mid Q \sim P_2 \mid Q$

$P_1 \setminus L \sim P_2 \setminus L$

Similarly, if P_1 and P_2 are processes with $P_1 \approx P_2$ then

$P_1 \mid Q \approx P_2 \mid Q$

$P_1 \setminus L \approx P_2 \setminus L$

6.6 Bibliographical Notes

The term process algebra refers to a family of formal methods that are well-suited to describing systems of concurrent, communicating components. Process algebras, as their name suggests, place emphasis on the algebraic laws that hold for processes and the equivalence between them. They also typically describe processes using a small collection of operators (as we have seen in the case of CSP, LOTOS and CCS) and primitives (such as *stop* or *skip*). Interaction between independent processes is specified as communication, communication being either synchronous and asynchronous.

Beyond CSP, CCS [3] and the ISO standard LOTOS [4] which we have introduced here, other process algebras include ACP [5] and the π-calculus [6].

Introductions to CSP include the texts by Hoare [7], Roscoe [2, 8] and Schneider [1]. The latter provides a very accessible introduction. Bowman and Gomez in [9] provide a good introduction to LOTOS, and also a comparison between CSP, LOTOS and CCS, as well as discussing timed models.

CSP and CCS influenced one another throughout their development. CCS was developed in the '70s by Milner, with an initial version being published in 1980, and CSP appeared around a similar time. LOTOS had a different genesis from these two languages, and came out of the telecoms community from the need to define protocols formally and precisely. The name LOTOS was first used in the early 1980s to describe a language based on early versions of CCS and CSP. It was subsequently refined and became an international standard in 1989. An extended version of the language (E-LOTOS) was subsequently developed and standardised in 2001 [10].

ACP is a process algebra developed by Bergstra and Klop in the early '80s. It places much emphasis on the algebraic side of the language (this is something we have not stressed in this chapter). It has many similarities with CSP and other process algebras, with operations to denote choice, concurrency, communication and so forth. The π-calculus grew out of work on CCS, but crucially includes mobility and allows channel names to be communicated along the channels themselves, and in this way it is able to describe concurrent computations whose network configuration may change during the computation.

Must and *may* testing are defined in [11]. May testing is just trace inclusion as we have met already, intuitively representing that one process may pass every test that another passes. With must equivalence two processes are required to have the same convergent traces, and the same refusals after these traces, but they are just required to start diverging after the same traces and after that divergent point they may have completely different traces. Full details of its formulation are in [11].

References

1. Schneider S (1999) Concurrent and real time systems: the CSP approach. Wiley, New York
2. Roscoe AW (1998) The theory and practice of concurrency. International series in computer science. Prentice Hall, Upper Saddle River
3. Milner R (1989) Communication and concurrency. Prentice-Hall, Upper Saddle River
4. Bolognesi T, Brinksma E (1988) Introduction to the ISO specification language LOTOS. Comput Netw ISDN Syst 14(1):25–59
5. Bergstra JA, Klop JW (1984) Process algebra for synchronous communication. Inf Control 60(1):109–137
6. Milner R (1999) Communicating and mobile systems: the π-calculus. Cambridge University Press, New York
7. Hoare CAR (1985) Communicating sequential processes. Prentice Hall, Upper Saddle River
8. Roscoe AW (2010) Understanding concurrent systems. Springer, Berlin
9. Bowman H, Gomez R (2005) Concurrency theory: calculi an automata for modelling untimed and timed concurrent systems. Springer, New York
10. ISO/IEC. International standard 15437:2001: Information technology – Enhancements to LOTOS (E-LOTOS) (2001)
11. de Nicola R, Hennessy MCB (1984) Testing equivalences for processes. Theor Comput Sci 34(1):83–133

Chapter 7
State-Based Languages: Z and B

This chapter defines refinement in Z, and shows how it derives from the relational model in Chap. 4. It discusses the similarities and differences with refinement in B.

The approach taken in a state-based specification language is very different in emphasis from that in a process algebra. Process algebras stress the interaction between independent components (processes), so that communication and concurrency are key. State is implicit in such a description. A different approach is taken by a state-based language which, as the name suggests, considers the specification of state as the primary focus in a description. In this chapter we illustrate the approach to state-based specification by briefly introducing the Z and B notations, and showing how we can apply our theory of refinement to them.

7.1 Z - The Language

Z is a state-based specification language. It uses first order predicate logic and set theory to describe the possible states of a system, including the initial state. There are a number of styles of using Z, and the one that we will illustrate here is the most common, the so-called *states and operations* style of using it. In this style a system is described by specifying operations which describe changes to the state of the system. The state of the system and the operations acting on it are written in Z using *schemas* which structure the specification into convenient components. A *calculus* is provided to combine the schemas in appropriate ways, and this *schema calculus* helps to structure the specification.

To illustrate its general approach we specify the frequency server in Z. The description is going to consist of

- The types and global constants of the specification.
- A description of the abstract state, written using schemas.

© Springer International Publishing AG, part of Springer Nature 2018
J. Derrick and E. Boiten, *Refinement*, https://doi.org/10.1007/978-3-319-92711-4_7

- A description of the initial state of the system.
- One or more operations, which define the behaviour of the system. Again these will be written using schemas and the schema calculus.

In Z the formal description can be interleaved with informal text, as we will do below.

Types. Every value in Z has a *unique* type; when x is declared as $x{:}S$ then the type of x is the largest set containing S. In fact, Z provides a single built-in type, namely the type of integers . Although Z only provides a single pre-existing type, there are a number of ways for a specifier to define types relevant to the specification under construction.

One way to build further types is to simply declare them. A *given set* can be constructed through a declaration of the form

$$[PID, FREQ]$$

which introduces two new types: the sets PID and $FREQ$. The internal structure of these types is left unspecified.

To specify global values we use an *axiomatic definition*, containing a declaration and a (optional) predicate that constrains the declaration. For example, the following

$$\mid \ F : \mathbb{P}\,FREQ$$

introduces a global constant F as a subset of $FREQ$.

7.1.1   Using Schemas

To describe the state Z uses *schemas* which denote labelled products. Like axiomatic definitions they consist of declarations and optional predicates. So

```
┌─ State ──────────────────────────────────────
│  clients : ℙ PID
│  freq : ℙ FREQ
│
└──────────────────────────────────────────────
```

introduces a state consisting of two components: *clients* and *freq*, with no further predicates to constrain them. The operations will describe how they alter these state variables. First the initialisation is given by a special *Init* schema:

```
┌─ Init ───────────────────────────────────────
│  State'
│ ─────────────────────────────────────────────
│  freq' = F
└──────────────────────────────────────────────
```

Here we are using the standard Z convention that the prime on a variable (e.g., as in *freq'*) denotes its *after state*. The use of *State'* (so *State* with a prime symbol) here means to include all declarations and predicates of the schema *State*, with all variables and all occurrences of them in predicates decorated with that prime.

So the effect of this initialisation is to constrain the initial value of *freq* to be the set *F*. The behaviour of the system is described by specifying operations which change the state. The following describes an operation called *Allocate* - which allocates a frequency.

Allocate
ΔState
pid? : *PID*
reply! : *ok* | *error*
freq! : *FREQ*

---
pid? ∈ *clients*
clients' = *clients*
(*freq* = ∅ ∧ *reply!* = *error* ∧ *freq'* = *freq*)
∨
(*freq* ≠ ∅ ∧ *reply!* = *ok* ∧ *freq!* ∈ *freq* ∧ *freq'* = *freq* \ {*freq!*})

The inclusion of *ΔState* means that the schema includes both the before state *State* and the after state *State'*. Inputs and outputs to an operation are given in the declaration, so the above contains an input *pid?* and two outputs *reply!* and *freq!* (note the ! is part of the name, so that *freq!* and *freq* refer to different things). The constraints on these are given by the predicate below the line. Here this says that the input *pid?* must be one of the *clients*. Then after the operation *clients* is not altered, but a frequency *freq!* is allocated if *freq* is non-empty (if it is empty an error is reported via *reply!*). This frequency is removed from the state variable *freq*. In this description we use a type *ok* | *error* which has the obvious interpretation.

In a similar way one can specify the operation that deallocates a frequency as follows:

Deallocate
ΔState
pid? : *PID*
freq? : *FREQ*

---
pid? ∈ *clients*
clients' = *clients*
freq' = *freq* ∪ {*freq?*}

The effect of this operation is to take in two inputs, the operation being applicable whenever *pid*? ∈ *clients*. The effect of the operation is that *clients* is unchanged, but that the input frequency is added to the set *freq*.

7.1.2   The Z Schema Calculus

Much of the power of Z as a specification notation derives from the operators that are provided for combining schemas. This *schema calculus* provides the ability to specify a complex operation by combining smaller components using schema conjunction, disjunction etc. Here we don't have occasion to use the schema calculus as a structuring mechanism in a specification, we do, however, find it convenient as a way to express the refinement proof obligations directly in Z.

We have seen, by example, that schemas consist of a declaration and a predicate. We've also seen that schemas can be *included* in another schema. An example of this is the inclusion of Δ*State* in the definition of an operation schema. This can be extended to any schema where the effect of inclusion is obtained by expanding all declarations and conjoining all predicates.

We have also seen schema *decoration* in writing *State'*. These are all part of the schema calculus. In addition, the schema calculus provides the schema operators of conjunction and implication which we will use in the refinement proof obligations.

The schema *conjunction* operator is closely related to schema inclusion, where the conjunction of two schemas *S* and *T* is identical to a schema which includes both *S* and *T* (and nothing else). The definition of *implication* is similar - but we make sure that all implicit constraints included in any typing information are included in the predicates of the schemas involved.

Schemas can also be used as declarations in quantification - again with the obvious interpretation. Thus we will write expressions such as

$$\forall AState; \; CState \bullet \cdots$$

and

$$\exists AState' \bullet \cdots$$

again with the obvious interpretation of quantification over all the variables in the named state spaces, as well as restricting the variables to those satisfying the predicates in the named state spaces.

A crucial use of the schema calculus is to define the precondition of a Z operation schema. This is defined as follows.

Definition 7.1 (*The Z operation precondition*)
For an operation *Op* on state *State*, with inputs *Inps* and outputs *Outs*, its precondition is defined by

$$preOp = \exists State'; \; Outs \bullet Op \qquad \qquad \square$$

Thus, *preOp* will be a schema on *State* and *Inps* indicating for which before-states and inputs *Op* provides a possible after-state and output.
For example,

$$\text{pre } Deallocate = [State; \ pid? : PID; \ freq? : FREQ \mid pid? \in clients]$$

(this incidentally illustrates that we can write our schemas in horizontal form as well as vertically).

We shall also find it convenient to extract the inputs and outputs of an operation in the following way:

Definition 7.2 (*Input and output signature*)
The input signature of an operation schema *Op* on state *State* is its projection on input components only. This is written $?Op$.

The output signature of an operation schema *Op* on state *State* is its projection on output components only. This is written $!Op$.   □

Thus $?Deallocate = [pid? : PID; \ freq? : FREQ]$.

Finally, we can use schemas as types. Our use of it here is restricted to using the θ operator on the state *State*. Specifically, $\theta State$ gives the mapping of values to components as a tuple of the labelled product that represents the schema. So, for example in a schema which contains $\Delta State$, the value $(\theta State, \theta State')$ is a pair, each element of which is a labelled tuple of the signature of *State*, one being the before state and the other the after state. Where we need to denote such tuples explicitly, they will look like $\langle\!\mid b == true, x == 17 \mid\!\rangle$: a tuple containing a Boolean field named b and an integer field named x.

Much more can be written about the Z schema calculus, we have given a brief introduction sufficient to motivate its use within the refinement framework. What should be clear throughout though, is the very different type of description one arrives at when using a state-based language such as Z compared to using a process algebra. None of the concerns of a process algebra: process, communication, concurrency ...., have been given an explicit treatment in Z. Instead it has concentrated on a description of the state and the effect an operation has on that state, including how the inputs and outputs are treated. There are some obvious parallels however, specifically, both styles are concerned with changes to a system upon occurrences of events or operations, and we will use this later as our starting point to reconcile the different semantic approaches to refinement. First, we consider how refinement is defined in Z. To do so we are going to take a Z specification and consider it as a data type in the following sense:

Definition 7.3 (*Standard Z ADT*)
A standard Z ADT is a 3-tuple $(State, Init, \{Op_i\}_{i\in I})$ such that *State* is a state schema, *Init* is a schema on *State'*, and Op_i are operations on $\Delta State$. The index set I is the *alphabet* of the ADT.   □

We now consider how we can apply our relational theory of refinement to it to derive proof obligations expressed in Z itself.

7.2   Z – Refinement

As we commented in the previous chapter, once the semantics of a language has been
defined, the definition of refinement should follow naturally from it. For Z we will
use a relational semantics as defined in Chap. 4 to define refinement. Specifically, we
will consider a Z specification to define a relational data type in the sense of Sect. 4.2.
The Z data type defines a state, an initialisation and a collection of operations which
can be considered as relations between the before and after state.

Taking this approach means that refinement can then be defined in terms of programs in the manner we did in Definition 4.5. To do so we formalise the Z relational
semantics in the following manner.

7.2.1   The Relational Semantics of a Z Specification

The relational data types we introduced earlier had the following form:
$(\mathsf{State}, \mathsf{Init}, \{\mathsf{Op}_i\}_{i\in I}, \mathsf{Fin})$, which used a global state G whereas as we have just
seen a Z specification can be thought of as defining a tuple

$$(State, Init, \{Op_i\}_{i\in I})$$

of state, initialisation and operations. Whilst there might be an obvious correspondence between some of the components, we have not mentioned a finalisation when
writing a Z description. Nor have we indicated how inputs and outputs are going to
be embedded in a relational model that doesn't normally have them.

In fact, the inputs and outputs of a specification are modelled by sequences whose
elements are produced and consumed one by one by the operations of the ADT. Inputs
and outputs are observable, and are thus part of the global state, as well as of the
local state since they are consumed and produced by the individual operations. For
simplicity, we assume that all operations Op_i have input of type *Input*, and output of
type *Output*. Initialisation and finalisation will be concerned with copying the input
and output sequences between the global and local state. We use a sans serif font
to distinguish the relational interpretations from the Z specifications.

State The global state contains just sequences of inputs and outputs, whilst the local
state contains both of those plus a representation of the Z ADT state:

$$\mathsf{G} == \mathrm{seq}\, Input \times \mathrm{seq}\, Output$$
$$\mathsf{State} == \mathrm{seq}\, Input \times \mathrm{seq}\, Output \times State$$

Initialisation The initialisation transfers the sequence of inputs from the global
state to the local state, and picks an initial local ADT state that satisfies the ADT's
initialisation.

Init == {*Init*; *is* : seq *Input*; *os* : seq *Output* • (*is*, *os*) ↦ (*is*, ⟨⟩, θ*State*′)}

Operations The effect of an operation *Op* is modelled as follows. The first element is taken from the input sequence, and used as the input for the operation. The remainder of the input sequence is left for the following operations. The output produced by the operation is appended to the output sequence. The state is transformed according to the operation.

Op$_i$ == {*Op$_i$*; *is* : seq *Input*; *os* : seq *Output* •
$\qquad$ (⟨θ*Input*⟩ ⌢ *is*, *os*, θ*State*) ↦ (*is*, *os* ⌢ ⟨θ*Output*⟩, θ*State*′)}

Finalisation The finalisation makes visible the outputs produced by the program:

Fin == {*State*; *is* : seq *Input*; *os* : seq *Output* • (*is*, *os*, θ*State*) ↦ (⟨⟩, *os*)}

This is quite a significant choice, as one can see here clearly that you could have taken an alternative view of what would be visible. We will return to this point later. Sufficient to say for the moment the above is the 'standard' finalisation that produces the 'standard' definition of refinement in Z as we give it below.

7.2.2 Data Refinement and Simulations for Z

Now we have given a relational semantics to a Z specification, we can directly apply Definition 4.5. However, in the literature refinement in Z isn't usually defined in those terms - but given in terms of the underlying *simulations* that, due to the theory in Chap. 4, are sound and complete for that definition of refinement.

However, the theory in Sect. 4.3 was defined for total relations - and the operations in Z aren't necessarily total. For example, *Deallocate* has a precondition that *pid*? ∈ *clients*. What happens if this does not hold? We know from Sect. 4.4 how to encode partial relations as total ones, and that is what we are going to do here. Note that here we have a choice, as Sect. 4.4 discussed two models with slightly different characteristics: the non-blocking interpretation and the blocking interpretation.

For Z we will use the non-blocking interpretation defined in Sect. 4.4.1.1, noting that other languages can make other choices. Specifically, Object-Z [1], an object oriented version of Z, uses the blocking interpretation. However, for the moment let us fix on the non-blocking interpretation. We know then that the precondition defines the region where an operation is defined, and that outside this region *anything might happen*. As we discussed in Sect. 4.4 the simulation rules can be unwound to define the forward and backward simulation rules for partial relations - see Definitions 4.12 and 4.13.

We start with two Z specifications given as data types $(AState, AInit, \{AOp_i\}_{i \in I})$ and $(CState, CInit, \{COp_i\}_{i \in I})$. To show a simulation between them it is necessary to postulate a retrieve relation R between the local state spaces $AState$ and $CState$.

We can derive the relational interpretations of the specifications as above. Finally, we just need the relational interpretation of a retrieve relation which in the non-blocking model will be along the following lines.

As a retrieve relation does not normally refer to inputs and outputs, the most obvious interpretation is to assume identical inputs and outputs, which we do here. If R is the retrieve relation between $AState$ and $CState$, the relational interpretation is:

$$R == \{R;\ is : \text{seq } Input;\ os : \text{seq } Output \bullet$$
$$(is, os, \theta AState) \mapsto (is, os, \theta CState)\}$$

Remember here that $\theta State$ gives the mapping of values to components in the labelled product. Note further that this embedding of the retrieve relation confirms the requirement of conformity of inputs and outputs between concrete and abstract ADT.

We now consider the simulation conditions in turn. Although we haven't stressed the use of the schema calculus in Z, one of the beauties of it is that we can turn the relational expressions into conditions in the Z schema calculus itself. We start with Definition 4.12 and represent the conditions directly in Z. First a forward simulation. The initialisation condition $CInit \subseteq AInit \mathbin{\mathring{,}} R$ becomes

$$\forall CState' \bullet CInit \Rightarrow \exists AState' \bullet R' \wedge AInit$$

By construction of the finalisations in the embedding, it holds that

$$R \mathbin{\mathring{,}} CF \subseteq AF \equiv true$$

The applicability condition for operations can be re-expressed as follows:

$$\text{ran}(\text{dom } AOp_i \vartriangleleft R) \subseteq \text{dom } COp_i$$
$$\equiv \forall CState;\ AState;\ ?AOp_i \bullet R \wedge \text{pre } AOp_i \Rightarrow \text{pre } COp_i$$

Finally, for the correctness of operations, we have:

$$(\text{dom } AOp_i \vartriangleleft R) \mathbin{\mathring{,}} COp_i \subseteq AOp_i \mathbin{\mathring{,}} R$$
$$\equiv \forall AState;\ ?AOp_i;\ CState;\ CState';\ !AOp_i \bullet$$
$$R \wedge \text{pre } AOp_i \wedge COp_i \Rightarrow \exists AState' \bullet AOp_i \wedge R'$$

This derivation completes the full forward simulation rule for Z ADTs with inputs and outputs. This is expressed in the following definition.

Definition 7.4 (*Forward simulation for Z*)
Let $A = (AState, AInit, \{AOp_i\}_{i \in I})$ and $C = (CState, CInit, \{COp_i\}_{i \in I})$ be Z data types, where the operations have conformal inputs and outputs. The relation R on $AState \wedge CState$ is a *forward simulation* from A to C if

$$\forall CState' \bullet CInit \Rightarrow \exists AState' \bullet AInit \wedge R'$$

and for all $i \in I$:

$$\forall AState;\ CState;\ ?AOp_i \bullet \operatorname{pre} AOp_i \wedge R \Rightarrow \operatorname{pre} COp_i$$
$$\forall AState;\ CState;\ CState';\ ?AOp_i;\ !AOp_i \bullet$$
$$\operatorname{pre} AOp_i \wedge R \wedge COp_i \Rightarrow \exists AState' \bullet R' \wedge AOp_i$$

If such a simulation exists, we also say that C is a forward simulation of A, also denoted $A \sqsubseteq_{FS} C$, and similarly for corresponding operations of A and C.
$\square$

We can make a similar derivation for backward simulations, resulting in the following set of conditions.

Definition 7.5 (*Backward simulation for Z*)
Let $A = (AState, AInit, \{AOp_i\}_{i \in I})$ and $C = (CState, CInit, \{COp_i\}_{i \in I})$ be Z data types, where the operations have conformal inputs and outputs. Then the relation T on $AState \wedge CState$ is a *backward simulation* from A to C if

$$\forall CState \bullet \exists AState \bullet T$$
$$\forall AState';\ CState' \bullet CInit \wedge T' \Rightarrow AInit$$

and for all $i \in I$:

$$\forall CState;\ ?AOp_i \bullet (\forall AState \bullet T \Rightarrow \operatorname{pre} AOp_i) \Rightarrow \operatorname{pre} COp_i$$
$$\forall AState';\ CState;\ CState';\ ?AOp_i;\ !AOp_i \bullet$$
$$(\forall AState \bullet T \Rightarrow \operatorname{pre} AOp_i) \Rightarrow (COp_i \wedge T' \Rightarrow \exists AState \bullet T \wedge AOp_i)$$

If such a simulation exists, we also say that C is a backward simulation of A, also denoted $A \sqsubseteq_{BS} C$, and similarly for corresponding operations of A and C.
$\square$

We have assumed that partial operations are to be interpreted in the non-blocking model. The alternative is to assume a blocking interpretation. If we do so then we can easily derive a set of forward and backward simulation conditions in the same way. When we do so the rules stay the same apart from the correctness condition. Specifically in the blocking model, the forward simulation correctness condition becomes

$$\forall AState;\ CState;\ CState';\ ?AOp_i;\ !AOp_i \bullet$$
$$R \wedge COp_i \Rightarrow \exists AState' \bullet R' \wedge AOp_i$$

Similarly the backward simulation correctness condition becomes

$$\forall AState';\ CState;\ CState';\ ?AOp_i;\ !AOp_i \bullet$$
$$(COp_i \wedge T') \Rightarrow \exists AState \bullet T \wedge AOp_i$$

7.2.3 Z Refinement in Practice

Having derived the simulation rules for Z it is worth considering how they are applied in practice. The first point to note is that a refinement is never verified by direct appeal to Definition 4.5. Verification according to that definition involves quantification over all possible programs. The whole point of simulations was that they reduced that to a condition applied on a per-operation basis. All Z refinements are verified in that manner. This involves postulating a retrieve relation - and of course one could make a mistake in the one that is chosen. One has to be careful to understand that just because a particular retrieve relation doesn't verify a simulation, it doesn't mean that no simulation exists but just that the chosen one doesn't work.

We have seen that in a process algebra, refinement can allow a number of changes in a specification. Trace refinement allows one to refine all the behaviour away, however, other refinement relations that we have considered are usually centred around the reduction of non-determinism. The same is true of refinement in Z, in that:

Refinement in Z allows one to reduce non-determinism by weakening an operation's precondition or strengthening an operation's post condition.

Example 7.1 The *Deallocate* operation in our frequency server specification has a precondition that $pid? \in clients$. We can weaken that to say what happens if $pid? \notin clients$ - and here we say that in this case nothing in the state changes. So we producea

new more concrete specification with the same state and initialisation but with the new deallocate operation. That is we set:

$CState == State$
$CInit == Init$
$CAllocate == Allocate$

with

```
┌─ CDeallocate ─────────────────────────────────────────────
│ ΔCState
│ pid? : PID
│ freq? : FREQ
├───────────────────────────────────────────────────────────
│ (pid? ∈ clients ∧ clients' = clients ∧ freq' = freq ∪ {freq?})
│ ∨
│ (pid? ∉ clients ∧ clients' = clients ∧ freq' = freq)
└───────────────────────────────────────────────────────────
```

Since the state spaces are the same we use the identity retrieve relation. That is, set R to be

```
┌─ R ───────────────────────────────────────────────────────
│ State
│ CState
└───────────────────────────────────────────────────────────
```

We now apply one of the simulation rules. Here we just need a forward simulation. The initialisation condition is trivially true, as are the conditions needed for the *Allocate* operation since it is unchanged. For the *Deallocate* operation we note that pre *Deallocate* is the condition $pid? \in clients$ whereas pre *CDeallocate* is always true. Applicability follows trivially. Similarly for correctness we note that

pre $Deallocate \wedge R \wedge CDeallocate \equiv Deallocate$

trivially follows.   □

There is another facet of refinement in Z which is due to the explicit representation of state in a Z specification. Specifically, although we have been explicit about the state in our specification, the state is internal, and the internal representation of a state is not part of the visible interface - none of it appears in the finalisation in the semantics. Thus this can be changed in a refinement - as long as the visible behaviour remains the same.

Example 7.2 In our frequency server *freq* was defined to be a set. In practice in an implementation some sort of queue or list is likely to be used. We introduce a new specification to reflect this design choice. The description is similar, except this version uses an injective sequence (iseq, i.e. without duplicates) of frequencies as follows:

```
┌─ CState ──────────────────────
│ cclients : ℙ PID
│ cfreq : iseq FREQ
└───────────────────────────────
```

```
┌─ CInit ───────────────────────
│ CState′
├───────────────────────────────
│ ran cfreq′ = F
└───────────────────────────────
```

```
┌─ CAllocate ──────────────────────────────────────────────────────────
│ ΔCState
│ pid? : PID
│ reply! : ok │ error
│ freq! : FREQ
├──────────────────────────────────────────────────────────────────────
│ pid? ∈ cclients
│ cclients′ = cclients
│ (cfreq = ⟨ ⟩ ∧ reply! = error ∧ cfreq′ = cfreq)
│ ∨
│ (cfreq ≠ ⟨ ⟩ ∧ reply! = ok ∧ freq! ∈ ran cfreq ∧ ran cfreq′ = ran cfreq \ {freq!})
└──────────────────────────────────────────────────────────────────────
```

```
┌─ CDeallocate ────────────────────────────────────────────────────────
│ ΔCState
│ pid? : PID
│ freq? : FREQ
├──────────────────────────────────────────────────────────────────────
│ pid? ∈ cclients
│ cclients′ = cclients
│ ran cfreq′ = ran cfreq ∪ {freq?}
└──────────────────────────────────────────────────────────────────────
```

This time the retrieve relation is not the identity as it must document the change in the state space. We use the following

```
┌─ R ──────────────────────────────────────────────────
│ State
│ CState
│ ─────────────────────────
│ cclients = clients
│ ran cfreq = freq
└──────────────────────────────────────────────────────
```

Using this the conditions for a forward simulation are easily verified. □

This illustrates the following

> Refinement in Z allows one to change the state-space of a specification as long as the external behaviour remains consistent.

The description in Example 7.2 contains a lot of non-determinism. Specifically, the allocated frequency can be any of those in the sequence *cfreq*, and furthermore that list may be reordered in the deallocate operation. Both of these are unlikely in a real implementation. We can reduce this non-determinism by choosing the head of the sequence as the output frequency in the allocate operation. That is, replacing *CAllocate* by the following.

```
┌─ CCAllocate ─────────────────────────────────────────
│ ΔCState
│ pid? : PID
│ reply! : ok | error
│ freq! : FREQ
│ ─────────────────────────
│ pid? ∈ cclients
│ cclients' = cclients
│ (cfreq = ⟨⟩ ∧ reply! = error ∧ cfreq' = cfreq)
│ ∨
│ (cfreq ≠ ⟨⟩ ∧ reply! = ok ∧ freq! = head cfreq ∧ cfreq' = tail cfreq)
└──────────────────────────────────────────────────────
```

It is then a simple matter to verify the applicability and correctness conditions for this new operation schema.

Example 7.3 Simple refinements use retrieve relations which are actually functions, although this is not always the case as this nice example illustrates. Here there is one operation *Pick* that outputs an unused natural number. In the abstract specification this value is chosen non-deterministically.

```
┌─ State ─────────────────────      ┌─ Init ────────────────────────
│ s : ℙ ℕ                           │ State′
└─────────────────────────────      ├────────────────────────────────
                                    │ s′ = ∅
                                    └────────────────────────────────
```

```
┌─ Pick ───────────────────────────────────────────────────────────
│ ΔState
│ r! : ℕ
├──────────────────────────────────────────────────────────────────
│ s′ = s ∪ {r!}
│ r! ∉ s
└──────────────────────────────────────────────────────────────────
```

In the refinement we use a single natural number n in place of the set s, now the operation *Pick* is no longer non-deterministic.

```
┌─ CState ──────────────────────    ┌─ CInit ───────────────────────
│ n : ℕ                             │ CState′
└─────────────────────────────      ├────────────────────────────────
                                    │ n′ = 0
                                    └────────────────────────────────
```

```
┌─ CPick ──────────────────────────────────────────────────────────
│ ΔCState
│ r! : ℕ
├──────────────────────────────────────────────────────────────────
│ n′ = n + 1
│ r! = n
└──────────────────────────────────────────────────────────────────
```

The retrieve relation between the two state spaces maps n to $max(s) + 1$ if s is not empty, and n to 0 if s is empty.   □

Of course, just as in the relational theory discussed in Sect. 4.4 not all refinements can be verified by a forward simulation. For example, it is easy to code up in Z the example illustrating this from Example 4.2 to specify an example that needs a backward simulation in its verification.

7.2.3.1   The Completeness of the Simulation Rules in Z

In Sect. 4.4.3 we discussed the circumstances by which the simulation rules were *complete* - that is whether every refinement can be verified using a combination of forward and backward simulation rules. Of course these results carry over to Z in the following way.

We know that simulations are jointly complete for total data types - however, it is rare that a Z specification only contains operations that are total. The use of Z forces to use one of the two partial interpretations: non-blocking or blocking. The two relevant results are the following:

Theorem 4.6 tells us that the non-blocking simulation rules are jointly complete in the non-blocking interpretation (i.e., the one that is standard in Z).

The counter-example in Sect. 4.4.3 shows us that the blocking simulation rules are not complete in the blocking interpretation - that is the interpretation used in, for example, Object-Z.

Example 7.4 A simple example is the following, with two data types A and C, where $A = (State, AInit, \{Dec\})$ and $C = (State, CInit, \{Dec\})$. They are mutual refinements in the blocking relational embedding, but the refinement of A by C cannot be proved using the non-blocking simulation rules in Z.

$$
\begin{array}{|l}
\hline
State \\
\hline
x : \mathbb{N} \\
\hline
\end{array}
\qquad
\begin{array}{|l}
\hline
Dec \\
\hline
\Delta State \\
\hline
x' = x - 1 \\
\hline
\end{array}
$$

$$
\begin{array}{|l}
\hline
AInit \\
\hline
State' \\
\hline
x' \in \{1, 3\} \\
\hline
\end{array}
\qquad
\begin{array}{|l}
\hline
CInit \\
\hline
State' \\
\hline
x' \in \{1, 2, 3\} \\
\hline
\end{array}
$$

$\square$

7.3   The B-Method

B is another state-based notation which has a well-defined refinement methodology. Indeed, it is called the B-*method* to stress the methodology of development as opposed to just a language for formalising system descriptions. The notation it uses to describe systems is known as the *Abstract Machine Notation*, or *AMN*, and provides for a common framework for specifications, refinements and implementations. The style of AMN is similar to Z but is closer to a pseudo programming language with the use of constructs familiar from an imperative style of programming as well as using first order predicate logic and set theory. Its method is based on step-wise refinement from abstract descriptions down to descriptions which are close to code. To aid development the method has been supported by a variety of toolsets, developed alongside the language and very much part of its development methodology.

The basic building block of a specification in the B-notation is called an *abstract machine*. These can be used as components in larger specifications using various structuring mechanisms. Within a machine one declares variables, invariants, an initialisation and a collection of operations, in a way that is familiar to those knowing Z.

To illustrate the general approach we specify the frequency server using the B-notation. The specification of such a machine is as follows.

```
MACHINE          FreqServer(PID, FREQ, f)
CONSTRAINTS      f ∈ ℙ FREQ
SETS             REPLY = {ok, error}
VARIABLES        clients, freq
INVARIANT        clients ∈ ℙ PID ∧ freq ∈ ℙ FREQ
INITIALISATION   freq := f
OPERATIONS
Deallocate(pid?, freq?) ==
    PRE    pid? ∈ clients ∧ freq? ∈ FREQ
    THEN   clients, freq := clients, freq ∪ {freq?}
    END ;
reply!, freq! ⟵ Allocate(pid?) ==
    PRE    pid? ∈ clients ∧ freq! ∈ FREQ ∧ reply! ∈ REPLY
    THEN   (freq = ∅ ∧ reply! = error ∧ freq := freq)
           ∨
           (freq ≠ ∅ ∧ reply! = ok ∧ freq! :∈ freq ∧ freq := freq \ {freq!})
    END
END
```

We discuss each part in turn.

Machines. Machines have specific names so they can be used as components in more complex descriptions, here we call this machine *FreqServer*. Parameters to machines can be specified after the machine name - its optional to have them, but in the above we have two in upper case, and these two correspond to the two given sets we used in Z. Parameters in lower case, here just one f, are values, they are given in lower case (hence we must depart from the Z here) and their types are given in the subsequent CONSTRAINTS clause which we give next - here describing the obvious thing. In addition to the two given sets, the Z specification gave an explicit type to the output *reply!*. Here we give that type the name *REPLY* and specify it in the SETS clause.

Variables. Variables, but without giving their types, are defined in the VARIABLES clause. Their types and any invariants that need to hold for the machine are given in the INVARIANT. The initialisation is given next. Here we can see the first use of programming pseudo-code, where the use of the after-state prime in Z is replaced by programming-like assignment.

Operations. Outputs and inputs of an operation Op are described by writing: $outputs \leftarrow Op(inputs)$. So in the above, $Deallocate(pid?, freq?)$ specifies an operation called $Deallocate$ with two inputs but no outputs. Likewise $reply!, freq! \leftarrow Allocate(pid?)$ says that $Allocate$ has one input and two outputs. The decorations of ? and ! are not necessary in the B-notation, we have simply used them here to be consistent with the Z specification in Sect. 7.1.

Operations have explicit preconditions - listed under PRE. This is in contrast to Z where preconditions are implicit and need to be calculated if necessary using the schema operator pre. The effect of an operation is given after the THEN clause. Here we update the variables in the obvious fashion in both operations. The one piece of syntax and semantics to note is the expression $freq! :\in freq$ which is the non-deterministic assignment of $freq!$ to be any member of $freq$.

The B-notation also provides an explicit *choice* statement that could be used instead of the disjunction in the effect in the allocate operation. This would be written as

$reply!, freq! \leftarrow Allocate(pid?) ==$
    PRE $pid? \in clients \wedge freq! \in FREQ \wedge reply! \in REPLY$
    THEN
        CHOICE $(freq = \varnothing \wedge reply! = error \wedge freq := freq)$
        OR $(freq \neq \varnothing \wedge reply! = ok \wedge freq! :\in freq \wedge freq := freq \setminus \{freq!\})$
        END
    END

There are further constructs available in the AMN, and, as commented above there are a variety of structuring mechanisms such as the ability to include one machine in another or use one in a different ways. We will not cover them here since they are not central to our theory of refinement, and the literature on B contains full descriptions of their use.

7.3.1 Machine Consistency

There are some explicit consistency conditions that a machine needs to fulfil to ensure a machine is internally coherent. These include checking that an invariant is consistent, that the initialisation actually establishes an initial state in which the invariant holds, and that the operations preserve the invariant. Finally, any parameters must meet the constraints. These conditions can be expressed as

$$C \Rightarrow \exists v. I$$
$$C \Rightarrow [Init] I$$
$$C \wedge I \wedge P \Rightarrow [S]I$$
$$\exists p \bullet C$$

for a machine with variables v, invariant I, initialisation *Init* and for an operation with precondition P and effect S, parameters p and constraint C. Some of this notation needs explaining, and is known as the weakest precondition notation.

7.3.1.1   Weakest Preconditions

Informally the weakest precondition of a statement is the largest set of states from which that statement will reach a certain postcondition. So for a predicate P and statement S, $[S]P$ is a predicate that holds for any state that is guaranteed to achieve P as its post-state. In the AMN that is used in B it is possible to *calculate* the weakest precondition for any statement S and postcondition P.

First note that it distributes through some of the propositional connectives, in that we have:

$$[S](P \vee Q) = [S]P \vee [S]Q$$
$$[S](P \wedge Q) = [S]P \wedge [S]Q$$
$$[S](P \Rightarrow Q) = [S]P \Rightarrow [S]Q$$

The basic calculation one can make in AMN is the following:

$$[x := E]P = P[E/x]$$

for a variable x and expression E. Multiple assignment and the other AMN operators are similar, for example:

IF E THEN S ELSE T END $= (E \Rightarrow [S]P) \wedge (\neg E \Rightarrow [T]P)$

very much along the lines one would expect.

With this notation in place one can see that

$$C \Rightarrow [Init] I$$
$$C \wedge I \wedge P \Rightarrow [S]I$$

requires, firstly, that under the context C the initialisation *Init* must establish the invariant I, and, secondly, that, under the context C invariants must be preserved by the operations.

There is much more to be said about the weakest precondition, its derivation and use in specification and development. However, for our purposes, this very brief introduction is sufficient to define refinement in the B-method, which we do now.

7.4 Refinement in the B-Method

The B-method comes with a well defined notion of refinement as part of its methodology, defined, not in terms of a semantic model, but in terms of some proof obligations as we now describe.

Refinements are specified in B via machines, known unsurprisingly as *refinement machines*, using a specific REFINEMENT header. A refinement machine has the same signature as the machine that it refines, in the same sense that refinement in Z preserved the operations with their input and output parameters. So again as one would expect, refinement in B is all about preserving observable behaviour whilst having the freedom to make some specific design and implementation choices. This immediately gives one a template for the refinement. So, for example, to refine the frequency server we know it will take the following form:

```
REFINEMENT  FreqServerR
REFINES  FreqServer
...
OPERATIONS
Deallocate(pid?, freq?) ==
...
reply!, freq! ← Allocate(pid?) ==
...
END
```

A refinement machine needs to describe the relationship between its state and the state of the machine that it refines, given as a *linking invariant*, which is another name for a retrieve relation. This is done explicitly within the refinement machine in its invariant.

The name of a refinement machine is not allowed to contain any parameters - the parameters of the original machine are visible to it. The convention is, like we have done here, to add an R to the name of the machine being refined.

The *sets*, *constraints*, and *parameters* of the machine being refined are visible to any refinement, but the state is not visible. Additional sets and constraints can be defined in the refinement machine, and, of course, it will have to define its own variables for its own state representation. These variables will need to be initialised, and additional invariants can be placed over them.

As in Z, refinement in B concerns the allowable changes of observable behaviour. Rather than a semantic interpretation being provided - and simulation rules being derived - proof obligations for refinement are given as the primary definition. These will be seen to correspond to those contained in the forward simulations that we discussed above. However, there are no rules that correspond to a backward simulation in the B-methodology.

All operations, with the same inputs and outputs, must also be given within the refinement. Applicability, as in Z, must hold for the operations. Specifically, operations in the refined machine must be enabled (i.e., their precondition be true) whenever the operation in the machine they refine is true. Similarly, correctness must hold. That is, when invoked within its precondition, the effect of an operation in a refined machine must correspond to some effect of the operation in the original machine, modulo the states being linked by the linking invariant. These conditions can be seen to be analogous to the definition of a *forward simulation* in Z.

Given this observation, it is unsurprising that refinement in the B-method allows non-determinism to be reduced in exactly the same way as a forward simulation does in Z. Non-determinism can also be 'moved earlier' in a refinement in the way that a forward simulation allows, but in the absence of any backward simulation proof obligations the methodology is not complete in the way that it is in Z.

Example 7.5 We can refine our frequency server machine in a similar fashion to how we performed the refinement in Z: replacing the set by an injective sequence, and making the operations deterministic. This is given as a refinement machine *FreqServerR* as follows.

```
REFINEMENT          FreqServerR
REFINES             FreqServer
VARIABLES           cclients, cfreq
INVARIANT     cclients ∈ ℙ PID ∧ cfreq ∈ iseq(FREQ) ∧ ran(cfreq) = freq
INITIALISATION      cfreq :| ran cfreq = f ∧ cfreq ∈ iseq(FREQ)
OPERATIONS
Deallocate(pid?, freq?) ==
    PRE    pid? ∈ cclients ∧ freq? ∈ FREQ
    THEN   (freq? ∈ ran cfreq ∧ cclients, cfreq := cclients, cfreq)
             ∨
           (freq? ∉ ran cfreq ∧ cclients, cfreq := cclients, cfreq ⌢ [freq?])
    END ;
reply!, freq! ← Allocate(pid?) ==
    PRE    pid? ∈ cclients ∧ freq! ∈ FREQ ∧ reply! ∈ REPLY
    THEN   (cfreq = [] ∧ reply! = error ∧ cfreq := cfreq)
             ∨
           (cfreq ≠ [] ∧ reply! = ok ∧ freq! = first(cfreq) ∧ cfreq := tail(cfreq))
    END
END
```

The variables here are the variables needed in the state space of the concrete machine. They have the associated invariant that defines their types. In B we also include the invariant that defines the linking invariant, here (as in the Z) described by ran(*cfreq*) = *freq*. Any sets and parameters of *FreqServer* are visible in *FreqServerR*, thus we can make reference here to *PID*, *FREQ*, *f*, and *REPLY*.

$\square$

7.4.1   Proof Obligations for Refinement

To understand the proof obligations for refinement in B consider a machine *Spec* and its refinement *SpecR*.

```
MACHINE          Spec
...
INVARIANT        I
INITIALISATION   Init
OPERATIONS
outputs ← Op(inputs) == PRE    P THEN   S END
...
END
```

```
REFINEMENT       SpecR
REFINES          Spec
...
INITIALISATION   InitC
OPERATIONS
outputs ← Op(inputs) == PRE    PC THEN   SC END
...
END
```

where the linking invariant between the two state spaces is called *J*.

Initialisation. As in the forward simulations we have met so far, every possible state that *InitC* can reach must be, modulo *J* some possible state that *Init* can reach. That is, in terms of weakest precondition, ¬[*Init*] ¬*J* must be true for any state that *InitC* can reach. This can written as:

[*InitC*]¬[*Init*] ¬*J*

A comment about non-termination is in order here. $\neg[Init] \neg J$ might be true because some *Init* has some execution which does not terminate. However, we are only interested in machines that are internally consistent (in the sense discussed in Sect. 7.3.1), and one of the proof obligations there was that $[Init] I$. And if this holds then *Init* is guaranteed to terminate.

Operations. As in any forward simulation, we place a proof obligation on each operation. Specifically, in a way similar to a forward simulation in Z we require a correctness proof rule. The initial formulation of this is the following (in the absence of outputs)

$$I \wedge J \wedge P \Rightarrow [SC]\neg[S] \neg J$$

However, if (as is usual) our operation has an output we must ensure that the outputs of the refinement are possible outputs of the original, recognising that, like reducing a non-deterministic after-state, we're allowed to reduce non-determinism in the refinement of outputs. To do so we need to add some additional syntax in the above rules to record this:

$$I \wedge J \wedge P \Rightarrow [SC[outc/outputs]]\neg[S] \neg J \wedge (outc = outputs)$$

In general in a refinement machine, it is not necessary to give an explicit precondition - as it inherits that of the machine being refined. However, in cases that it does, as in our abstract example above, we need to check that the precondition *PC* is true whenever *P* is true - modulo the invariant and linking invariant. This is expressed as:

$$I \wedge J \wedge P \Rightarrow PC$$

Thus to summarise, machine *SpecR* is a valid refinement of machine *Spec* whenever:

$$[InitC]\neg[Init] \neg J$$
$$I \wedge J \wedge P \Rightarrow [SC[outc/outputs]]\neg[S] \neg J \wedge (outc = outputs)$$
$$I \wedge J \wedge P \Rightarrow PC$$

In this formulation we have just considered the refined initialisation and operations. In addition, a refinement machine might well have its own sets, constants and collection of properties on them. These introduce their own proof obligations - firstly by a consistency check between the two lots of sets, constants etc, and secondly by the necessity to add this information into the conditions above. We do not detail these here, since they don't add to the essence of the refinement conditions discussed here. Full accounts are given in the literature.

Example 7.6 To show that *FreqServerR* is a refinement of *FreqServer* one first verifies the initialisation condition that

$$[cfreq :| \text{ ran } cfreq = f]\neg[freq := f] \neg(\text{ran}(cfreq) = freq)$$

since ran$(cfreq) = freq$ is the linking invariant. This is easy to verify applying the law for weakest precondition calculation for assignment twice.

Then one has to show that the precondition in the refinement is true whenever it holds in the abstract specification. Since the preconditions for the two operations are the same in each specification this easily follows. Finally, one has to show correctness for each operation. For *Deallocate*, where we have no outputs, this amounts to showing that

$$
\begin{aligned}
&clients \in \mathbb{P}\,PID \wedge freq \in \mathbb{P}\,FREQ \wedge cfreq \in \text{iseq } FREQ \\
&\wedge(\text{ran}(cfreq) = freq) \\
&\wedge(pid? \in clients \wedge freq? \in FREQ) \\
&\wedge freq? \notin \text{ran } cfreq \\
&\quad\Rightarrow [cclients, cfreq := cclients, cfreq \frown [freq?]] \\
&\qquad\qquad \neg[clients, freq := clients, freq \cup \{freq?\}] \neg(\text{ran}(cfreq) = freq)
\end{aligned}
$$

which is again true by direct calculation, and a similar proof for the case *freq?* ∈ ran *cfreq*. □

7.4.2 Implementation Machines

The type of refinement we have just illustrated in Example 7.6 is a typical *data refinement* where we resolve some of the design decisions in moving the description closer to an implementation. It is, however, still some way from being at a level where one would start coding. The refinements in Z we discussed earlier had a similar flavour, and Z in this sense is very much a specification language. The B-method, on the other hand, goes further by providing an explicit methodology for refining down to code level. As part of this B has the concept of *implementation machines*, which is a specific kind of refinement machine from which code can be produced in a direct fashion.

To signify that this really is the implementation step, there can only be one implementation machine in any refinement derivation, whereas there can be as many refinement steps as needed. To ensure that implementation machines really are close to code they have to conform to some specific constraints, including the following:

• Implementation machines have no state of their own
• Developments are structured using a special *imports clause*
• Implementation machines cannot use non-deterministic choice or parallel composition

Data refinement is supported by implementation machines in the same way as before - although the state is not directly included in the implementation machine itself.

7.5 Bibliographical Notes

There is a large literature on state-based languages and their use.

For example, introductory texts on Z include *An Introduction to Formal Specification and Z* by Potter *et al* [2] and books by Ratcliff [3], Bottaci and Jones [4], Bowen [5] and Jacky [6]. *Specification Case Studies* edited by Hayes [7] served as an early definition of the Z language and contains many examples of particular aspects of the notation. Spivey's *The Z Notation: A Reference Manual* [8] came to be the *de facto* definition of the language, and until the standard [9] appeared, [10] was the main resource for Z semantics.

More advanced books include *Z in Practice* [11] by Barden, Stepney and Cooper aimed at those who already understood the basics of Z, and *Using Z: Specification, Refinement and Proof* [12] by Woodcock and Davies. The latter discusses proof and refinement in Z in some detail. The relationship between temporal logic and refinement in Z is discussed in [13, 14].

Refinement in Z and Object-Z [15] provides a comprehensive account of refinement in Z and Object-Z and its generalisations. The generalisations include non-atomic (or action) refinement whereby the conformality assumption is broken and one operation can be split into several upon refinement (see also [16, 17] and [18]); the consideration of internal operations in Z refinements (along the lines of the treatment in a process algebra, see [19, 20]); and notions of refinement where part of the internal state is made visible.

Z lacks the comprehensive tool-support that B and Event-B benefit from. There is, however, some work on tool support for the verification of refinements in Z, and this includes [21–24].

Introductory texts on B include the following: [25–28], which discuss both specification and refinement in B. A collection of case studies in B refinement is presented in [29]. Further examples of refinement in B are given in [28, 30]. B also benefits from extensive tool-support, including that provided by the *B-toolkit* as well as *Atelier B*. The B method has been used in some major safety-critical system applications in Europe (such as in Paris Metro Line 14 and Ariane 5 rocket).

The regular series of conferences, *ZUM: The Z Formal Specification Notation* ran throughout the 1990s [31–36] and has since developed into joint conferences with users of the B notation [37–40], and most recently also with ASM, Alloy and VDM in the ABZ series [41–43]. The *FME* (since 2005: FM) conferences also regularly contain papers concerning aspects of the notation.

There is a body of work on combining state-based and process algebraic languages to produce an integrated notation. These include combinations of CSP and Object-Z as well as CSP and B and so forth. The relationship between the different notions of refinement (see Part III) allows a well-defined notion of refinement to be defined in these integrated languages. For example, work on refinement in integrations of Object-Z and CSP includes [44–48]. A correspondence between B and action systems has been used as a vehicle to specify and refine concurrent systems, see, for example, [49].

References

1. Smith G (2000) The Object-Z specification language. Kluwer Academic Publishers, Boston
2. Potter B, Sinclair J, Till D (1996) An introduction to formal specification and Z. International series in computer science, 2nd edn. Prentice Hall, New York (1991)
3. Ratcliff B (1994) Introducing specification using Z: a practical case study approach. McGraw-Hill, London
4. Bottaci L, Jones J (1995) Formal specification using Z: a modelling approach. International Thomson Publishing, London
5. Bowen JP (1996) Formal specification and documentation using Z: a case study approach. International Thomson Computer Press, London
6. Jacky J (1997) The way of Z: practical programming with formal methods. Cambridge University Press, Cambridge
7. Hayes IJ (ed) (1987) Specification case studies. International series in computer science, 2nd edn. Prentice Hall, New York (1993)
8. Spivey JM (1992) The Z notation: a reference manual. International series in computer science, 2nd edn. Prentice Hall, New York
9. ISO/IEC (2002) International standard 13568:2002 Information technology – Z formal specification notation – Syntax, type system and semantics
10. Spivey JM (1988) Understanding Z: a specification language and its formal semantics. Cambridge University Press, Cambridge
11. Barden R, Stepney S, Cooper D (1994) Z in practice. BCS practitioner series, Prentice Hall, New York
12. Woodcock JCP, Davies J (1996) Using Z: specification, refinement, and proof. Prentice Hall, New York
13. Derrick J, Smith G (2004) Linear temporal logic and Z refinement. In: Rattray C, Maharaj S, Shankland C (eds) AMAST. Lecture notes in computer science, vol 3116. Springer, Berlin, pp 117–131
14. Derrick J, Smith G (2012) Temporal-logic property preservation under Z refinement. Form Asp Comput 24(3):393–416
15. Derrick J, Boiten EA (2014) Refinement in Z and Object-Z, 2nd edn. Springer, Berlin
16. Derrick J, Wehrheim H Using coupled simulations in non-atomic refinement. In: Bert et al [39], pp 127–147
17. Derrick J, Wehrheim H Non-atomic refinement in Z and CSP. In: Treharne et al [40], pp 24–44
18. Boiten EA (2014) Introducing extra operations in refinement. Form Asp Comput 26(2):305–317
19. Derrick J, Boiten EA, Bowman H, Steen MWA Weak refinement in Z. In: Bert et al [39], pp 369–388
20. Derrick J, Boiten EA, Bowman H, Steen MWA (1998) Specifying and refining internal operations in Z. Form Asp Comput 10:125–159
21. Derrick J, Wehrheim H (2007) On using data abstractions for model checking refinements. Acta Inf 44(1):41–71
22. Derrick J, North S, Simons T (2006) Issues in implementing a model checker for Z. In: Liu Z, He J (eds) ICFEM. Lecture notes in computer science, Springer, Berlin, pp 678–696

23. Smith G, Derrick J (2006) Verifying data refinements using a model checker. Form Asp Comput 18(3):264–287
24. Smith G, Derrick J (2005) Model checking downward simulations. Electron Notes Theor Comput Sci 137(2):205–224
25. Abrial J-R (1996) The B-book: assigning programs to meanings. Cambridge University Press, New York
26. Schneider S (2001) The B-method: an introduction. Palgrave Macmillan, London
27. Wordsworth JB (1996) Software engineering with B. Addison-Wesley, Longman Publishing Co., Inc., Boston
28. Lano K (1996) The B language and method: a guide to practical formal development. FACIT series, Springer, Berlin
29. Sekerinski E, Sere K (eds) (1999) Program development by refinement - case studies using the B method. FACIT, Springer, Berlin
30. Abrial J-R, Mussat L (1997) Specification and design of a transmission protocol by successive refinements using B. In: Broy M, Schieder B (eds) Mathematical methods in program development. NATO ASI series F: computer and systems sciences, vol 158. Springer, Berlin, pp 129–200
31. Nicholls JE (ed) (1990) Z user workshop, Oxford 1990. Workshops in computing, Springer, Berlin
32. Bowen JP, Nicholls JE (eds) (1992) Seventh annual Z user workshop. Springer, London
33. Bowen JP, Hall JA (eds) (1994) ZUM'94. Z user workshop. Workshops in computing, Springer, Cambridge
34. Bowen JP, Hinchey MG (eds) (1995) ZUM'95: The Z formal specification notation. Lecture notes in computer science, vol 967. Springer, Limerick
35. Bowen JP, Hinchey MG, Till D (eds) (1997) ZUM'97: The Z formal specification notation. Lecture notes in computer science, vol 1212. Springer, Berlin
36. Bowen JP, Fett A, Hinchey MG (eds) (1998) ZUM'98: The Z formal specification notation. Lecture notes in computer science, vol 1493. Springer, Berlin
37. Bowen JP, Dunne S, Galloway A, King S (eds) (2000) ZB2000: Formal specification and development in Z and B. Lecture notes in computer science, vol 1878. Springer, Berlin
38. Bert D, Bowen JP, Henson MC, Robinson K (eds) (2002) ZB 2002: formal specification and development in Z and B, 2nd international conference of B and Z users. Lecture notes in computer science, vol 2272. Springer, Berlin
39. Bert D, Bowen JP, King S, Waldén MA (eds) (2003) ZB 2003: formal specification and development in Z and B, third international conference of B and Z users. Lecture notes in computer science, vol 2651. Springer, Berlin
40. Treharne H, King S, Henson MC, Schneider SA (eds) (2005) ZB 2005: formal specification and development in Z and B, 4th international conference of B and Z users, Guildford, UK, 13–15 April 2005, proceedings. Lecture notes in computer science, vol 3455. Springer, Berlin
41. Börger E, Butler MJ, Bowen JP, Boca P (eds) (2008) ABZ 2008. Lecture notes in computer science, vol 5238. Springer, Berlin
42. Frappier M, Glässer U, Khurshid S, Laleau R, Reeves S (eds) (2010) ABZ 2010. Lecture notes in computer science, vol 5977. Springer, Berlin
43. Derrick J, Fitzgerald JA, Gnesi S, Khurshid S, Leuschel M, Reeves S, Riccobene E (eds) (2012) Abstract state machines, Alloy, B, VDM, and Z - third international conference, ABZ 2012. Lecture notes in computer science, vol 7316. Springer, Berlin
44. Smith G (1997) A semantic integration of Object-Z and CSP for the specification of concurrent systems. In: Fitzgerald J, Jones CB, Lucas P (eds) FME'97: industrial application and strengthened foundations of formal methods. Lecture notes in computer science, vol 1313. Springer, Berlin, pp 62–81
45. Smith G, Derrick J Refinement and verification of concurrent systems specified in Object-Z and CSP. In: Hinchey and Liu [50], pp 293–302
46. Smith G, Derrick J (2001) Specification, refinement and verification of concurrent systems - an integration of Object-Z and CSP. Form Methods Syst Des 18:249–284

47. Smith G, Derrick J, George C, Miao H (eds) (2002) Abstract specification in Object-Z and CSP. Formal methods and software engineering. Lecture notes in computer science, vol 2495. Springer, Berlin, pp 108–119
48. Derrick J, Smith G (2003) Structural refinement of systems specified in Object-Z and CSP. Form Asp Comput 15(1):1–27
49. Butler M An approach to the design of distributed systems with B AMN. In: Bowen et al [35], pp 223–241
50. Hinchey MG, Liu S (eds) (1997) First international conference on formal engineering methods (ICFEM'97). IEEE Computer Society Press, Hiroshima, Japan

Chapter 8
State-Based Languages: Event-B and ASM

In this chapter we consider two further state-based notations, specifically Event-B and the ASM notation. Both have similarities to Z and B, and indeed as the name suggests Event-B grew out of the B notation. Both offer more flexibility in their approach to refinement than Z and B – by adopting models closer to those in Chap. 3. One aspect of this that we discuss in this chapter is how they support refinements, and simulations, where one event or operation can be refined by several. That is, the assumption of conformality is dropped, and we discuss this below.

8.1 Event-B

Event-B is a notation, and method, for describing and refining systems that can be modelled as discrete transition systems. In that sense it is similar to other notations we have introduced earlier in this part. However, instead of stressing communication and concurrency, as in a process algebra, or the state in a system, as in a state-based system, it is centred around the idea of an *event*. In this sense it has many similarities with notations such as Action Systems. Event-B descriptions have additional structure, however, and the *B* in Event-B denotes the fact that it is an evolution of the B notation.

Specifications in Event-B consist of two basic parts: *contexts* and *machines*. As in B, machines define the dynamic part, that is the specification of behaviour, whereas contexts specify the static part. A context may contain carrier sets (i.e., user-defined types), constants, axioms, and theorems. These are accessible to a machine when the machine *sees* the context - the Event-B way of importing contexts.

The idea of the machines is to encapsulate a transition system, where the transitions will be modelled as a set of guarded events. Machines can contain *variables*, *invariants*, *theorems*, *events*, and a *variant*. Although Event-B is sometimes called an event-based notation, state is, in fact, explicit in that the variables of a machine define the state of that machine, and these variables are constrained by the invariant.

© Springer International Publishing AG, part of Springer Nature 2018   149
J. Derrick and E. Boiten, *Refinement*, https://doi.org/10.1007/978-3-319-92711-4_8

Possible state changes are described by events, which we describe below. As in B, Event-B requires that certain proof obligations hold for a constructed system so ensuring the consistency of the specification.

Developments are supported by refinements, and, as in B, one machine can refine another. These refinements are supported by the use of both *forward* and *backward* simulations, as in other similar notations such as Z and B.

In this chapter we briefly introduce Event-B and its approach to refinement. The latter is based on a relational semantics similar to that used earlier in Z. As with the other notations that we study, we do not attempt to introduce the whole language here, and, for example, don't discuss contexts nor give the formal syntax that Event-B specifications must conform to. We begin with a brief introduction to specifying machines in Event-B.

8.1.1   Specifying Machines in Event-B

To illustrate machines, we respecify in Event-B the small system given in Example 7.1.

Example 8.1 Remember that in this system we are just interested in picking an unused natural number. This first Event-B machine, M_0, will just have one event, $pick_0$.

> **machine** M_0
> **variables** s_0, r_0
> **invariants**
>   inv1: $s_0 \in \mathbb{P}\,\mathbb{N}$
>   inv2: $r_0 \in \mathbb{N}$
> **events**
> $initialization_0 \mathrel{\widehat{=}}$
> $s_0 := \varnothing$
> $pick_0 \mathrel{\widehat{=}}$
> $r_0, s_0 :\mid s_0' = s_0 \cup \{r_0'\} \wedge r_0' \notin s_0$
> **end**

Here we see we have, in the same way as we did in B, introduced two variables s_0, r_0, each given their type in the invariants clause. The machine also specifies two events. The initialisation is one of the events, and sets s_0 to be the empty set. The event $pick_0$ chooses the new value of r_0 non-deterministically, and the syntax for non-deterministic selection is the same as in B. $\square$

One key difference to note here is that we are not specifying any *input* or *output* in this machine. Indeed, one facet of the emphasis on events and event-based description is that our Event-B specifications will be concerned with transitions in our system and not the input/output behaviour.

In this chapter we will use events which conform to the following template (but note that in full generality the syntax is richer).

> *eventname*
> > **status**...
> > **refines**...
> > **when**...
> > **then**...
> > **end**

where, within this:

- **status** is one of *ordinary*, *convergent* or *anticipated*. This relates to potential *divergence* of *perspicuous* events, and will be discussed later. The default status is *ordinary*;
- **refines** is a list of events that this event refines - in general, and in contrast to B, events in a refinement are not necessarily in 1–1 correspondence;
- the guards of an event are contained in the **when** clause;
- and the behaviour of the event is given in the **then** clause as a list of, potentially named, actions.

We can abbreviate this syntax and, as in our simple example above, omit some of the clauses and keywords when the effect of the specified action is obvious.

As in B the actions can be both simple assignments, as in $s := \varnothing$, or non-deterministic, as in $r, s :| \ s' = s \cup \{r'\} \wedge r' \notin s$. The names of the actions, if used, have no effect on the semantics of the machine, and are thus similar in status to the names of an invariant or theorem.

The contexts, which we don't discuss in any depth here, enable a variety of mathematical data types to be defined and used within the Event-B machines. For more details of contexts and the full language see [1] or [2].

8.1.2 Proof Obligations for Event-B Machines

The Event-B development methodology defines a number of proof obligations for a specification. The proof obligations that are defined for an Event-B machine are similar to those needed in B (see Sect. 7.3.1). First, there is an *invariant preservation* proof obligation, that ensures that each invariant in a machine is preserved by every event. Second, there is the *feasibility* proof obligation that ensures that every event is feasible, that is, has some well-defined after state.

For example, suppose a machine *Machine* and event *event* have the following form

machine *Machine*	*event* $\widehat{=}$
variables *v*	**when** $G(v)$
invariant $I(v)$	**then** $v :\mid BA(v, v')$
events *init*, *event*, ...	**end**
end	

This machine has invariant $I(v)$, and the event has guard $G(v)$ and action given as the predicate $BA(v, v')$ on before and after states. Then the invariant preservation proof obligation INV requires that

$$\text{INV:} \quad I(v) \wedge G(v) \wedge BA(v, v') \Rightarrow I(v')$$

and the feasibility proof obligation FIS that

$$\text{FIS:} \quad I(v) \wedge G(v) \Rightarrow \exists v' \bullet BA(v, v')$$

Application of these two rules to the above example is trivial[1].

There is also an optional deadlock-freedom proof obligation saying that at least one event in a machine guard is always true, thus ensuring progress is always feasible.

8.2   Refinement in Event-B

Refinement in Event-B is, on the surface, very similar to refinement and development in B. One machine can refine another, individual events are refined allowing the reduction of non-determinism and data refinement to be supported. Furthermore, simulation proof obligations are defined to support the verification of refinement.

However, there are some key semantic differences. In particular, as mentioned above, in a refinement events do not need to be in a 1–1 correspondence, specifically events might be merged or new events introduced as part of the refinement step. That is, we do not assume data types are *conformal*. This is a clear departure from the refinement framework in Z or B, and arises because in the relational semantic model of Event-B, the event names do not have the same significance as they do, for example, in Z. We will discuss this more below. First of all a simple example.

---

[1] Texts on Event-B express the proof obligations in the sequent calculus. Without loss of generality we use implication here to be consistent with other notations in this book.

Example 8.2 We refine the machine given in Example 8.1. As before we use a single natural number n_1 in place of the set s_0. As before the event *pick* is no longer non-deterministic.

> **machine** M_1
> **refines** M_0
> **variables** n_1, r_1
> **invariants**
>   inv1: $n_1 \in \mathbb{N}$
>   inv2: $r_1 \in \mathbb{N}$
>   gluing: $((n_1 = max(s_0) + 1 \wedge s_0 \neq \varnothing)$
> $\vee (n_1 = 0 \wedge s_0 = \varnothing)) \wedge (r_1 = r_0)$
> **events**
>   initialization$_1 \mathrel{\widehat{=}}$
> $n_1 := 0$
>   pick$_1 \mathrel{\widehat{=}}$
> $r_1 := n_1 \wedge n_1 := n_1 + 1$
> **end**

As we can see in this example, where the event correspondence is 1–1 we drop the explicit indication about which event is refined by which other event. □

When one machine M_0 is refined by another machine M_1 we write, as usual, $M_0 \sqsubseteq M_1$. The gluing invariant, which above is $((n_1 = max(s_0) + 1 \wedge s_0 \neq \varnothing) \vee (n_1 = 0 \wedge s_0 = \varnothing)) \wedge (r_1 = r_0)$ plays exactly the same role as a retrieve relation in Z or a linking invariant in B.

To verify this refinement it is sufficient to verify a number of simulation conditions. Suppose an abstract event has guard G and action BA (as above), and concrete event has guard H and action $BA1$. Then with abstract invariant I and gluing invariant J the rules we will use are the following (we comment on why they are sufficient below).

GRD: $I(v) \wedge J(v, w) \wedge H(w) \Rightarrow G(v)$
SIM: $I(v) \wedge J(v, w) \wedge H(w) \wedge BA1(w, w') \Rightarrow \exists v' \bullet BA(v, v') \wedge J(v', w')$

The first is guard strengthening, requiring that when a concrete event is enabled then so is the abstract one. The second rule is event correctness, essentially as we have already seen it in Z and B. In addition, one would show INV and FIS for the refined machine.

Notice that the first rule is not applicability, it is the opposite, saying that the concrete precondition must imply the abstract one. In essence, it also derives from event correctness on events with explicitly specified guards. To counter this, and to stop events being all refined to deadlock a *relative deadlock freedom* rule is used that asserts at least one of the guards in a machine must be true. This has the following form:

$$\text{DLF:} \quad I(v) \wedge J(v, w) \wedge (G_1(v) \vee \ldots \vee G_n(v)) \Rightarrow (H_1(w) \vee \ldots \vee H_n(w))$$

where there are n events, and the abstract machine has events with guards $G_i(v)$ and the corresponding concrete machine has guards $H_i(w)$. Another way of looking at this is that it ensures that the concrete system does not terminate more often than the abstract system does; however, this condition trivially holds in any system where one of the events is always enabled.

Example 8.3 We can apply these rules to show the refinement of the above machines. To do so we note that the guards of $pick_0$ and $pick_1$ are true. Furthermore, the typing information is preserved by all events.

FIS and INV are seen to hold for the refined machine. Furthermore, since the events are always enabled, GRD holds. DLF also holds because all events are always enabled. The key condition to check therefore is SIM - and the reasoning is as in the previous formulation of this example.   □

8.2.1   A Relational Semantics for Event-B

In Sect. 7.2.1 we discussed how a relational semantics for Z could be used to derive practical simulation rules for use in Z. In this section we undertake the same task for Event-B. To do so we will

1. decide what we consider to be observable,
2. write this in a relational framework,
3. derive forward and backward simulation rules for the verification of refinements, and
4. show how to interpret an Event-B specification in this relational framework.

We do this in turn.

8.2.1.1   Observations

Our starting point for observations will be to observe *sequences of states*, and consider that these make up the *observable traces* of an Event-B specification. This is conceptually close to the state traces semantics of CSMATs (Definition 3.7), with the difference that we do observe the occurrence of individual events as we did in later versions of simple state based systems.

This is fundamentally different from the traces we have considered in most semantic models or in our treatment of a process algebra, where traces were sequences of *events* rather than sequences of *states*. So, for example, we had traces such as ⟨*pound*, *coffee_button*⟩. Semantic models like those discussed in Chap. 3 allow us to lose the 1–1 correspondence between events in a refinement. In the particular context of Event-B, we will be asking for inclusion of traces which do not mention event names, only the states. In this sense we will end up with quite a flexible model.

With this view of traces as sequences of states, and these traces being our observations, we also take the view here that deadlock after a trace be observable. This is akin to the notion of *completed trace refinement* introduced in Sect. 1.4 and the partial correctness models of Chap. 3 where traces were observed along with the observation when traces could not be extended – that is, when we have reached a deadlock state. Here we are making the same observations where our traces are sequences of states as opposed to sequences of events.

Refinement then requires, as usual, that these observations are consistent in any refinement. This gives rise to two aspects corresponding to the two observations (traces and reaching a deadlock state). The first is that we require trace inclusion. The second is that no new deadlocks are introduced in a refinement, that is, any deadlock of the concrete system was also present in the abstract system. This stops one refining the whole system to a deadlocked state.

8.2.1.2 A Relational Framework

We now encode these ideas in a simple relational framework. To do so in full generality we consider a global state space G, which consists of all the external variables. We can then consider an abstract system A to be defined as a triple $(S, L, ae_i)_{i \in X}$ and a concrete system C defined by its triple $(T, M, ce_i)_{i \in Y}$, where S and T are sets of states, L and M the initial states, and ae_i and ce_i are the events described as transition relations (from S to S and T to T respectively). We immediately have the following simple constraints:

$$L \subseteq S \quad L \neq \varnothing \quad ae_i \in S \leftrightarrow S$$
$$M \subseteq T \quad M \neq \varnothing \quad ce_i \in T \leftrightarrow T$$

The local state spaces S and T are related to the global state space G by two functions f and g as follows

$$f : S \to G$$
$$g : T \to G$$

This scenario is akin to comparing two different state abstractions in CSMATs (Definition 3.11), where the functions f and g could be projections on observable variables, for example. They are also similar to the initialisation and finalisation used in the relational semantics introduced in Chap. 4, with initialisation and finalisation chosen to be each other's converse relations in this case.

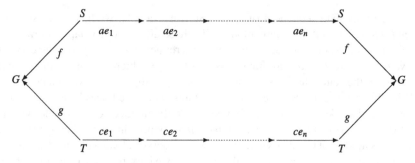

Fig. 8.1 Relational refinement for Event-B

Our notions of observation then lead to the following. First, the empty trace must be indistinguishable, modulo the projection onto the global state space, that is (where $g(M)$ denotes the relational image of M under g):

$$g(M) \subseteq f(L)$$

Second, every refined trace must also be an abstract trace, again modulo the projection onto the global state space. See Fig. 8.1 which illustrates the basic set up, and which should be familiar from Chap. 4. To consider this we form the single transition relation which represents the effect of all of the individual events. That is we define (assuming that $X = 1..n$ and $Y = 1..m$):

$$ae = ae_1 \cup \ldots \cup ae_n$$
$$ce = ce_1 \cup \ldots \cup ce_m$$

The condition on traces can then be unwound to the two (together sufficient but slightly stronger) conditions that:

$$g^{-1} \,\fatsemi\, ce \,\fatsemi\, g \subseteq f^{-1} \,\fatsemi\, ae \,\fatsemi\, f$$
$$f(\operatorname{dom}(ae)) \subseteq g(\operatorname{dom}(ce))$$

A reminder that $\fatsemi$ is the forward relational composition.

It is important to note here that the conditions are expressed as conditions on the whole transition relations ae and ce, not on each individual event ae_i. Our next task, therefore, is to unwind these conditions into a set of simulation conditions, and we do this now.

8.2.1.3 Simulation Conditions

To derive the simulation conditions, we first consider the case where the events are in 1–1 correspondence. That is, in the above abstract and concrete systems we have

$X = Y$, and we expect the behaviours of ae_i and ce_i to match up. We can thus use the following two requirements (where the first is required for all $i : 1..n$):

$$g^{-1} \mathbin{\fatsemi} ce_i \mathbin{\fatsemi} g \subseteq f^{-1} \mathbin{\fatsemi} ae_i \mathbin{\fatsemi} f$$
$$f(\!|\operatorname{dom}(ae)|\!) \subseteq g(\!|\operatorname{dom}(ce)|\!)$$

Next we fix a gluing invariant (remember that this is essentially the same as a linking invariant in B or retrieve relation in Z). As the gluing invariant is explicitly specified in Event-B (unlike in Z where it needs to be found as part of the verification effort), we can model the concrete system as containing *only* states that are linked to abstract states. Thus, r will be a *total* relation from local state space T to local state space S:

$$r : T \leftrightarrow S \qquad \operatorname{dom}(r) = T$$

Forward simulations. We can now extract conditions that are *sufficient* to guarantee the refinement conditions outlined above. The first is a set of forward simulation conditions. They are that (for all $i:1..n$):

$$r^{-1} \mathbin{\fatsemi} g \subseteq f$$
$$M \subseteq r^{-1}(\!|L|\!)$$
$$r^{-1} \mathbin{\fatsemi} ce_i \subseteq ae_i \mathbin{\fatsemi} r^{-1}$$
$$r^{-1}(\!|\operatorname{dom}(ae)|\!) \subseteq \operatorname{dom}(ce)$$

The first is a consistency condition on the projections onto the external global state space, which ensures equal observations, i.e. consistency of finalisation. Together with the second condition, it establishes the required condition for the empty trace without assuming any other properties of the observation function g:

$$g(\!|M|\!) \subseteq f(\!|L|\!)$$
$$\qquad \Leftarrow \{r^{-1} \mathbin{\fatsemi} g \subseteq f\}$$
$$g(\!|M|\!) \subseteq (r^{-1} \mathbin{\fatsemi} g)(\!|L|\!)$$
$$\qquad \equiv \{(p \mathbin{\fatsemi} q)(\!|A|\!) = q(\!|p(\!|A|\!)|\!)\}$$
$$g(\!|M|\!) \subseteq g(\!|r^{-1}(\!|L|\!)|\!)$$
$$\qquad \Leftarrow \{\text{independence from } g\}$$
$$M \subseteq r^{-1}(\!|L|\!)$$

The first step in this proof is a formal strengthening, essentially assuming that the required consistency in initial observations between concrete and abstract systems will be achieved from states linked by the gluing invariant. The final step could be strengthened to an equivalence if g were injective, i.e. the concrete state is essentially observable, which is a too strong assumption in practice.

The third condition is a correctness condition on individual operations that will ensure overall correctness:

$$f^{-1} \, \mathring{,} \, ae_i \, \mathring{,} \, f$$
$$\supseteq \{r^{-1} \, \mathring{,} \, g \subseteq f, \text{twice}\}$$
$$g^{-1} \, \mathring{,} \, r \, \mathring{,} \, ae_i \, \mathring{,} \, r^{-1} \, \mathring{,} \, g$$
$$\supseteq \{r^{-1} \, \mathring{,} \, ce_i \subseteq ae_i \, \mathring{,} \, r^{-1}\}$$
$$g^{-1} \, \mathring{,} \, r \, \mathring{,} \, r^{-1} \, \mathring{,} \, ce_i \, \mathring{,} \, g$$
$$\supseteq \{r \text{ is a total function: } r \, \mathring{,} \, r^{-1} \supseteq id\}$$
$$g^{-1} \, \mathring{,} \, ce_i \, \mathring{,} \, g$$

It will also lead us to the two forward simulation conditions GRD and SIM detailed above when we express it in terms of Event-B machines. Finally, the fourth condition $r^{-1} (\mathrm{dom}(ae)) \subseteq \mathrm{dom}(ce)$ will lead us to the deadlock freedom condition DLF when expressed in Event-B.

Backward simulations. Using the same approach the backward simulation conditions are that (for all $i{:}1..n$):

$$r^{-1} \, \mathring{,} \, g \subseteq f$$
$$M \subseteq r^{-1} (L)$$
$$ce_i \, \mathring{,} \, r \subseteq r \, \mathring{,} \, ae_i$$
$$r^{-1} (\mathrm{dom}(ae)) \subseteq \mathrm{dom}(ce)$$

All but the third of these are the same as those for a forward simulation. The third is the backwards version of the SIM rule. The similarity of the SIM rules with those as presented for the relational semantics for Z should be clear.

8.2.2   Data Refinement and Simulations for Event-B

Having defined our relational framework, and derived the simulation conditions within it, we can now express those in Event-B. To do so suppose M_0 is given by:

machine M_0
variables v
invariant $I(v)$
events $ainit, aevent_1, \ldots$
end

with $ainit$ and $aevent_i$ defined as:

$ainit \, \widehat{=}$
  $v :\mid K(v')$

$aevent_i \, \widehat{=}$
  when $G_i(v)$
  then $v :\mid BA_i(v, v')$
  end

Suppose now that machine M_1 refines M_0 and is given by

> **machine** M_1
> **refines** M_0
> **variables** w
> **invariant** $J(v, w)$
> **events** $cinit, cevent_1, \dots$
> **end**

with $cinit$ and $cevent_i$ defined as:

$cinit \widehat{=}$	$cevent_i \widehat{=}$
$\quad w :\mid N(w')$	$\quad$ **refines** $aevent_i$
	$\quad$ **when** $H_i(w)$
	$\quad$ **then** $w :\mid CBA_i(w, w')$
	$\quad$ **end**

We can give a relational interpretation to these machines in order to apply the refinement theory of the preceding section. Most of these are obvious, for example, the state space S will be those states that satisfy the invariant I. Similarly the state space T consists of those states that satisfy both I and J. The initial states are defined by the predicates in the initialisations of the machines, and so forth. This leads to the following definitions for the abstract machine:

$$S = \{v \mid I(v)\}$$
$$L = \{v \mid K(v)\}$$
$$ae_i = \{(v, v') \mid I(v) \wedge G_i(v) \wedge BA_i(v, v')\}$$
$$\text{dom } ae_i = \{v \mid I(v) \wedge G_i(v)\}$$

Deriving proof obligations for Event-B machines. Even before we consider the simulation conditions, we can use this relational formulation to derive the basic Event-B proof obligations as follows. The conditions that $L \neq \varnothing$ and $L \subseteq S$ yield the following feasibility and invariant conditions in Event-B:

FIS: $\quad \exists v \bullet K(v)$
INV: $\quad K(v) \Rightarrow I(v)$

There are also feasibility and invariant conditions for each event. The feasibility condition arises from the definition of ae_i together with the assertion that dom $ae_i = \{v \mid I(v) \wedge G_i(v)\}$. For the latter to be true we need to show:

FIS: $\quad I(v) \wedge G_i(v) \Rightarrow \exists v' \bullet BA_i(v, v')$

Finally, $ae_i \in S \leftrightarrow S$ combined with the definition of ae_i gives

INV: $I(v) \wedge G_i(v) \wedge BA_i(v, v') \Rightarrow I(v')$

Deriving simulation conditions for Event-B machines. To derive the simulation conditions we first encode the refined machine in the relational framework as follows:

$$T = \{w \mid \exists v \bullet (I(v) \wedge J(v, w))\}$$
$$M = \{w \mid N(w)\}$$
$$ce_i = \{(w, w') \mid \exists v \bullet (I(v) \wedge J(v, w)) \wedge H_i(w) \wedge CBA_i(w, w')\}$$
$$\text{dom } ce_i = \{v \mid \exists v \bullet (I(v) \wedge J(v, w)) \wedge H_i(w)\}$$

We also translate the gluing invariant as the following:

$$r = \{(w, v) \mid I(v) \wedge J(v, w)\}$$

We now translate the relational simulation conditions to Event-B. For a forward simulation the conditions were:

$$M \subseteq r^{-1}(\!| L |\!)$$
$$r^{-1} \mathbin{\mathring{,}} ce_i \subseteq ae_i \mathbin{\mathring{,}} r^{-1}$$
$$r^{-1}(\!| \text{dom}(ae) |\!) \subseteq \text{dom}(ce)$$

Now $M \subseteq r^{-1}(\!| L |\!)$ translates to

INV_INIT: $N(w) \Rightarrow \exists v \bullet (K(v) \wedge J(v, w))$

The constraint on the domain of the concrete transition relations leads to the following, which is FIS for a refinement:

FIS_REF: $I(v) \wedge J(v, w) \wedge H_i(w) \Rightarrow \exists w' \bullet CBA_i(w, w')$

The requirement that $r^{-1} \mathbin{\mathring{,}} ce_i \subseteq ae_i \mathbin{\mathring{,}} r^{-1}$ can be split into two conditions yielding precisely GRD and SIM used above:

GRD: $I(v) \wedge J(v, w) \wedge H_i(w) \Rightarrow G_i(v)$
SIM: $I(v) \wedge J(v, w) \wedge H_i(w) \wedge CBA_i(w, w') \Rightarrow \exists v' \bullet BA_i(v, v') \wedge J(v', w')$

Finally, the condition $r^{-1}(\!| \text{dom}(ae) |\!) \subseteq \text{dom}(ce)$ is a condition on the whole transition relation, and can easily be seen to translate into the deadlock freedom condition

DLF : $I(v) \land J(v, w) \land (G_1(v) \lor \ldots \lor G_n(v)) \Rightarrow (H_1(w) \lor \ldots \lor H_n(w))$

Summarising, we have the following conditions for a forward simulation in Event-B

Definition 8.1 (*Forward simulation in Event-B*)
Let machines M_0 and M_1 be as above. Then M_1 is a forward simulation of
machine M_0 whenever the following conditions hold for all $i:1..n$:

INV_INIT: $N(w) \Rightarrow \exists v \bullet (K(v) \land J(v, w))$
FIS_REF: $I(v) \land J(v, w) \land H_i(w) \Rightarrow \exists w' \bullet CBA_i(w, w')$
GRD: $I(v) \land J(v, w) \land H_i(w) \Rightarrow G_i(v)$
SIM: $I(v) \land J(v, w) \land H_i(w) \land CBA_i(w, w') \Rightarrow \exists v' \bullet BA_i(v, v') \land J(v', w')$
DLF: $I(v) \land J(v, w) \land (G_1(v) \lor \ldots \lor G_n(v)) \Rightarrow (H_1(w) \lor \ldots \lor H_n(w))$ $\square$

Similarly one can translate the relational conditions for a backward simulation
into Event-B, and doing so yields the following:

Definition 8.2 (*Backward simulation in Event-B*)
Let machines M_0 and M_1 be as above. Then M_1 is a backward simulation of
machine M_0 whenever the following conditions hold for all $i:1..n$:

INV_INIT: $N(w) \Rightarrow \exists v \bullet (K(v) \land J(v, w))$
FIS_REF: $I(v) \land J(v, w) \land H_i(w) \Rightarrow \exists w' \bullet CBA_i(w, w')$
COR_BW: $H_i(w) \land CBA_i(w, w') \land (\exists v \bullet I(v) \land J(v, w)) \land J(v', w')$
                $\Rightarrow \exists v \bullet I(v) \land J(v, w) \land BA_i(v, v') \land G_i(v)$
DLF: $I(v) \land J(v, w) \land (G_1(v) \lor \ldots \lor G_n(v)) \Rightarrow (H_1(w) \lor \ldots \lor H_n(w))$ $\square$

Unlike for forward simulation, it is not sound to split the COR_BW condition into
guard and effect conditions – as all four conjuncts in the consequence depend on the
same abstract witness before-state v.

Example 8.4 In this example we assume the definition of a number of sets and
constants as follows which would normally be given as *contexts* of the Event-B
machines:

- A finite set *PHONES* and constant $m > 0$, with $card(PHONES) \geq m$

Our initial machine M_0 has a variable *phones* denoting a finite set of up to m mobile
phones - which will later belong to a particular person. In addition to the initialisation,
two events are specified, one allocating a new set of phones, the other deallocating
these numbers from the collection *phones*.

machine M_0
variables   *phones*
invariants
    inv1:   *phones* $\subseteq$ *PHONES*
    inv2:   *card*(*phones*) $\leq m$
events
    initialization$_0$ $\widehat{=}$
       phones := $\varnothing$
    OpenPhones $\widehat{=}$
       status *ordinary*
       when *card*(*phones*) $\neq m \wedge$ *phones* $\neq$ *PHONES*
       then
          phones $:\mid$ *phones* $\subset$ *phones*$' \wedge$ *card*(*phones*$'$) $\leq m$
       end
    ClosePhones $\widehat{=}$
       status *ordinary*
       when *phones* $\neq \varnothing$
       then
          phones $:\mid$ *phones*$' \subset$ *phones*
       end
end

OpenPhones enlarges the set *phones*, and *ClosePhones* decreases its size - both are non-deterministic. We can show the necessary proof obligations for these events. For example, FIS for *OpenPhones* is the following:

$$\dots \wedge card\,(phones) \neq m \wedge phones \neq PHONES$$
$$\Rightarrow \exists\, phones' \bullet phones \subset phones' \wedge card\,(phones') \leq m$$

where … represents the invariants in the machine and context. Similarly, the obligation INV for *ClosePhones* is the following:

$$card\,(phones) \leq m \wedge phones \neq \varnothing \wedge phones' \subset phones \Rightarrow card\,(phones') \leq m$$

Deadlock freedom is the requirement that one of the events is always applicable. Again this is easy to discharge.

We now introduce a refinement. To do so we introduce new sets (again in a full specification this would be part of a context). Here these are as follows:

- A finite set *MEM* .
- A finite set *PEOPLE* $\subseteq$ *MEM* .
- A set of *OWNERS* $\subseteq$ *MEM* .
- A total function *owner* which maps each phone to its owner, i.e., *owner* : *PHONES* $\rightarrow$ *OWNERS*.

Using these we define a refinement which will be a machine M_1 that has a new variable *contacts* which will represent the contact list for a phone. Initially this will be set to empty.

> **machine** M_1
> **refines** M_0
> **variables** *phones, contacts*
> **invariants**
>   inv3 : *contacts* : *phones* $\leftrightarrow$ *OWNERS*
>   inv4 : $\forall p$: *phones* • *owner*(p) $\notin$ *contacts*({p})
> **events**
>   initialization$_1$ $\widehat{=}$
>   *contacts* := $\varnothing$
> . . .

OpenPhones is unchanged in this refinement. *ClosePhones* is amended to update *contacts* by removing the information from the contacts about the phones that have shut down.

> ClosePhones $\widehat{=}$
>   **status** *anticipated*
>   . . .
>   **then**
>   . . .
>   *contacts* :| *contacts′* $= (phones′ \setminus phones) \lhd contacts$
>   **end**

Proof obligations GRD and SIM are easy to verify for these two refined events: because the refinement does not change guards and only adds additional conjuncts in refinement, it only needs to be established that the (gluing) invariant holds in the after state.

Matching the elements of the specifications with the variables in the forward simulation rules, we have:

v	*phones*
w	*phones, contacts*
$I(v)$	inv1 $\wedge$ inv2
$J(v,w)$	inv3 $\wedge$ inv4
$K(v′)$	*phones′* $= \varnothing$
$N(w′)$	*phones′* $= \varnothing \wedge contacts′ = \varnothing$

and for example `INV_INIT` is:

$$phones = \varnothing \wedge contacts = \varnothing \Rightarrow \exists phones \bullet phones = \varnothing \wedge \texttt{inv1} \wedge \ldots \wedge \texttt{inv4}$$

where all four invariants are indeed true for both *phones* and *contacts* equal to the empty set. (Note that the initialisation predicates refer to after state variables, but the corresponding refinement conditions in Event-B systematically remove all primes, as there are no before state variables in the initialisation predicates in any case.)

For the operations, the only non-trivial condition is `FIS_REF`: $I(v) \wedge J(v, w) \wedge H_i(w) \Rightarrow \exists w' \bullet CBA_i(w, w')$. For *ClosePhones*, that amounts to the easily provable

$$\texttt{inv1} \wedge \ldots \wedge \texttt{inv4} \wedge phones \neq \varnothing \Rightarrow$$
$$\exists contacts' \bullet phones' \subset phones \wedge contacts' = (phones' \setminus phones) \lhd contacts$$

$\square$

8.2.2.1   Splitting and Merging Events in a Refinement

The original conditions for a refinement were given in Sect. 8.2.1.2 as conditions on the entire transition relation which coded up all the behaviour of a machine as one relation. Specifically, the key condition was that:

$$g^{-1} \mathbin{\substack{\circ \\ \circ}} ce \mathbin{\substack{\circ \\ \circ}} g \subseteq f^{-1} \mathbin{\substack{\circ \\ \circ}} ae \mathbin{\substack{\circ \\ \circ}} f$$

We then derived some simpler sufficient conditions when the events in a refinement were in a 1–1 correspondence between abstract and refined machines. However, Event-B allows events to be split or merged in refinement steps as long as the above condition holds. This is an additional level of flexibility not offered by the state-based notations discussed so far.

The requirements on a refinement when we split or merge events are simple. When two concrete events both refine the same abstract one we can "split" the abstract one. That is, if ae_i is split into ce_{i1} and ce_{i2}, then one proves that both ce_{i1} and ce_{i2} refine ae_i using the above forward or backward simulation conditions.

One can also merge events, so that, for example, two abstract events ae_i and ae_j are replaced by a single event ce_{ij} in a refinement step. This is only allowed if the two abstract events have identical actions, though possibly different guards. The requirement then is simply that ce_{ij} refines $ae_i \cup ae_j$. To express this in Event-B, suppose in a machine with invariant $I(v)$ we have abstract events as follows:

$$aevent_1 \,\widehat{=}$$
    when $G_1(v)$
    then $v :| BA(v, v')$
    end

$$aevent_2 \,\widehat{=}$$
    when $G_2(v)$
    then $v :| BA(v, v')$
    end

and concrete event that merges the two:

$$cevent_{12} \,\widehat{=}$$
    refines $aevent_1, aevent_2$
    when $H(v)$
    then $v :| BA(v, v')$
    end

The resultant proof obligation is simply that

$$I(v) \wedge H(v) \Rightarrow G_1(v) \vee G_2(v)$$

8.2.2.2 Introducing New Events in a Refinement

More general than splitting or merging events is the ability to introduce new events in a refinement step. So far we have not discussed an event's *status* in detail, but when we introduce new events in a refinement step this is where it becomes relevant. In general, each event has a status which can be *ordinary*, *convergent* or *anticipated*. So far all our events have been *ordinary*.

Newly introduced events in Event-B are perspicuous: they "refine skip". As is explained in Chap. 5, that means that they run the risk of introducing divergence: infinite executions of only concrete perspicuous events which make no change in the abstract state whatsoever.

Event-B is (mostly – explanation following soon) free of divergence. To maintain that, extra work is needed with the introduction of perspicuous events. This involves the introduction of a *variant*, a natural number-valued expression. Then there are two possibilities:

- the simplest approach is for the new perspicuous event to be labelled *convergent*, which incurs an immediate proof obligation that the new event strictly reduces the variant on every execution;
- however, sometimes it may not be possible or convenient to prove the new event's convergence yet. This may occur, for example, if the intended variant is defined in terms of variables that are due to appear at a lower level of abstraction in a future refinement step. In this case, the event is labelled *anticipated*, and it is only required for this event to not increase any variants already defined. In this case, the Event-B specification is temporarily divergent if considering traces that also

include the anticipated event(s). Looking at traces that cross out any anticipated events, there is still no divergence.

The operations added in this way are *not* internal operations: in any next refinement, *convergent* events become *ordinary*, and are subject to the same refinement conditions as any other operation introduced initially or in earlier refinement steps. The *anticipated* event becomes *convergent* in the step that the postponed convergence proof is added, and also *ordinary* after that. This supports the Event-B philosophy of gradually introducing detail of modelling as well as of implementation in refinement – refinement does not just establish correctness with respect to the very first specification, but also consistency with any detail added since that point.

To understand the proof obligations associated with introducing a new event in a refinement step, suppose that in our relational framework ae_i is refined by ce_i but that the refinement step also introduces new events ne_i (for all i: $1..m$).

These new events are perspicuous, which means they must refine *skip*. That is, one would need to prove, for a forward simulation, that:

$$r^{-1} \, \stackrel{\circ}{\circ} \, ne_i \subseteq r^{-1}$$

or, for a backward simulation, that:

$$ne_i \, \stackrel{\circ}{\circ} \, r \subseteq r$$

We can translate this into a condition on Event-B events as follows. Suppose the new event is of the following form:

$$new\_event_i \widehat{=}$$
   when $NE_i(w)$
   then $w :| NBA_i(w, w')$
   end

Adapting Fig. 8.1 to the situation with perspicuous events produces a diagram representing refinement and simulations along the lines of that in Fig. 8.2 and in the spirit of Definition 5.1:

Then, what we have to prove for forward simulation invariant preservation is the simplified INV rule:

INV_NE: $I(v) \wedge J(v, w) \wedge NE_i(w) \wedge NBA_i(w, w') \Rightarrow J(v, w')$

Since new events can occur at arbitrary points we have to adapt the deadlock freedom condition to require that always either a newly added or an original event is enabled. That is, it becomes the following:

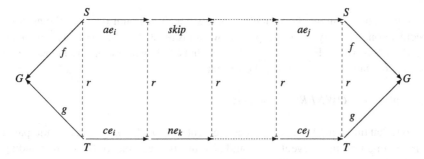

Fig. 8.2 Relational refinement for Event-B with perspicuous events

DLF: $\quad I(v) \wedge J(v, w) \wedge (G_1(v) \vee \ldots \vee G_n(v)) \Rightarrow$
$$(H_1(w) \vee \ldots \vee H_n(w) \vee NE_1(w) \vee \ldots \vee NE_m(w))$$

In order to prove that convergent events are not executed forever, one specifies a variant V which maps a state v to a natural number. One then proves that each convergent event strictly decreases V. This is encapsulated in Event-B by the following two proof obligations that apply to every convergent event, where VAR ensures the decrement of the variant and NAT ensures that the variant is a natural number when the event is enabled:

NAT: $\quad I(v) \wedge J(v, w) \wedge NE_i(w) \Rightarrow V(w) \in \mathbb{N}$
VAR: $\quad I(v) \wedge J(v, w) \wedge NE_i(w) \wedge NBA_i(w, w') \Rightarrow V(w') < V(w)$

For an *anticipated* event, we must prove that $V(w') \leq V(w)$, that is, these anticipated events do not increase the variant. Thus anticipated events must obey NAT and the following proof obligation rule, which we also denote as VAR:

VAR: $\quad I(v) \wedge J(v, w) \wedge NE_i(w) \wedge NBA_i(w, w') \Rightarrow V(w') \leq V(w)$

Example 8.5 Continuing with our specification from Example 8.4, as part of the first refinement M_1 we also introduce a new event *AddContact* which adds a contact for a phone belonging to a user.

```
AddContact ≙
    status convergent
    then
        contacts :| ∃o : OWNERS, p : phones • o ≠ owners(p)∧
                (p, o) ∉ contacts ∧ contacts' = contacts ∪ {(p, o)}
    end
```

Since this only changes the variable *contacts* which does not occur in the abstract specification, it clearly refines skip - as new events must. There is no data refinement, so INV_NE is trivial. Finally we must prove that convergent events are not executed forever. To show this we can use the variant

$$\#(phones \times OWNERS) \setminus contacts$$

to show, that the event *AddContact* is convergent. If *ClosePhones* were an anticipated rather than an ordinary event, we could also use this variant for the corresponding proof obligation: that *ClosePhones* does not increase it.   □

8.3   ASM

The Abstract State Machine (ASM for short) method is another state-based methodology for the specification and refinement of systems. It has similarities to both B and Event-B, and its specifications define finite state machines that update an abstract state. The interest to us here is not so much the style of its syntax, which in the basic form is simple, but its approach to refinement which generalises the approach we have seen so far in the state-based systems we have looked at.

In its simplest form (basic ASM), an ASM is a finite set of *transition rules* of the form

if *Condition* **then** *Updates*

which transform abstract states. Naturally in this *Condition* is the guard of the transition, whilst *Updates* is a finite set of assignments of the form

$$f(t_1, \ldots, t_n) := t$$

In the original formulation, an ASM consisted of a single agent executing a program in a sequence of steps, possibly interacting with its environment. Later this idea was extended to capture distributed computations, in which multiple agents execute their programs concurrently. ASM specifications consist of a series of ASM models each being a refinement of the previous one.

A very simple example, and sufficient for our purposes, is a *control state ASM* which defines a simple finite state machine branching. It is often given pictorially, as we do in Fig. 8.3, which is interpreted to mean:

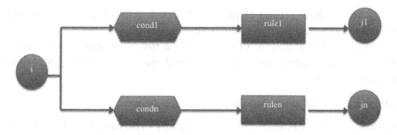

Fig. 8.3 A simple control state ASM

if $cond_1 \wedge ctl\_state = i$
then $ctl\_state := j_1$
    $rule_1$

$\vdots$

if $cond_n \wedge ctl\_state = i$
then $ctl\_state := j_n$
    $rule_n$

With this in mind one could write a very simple ASM for the frequency server (simple as it has just one frequency).

Example 8.6 This ASM has signature of just x, with initial state S_0 where $x = 0$. It has two components: *allocate* and *deallocate* defined by the transition rules as follows:

$allocate = \{$if $x = 0$ then $x := 1\}$
$deallocate = \{$if $x = 1$ then $x := 0\}$

Then $FS = allocate \cup deallocate$ is the (sequential) ASM specification. $\qquad\Box$

For our purposes this is a sufficient amount of the ASM language to introduce, of course there are substantial examples of specification of real systems in the literature using the full force of the language.

8.3.1 ASM Semantics and ASM Refinement

The definition of ASM refinement is based on the ASM semantics which represents ASMs as *transition systems*, which are state machines with anonymous transitions similar to those described in Chap. 3. In particular, a transition system here is of the form: $M = (States, T, IN)$ where *States* is a non-empty set of states, $IN \subseteq States$ is the set of initial states, and $T \subseteq States \times States$ is a transition relation. For full generality we assume $\perp$ is an element of *States* in order that divergence may be encoded in the standard fashion as we have done before.

One can then define notions of a *trace* and a *run* of an abstract state machine, and in the ASM semantics the notion of a *final state* is necessary. The following definition is needed.

Definition 8.3 (*Final states, traces, runs and I/O behaviour*)

Final state   A state $s \in$ *States* is final if $s \notin \text{dom} T$. The set of final states is denoted *OUT*.

Traces   A trace σ is a finite or infinite sequence of states where $(\sigma(i), \sigma(i+1)) \in T$ for $i < len(\sigma)$. For a finite trace the last state must be a member of *OUT*. (So in the terminology of the early chapters, finite traces are *completed* ones.)

Run   A run is a trace that starts with an initial state, i.e., $\sigma(0) \in IN$.

Partial I/O behaviour   The partial I/O behaviour of a machine M is the relation $(IN \setminus \{\perp\}) \times (OUT \setminus \{\perp\}) \cap T^*$. We denote this $PIO(M)$.

Total I/O behaviour   The total I/O behaviour of a machine M is the relation $PIO(M) \cup \{(s, \perp)|$ when s is an initial state with an infinite run$\}$. $\square$

The notion of trace should be compared with that in Definition 1.2. Two differences are worth noting. First, traces here are (like in Event-B) sequences of states rather than sequences of events. Second, we allow infinite traces in this definition. However, unlike in CSP where we had divergences and infinite traces separately (possible because we could distinguish infinite *internal* behaviour), infinite traces here are interpreted as essentially divergent. In an alternative view where *all* traces are infinite, any finite trace can be interpreted as an infinite trace by adding infinite stuttering in the final state, similar to considering the transition relation T as reflexive like we did in Chap. 3. The partial I/O behaviour corresponds to relational semantics of CSMATs (Definition 3.8).

These definitions allow one to define a number of different notions of refinement correctness depending on whether total or partial correctness is needed. In the definitions we supposed that an abstract transition system $AM = (AS, AIN, AT)$ is refined to a concrete transition system $CM = (CS, CIN, CT)$.

The first two notions do not consider intermediate states of AM and CM, but just look at their input / output behaviour. To do so they use two relations $IR \subseteq AIN \times CIN$ and $OR \subseteq AOUT \times COUT$ to determine when initial and final states are considered to be equivalent.

Definition 8.4 (*Preservation of partial correctness in ASM*)
A refinement of AM to CM preserves partial correctness with respect to (IR, OR), if for every finite run σ_C of CM there exists a finite run σ_A such that the initial states are related by IR and the final states are related by OR. $\square$

Informally, the definition says, as one would expect, that the effects of runs of CM are consistent with those of AM. In particular, terminating refined runs simulate terminating abstract runs via the input / output correspondence given by the two relations IR and OR.

This notion of refinement or preservation of partial correctness can be specified as $PIO(CM) \subseteq IR^{-1} \, \mathring{,} \, PIO(AM) \, \mathring{,} \, OR$. Note also that if the mappings are the identity (that is the state spaces are the same and $IR = OR = id$), then this notion of refinement corresponds to relational partial correctness refinement as in Definition 3.9.

Two points are worth noting. The first is that the correspondences between the states are part of the definition of refinement. This has the flavour already of a simulation (specifically the retrieve relation linking abstract and concrete states), yet is in the basic definition of refinement for ASMs. This is in contrast to both the LTS notions of refinement (cf. Chap. 1) as well as the relational view (cf. Chap. 4). Specifically there is no jointly accessible global state G that was present in the definitions of refinement in a relational context (and used in Z, Event-B etc). Second, it is a weak notion of refinement since we quantify over finite runs from CM, and the definition allows a finite abstract run to be implemented by a divergent one.

To tackle the latter issue, a strengthened definition can be given as follows.

Definition 8.5 (*Preservation of total correctness in ASM*)
A refinement from AM to CM preserves total correctness if it preserves partial correctness, and if for any infinite run σ_C of CM there exists an infinite run σ_A of AM such that the initial states are related by IR. □

This stronger definition implies that finite as well as infinite runs simulate an abstract run via the input / output correspondence given by the two relations IR and OR. Given the property, then the following holds: $TIO(CM) \subseteq IR^{-1} \, \mathring{,} \, TIO(AM) \, \mathring{,}$ $(OR \cup \{(\bot, \bot)\})$. Again, if the state spaces are the same and the relations IR and OR are the identity, then all total correctness assertions for the programs are preserved.

However, although this strengthened definition does not allow finite runs to be implemented by divergent ones, there is little requirement of consistency on them between abstract and concrete systems - all that is required is that their initial states are related. Clearly one cannot relate final states with an infinite run, so how should we compare infinite runs? The answer lies in a retrieve relation-like correspondence as we pass through the infinite run. We don't require a step-by-step correspondence though, that would give us a simulation, but just that we 'touch base' between abstract and concrete system infinitely often as we pass through it. The following definition makes this more precise.

Definition 8.6 (*Partial and total preservation of traces in ASM*)
Given a relation $IO \subseteq AS \times CS$, a refinement from AM to CM totally preserves traces with respect to IO if it preserves total correctness for $IR = IO \cap (AIN \times CIN)$ and $OR = IO \cap (AOUT \times COUT)$, and if for any infinite run σ_C there is an infinite run σ_A and two strictly monotone sequences $i_0 < i_1 < \ldots$ and $j_0 < j_1 < \ldots$ of natural numbers, such that for all k, $IO(\sigma_A(i_k), \sigma_C(j_k))$ holds.

For a refinement to partially preserve traces, the refinement must preserve partial correctness and the sequence $i_0 \leq i_1 \leq \ldots$ is only required to be monotone. □

Fig. 8.4 Refinement for
ASM

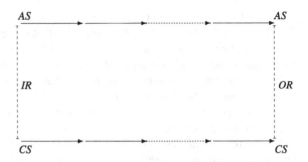

So, in this definition the correspondence between states in the infinite run is given by the relation *IO*. Typically *IO* will compare intermediate input and output of the ASMs, which is usually modelled by reading or writing external functions in the ASM notation. In fact, in the above definition there is some freedom in the exact choice of *IO*, and we discuss this later.

We're still working with the basic definition of refinement here. Let us now consider how simulations might be used to verify such refinements as we have done for other state-based notations. As previously we will use a *coupling invariant* between the abstract and concrete state spaces. However, in a generalisation to the framework that we have used previously, we won't require a strict step-by-step correspondence preserving the coupling invariant, and in pictorial terms will allow *m* − *n* steps instead of just 1–1. This is consistent with the view, like in Chap. 3, that it is the state changes caused, rather than the names of events, which carries the main emphasis.

To illustrate refinement and simulations in ASM, Fig. 8.4 illustrates an arbitrary refinement in ASM - where it should be noted that the number of steps in the abstract and concrete systems are not necessarily the same. Then Fig. 8.5 illustrates a generalised simulation in a schematic fashion - where again the number steps in a simulation is not 1–1.

Fig. 8.5 Generalised
simulations in ASM

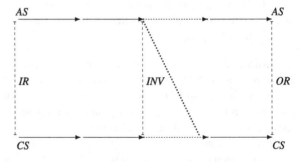

One immediate question is to ask how the coupling invariant *INV* interacts with the relations *IR* and *OR* - since they already link abstract and concrete states. In Definition 8.6, *IR* and *OR* were defined in terms of the relation *IO* (which will typically compare input and output in the two systems). So if one wants to preserve traces with respect to *IO*, then *INV* has to be stronger than *IO*. Typically *INV* will be a conjunction of a predicate *IO* relating observable inputs and outputs between the abstract and concrete state plus other predicates which relate the internal data representations across the two state spaces.

To build the correct simulation definition we have to take into account several aspects.

Firstly, we must start the simulation off. In our previous relational approach this was done by embedding the global state *G* into the two local states. Now we don't have a global state, rather we have an initial pairing of states given by *IR*. So initialisation will do two things: set up initial states linked by *IR*, then from this establish *INV* 'at some point' down the line. "At some point" means we do not have to establish *INV* after the next step in the trace. To express this we will use some temporal operators *AF* and *EF* defined below. Secondly, there will be a simulation step in the middle, and thirdly a finalisation step, which from states being linked by *INV* will establish *OR* as needed at the end of a refinement.

The simulation step is also complicated by the fact that from *INV* we don't require *INV* in the next pair of states but some point in the future. A general simulation step will be *m:n*, that is for *n* concrete steps we look forward *m* abstract steps. So if *as* and *cs* are related by *INV*, and they are not both final states, then we are going to add a commuting diagram with *INV* holding at the other end. This diagram might be one of a number of shapes depending on whether *m* or *n* are zero (in which case we get triangles). The commuting diagram might have 0 concrete steps ($n = 0$), in which case we use a well-founded predicate $<_{m0}$ on states which is forced to decrease, stopping an infinite sequence of *m*:0 triangles from occurring. To stop an infinite sequence of 0:*n* diagrams we use another well-founded predicate $<_{0n}$ which in a similar fashion must also decrease. Finally, if $m, n > 0$ then the condition asks that states that are *m* and *n* steps ahead, respectively, are chosen that complete the simulation.

To give the definition we first define the temporal operators we need. Specifically, we introduce operators $AF(s, p)$ meaning for all executions starting with *s* predicate *p* will eventually hold, and $EF(s, p)$ meaning for some execution starting in *s* it will be the case that eventually *p* holds. Two further operators are used if the number of steps in a simulation step is positive: $AF^+(s, p)$ and $EF^+(s, p)$.

These can all be defined as follows (where $trace(\sigma)$ means σ is a trace):

$$AF(s, p) = \forall \sigma \bullet \sigma(0) = s \wedge trace(\sigma) \Rightarrow \exists n \bullet p(\sigma(n))$$
$$EF(s, p) = \exists \sigma \bullet \sigma(0) = s \wedge trace(\sigma) \wedge \exists n \bullet p(\sigma(n))$$
$$AF^+(s, p) = s \notin OUT \wedge (\forall s_0 \bullet T(s, s_0) \Rightarrow AF(s_0, p))$$
$$EF^+(s, p) = s \notin OUT \wedge (\exists s_0 \bullet T(s, s_0) \wedge EF(s_0, p))$$

We can finally give the definition of a *generalised forward simulation*.

Definition 8.7 (*Generalised forward simulation in ASM*)
INV is a generalised forward simulation with respect to *IR* and *OR* from *AM* to *CM* whenever the following conditions hold:

initialisation	$\forall cs \in CIN \bullet \exists as \in AIN \bullet IR(as, cs)$
correctness	$\forall as, cs \bullet IR(as, cs) \Rightarrow AF(cs, \lambda cs' \bullet EF(as, \lambda as' \bullet$ $INV(as', cs')))$
finalisation	$\forall as, cs \bullet as \in AOUT \wedge cs \in COUT \wedge INV(as, cs) \Rightarrow$ $OR(as, cs)$
non-divergence	We have expressions $<_{m0}$ and $<_{0n}$ satisfying properties as described above. □

The following results then hold:

1. If there exists a generalised forward simulation *INV* from *AM* to *CM* then the refinement preserves total correctness.
2. If in addition *INV* implies *IO* then the refinement totally preserves traces.
3. To just ensure preservation of partial correctness and partial preservation of traces, the condition that $<_{0n}$ decreases for 0:*n* diagrams can be omitted in the correctness part of Definition 8.7.

The simulation definition in Definition 8.7 is expressed in terms of the semantics. However, for direct application these are normally turned into expressions in dynamic logic to allow the application to ASM specifications.

8.4   Bibliographical Notes

A comprehensive introduction to Event-B is given in [1], which provides a good introduction to the basics as well as its proof method and approach to refinement. It introduces the relational semantics discussed in this chapter, and we have conformed to its notation and retained the structure of the development of simulation rules. The book also works through a series of case studies of specification and refinement in Event-B. Further information on Event-B is provided in [2].

Event-B benefits from extensive tool support. In particular, the *Rodin Platform* is an Eclipse-based IDE for Event-B which provides tool support for refinement of Event-B specifications and support to discharge their proof obligations. The platform is open source, contributes to the Eclipse framework and is further extendable with plugins. It was developed under a series of EU funded research projects. A good introduction to the Rodin tool is given in [3]. The website http://www.event-b.org provides resources on Event-B and the Rodin tool can be downloaded from there.

Event-B has taken a rather flexible approach to its semantics. Prior to [1] there was no formal justification to the proof obligations, nor the refinement rules. Indeed, [4] argues that the lack of a fixed semantics is an advantage since it increases the flexibility of the specification formalism. There is some validity to this claim and many of the proof obligations are clearly desirable with or without a formal semantics. Boiten [5] analyses implicit compromises in the set-up of Event-B refinement, drawing the conclusion that imposing stronger refinement rules such as failures refinement would prohibit the current approach to increasing the granularity of Event-B events.

Alternative approaches to the semantics of Event-B are to use action systems, as is done by Butler in [6], or to interpret Event-B specifications in CSP, which is done in [7]. The latter provides the most comprehensive account of refinement in Event-B in some senses. It provides the clearest definition of what it means for events to be *anticipated* and *convergent*, which we have adopted. It defines a behavioural semantics for Event-B refinement by defining a CSP semantics for Event-B. It shows how the different forms of Event-B refinement can be captured as CSP refinement relations, and provides a formal semantics for refinements involving splitting events and the use of anticipated events. Specifically, it defines two, what it calls, *development strategies*, which take different choices as to whether a machines interface is extended by new events.

The origin of abstract state machines was in the work of Yuri Gurevich, who first proposed it in the mid-1980s as a way of improving on Turing's thesis that every algorithm is simulated by an appropriate Turing machine. By the 1990s, work on ASMs was done as a means for the specification and verification of both hardware and software. ASMs have now been used in a wide variety of applications, including the specification of standards of languages such as Prolog and Java; the engineering of industrial control systems; e-commerce; compilers and many more.

A website containing material on ASM including references to introductory material, case studies and tools can be found at: http://web.eecs.umich.edu/gasm/intro.html.

A good introduction to the language and some of its applications is provided in [8]. There are two books on the ASM methodology: [9] and [10]. Other good introductory material includes [11] and [12].

The definition of the semantics of ASMs as transition systems is given in [13]. There are a number of papers which describe the approach to refinement in ASM. [14] provides a good high-level overview of the approach and the basic definition of refinement in ASM by generalised simulations.

There are a number of examples of the use of ASM refinement in the AsmBook [9], a large real-life case study which makes widely use of that scheme is the book [10]. A full technical description of generalised simulations is given by Schellhorn in [15]. The KIV theorem prover has been used to verify refinements, and the approach is explained in [16]. The link between generalised forward simulations and a relational approach to data refinement is explored by Schellhorn in [17].

References

1. Abrial J-R (2010) Modeling in Event-B: system and software engineering, 1st edn. Cambridge University Press, New York
2. Métayer C, Abrial J-R, Voisin L (2005) Event-B language, RODIN Project Deliverable 3.2. http://rodin.cs.ncl.ac.uk/deliverables/D7.pdf. Accessed 15 June 2018
3. Abrial J-R, Butler M, Hallerstede S, Hoang TS, Mehta F, Voisin L (2010) Rodin: an open toolset for modelling and reasoning in Event-B. STTT 12(6):447–466
4. Hallerstede S (2011) On the purpose of Event-B proof obligations. Form Asp Comput 23(1):133–150
5. Boiten EA (2014) Introducing extra operations in refinement. Form Asp Comput 26(2):305–317
6. Butler M (2012) External and internal choice with event groups in Event-B. Form Asp Comput 24(4):555–567
7. Schneider S, Treharne H, Wehrheim H (2014) The behavioural semantics of Event-B refinement. Form Asp Comput 26(2):251–280
8. Börger E (2005) The ASM method for system design and analysis. A tutorial introduction. In: Gramlich Bernhard (ed) Frontiers of combining systems: 5th international workshop, FroCoS 2005, Vienna, Austria. Lecture notes in artifical intelligence, vol 3717. Springer, Berlin, pp 264–283
9. Börger E, Stark RF (2003) Abstract state machines: a method for high-level system design and analysis. Springer, New York
10. Stark RF, Börger E, Schmid J (2001) Java and the Java virtual machine: definition, verification, validation. Springer, New York
11. Reisig W (2008) Abstract state machines for the classroom. In: Bjørner D, Henson MC (eds) Logics of specification languages. Springer, Berlin, pp 15–46
12. Börger E, Raschke A (2018) Modeling companion for software practitioners. Springer, Berlin
13. Gurevich Y (1995) Evolving algebras 1993: lipari guide. Oxford University Press, Oxford, pp 9–36
14. Börger E (2003) The ASM refinement method. Form Asp Comput 15(2):237–257
15. Schellhorn G (2001) Verification of ASM refinements using generalized forward simulation. J Univers Comput Sci 7(11):952–979. http://www.jucs.org/jucs_7_11/verification_of_asm_refinements
16. Schellhorn G, Ahrendt W (1998) The WAM case study: verifying compiler correctness for prolog with KIV. In: Bibel W, Schmitt PH (eds) Automated deduction - a basis for applications, vol III. applications. Springer, Dordrecht, pp 165–194
17. Schellhorn G (2005) ASM refinement and generalizations of forward simulation in data refinement: a comparison. Theor Comput Sci 336(2–3):403–436

Part III
Relating Notions of Refinement

The first part of this book introduced some of the differing approaches there are to the semantics of refinement, and the second part showed how these were reflected in different specification languages. A natural question that might be in a reader's mind right now is *"why all these different ones"*? Some of these differences in refinement relations are due to different notions of observation—as we have already covered in Part I—but that is not the whole story... and this part describes the relationships between notions of refinement across the different languages and semantics.

Chapter 9
Relational Concurrent Refinement

9.1 Introduction

In Part I of this book we introduced several differing approaches to refinement. Specifically, in models of concurrency (see Chap. 1), refinement was defined in terms of sets of observations, which can include the events a system is prepared to accept or refuse, or depend on explicit properties of states and transitions. By varying the observation we defined a whole spectrum of refinement relations including trace refinement, failures refinement, and so forth.

A very different approach was taken in Chap. 4 where data refinement was defined in terms of the relational inclusion of the behaviour of abstract programs.

The refinement relations from Chap. 1 found realisation in process algebras, and we discussed this in Chap. 6, and the relational view of refinement discussed in Chap. 4 was used in Z and B in Chap. 7, and then for Event-B and ASM in Chap. 8.

The natural question we seek to answer in this chapter is the following: *how can these approaches be reconciled?* To do so it is necessary to define a correspondence between the relational model and the process model. This is usually done either by defining a *corresponding process* in, say, CSP for each ADT, and then deriving the process semantics, or by defining a process semantics directly for an ADT. Either way, a process semantics $[\![A]\!]$ can be given for an ADT A. The central aim is to derive results of the following form:

In relational model X, $A \sqsubseteq_{data} C$ if and only if $[\![A]\!] \sqsubseteq_{ps} [\![C]\!]$.

where $\sqsubseteq_{data}$ denotes relational data refinement, and $\sqsubseteq_{ps}$ the refinement relation induced by the given process semantics. Varying X, and to some extent $\sqsubseteq_{data}$, gives different process semantics. In particular, we are interested in the semantic models of CSP, for example, traces, failures, or failures-divergences and how they are related to data refinement in a relational model.

To begin to understand the relationship between different types of refinement, in this chapter we embed the concurrent refinement relations into the relational framework, and this is done by exploiting the role of *finalisation* in the relational semantics

© Springer International Publishing AG, part of Springer Nature 2018   179
J. Derrick and E. Boiten, *Refinement*, https://doi.org/10.1007/978-3-319-92711-4_9

by adding in more information about possible observations. We thus gain results such
as:

> In the non-blocking relational model with standard observations, A $\sqsubseteq_{data}$ C if and only if
> $[\![A]\!]$ is traces-divergences refined by $[\![C]\!]$.

By deriving results such as this we achieve two things:

1. An understanding of the relationship between concurrent refinement semantics
   and their relational counterpart.
2. Using this we derive simulation-based methods for the verification of concurrent
   refinement relations.

We will look at three instantiations of these questions in this chapter. First of all
we will discover how to embed process algebraic refinement in a relational model.
This will tell us, for example, what relational model corresponds to trace refinement,
and so forth. Then we will look at the dual question and look at different relational
models (blocking, non-blocking etc) and determine which concurrent model they
map to. Finally, we will look at automata, and the simulations introduced in that
model (see Chap. 2), introducing along the way the *IO automata* model which adds
input and output actions into a basic automata framework.

To begin, however, we recap on the approach to refinement defined in Chaps. 1
and 4 from Part I.

9.2   Background

In a process algebra such as CSP, LOTOS, or CCS a system is defined in terms
of actions (or events) which represent the interactions between a system and its
environment. As we have seen, the exact way in which the environment is allowed to
interact with the system varies between different semantics. Typical semantics are set-
based, associating one or more sets with each process, for example traces, refusals,
divergences. Refinement was then defined in terms of set inclusions and equalities
between the corresponding sets for different processes. We use the same notation we
introduced earlier, in particular the definition of labelled transition system given in
Definition 1.1 and related definitions.

On the other hand, in a state-based system, specifications are considered to define
abstract data types (ADTs), consisting of an initialisation, a collection of operations
and a finalisation, all of which are relations using a global state G and a local state
State. A program over an ADT is a sequential composition of these elements, trans-
forming a global visible state into another one via a sequence of hidden local states.
The *initialisation* of the program takes a global state to a local state, on which the
operations act, a *finalisation* translates back from local to global. Refinement was
defined to be the subset relation over program behaviours, where what is deemed
visible (i.e., the domain of the initialisation and the range of the finalisation) is the
input/output relation.

Thus a (concrete) ADT C refines a (more abstract) ADT A if for every program and initial global state (for example representing a sequence of inputs), the global state that C produces (for example representing a sequence of outputs) is one that A could also have produced. To make the verification of refinements tractable, *simulations* have become the accepted approach, and for a complete method, two kinds of simulations were defined: forward and backward simulations. The use of these simulations in specific formal methods was discussed extensively in Part II of this book.

The relational theory we discussed in Chap. 4 was defined for total relations, and in order to apply it to Z we totalised the partial relations to derive the simulation rules. In fact, the restriction to total relations is unnecessary, as soundness and joint completeness of the same set of simulation rules also hold in the more general case of when the relations can be partial. It simplifies the following theory to use this partial framework, although the same set of results are obtained if one uses a total framework.

Previously we have defined the notion of an abstract data type in Definition 4.1. Using this, data refinement is defined in Definition 4.5 and then forward and backward simulations in Definitions 4.6 and 4.7 respectively. Totalisations as defined in Sect. 4.4.1 lead to simulations for partial relations (Definitions 4.12 and 4.13). A state-based realisation of these simulations was given as in Chap. 7.

We will use these ideas as the setting and context of this part, specifically using embeddings of process algebraic semantics into abstract data types, and the resultant representation of simulation rules within the Z schema calculus, since this offers a very convenient form to represent the key ideas and differences between the simulation rules.

9.3 Relating Process Algebraic and Relational Refinement

In order to relate the state-based and relational approaches to refinement we exploit the idea that the finalisation in a relational framework represents the observations one makes. The link to process algebras is made by defining a process algebraic framework within the relational framework, by constructing a kind of ADT, specified using a Z data type, that embeds the process algebraic refinement observations in the relational finalisation. One can then see the relationship between process algebraic refinement and relational refinement as well as extract simulation rules for each process algebraic instantiations.

In particular, we will do the following:

1. define a relational embedding of the Z data type, that is, define a data type (specifically define the finalisation operation) so as to facilitate the proof that data refinement equals the correct inclusion of observations in the event based semantics. The choice of finalisation is taken so that we observe the characteristics of inter-

est. Thus in the context of trace refinement we are interested in observing traces, but in that of failures refinement we will need to observe more.

2. We then describe how to calculate the relevant LTS aspect from the Z data type. For example, for trace refinement we work out what denotes traces in the Z data type.

3. We then prove that data refinement equals the relevant event based definition of refinement.

4. Finally, we extract a characterisation of refinement as simulation rules on the operations of the Z data type.

We will look at different process algebraic refinement relations in turn. Many steps we undertake in this are the same or very similar for the different refinement relations, but the proof of equivalence of refinement followed by the characterisation of simulation rules provides the largest variation between cases.

Due to their construction the simulation rules for each refinement relation are guaranteed to provide a sound proof method for the given notion of refinement. However, their joint completeness requires a separate proof – either an independent one, or one that shows that a standard construction of an intermediate data type in a completeness proof occurs within the range of the given embedding – avoiding situations like described in Sect. 4.4.3.

To give a flavour of the approach consider the basic relational framework, where programs are relations over an augmented global state $G_\perp$ where $G == \{*\}$. Observations of a program thus merely record whether the sequence of operations terminated correctly (output $*$) or whether they aborted with an output of $\perp_G$ through either non-termination (non-blocking contract approach) or inapplicability (blocking behavioural approach).

The basic 'observations' the relational model makes are very weak, sufficient perhaps for a sequential setting, but certainly not discriminating enough for a concurrent setting. The solution is simple: make more observations, and the only way we can do this is to increase the expressiveness of the finalisation, since this represents what is observable. To illustrate this, we sketch an embedding that includes refusal information.

To include extra information, we generalise the finalisation from being $\{State \bullet \theta State \mapsto *\}$ (recording "success" in every state that we can reach) to becoming $\{State \bullet \theta State \mapsto E\}$. Here E will represent the observations made, and what goes in E depends on what we want to observe, for example, we could consider E to be a set of operation names representing what operations could be *refused* at the state in which we have just finalised. (The result type of finalisation and the input of initialisation should both be the "global state", and thus for consistency, initialisation should also take a set of operations as its input.) An example illustrates the general approach:

Example 9.1 A basic switch is specified as the standard Z ADT $(B, Init, \{On, Off\})$ where

$$\begin{array}{l} \underline{\;B\;} \\ b : \mathbb{B} \end{array}$$

$$\begin{array}{l} \underline{\;Init\;} \\ B' \\ \overline{} \\ b' \end{array}$$

$$\begin{array}{l} \underline{\;On\;} \\ \Delta B \\ \overline{} \\ \neg b \wedge b' \end{array}$$

$$\begin{array}{l} \underline{\;Off\;} \\ \Delta B \\ \overline{} \\ b \wedge \neg b' \end{array}$$

This is interpreted as the relational data type (B, Init, {On, Off}, Fin) which records refused operations at the end of the program:

$$B == \{ (\!| \; b == true \; |\!), \; (\!| \; b == false \; |\!) \}$$
$$Init == \{ g : \mathbb{P}\{On, Off\} \bullet g \mapsto (\!| \; b == true \; |\!) \}$$
$$On == \{ (\!| \; b == false \; |\!) \mapsto (\!| \; b == true \; |\!) \}$$
$$Off == \{ (\!| \; b == true \; |\!) \mapsto (\!| \; b == false \; |\!) \}$$
$$Fin == \{ (\!| \; b == true \; |\!) \mapsto \{On\}, \; (\!| \; b == true \; |\!) \mapsto \varnothing,$$
$$(\!| \; b == false \; |\!) \mapsto \{Off\}, \; (\!| \; b == false \; |\!) \mapsto \varnothing \} \qquad \square$$

With this approach one can then do two things. First, one can formally show the two notions of refinement coincide. Second, one can derive simulation rules for each specific embedding. For each refinement relation that we now consider we do both.

Let us begin with trace refinement.

9.3.1   Trace Refinement

First of all a reminder that trace refinement is defined by $p \sqsubseteq_{tr} q$ iff $traces(q) \subseteq traces(p)$, using the notation from Chap. 1.

According to the methodology above we now define a relational embedding of this trace model. The partial relations model records exactly trace information for the embedding when one uses a very trivial finalisation.[1] In this embedding $G == \{*\}$, and the local state is State $== State$. Then the Z data type $(State, Init, \{Op_i\}_{i \in I})$ is interpreted relationally as (State, Init, $\{Op_i\}_{i \in I}$, Fin) where

$$Init == \{ Init \bullet * \mapsto \theta State' \}$$
$$Op == \{ Op \bullet \theta State \mapsto \theta State' \}$$
$$Fin == \{ State \bullet \theta State \mapsto * \}$$

---

[1] See [1].

Note that this relational interpretation and finalisation is simpler than that given in Sect. 7.2.1, reducing it to the situation where there are no inputs or outputs. Inputs and outputs add some complexity and subtlety and are discussed in depth in Chap. 10. With the simple embedding given above, possible traces lead to the single global value; impossible traces have no relational image. We use these ideas to define the *trace embedding* as follows:

Definition 9.1 (*Trace embedding*)
A Z data type (*State*, *Init*, $\{Op_i\}_{i \in I}$) has the following trace embedding into the relational model.

$$G == \{*\}$$
$$State == State$$
$$Init == \{Init \bullet * \mapsto \theta State'\}$$
$$Op == \{Op \bullet \theta State \mapsto \theta State'\}$$
$$Fin == State \times G$$

To distinguish between the different embeddings we denote the trace embedding of a data type A as $A \mid_{tr}$. We drop the $\mid_{tr}$ if the context is clear.   □

To prove the correspondence between trace preorder and data refinement we need to provide an understanding of what constitutes the traces of an abstract data type. This is done in a natural fashion in the following definition.

Definition 9.2 (*Traces of a relational data type*)
The *traces* of a Z data type (*State*, *Init*, $\{Op_i\}_{i \in I}$) are all sequences $\langle i_1, \cdots, i_n \rangle$ such that

$$\exists State' \bullet Init \, \overset{\circ}{\scriptscriptstyle\circ} \, Op_{i_1} \, \overset{\circ}{\scriptscriptstyle\circ} \cdots \overset{\circ}{\scriptscriptstyle\circ} \, Op_{i_n}$$

We denote the traces of an ADT A by $\mathscr{T}(A)$.   □

The central result for each refinement relation is the correctness of this embedding. This is expressed as follows.

Theorem 9.1 *With the trace embedding, data refinement corresponds to trace preorder. That is, when Z data types A and C are embedded as A and C,*[2]

$$A \mid_{tr} \sqsubseteq_{data} C \mid_{tr} \ \textit{iff} \ \mathscr{T}(C) \subseteq \mathscr{T}(A)$$

Proof From the definition of traces for Z data types and the embedding given it is obvious that for any sequence p, $(*, *) \in p_A$ iff $p \in \mathscr{T}(A)$. Also, for any p, $p_A = \{(*, *)\}$ or $p_A = \varnothing$. Thus, data refinement ($p_A \subseteq p_C$ for all p) corresponds to trace refinement.   □

---

[2]This condition is left implicit in the rest of this chapter.

From this result it can be seen that observations in the testing scenario, here a display with an action name displayed, are distributed in the relational notion of refinement. That is, although finalisations are often taken to be the 'observations', in fact, some of the observations are implicit in the program p and the relational inclusion $p_C \subseteq p_A$ (since finalisations only contain the information as to whether the trace was defined or not).

With this embedding in place, we can now extract the simulation rules that correspond to this notion of refinement. These are the rules for standard Z refinement but omitting applicability of operations.

The conditions for a forward simulation in this partial relational model are:

$$CInit \subseteq AInit \,\mathbin{\substack{\circ \\ \circ}}\, R$$
$$R \,\mathbin{\substack{\circ \\ \circ}}\, CFin \subseteq AFin$$
$$\forall i : I \bullet R \,\mathbin{\substack{\circ \\ \circ}}\, COp_i \subseteq AOp_i \,\mathbin{\substack{\circ \\ \circ}}\, R$$

The first and last of these are just the standard initialisation and correctness conditions, respectively. The finalisation condition, in fact, places no further requirements with the trace embedding. For a backwards simulation, the finalisation condition simplifies to totality of T. We thus have the following conditions for the trace embedding.

Definition 9.3 (*Trace simulations in Z*)
Given Z data types A and C, the relation R on $AState \wedge CState$ is a *trace forward simulation* from A to C if

$$\forall CState' \bullet CInit \Rightarrow \exists AState' \bullet AInit \wedge R'$$
$$\forall i \in I \bullet \forall AState;\; CState;\; CState' \bullet R \wedge COp_i \Rightarrow \exists AState' \bullet R' \wedge AOp_i$$

The total relation T on $AState \wedge CState$ is a *trace backward simulation* from A to C if

$$\forall AState';\; CState' \bullet CInit \wedge T' \Rightarrow AInit$$
$$\forall i : I \bullet \forall AState';\; CState;\; CState' \bullet$$
$$(COp_i \wedge T') \Rightarrow (\exists AState \bullet T \wedge AOp_i) \qquad \square$$

9.3.2 Completed Trace Refinement

We can follow the same approach with other process algebraic refinement relations. For example, consider *completed trace refinement* as defined in Sect. 1.4. Remember that the completed trace preorder, $\sqsubseteq_{ctr}$, is defined by $p \sqsubseteq_{ctr} q$ iff $\mathscr{T}(q) \subseteq \mathscr{T}(p)$ and $\mathscr{CT}(q) \subseteq \mathscr{CT}(p)$.

For this refinement relation we will use the following relational embedding where the global state has been augmented with an additional element $\checkmark$, which denotes that the given trace is complete (i.e., no operation is applicable). We will now use a generalised finalisation to record these observations in the manner we discussed in the introduction.

Definition 9.4 (*Completed trace embedding*)
The Z data type (*State*, *Init*, $\{Op_i\}_{i \in I}$) has the following completed trace embedding into the relational model.

> G $==$ $\{*, \checkmark\}$
> State $==$ *State*
> Init $==$ G $\times$ $\{Init \bullet \theta State'\}$
> Op $==$ $\{Op \bullet \theta State \mapsto \theta State'\}$
> Fin $==$ $\{State \bullet \theta State \mapsto *\} \cup \{State \mid (\forall i : I \bullet \neg \operatorname{pre} Op_i) \bullet \theta State \mapsto \checkmark\}$

This embedding is denoted A $\vert_{ctr}$.   □

In a similar way to trace refinement we now define the completed traces of a data type:

Definition 9.5 (*Complete traces of a relational data type*)
The *completed traces* of a Z data type (*State*, *Init*, $\{Op_i\}_{i \in I}$) are all sequences $\langle i_1, \cdots, i_n \rangle$ such that

$$\exists State' \bullet Init \,\overset{\circ}{\scriptstyle 9}\, Op_{i_1} \,\overset{\circ}{\scriptstyle 9}\, \cdots \,\overset{\circ}{\scriptstyle 9}\, Op_{i_n} \wedge \forall i : I \bullet \neg(\operatorname{pre} Op_i)'$$

We denote the complete traces of an ADT A by $\mathscr{C}\mathscr{T}(A)$.   □

This definition allows us to prove the correctness result for this embedding:

Theorem 9.2 *With the completed trace embedding, data refinement corresponds to completed trace preorder. That is,*

$$A \vert_{ctr} \sqsubseteq C \vert_{ctr} \ \textit{iff} \ \mathscr{C}\mathscr{T}(C) \subseteq \mathscr{C}\mathscr{T}(A) \ \textit{and} \ \mathscr{T}(C) \subseteq \mathscr{T}(A)$$

Proof 1. Suppose that $\mathscr{C}\mathscr{T}(C) \subseteq \mathscr{C}\mathscr{T}(A)$ and $\mathscr{T}(C) \subseteq \mathscr{T}(A)$. To show $A \sqsubseteq C$ we need $p_C \subseteq p_A$ for all programs p. Given p, if p is not a trace of C then $p_C = \varnothing$, and thus the inclusion is trivial. Otherwise, either $(*, \checkmark)$ and $(*, *)$ are both in p_C or just $(*, *)$ is in p_C.

If $(*, \checkmark)$ is in p_C then p is a completed trace in C, and thus also in A. Hence $(*, \checkmark)$ is in p_A, and so is $(*, *)$. If just $(*, *)$ is in p_C then p is a trace which is not a completed trace in C. Since $\mathscr{T}(C) \subseteq \mathscr{T}(A)$, p is also a trace in A. Hence $(*, *)$ is in p_A.

2. Suppose $A \sqsubseteq C$. Given $p \in \mathscr{CT}(C)$. Thus $(*, \checkmark) \in p_C \subseteq p_A$, and hence $p \in \mathscr{CT}(A)$. For a similar reason we also get trace inclusion. ☐

We now extract the simulation rules that correspond to this notion of refinement. Given the completed trace embedding in the relational model, only the finalisation is non-trivially altered from the embedding given for the trace embedding. Thus we just have to consider the effect of the finalisation requirement:

Forward simulations: $R \,_9^\circ\, \mathsf{CFin} \subseteq \mathsf{AFin}$ is equivalent to

$$\forall AState; \ CState \bullet R \wedge (\forall i : I \bullet \neg \operatorname{pre} COp_i) \Rightarrow \forall i : I \bullet \neg \operatorname{pre} AOp_i$$

Backward simulations: $\mathsf{CFin} \subseteq \mathsf{T} \,_9^\circ\, \mathsf{AFin}$ is equivalent to T being total and

$$\forall CState \bullet (\forall i : I \bullet \neg \operatorname{pre} COp_i) \Rightarrow \exists AState \bullet T \wedge \forall i : I \bullet \neg \operatorname{pre} AOp_i$$

Pulling this together we have the following conditions for the completed trace embedding.

Definition 9.6 (*Completed trace simulations in Z*)
Given Z data types A and C. The relation R on $AState \wedge CState$ is a *completed trace forward simulation* from A to C if

$$\forall CState' \bullet CInit \Rightarrow \exists AState' \bullet AInit \wedge R'$$
$$\forall i \in I \bullet \forall AState; \ CState; \ CState' \bullet R \wedge COp_i \Rightarrow \exists AState' \bullet R' \wedge AOp_i$$
$$\forall AState; \ CState \bullet R \wedge (\forall i : I \bullet \neg \operatorname{pre} COp_i) \Rightarrow \forall i : I \bullet \neg \operatorname{pre} AOp_i$$

The total relation T on $AState \wedge CState$ is a *completed trace backward simulation* from A to C if

$$\forall AState'; \ CState' \bullet CInit \wedge T' \Rightarrow AInit$$
$$\forall i \in I \bullet \forall AState'; \ CState; \ CState' \bullet$$
$$(COp_i \wedge T') \Rightarrow (\exists AState \bullet T \wedge AOp_i)$$
$$\forall CState \bullet (\forall i : I \bullet \neg \operatorname{pre} COp_i) \Rightarrow \exists AState \bullet T \wedge \forall i : I \bullet \neg \operatorname{pre} AOp_i \qquad \square$$

9.3.3   *Failure Refinement*

Failures refinement was introduced in Sect. 1.5, where the failures semantics recorded both the traces that a process can do, and also sets of actions which it can refuse, that is, actions which are not enabled. These are recorded as failures of a process.

We will discuss this embedding and the relationship between failures refinement and data refinement in more detail in Chap. 10. For the moment we give the general approach without much comment. The embedding we use is the following.

Definition 9.7   (*Failures embedding*)
A Z data type (*State*, *Init*, $\{Op_i\}_{i \in I}$) in the refusals interpretation is embedded in the relational model as follows.

$$G == \mathbb{P}\,I$$
$$\text{State} == State$$
$$\text{Init} == \{Init;\ E : \mathbb{P}\,I \bullet E \mapsto \theta State'\}$$
$$\text{Op} == \{Op \bullet \theta State \mapsto \theta State'\}$$
$$\text{Fin} == \{State;\ E : \mathbb{P}\,I \mid (\forall i \in E \bullet \neg \operatorname{pre} Op_i) \bullet \theta State \mapsto E\}$$

This embedding is denoted $\mathsf{A}\mid_f$.   □

In the relational embedding failures are pairs (tr, X), where tr is a trace ending in state S' such that $\forall i : X \bullet S' \notin \operatorname{dom} \mathsf{Op}_i$. The correctness theorem is the following.

Theorem 9.3   *With the failures embedding, data refinement corresponds to the failures preorder. That is,*

$$\mathsf{A}\mid_f \sqsubseteq \mathsf{C}\mid_f\ \ iff\ \mathscr{F}(C) \subseteq \mathscr{F}(A)$$ □

Given the failures embedding the simulation conditions are the usual conditions on initialisation and operations, extended with conditions derived from finalisation as follows (see subsequent chapter, and note that we are not considering input and output at this stage):

Forward simulations: $\mathsf{R}\,\mathring{\,}\,\mathsf{CFin} \subseteq \mathsf{AFin}$ is equivalent to

$$\forall i : I;\ AState;\ CState \bullet R \wedge \operatorname{pre} AOp_i \Rightarrow \operatorname{pre} COp_i$$

Backward simulations: $\mathsf{CFin} \subseteq \mathsf{T}\,\mathring{\,}\,\mathsf{AFin}$ is equivalent to

$$\forall CState \bullet \exists AState \bullet T \wedge \forall i : I \bullet (\operatorname{pre} AOp_i \Rightarrow \operatorname{pre} COp_i)$$

Using the notation that

$$Ref(State) = \{i : I \mid \neg\, pre\, Op_i\}$$

(i.e., *Ref* denotes the maximal refused set of operations in a given state), we can also write the last condition as

$$\forall\, CState \bullet \exists\, AState \bullet T \wedge Ref(CState) \subseteq Ref(AState)$$

The observant will notice that this backward simulation rule is stronger than the normal applicability condition. We defer discussion of this until Chap. 10.

9.3.4 Failure Trace Refinement

The *failure trace semantics*, see Sect. 1.7, considers refusal sets not only at the end of a trace, but also between each action in a trace. The relational embedding we use is an obvious generalisation of the failures embedding. The observation of refusals at finalisation is retained, but a similar observation is also made before every operation; these observations are collected in a sequence, which is initialised as empty and copied to the global state at finalisation (similar to the standard treatment of outputs in Z, see Sect. 7.2.1).

Definition 9.8 (*Failure trace embedding*)
A Z data type $(State, Init, \{Op_i\}_{i \in I})$ in the failure trace interpretation is embedded in the relational model as follows.

$$G == seq\, \mathbb{P}\, I$$
$$State == seq\, \mathbb{P}\, I \times State$$
$$Init == G \times \{Init \bullet (\langle\,\rangle, \theta State')\}$$
$$Op == \{Op;\ fs : seq\, \mathbb{P}\, I;\ E : \mathbb{P}\, I \mid (\forall i : E \bullet \neg\, pre\, Op_i) \bullet$$
$$(fs, \theta State) \mapsto (fs \frown \langle E \rangle, \theta State')\}$$
$$Fin == \{State;\ fs : seq\, \mathbb{P}\, I;\ E : \mathbb{P}\, I \mid (\forall i : E \bullet \neg\, pre\, Op_i) \bullet$$
$$(fs, \theta State) \mapsto fs \frown \langle E \rangle\}$$

The embedding is denoted $\mathsf{A}\mid_{ft}$.   □

In the relational embedding failure traces are the obvious generalisation of failures.

Theorem 9.4 *With the failure traces embedding, data refinement corresponds to the failure traces preorder. That is,* $\mathsf{A}\mid_{ft} \sqsubseteq \mathsf{C}\mid_{ft}$ *iff* $\mathscr{F}\mathscr{T}(C) \subseteq \mathscr{F}\mathscr{T}(A)$.   □

In the failure trace embedding, both the correctness and finalisation conditions are potentially amended due to the record of failures at each operation step; initialisation conditions are unchanged from the trace simulations. The extended retrieve relation will necessarily relate only identical sequences of previous observations. The derivations of simulation conditions are very similar to those for failures refinement.

Forward simulations: The finalisation condition here leads to the traditional "applicability" condition for operations, namely

$$\forall \, AState; \; CState; \; i : I \bullet (R \land \operatorname{pre} AOp_i) \Rightarrow \operatorname{pre} COp_i$$

The correctness condition $R \,\S\, COp_i \subseteq AOp_i \,\S\, R$ expands to the following

$$\forall \, i : I; \; AState; \; CState; \; CState' \bullet \forall E \bullet \\ R \land COp_i \land Fcond(E, \theta CState) \Rightarrow \\ \exists \, AState' \bullet R' \land AOp_i \land Fcond(E, \theta AState)$$

where $Fcond(E, s) == \forall i : E \bullet \neg \exists Op_i \bullet s = \theta State$. However, taking the finalisation condition into account, this simplifies to the standard correctness condition:

$$\forall \, i : I; \; AState; \; CState; \; CState' \bullet \\ R \land COp_i \Rightarrow \exists \, AState' \bullet R' \land AOp_i$$

Backward simulations: The finalisation condition here expands to the stronger "applicability" condition also known from failures refinement:

$$\forall \, CState \bullet \exists \, AState \bullet T \land Ref(CState) \subseteq Ref(AState)$$

The correctness condition for operations $COp_i \,\S\, T \subseteq T \,\S\, AOp_i$ expands to

$$\forall \, i : I; \; AState'; \; CState; \; CState' \bullet \\ (COp_i \land T') \Rightarrow \exists \, AState \bullet T \land AOp_i \land Ref(CState) \subseteq Ref(AState)$$

which does not imply the finalisation condition (e.g. it does not insist on an abstract state linked via T to a concrete state in which no operation COp_i is possible).

9.3.5   Extension and Conformance

In Chap. 1 we also discussed two refinement relations, *conformance* and *extension*, which were motivated by work on the process algebra LOTOS. These relations are denoted by *conf* and *ext* respectively, where $p \sqsubseteq_{conf} q$ whenever q deadlocks less often than p in any environment whose traces are limited to those of p; and $p \sqsubseteq_{ext} q$ whenever q has at least the same traces as p, but in an environment whose traces are limited to those of p, it deadlocks less often.

We will define an embedding below such that data refinement induces extension. However, note that this is not possible for conformance. This is because conformance is not a preorder, whereas we know that data refinement is a preorder. Thus no embedding as a data refinement theory will produce a model equivalent to it.

Hence we will have to restrict ourselves here to extension, and the relational embedding we use is just the totalisation over the space of partial relations that is the standard *non-blocking* model (as defined above).

Definition 9.9 (*Extension embedding*)
A Z data type (*State*, *Init*, $\{Op_i\}_{i \in I}$) in the extension interpretation is embedded in the relational model as follows.

$$
\begin{aligned}
&\mathsf{G} == \mathbb{P}\,I \cup \{\bot\} \\
&\mathsf{State} == State \cup \{\bot\} \\
&\mathsf{Init} == \mathsf{G} \times \{Init \bullet \theta State'\} \\
&\mathsf{Op} == \mathsf{OpB} \cup \{\mathsf{x}, \mathsf{y} : \mathsf{State} \mid \mathsf{x} \notin \mathrm{dom}\,\mathsf{OpB} \bullet (\mathsf{x}, \mathsf{y})\} \\
&\text{where } \mathsf{OpB} == \{Op \bullet \theta State \mapsto \theta State'\} \\
&\mathsf{Fin} == \{State;\ E : \mathbb{P}\,I \mid (\forall\,i : E \bullet \neg\,\mathrm{pre}\,Op_i) \bullet \theta State \mapsto E\} \cup \{\bot\} \times \mathsf{G}
\end{aligned}
$$

This embedding is denoted $\mathsf{A}\,|_{ext}$. □

Theorem 9.5 *With the extension embedding, data refinement corresponds to the extension preorder. That is,*

$$
\begin{aligned}
\mathsf{A}\,|_{ext} &\sqsubseteq \mathsf{C}\,|_{ext} \quad \textit{iff} \\
&\mathscr{T}(A) \subseteq \mathscr{T}(C)\ \textit{and} \\
&\forall\,\sigma \in \mathscr{T}(A);\ X \subseteq Act \bullet C\ \textbf{after}\ \sigma\ \textbf{ref}\ X\ \textit{implies}\ A\ \textbf{after}\ \sigma\ \textbf{ref}\ X
\end{aligned}
$$

Proof 1. Suppose that $\mathscr{T}(A) \subseteq \mathscr{T}(C)$ and
$\forall\,\sigma \in \mathscr{T}(A);\ X \subseteq Act \bullet C\ \textbf{after}\ \sigma\ \textbf{ref}\ X$ implies $A\ \textbf{after}\ \sigma\ \textbf{ref}\ X$.

Consider a trace p. If $p \notin \mathscr{T}(A)$ then the embedding (through the totalisation) ensures that $p_A = \mathsf{G} \times \mathsf{G}$ and thus $p_C \subseteq p_A$ trivially holds. If $p \in \mathscr{T}(A)$ then by assumption also $p \in \mathscr{T}(C)$. Now although p is a trace in C, it is still possible that $p_C = \mathsf{G} \times \mathsf{G}$. In this case, p is "blocked along the way" in C, i.e., there is an action a and strings p' and p'' such that $p = p'ap''$ and $C\ \textbf{after}\ p'\ \textbf{ref}\ \{a\}$. Then refusal inclusion ensures that $A\ \textbf{after}\ p'\ \textbf{ref}\ \{a\}$ and the embedding ensures that $p_A = \mathsf{G} \times \mathsf{G}$, thus $p_C \subseteq p_A$. When $p_C \neq \mathsf{G} \times \mathsf{G}$, all observations made record genuine refusals, and $(g, X) \in p_C$ implies $C\ \textbf{after}\ p\ \textbf{ref}\ X$, by assumption then also $A\ \textbf{after}\ p\ \textbf{ref}\ X$ and thus $(g, X) \in p_A$ and $p_C \subseteq p_A$.

2. Suppose $A \sqsubseteq C$. Then trace inclusion can be proved by induction over the length of the trace, and refusals subsetting follows as a consequence of using the non-blocking totalisation. $\square$

The use of the non-blocking totalisation for modelling extension means we can easily extract the simulation conditions as follows:

Definition 9.10 (*Extension forward simulation in Z*)
Given Z data types A and C. The relation R on $AState \wedge CState$ is a *extension forward simulation* from A to C if

$$\forall CState' \bullet CInit \Rightarrow \exists AState' \bullet AInit \wedge R'$$
$$\forall i : I;\ AState;\ CState \bullet \operatorname{pre} AOp_i \wedge R \Rightarrow \operatorname{pre} COp_i$$
$$\forall i : I;\ AState;\ CState;\ CState' \bullet \operatorname{pre} AOp_i \wedge R \wedge COp_i$$
$$\Rightarrow \exists AState' \bullet R' \wedge AOp_i \qquad \square$$

Definition 9.11 (*Extension backward simulation in Z*)
Given Z data types $A\ C$. The total relation T on $AState \wedge CState$ is an *extension backward simulation* from A to C if

$$\forall AState';\ CState' \bullet CInit \wedge T' \Rightarrow AInit$$
$$\forall CState \bullet \exists AState \bullet \forall i : I \bullet T \wedge (\operatorname{pre} AOp_i \Rightarrow \operatorname{pre} COp_i)$$
$$\forall i : I;\ AState';\ CState;\ CState' \bullet$$
$$(COp_i \wedge T') \Rightarrow (\exists AState \bullet T \wedge (\operatorname{pre} AOp_i \Rightarrow AOp_i)) \quad \square$$

9.4   Relating Data Refinement to Process Algebraic Refinement

The previous section has shown how to embed observations into a relational model to define simulation rules for various process algebraic refinement relations. We know, therefore, which simulation rules correspond to, for example, trace or failures refinement.

The other obvious question is the dual to this: if we start with relational data refinement, and the standard simulation rules, what process algebraic refinement does this induce? In this section we survey answers to this question.

As an overview of the results the following table summarises the known correspondences. For completeness we give the reference to where these results were first defined.

Relational refinement	Process model	Citation
Non-blocking data refinement	traces-divergences	[2]
Blocking data refinement with deterministic outputs	singleton failures	[3, 4]
Blocking data refinement	singleton failures of process and input process	[3, 4]
Blocking data refinement with strengthened applicability but no input/output	failures	[5]
Blocking data refinement with extended finalisations	failures-divergences	[1, 6]
Non-blocking data refinement with extended finalisations but no input/output	failures-divergences	[1, 6]

The immediate point to note is that somewhat surprisingly neither non-blocking or blocking data refinement correspond to traces, failures or failure-divergences refinement. One might have thought that the 'natural' refinement relations in the two semantic models would correspond to each other. This table shows that this is not true - and, of course, this is due to the slightly different types of observation made in each model.

In the table, *strengthened applicability* refers to the additional condition in a backward simulation discussed in Sect. 9.3.3 above. And *extended finalisations* refer to the additional refusal embedding needed to recover failure-divergences refinement and discussed in depth in Chap. 10.

The two additional semantics models for CSP not previously introduced but referenced above are the *traces-divergences semantics* and the *singleton failures semantics* - the latter only arising in discussions relating notions of refinement.

Traces-divergences semantics The traces-divergences semantics is just the failures-divergences semantics with the refusal information removed. A process P is now modelled by (A, T, D), where T are the traces of P. It is obtained from the failures-divergences semantics by defining the traces as $T(P) == \{tr \mid (tr, \varnothing) \in F(P)\}$.

The traces-divergences semantics induces a refinement ordering, where $P \sqsubseteq_{td} Q$ iff $T(Q) \subseteq T(P)$ and $D(Q) \subseteq D(P)$.

Singleton failures semantics The singleton failures semantics for CSP was introduced solely in order to define an appropriate correspondence with blocking data refinement. Essentially the singleton failures semantics is a failures semantics where the refusal sets have cardinality at most one. Specifically, a process is now modelled by (A, S) where $S \subseteq A^* \times \mathbb{P}_1 A$ (and $\mathbb{P}_1$ forms subsets of cardinality at most one).

If P is a process expressed in terms of *stop*, $\rightarrow$, $\sqcap$, $\square$ and $\parallel$, then its singleton failures are given as the obvious projection from its failures, that is:

$$S(P) = F(P) \cap (A^* \times \mathbb{P}_1 A)$$

This does not hold for processes containing hiding.

The singleton failures semantics induces a refinement ordering, where $P \sqsubseteq_{singf} Q$ iff $S(Q) \subseteq S(P)$.

Clearly, failures-divergences refinement is stronger than traces-divergences refinement, that is, $P \sqsubseteq_{fd} Q \Rightarrow P \sqsubseteq_{td} Q$. For divergence-free processes we have $P \sqsubseteq_{singf} Q \Rightarrow P \sqsubseteq_{td} Q$, and for divergence-free basic processes (i.e., ones expressed in terms of $stop$, $\rightarrow$, $\sqcap$, $\square$ and $\parallel$) we have $P \sqsubseteq_{fd} Q \Rightarrow P \sqsubseteq_{singf} Q$.

The methodology for showing the correspondences in the first three lines of the table above is, by nature, different from that used so far. It has to be different because until now we have been altering the standard data refinement rules to meet the requirements in various process algebraic refinement relations. Now, we want to fix on the standard data refinement definition and understand which process algebraic refinement relation it corresponds to.

The usual methodology to do this is to define some sort of *corresponding process* in CSP for an abstract data type. We illustrate this briefly in the following two subsections.

9.4.1 Non-blocking Data Refinement and the Traces-Divergences Semantics

We take as our starting point ADTs that (could have) resulted from embedding Z datatypes, i.e. with input and output sequences included in local and global state and the usual "plumbing" on these components of the state, as given in Sect. 7.2.1.

To prove the equivalence between non-blocking data refinement and traces-divergences refinement, relational ADTs are translated into CSP directly such that, for an ADT A, the corresponding CSP process $process(A)$ is given by

$$process(A) == \sqcap s \in State, (\exists is \bullet (is, \langle \rangle, s) \in \operatorname{ran} Init) \bullet Proc_A(s)$$

$Proc_A(s) ==$
  $\square i \in I, in \in Input, (\langle in \rangle, \langle \rangle, s) \in \operatorname{dom} AOp_i \bullet$
    $\sqcap s' \in State, out \in Output,$
      $(\langle in \rangle, \langle \rangle, s) \mapsto (\langle \rangle, \langle out \rangle, s') \in AOp_i \bullet AOp_i.in.out \rightarrow Proc_A(s')$
  $\square$
  $\square i \in I, in \in Input, (\langle in \rangle, \langle \rangle, s) \notin \operatorname{dom} AOp_i \bullet$
    $\sqcap out \in Output \bullet AOp_i.in.out \rightarrow div$

Note that here 'div' is the divergent CSP process, which ensures that all events are possible after an operation has been called outside its precondition. The following can then be proved:

Theorem 9.6

In the non-blocking model, $A \sqsubseteq_{data} C$ if and only if $process(A) \sqsubseteq_{td} process(C)$. $\square$

9.4.2 Blocking Data Refinement and the Singleton Failures Semantics

Blocking data refinement has a less natural correspondence than non-blocking data refinement - less natural in the sense that it does not correspond to a process semantics that arises naturally in CSP or other process algebra. For the blocking model, the translation of an ADT A into a CSP process $process_b(A)$ is given by the following:

$$process_b(A) == \sqcap s \in State, (\exists is \bullet (is, \langle \rangle, s) \in ran\, Init) \bullet P_A(s)$$

$$
\begin{aligned}
P_A(s) == \\
&\square i \in I, in \in Input, (\langle in \rangle, \langle \rangle, s) \in dom\, AOp_i \bullet \\
&\quad \sqcap s' \in State, out \in Output, \\
&\qquad (\langle in \rangle, \langle \rangle, s) \mapsto (\langle \rangle, \langle out \rangle, s') \in AOp_i \bullet AOp_i.in.out \to P_A(s')
\end{aligned}
$$

As can be seen the enabling of this process is identical to that used in the non-blocking case. However, the effect of calling an operation outside its precondition is not now divergence but, since we are in the blocking model, simply inability to perform any event associated with that operation. This thus correctly reflects the intended meaning to the blocking model and with it data refinement corresponds to singleton failures refinement in the process model.

The inclusion of non-deterministic outputs complicates the process semantics needed, and an additional constraint is needed in order to characterise blocking data refinement. To do this a further partial translation is introduced, called *inputProcess* which provides a characterisation of when a particular input is in the domain. For the blocking model this is defined as:

$$inputProcess_b(A) == \sqcap s \in State, (*, s) \in Init \bullet P_A(s)$$

$$
\begin{aligned}
P_A(s) == \\
&\square i \in I, in \in Input, (\langle in \rangle, \langle \rangle, s) \in dom\, AOp_i \bullet \\
&\quad \sqcap s' \in State \mid (\exists out \in Output \mid (\langle in \rangle, \langle \rangle, s) \mapsto (\langle \rangle, \langle out \rangle, s') \in AOp_i) \bullet \\
&\qquad AOp_i.in \to P_A(s')
\end{aligned}
$$

As can be seen, this is the same as *process_b* except that the outputs are unobservable. We then get the following result:

Theorem 9.7

In the blocking model, $A \sqsubseteq_{data} C$ if and only if $process_b(A) \sqsubseteq_{singf} process_b(C)$ and $inputProcess_b(A) \sqsubseteq_{singf} inputProcess_b(C)$. For ADTs with deterministic outputs (or no input/output), this reduces to checking $process_b(A) \sqsubseteq_{singf} process_b(C)$. □

However, it is worth noting that the equivalence given in Theorem 9.7 only holds if the relational semantics includes a way of observing the exact point of deadlock, e.g., by producing trivial outputs, and preserving and counting those after deadlock.

Specifically, there is a key difference between two ways of producing a totalisation in the presence of outputs, in particular between $(State \times seq\ Output)_\bot$ and $(State_\bot \times seq\ Output)$. If you have the latter, you increase your observations in the relational world: you can observe how many outputs were produced before the state devolved to $\bot$. Having such an observation allows you to distinguish between, say, a trace $\langle a, b, c \rangle$ having blocked on b or on c. The standard relational treatment of e.g. Z specifications embeds outputs first, and then totalises the relation, so it doesn't allow this. In that model we can observe the outputs produced by any prefix of $\langle a, b, c \rangle$ that doesn't yet block, but they don't contain the additional information of whether blocking immediately after that was an option, if this prefix already allowed blocking.

9.5 Relating Automata and Relational Refinement

In Chap. 2 we discussed automata as an alternative semantic model for refinement, and in fact first introduced simulations in that context. A relational embedding can determine the exact correspondence between the use of simulations in automata and their relational counterpart.

Remember that an automaton was defined (see Definition 2.1) as a tuple $A = (States, Act, T, Start)$ where $States$ is a non-empty set of states, $Start \subseteq States$ is the set of initial states, Act is a set of actions which includes a special element τ, and $\longrightarrow \subseteq States \times Act \times States$ is a transition relation. The components of A are accessed as $states(A) = States$ and $start(A) = Start$.

With this definition, the most natural relational embedding of an automaton to use is the following.

Definition 9.12 (*Automata embedding*)
An automaton $A = (states(A), Act, \longrightarrow, start(A))$ has the following embedding into the relational model.

$$G == \{*\}$$
$$State == states(A)$$
$$Init == \{s : start(A) \bullet * \mapsto s\}$$
$$Op_i == \{s, s' : states(A) \mid s \xrightarrow{i} s' \bullet s \mapsto s'\}$$
$$Fin == \{s : states(A) \bullet s \mapsto *\}$$ □

Thus the automata embedding in Definition 9.12 is equivalent to the trace embedding. Furthermore, the automata simulations are equivalent to the trace simulations, so with this embedding relational data refinement is trace inclusion. A more interesting model is that offered by IO-automata, and we discuss this now.

9.5.1   IO Automata

IO automata are a class of automata that distinguish explicitly between the input and output of a system, and thus share characteristics with both standard automata and state-based languages such as Z and B. In such a model the set of actions is partitioned into input and output actions. A particular computational interpretation is taken, viz: output actions are actions initiated by the system, while input actions are under the control of the environment. A system can never refuse to perform its input actions, and its output actions can never be blocked by the environment.

Definition 9.13 (*Partitioned automaton; IO automata*)
A *partitioned automaton* is a LTS where the set of actions *Act* is partitioned into input actions L_I and output actions L_U ($L_I \cup L_U = Act$, $L_I \cap L_U = \varnothing$). An *IO automaton* p is a partitioned automaton for which all input actions are always enabled in any state. That is, for all states p:

$$\forall a \in L_I \bullet p \xrightarrow{a}$$

The class of IO automata with input and output actions L_I and L_U is denoted $IOTS(L_I, L_U)$.   □

Example 9.2 Four IO automata are given in Fig. 9.1 where they model a sweet dispensing machine for chocolate and liquorice, where $L_I = \{but\}$, $L_U = \{liq, choc\}$.

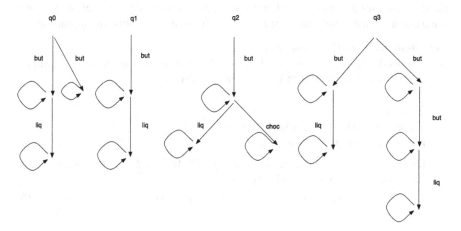

Fig. 9.1 Four IO automata

Input actions are always enabled, but may have no effect in a particular state; where this occurs it is denoted graphically with a self-loop without explicit label.   □

The input-output refinement relation, $\sqsubseteq_{iot}$ is defined via the notion of weakly quiescent traces, which are traces after which outputs are not immediately possible.

Definition 9.14 (*Weakly quiescent traces, IOTS refinement preorder*)
The weakly quiescent traces of a partitioned LTS A are denoted by $\delta\text{--}traces(A)$, and consist of all the traces $\sigma \in Act^*$ such that A **after** σ **ref** L_U. The IOTS refinement preorder is defined for IOTSs A and C by:

$$A \sqsubseteq_{iot} C \text{ iff } traces(C) \subseteq traces(A) \text{ and } \delta\text{--}traces(C) \subseteq \delta\text{--}traces(A) \qquad \square$$

Example 9.3 The following hold between the systems introduced above: $q_0 \sqsubseteq_{iot} q_1$ but $q_1 \not\sqsubseteq_{iot} q_0$, $q_2 \sqsubseteq_{iot} q_1$, $q_3 \sqsubseteq_{iot} q_1$, but $q_1, q_3 \not\sqsubseteq_{iot} q_2$ and $q_1, q_2 \not\sqsubseteq_{iot} q_3$.   □

The IOTS preorder can be defined for arbitrary partitioned LTSs, in which case it is usual to interpret these as under-specified IOTSs, where some input actions are not specified in some states. One might define an alternate relation, $\sqsubseteq_{ioconf}$, specifically for partitioned LTSs. Another approach is to give a *demonic semantics* for process expressions. In this semantics a transition is added for each non-specified input, and after this transition any behaviour is possible. We will follow the latter approach here. We give a relational characterisation of $\sqsubseteq_{iot}$, and in doing so derive simulation rules for it. To do this we will use the partial relational framework, but with some elements of totalisation used to deal with the demonic process semantics.

To define $\sqsubseteq_{iot}$ between arbitrary partitioned LTSs, we define $A \sqsubseteq_{iot} C$ iff $\widehat{A} \sqsubseteq \widehat{C}$, where $\widehat{A}$ is an appropriate relational embedding – i.e., rather than explicitly constructing the IOTS representing its demonic semantics, we give its relational version directly. This relational embedding needs to totalise operations in L_I to represent the fact that they are always enabled, and include a modification of L_U to represent the fact that after an unspecified input any behaviour is possible, and an appropriate finalisation to ensure subsetting of $\delta - traces$. We make the following definition.

Definition 9.15 (*IOTS embedding*)
A partitioned LTS $L = (States, L_I, L_U, \longrightarrow, Start)$ is embedded into the relational model as $\widehat{L} = (\mathsf{State}, \mathsf{Init}, \{\widehat{\mathsf{Op}}_i\}_{i \in L_I \cup L_U}, \mathsf{Fin})$, where

$\mathsf{G} == \{*, \delta\}$
$\mathsf{State} == States \cup \{\bot\}$, where $\bot \notin States$
$\mathsf{Init} == \{g : \mathsf{G}; \ s : Start \bullet g \mapsto s\}$
$\widehat{\mathsf{Op}}_i == \xrightarrow{i} \cup \{\bot \mapsto \bot\} \cup \{x : States, y : \mathsf{State} \mid i \in L_I \wedge x \xcancel{\xrightarrow{i}} \bullet x \mapsto y\}$
$\mathsf{Fin} == \{x : \mathsf{State} \bullet x \mapsto *\} \cup \{(\bot, \delta)\}$
$\qquad \cup \{x : States \mid (\forall i \in L_U \bullet x \xcancel{\xrightarrow{i}}) \bullet x \mapsto \delta\}$ □

Theorem 9.8 *With the IOTS embedding, data refinement corresponds to the IOTS preorder. That is, let $\widetilde{A}$ denote the IOTS obtained by giving the partitioned LTS A a demonic semantics, then*

$$\widehat{A} \sqsubseteq \widehat{C} \text{ iff } traces(\widetilde{C}) \subseteq traces(\widetilde{A}) \text{ and } \delta\text{-}traces(\widetilde{C}) \subseteq \delta\text{-}traces(\widetilde{A}) \qquad \square$$

We now extract the simulation rules that correspond to this notion of refinement. We have embedded an IOTS into a partial relational model, but one augmented with both refusals and a distinguished element, $\bot$. We will extract the underlying conditions in the usual fashion, however, one will obtain different conditions depending on whether an operation is in L_I or L_U.

First, the forward initialisation condition, which under the totalisation adds no extra constraints beyond normal. Second, if $i \in L_U$, then $\widehat{\mathsf{Op}}_i == \mathsf{Op}_i \cup \{(\bot, \bot)\}$, so that

$$\widehat{\mathsf{R}} \,\overset{\circ}{\circ}\, \widehat{\mathsf{COp}}_i \subseteq \widehat{\mathsf{AOp}}_i \,\overset{\circ}{\circ}\, \widehat{\mathsf{R}} \quad \text{iff} \quad \mathsf{R} \,\overset{\circ}{\circ}\, \mathsf{COp}_i \subseteq \mathsf{AOp}_i \,\overset{\circ}{\circ}\, \mathsf{R}$$

Third, if $i \in L_I$, then $\widehat{\mathsf{Op}}_i$ is the non-blocking totalisation over *states* $\cup \{\bot\}$, thus

$$\widehat{\mathsf{R}} \,\overset{\circ}{\circ}\, \widehat{\mathsf{COp}}_i \subseteq \widehat{\mathsf{AOp}}_i \,\overset{\circ}{\circ}\, \widehat{\mathsf{R}} \quad \text{iff} \quad \begin{array}{l} (\mathrm{dom}\,\mathsf{AOp}_i \lhd \mathsf{R}) \,\overset{\circ}{\circ}\, \mathsf{COp}_i \subseteq \mathsf{AOp}_i \,\overset{\circ}{\circ}\, \mathsf{R} \quad \text{and} \\ \mathrm{ran}\,(\mathrm{dom}\,\mathsf{AOp}_i \lhd \mathsf{R}) \subseteq \mathrm{dom}\,\mathsf{COp}_i \end{array}$$

Note, that for an IOTS (as opposed to an arbitrary partitioned LTS), input actions are always enabled, and thus in that case this correctness condition reduces to $\mathsf{R} \,\overset{\circ}{\circ}\, \mathsf{COp}_i \subseteq \mathsf{AOp}_i \,\overset{\circ}{\circ}\, \mathsf{R}$ for L_I.

Finally, the finalisation condition adds in the condition to check for refusals as needed for δ-*trace* inclusion. So $\widehat{\mathsf{R}} \,\overset{\circ}{\circ}\, \mathsf{CFin} \subseteq \mathsf{AFin}$ will become

$$\forall R \bullet (\forall i \in L_U \bullet \neg \operatorname{pre} COp_i) \Rightarrow (\forall i \in L_U \bullet \neg \operatorname{pre} AOp_i)$$

That is, if states are linked by the retrieve relation and C refuses output actions, then so must A.

For backward simulations, we use a similar line of reasoning to find that one requires the standard initialisation, blocking correctness for output actions, non-blocking applicability and correctness for input actions together with the refusal condition

$$\forall CState \bullet (\forall i \in L_U \bullet \neg \operatorname{pre} COp_i) \Rightarrow \exists AState \bullet T \wedge (\forall i \in L_U \bullet \neg \operatorname{pre} AOp_i)$$

which can be combined with the usual totality of backward simulation to give

$$\forall\, CState \bullet \exists\, AState \bullet T \wedge ((\forall\, i \in L_U \bullet \neg\, \mathrm{pre}\, COp_i) \Rightarrow (\forall\, i \in L_U \bullet \neg\, \mathrm{pre}\, AOp_i))$$

These are summarised in the following definition.

Definition 9.16 (*IOTS simulations in Z*)
Given Z data types A and C, both representing partitioned LTSs, $J = L_I \cup L_U$.
The relation R on $AState \wedge CState$ is an *IOTS forward simulation* from A to C
if

$\forall\, CState' \bullet CInit \Rightarrow \exists\, AState' \bullet AInit \wedge R'$
$\forall\, i : L_U;\ AState;\ CState;\ CState' \bullet R \wedge COp_i \Rightarrow \exists\, AState' \bullet R' \wedge AOp_i$
$\forall\, i : L_I;\ AState;\ CState \bullet \mathrm{pre}\, AOp_i \wedge R \Rightarrow \mathrm{pre}\, COp_i$
$\forall\, i : L_I;\ AState;\ CState;\ CState' \bullet \mathrm{pre}\, AOp_i \wedge R \wedge COp_i$
$\qquad\qquad\qquad\qquad\qquad\qquad\qquad \Rightarrow \exists\, AState' \bullet R' \wedge AOp_i$
$\forall\, R \bullet (\forall\, i : L_U \bullet \neg\, \mathrm{pre}\, COp_i) \Rightarrow (\forall\, i : L_U \bullet \neg\, \mathrm{pre}\, AOp_i)$

The relation T on $AState \wedge CState$ is an *IOTS backward simulation* from A to
C if

$\forall\, AState';\ CState' \bullet CInit \wedge T' \Rightarrow AInit$
$\forall\, i : L_U;\ AState';\ CState;\ CState' \bullet (COp_i \wedge T') \Rightarrow (\exists\, AState \bullet T \wedge AOp_i)$
$\forall\, i : L_I;\ CState \bullet \exists\, AState \bullet T \wedge (\mathrm{pre}\, AOp_i \Rightarrow \mathrm{pre}\, COp_i)$
$\forall\, i : L_I;\ AState';\ CState;\ CState' \bullet$
$\qquad\qquad (COp_i \wedge T') \Rightarrow (\exists\, AState \bullet T \wedge (\mathrm{pre}\, AOp_i \Rightarrow AOp_i))$
$\forall\, CState \bullet \exists\, AState \bullet T \wedge ((\forall\, i : L_U \bullet \neg\, \mathrm{pre}\, COp_i) \Rightarrow (\forall\, i : L_U \bullet \neg\, \mathrm{pre}\, AOp_i))$

$\qquad\qquad\qquad\qquad\qquad\qquad\qquad\qquad\qquad\qquad\qquad\qquad\qquad\quad \square$

So far we have used a totalisation to define $\sqsubseteq_{iot}$ between an LTS and an IOTS,
specifically using a *demonic* process semantics discussed. An alternative view of
under-specified input actions is that the under-specification represents an implicit
skip. Such an interpretation is called an *angelic* process semantics. The relational
embedding of such a semantics only alters the input action component from the one
we defined above. Thus, when deriving simulation conditions for such an embedding,
the initialisation, refusal conditions and correctness for output actions remain the
same.

For input actions, they are embedded as $\widehat{\mathsf{Op_i}} == \mathsf{Op_i} \cup \{(\textit{state}, \textit{state}) \mid \textit{state} \overset{i}{\not\longrightarrow} \}$ and the forward simulation condition $\widehat{\mathsf{R}} \, \fatsemi \, \widehat{\mathsf{COp_i}} \subseteq \widehat{\mathsf{AOp_i}} \, \fatsemi \, \widehat{\mathsf{R}}$ evaluates to

$$\mathsf{R} \, \fatsemi \, (\mathsf{COp_i} \cup (\overline{\mathrm{dom}\,\mathsf{COp_i}} \lhd \textit{skip})) \subseteq (\mathsf{AOp_i} \cup (\overline{\mathrm{dom}\,\mathsf{AOp_i}} \lhd \textit{skip})) \, \fatsemi \, \mathsf{R}$$

However, this does not have a particular interesting simplification.

9.6 Internal Events and Divergence

The consideration above has dealt with the basic structure of automata and IO automata, but without internal events or the potential consideration of divergence that they can give rise to. We briefly discuss some of these aspects here, continuing from the general discussion of these topics in Sect. 5.4. There we already discussed how to embed a relational data type with internal operations into a standard one, and noted that internal actions in a context where divergence is ignored can be dealt with by generalising all discussions based on $p \overset{a}{\longrightarrow} q$ to $p \overset{a}{\Longrightarrow} q$, i.e. inserting arbitrary internal behaviour (before and) after every observable event. For example, trace refinement ignoring divergence is defined in that way.

If a refinement relation does not ignore divergence, then the embeddings need to ensure the correct observations are made when the final state records divergence. In the case of catastrophic interpretations (i.e., ones where divergence is propagated to all further behaviours) the embeddings need to generate arbitrary behaviour from the point of divergence onwards, and propagate this into all subsequent operations, comparable to what we did for other catastrophic errors like the non-blocking totalisation and underspecified IOTS.

Where necessary, we record divergence using a special value ω which as usual is assumed not to be included in any local or global state space. For any set S, let $\mathsf{S}_\omega = \mathsf{S} \cup \{\omega\}$.

One of the simplest contexts in which divergence *is* taken into consideration is for trace refinement in the CSP failures-divergences model. Here, we need to make sure that every extension of a strictly divergent trace is recorded as a trace.

Definition 9.17 (*Embedding trace refinement (CSP f-d model)*)
A τ-data type $\mathsf{D} = (\mathsf{State}, \mathsf{Init}, \{\mathsf{Op_k}\}_{k \in I}, \tau, \mathsf{Fin})$ on global state $\mathsf{G} = \{*\}$ is embedded as the data type $\widehat{\mathsf{D}} = (\mathsf{State}_\omega, \widehat{\mathsf{Init}}, \{\widehat{\mathsf{Op_k}}\}_{k \in I}, \widehat{\mathsf{Fin}})$ where

$\widehat{\mathsf{Init}} = \mathsf{Init} \, \fatsemi \, \tau^* \cup \mathbf{if} \text{ divi Init } \mathbf{then} \, \mathsf{G} \times \mathsf{State}_\omega$

$\widehat{\mathsf{Op}} = \mathsf{Op} \, \fatsemi \, \tau^* \cup \mathrm{divOp} \times \mathsf{State}_\omega$

$\widehat{\mathsf{Fin}} = \mathsf{Fin} \cup \{\omega\} \times \mathsf{G}$

$\mathrm{divOp} =_{def} \{s : \mathsf{State} \mid \exists s' : \mathsf{State} \bullet (s, s') \in \mathsf{Op} \wedge s' \uparrow\}$

$\mathrm{divi\,Init} =_{def} \exists s : \mathrm{ran\,Init} \bullet s \uparrow$ □

The derivation of simulation rules leads to the following definition.

Definition 9.18 (*Simulations for trace refinement (CSP f-d mode)*)
A relation R on AState $\wedge$ CState is a forward simulation between τ-data types
A and C iff $\forall k : \mathsf{I}$ we have:

> **if** divi CInit **then** divi AInit **else** CInit $\fatsemi \tau_C^* \subseteq$ AInit $\fatsemi \tau_A^* \fatsemi$ R
>
> R $\fatsemi$ CFin $\subseteq$ AFin
>
> $(\mathrm{divAOp}_k) \lhd \mathsf{R} \fatsemi \mathsf{COp}_k \fatsemi \tau_C^* \subseteq \mathsf{AOp}_k \fatsemi \tau_A^* \fatsemi \mathsf{R}$
>
> $\mathrm{dom}(\mathsf{R} \rhd \mathrm{divCOp}_k) \subseteq \mathrm{divAOp}_k$

A relation T on CState $\wedge$ AState is a backward simulation between τ-data
types A and C iff $\forall k : \mathsf{I}$

> **if** divi CInit **then** divi AInit **else** CInit $\fatsemi \tau_C^* \fatsemi$ T $\subseteq$ AInit $\fatsemi \tau_A^*$
>
> CFin $\subseteq$ T $\fatsemi$ AFin
>
> $\mathrm{dom}(\mathsf{T} \rhd \mathrm{divAOp}_k) \lhd \mathsf{COp}_k \fatsemi \tau_C^* \fatsemi \mathsf{T} \subseteq \mathsf{T} \fatsemi \mathsf{AOp}_k \fatsemi \tau_A^*$
>
> $\mathrm{divCOp}_k \subseteq \mathrm{dom}(\mathsf{T} \rhd \mathrm{divAOp}_k)$ □

9.7   Bibliographical Notes

The last 20 years have seen significant research effort in comparing notions of refinement in different models of specification and computation, particularly motivated by the desire to integrate specification languages that use different paradigms.

Research on combining relational and concurrent refinement concentrated initially on providing joint semantics, and on identifying correspondences between variations of the relational models and concurrency semantics. In the latter category, see e.g. work by Bolton and Davies [3, 4] and Reeves and Streader [7]. The work on relational concurrent refinement started [1, 6] from the idea that the relational *finalisations* can encode the observations embedded in concurrency semantics. The relational simulation rules can then be used to extract simulations for concurrency. These provide a "canned induction" method of verifying concurrent refinement, by checking a fixed number of conditions for each possible action, rather than checking inclusion between potentially large sets. We derived simulation rules for failures-divergences refinement [1, 6], including also outputs and internal operations [8], and for readiness refinement [1]. These were mostly based on a relational model that was total.

However, trace refinement and other relations based on the partial relations model were considered in [9], and different interpretations of divergent behaviour in [10].

In all these cases, the refinement notions have been imported from a concurrency context, represented in a relational formalism, and then expressed in terms of Z data types. Thus it provides for an integration of paradigms by allowing specification using Z schemas and sets while adapting a concurrency-style semantics.

The singleton failures semantics for CSP was used by Bolton [11] (and published in [3, 4]) in order to define an appropriate correspondence with blocking data refinement. The relationship of singleton failures to other semantic models is discussed in [12] and later in [13] (which builds on [14]).

The results in the table at the start of Sect. 9.4 are due to Schneider [2], Bolton and Davies [3, 4], and Derrick and Boiten [1, 6]. Reeves and Streader [15] showed that the equivalence given in Theorem 9.7 only holds if the relational semantics includes a way of observing the exact point of deadlock.

For an introduction to the IO automata model, see [16]. For systems without internal evolution, IO automata do not differ from IO transition systems as discussed by Tretmans in [17]. IO transition systems offer the same perspective as the basic automata of [18] in that they include internal evolution in standard ways in their definition of refinement and simulation, and ignore divergence (indeed, only divergence-free systems are considered in [17]). Although internal actions do not alter the standard view of refinement, IO transition systems differ marginally from IO automata even for convergent systems since IO transition systems only require weak input enabling as opposed to the strong input enabling as required in [16].

The definition of $\sqsubseteq_{iot}$ that we use is the same as that given in [19, 20] for IO-automata, which is shown to be equivalent to the quiescent trace preorder of [21]. The use of weakly quiescent traces above differs from the (original) definition of quiescence given in [21], where quiescence requires the absence of both output and internal actions. Tretmans [17] comments that for divergence-free systems the two notions coincide but views the stronger quiescence to be counter-intuitive in the presence of divergence.

The *demonic semantics* for process expressions is defined in [22]. As we discussed above, the alternative view of under-specified input actions is that the under-specification represents an implicit *skip*. Such an interpretation was introduced in [21] and discussed in [22], where it is called the angelic process semantics.

References

1. Derrick J, Boiten EA (2003) Relational concurrent refinement. Form Asp Comput 15(1):182–214
2. Schneider S (2006) Non-blocking data refinement and traces-divergences semantics, personal communication
3. Bolton C, Davies J (2002) Refinement in Object-Z and CSP. In: Butler M, Petre L, Sere K (eds) Integrated formal methods (IFM 2002). Lecture notes in computer science, vol 2335. Springer, Berlin, pp 225–244
4. Bolton C, Davies J (2006) A singleton failures semantics for communicating sequential processes. Form Asp Comput 18(2):181–210
5. Josephs MB (1988) A state-based approach to communicating processes. Distrib Comput 3:9–18
6. Boiten EA, Derrick J (2002) Unifying concurrent and relational refinement. In: Derrick J, Boiten EA, von Wright J, Woodcock JCP (eds) ENTCS. Proceedings REFINE'02, vol 70
7. Reeves S, Streader D (2008) Data refinement and singleton failures refinement are not equivalent. Form Asp Comput 20(3):295–301
8. Boiten EA, Derrick J, Schellhorn G (2009) Relational concurrent refinement II: internal operations and outputs. Form Asp Comput 21(1–2):65–102
9. Derrick J, Boiten EA (2008) More relational refinement: traces and partial relations. Electron Notes Theor Comput Sci 214:255–276 (Proceedings of REFINE, Turku, 2008)
10. Boiten EA, Derrick J (2009) Modelling divergence in relational concurrent refinement. In: Leuschel M, Wehrheim H (eds) IFM 2009: Integrated formal methods. Lecture notes in computer science, vol 5423. Springer, Berlin, pp 183–199
11. Bolton C (2002) On the refinement of state-based and event-based models. PhD thesis, University of Oxford
12. van Glabbeek RJ (2001) The linear time - branching time spectrum I. The semantics of concrete sequential processes. In: Bergstra JA, Ponse A, Smolka SA (eds) Handbook of process algebra. Amsterdam, North-Holland, pp 3–99
13. Bolton C, Lowe G (2005) A hierarchy of failures-based models: theory and application. Theor Comput Sci 330(3):407–438
14. Bolton C, Lowe G (2003) A hierarchy of failures-based models. In: Corradini F, Westmann U (eds) Proceedings of express 2003: 10th international workshop on expressiveness in concurrency. Elsevier Science Publishers, Amsterdam
15. Reeves S, Streader D (2006) State- and event-based refinement. Technical report, University of Waikato, Department of computer science, University of Waikato, New Zealand
16. Lynch N, Tuttle M (1989) An introduction to input/output automata. CWI Q 2(3):219–246
17. Tretmans J (1996) Test generation with inputs, outputs, and quiescence. In: Margaria T, Steffen B (eds) Second international workshop on tools and algorithms for the construction and analysis of systems (TACAS'96). Lecture notes in computer science, vol 1055. Springer, Berlin, pp 127–146
18. Lynch N, Vaandrager FW (1995) Forward and backward simulations I: untimed systems. Inf Comput 121(2):214–233
19. Segala R (1997) Quiescence, fairness, testing, and the notion of implementation. Inf Comput 138(2):194–210
20. Segala R (1993) Quiescence, fairness, testing, and the notion of implementation (extended abstract). In: International conference on concurrency theory, pp 324–338

21. Vaandrager FW (1991) On the relationship between process algebra and input/output automata. Logic in computer science, pp 387–398
22. de Nicola R, Segala R (1995) A process algebraic view of I/O automata. Theor Comput Sci 138:391–423

Chapter 10
Relating Data Refinement and Failures-Divergences Refinement

10.1 Introduction

Chapter 9 discussed the general approach to relating process refinement and relational refinement by developing a relational framework general enough that we could embed some of the refinement relations we discussed in Chap. 1. This included a brief discussion of the simulation rules that arise in the context of failures refinement (see Sect. 9.3.3). In this chapter we consider failures refinement in more depth, and in particular start to discuss the role that inputs and outputs have in a relational framework and how they correspond to aspects of divergence and refusals.

10.2 The Basic Relational Embedding

Let us begin by considering the failures embedding first given in Sect. 9.3.3. Specifically, there we took the initialisation and finalisation to be

$$\mathsf{Fin} == \{State;\ E : \mathbb{P}\,I \mid (\forall\, i \in E \bullet \neg\, \mathsf{pre}\, Op_i) \bullet \theta State \mapsto E\}$$

and

$$\mathsf{Init} == \{Init;\ E : \mathbb{P}\,I \bullet E \mapsto \theta State'\}.$$

The local state and embedding of operations were unchanged from the embedding for standard data refinement. Notice that although the initialisation is altered it is purely to cope with a different global state. This does not affect the initialisation condition in the simulation rules. So the change to the finalisation is the only substantive alteration.

As we saw in each case we looked at in Chap. 9, when we generalise the finalisation, the simulation obligation on finalisation is not always satisfied by construction.

This is in contrast to the standard simulations. Remember that for forward simulations this was the condition that:

$$R \,\raisebox{0.1em}{$\scriptstyle 9$}\, CFin \subseteq AFin$$

However, letting $Ref(State) = \{i : I \mid \neg \operatorname{pre} Op_i\}$ upon expanding we find that

$$R \,\raisebox{0.1em}{$\scriptstyle 9$}\, CFin \subseteq AFin$$

$$\equiv$$

$$\forall R \bullet Ref(CState) \subseteq Ref(AState)$$

This condition is equivalent to the applicability condition, thus Definition 4.6 still represents the complete definition required.

This is *not* the case for backward simulations. Here, $CFin \subseteq T \,\raisebox{0.1em}{$\scriptstyle 9$}\, AFin$ leads to

$$\forall E : \mathbb{P} I; \; CState \bullet E \subseteq Ref(CState) \Rightarrow \exists AState \bullet (T \wedge E \subseteq Ref(AState))$$

which is equivalent to

$$\forall CState \bullet \exists AState \bullet T \wedge Ref(CState) \subseteq Ref(AState)$$

This is a condition which strengthens the traditional applicability condition, from

$$\forall i : I \bullet \forall CState \bullet \exists AState \bullet T \wedge (\operatorname{pre} AOp_i \Rightarrow \operatorname{pre} COp_i)$$

to

$$\forall CState \bullet \exists AState \bullet \forall i : I \bullet T \wedge (\operatorname{pre} AOp_i \Rightarrow \operatorname{pre} COp_i)$$

The difference between the two can be summarised as follows. The standard backward simulation applicability condition requires that we have to consider pairs of abstract and concrete states for each operation. The finalisation condition, on the other hand, requires that for every abstract state we can find a *single* concrete state such that all the preconditions of the abstract operations imply the preconditions of their concrete counterparts. This is a stronger condition and one that highlights the difference between sequential and concurrent refinement.

Definition 10.1 (*Backward simulation with refusals*)
Let $A = (AState, AInit, \{AOp_i\}_{i \in I})$ and $C = (CState, CInit, \{COp_i\}_{i \in I})$ be Z data types. Then the relation T on $AState \wedge CState$ is a *backward simulation with refusals* from A to C if

$\forall AState'; \; CState' \bullet CInit \wedge T' \Rightarrow AInit$
$\forall CState \bullet \exists AState \bullet T \wedge Ref(CState) \subseteq Ref(AState)$

and for all $i \in I$:

$\forall AState'; \; CState; \; CState' \bullet$
$\quad (\forall AState \bullet T \Rightarrow pre\,AOp_i) \Rightarrow (COp_i \wedge T' \Rightarrow \exists AState \bullet T \wedge AOp_i)$

The above rules assume the non-blocking interpretation of ADTs. In the block-ing interpretation, the rule for correctness becomes

$\forall AState'; \; CState; \; CState' \bullet (COp_i \wedge T') \Rightarrow \exists AState \bullet T \wedge AOp_i$ □

In summary, for *forward* simulation, the finalisation conditions are equivalent to the normal applicability condition. Thus, forward simulation, in the absence of input and output, is unchanged for this refusals embedding. However, for *backward* simulation, these finalisation conditions lead to a condition which strengthens the traditional applicability condition.

Example 10.1 The difference is illustrated in Fig. 10.1. This pictures an abstract and concrete system, in which the concrete system has no operations enabled at its single point but still satisfies the backward simulation conditions when finalisation is not considered.   □

Then, as we discussed in the last chapter, we can show the correspondence between relational and data refinement. Before we do that we need to understand how traces, refusals and divergences can arise in each relational model.

Blocking model: Traces arise from sequences of operations which are defined within their guards. Refusals indicate the impossibility of applying an operation outside its

Fig. 10.1 A backwards simulation which does not satisfy the finalisation condition

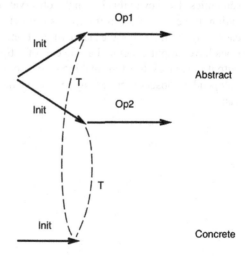

precondition. Furthermore, there are no divergences since each operation is either blocked or gives a well-defined result.

Non-blocking model: We will model the catastrophic error situation of applying an operation where it is not defined as a "divergence", slightly widening the definition of divergence from that given in Chap. 5. As no operation is blocked, every trace is possible: those that arise in the blocking model, and any other ones following divergence. There are no refusals beyond those after a divergence, since before the ADT diverges, no operation is blocked, it either gives a well-defined result or causes divergence. There are now, however, divergences, which arise from applying an operation outside its precondition.

These interpretations define the failures and divergences of an ADT. We can then prove the two central results.

Theorem 10.1 *In the blocking model, relational refinement with extended finalisations corresponds to failures-divergences refinement.*

Proof This is proved using the correspondence between traces and ADT programs that lead to a defined state (i.e., not $\perp_G$); the finalisations at the end of such programs contain the refusals. In this model, there are no divergences.   □

Theorem 10.2 *In the non-blocking model, relational refinement with extended finalisations corresponds to failures-divergences refinement.*

Proof Now ADT programs that lead to $\perp_G$ correspond to divergences rather than refusals. The sets of possible divergences are decreased by relational refinement; traces and well-defined programs are again in correspondence.   □

One observation to note is the following. We have started with the definition of refinement, which is a universal quantification over all traces, but we have obtained from this a semantic characterisation which is known to be more powerful than trace semantics. The key to this lies in the observation that, for *this* finalisation, the observation at the end of a full trace does *not* determine the observations possible after each of its prefixes. For the standard relational embedding (e.g., of Z) their finalisations have output generated at the end of a trace which determine the intermediate output sequences, too, thus making it an essentially sequential semantics. By making independent observations at any prefix, we have essentially made the choice points visible.

10.3 Dealing with Input and Output

Thus far we have considered the relationship between relational refinement of ADTs and failures-divergences refinement for simple ADTs where no input or output was present. We now generalise these results to specifications containing input and output. Crucial to this will, of course, be how we treat input and output in our framework, that is, how we define traces and, in particular, refusals for a system containing input and output.

Section 7.2.1 described the standard approach to deriving the simulation rules in the relational context when dealing with input and output. In this approach the global and local states are augmented with input and output sequences, which the operations affect in particular ways to mimic the effect of input consumption and output production.

One obvious route would be to apply the approach of the last section directly to this model, determining the failures-divergences refinement that then arises. However, when one works through the details of the construction it becomes clear that this approach is deficient.

The problem is that the input and output have an observable nature which is not captured when deriving the corresponding process (and its failures and divergences). In particular, the manipulation of the input and output sequences by an individual operation Op in a program is a key observable property, yet the corresponding process just considers this as a transition Op where only the operation name is visible and not the input and output.

The standard, and obvious, solution here is to describe a state change between $State$ and $State'$ due to an operation Op with input i and output o as a transition $State \xrightarrow{Op.i.o} State'$ due to the event $Op.i.o$. The traces arising from an ADT are then the traces arising from these transitions (cf. Definition 9.2 for the case without input and output).

The refusals and divergences are slightly more complicated. A consequence of including outputs in the events is that the traditional Z precondition, which excludes outputs, does not tell us whether a particular event is possible – only whether an event with *some* output value is possible for a particular input and before-state.

Let us for the moment consider the blocking model only.

What would the refusals need to be under the given interpretation? For a given input i and state $State$, if these lie outside the precondition of an operation Op, then $Op.i.o$ will be refused for all possible outputs o. What if an operation is applied in a state and input inside its precondition, can it ever be refused? If operations may contain a non-deterministic choice of outputs, the answer depends on how the environment reacts with it with respect to synchronisation on outputs. We have two choices:

- the environment cannot influence the output, and there are refusals of "possible" output values due to another output value being chosen, or
- the environment can influence the output, and there are no such refusals.

The first option deals with a situation when the outputs of an operation cannot be constrained by the environment: one can refuse all but one of the possible assignment of values to the outputs corresponding to a particular operation and assignment of values to the inputs. The alternative view is one where the coupling between a system and its environment is tighter and the environment can affect non-determinism in the outputs of operations by choosing a value to synchronise on if one can be found. We call the former a *demonic* choice of outputs, and the latter an *angelic* choice, noting that the former is the more common interpretation.

The refusals one gets differ slightly in each of the models. The refusal set E will also need to include input and output information since whether an operation is refused depends, as we have just seen, on the inputs and outputs. E will thus consist of *events* (in the process algebraic sense) that have been refused, which will be of the form $Op.i.o$ where Op is an operation index, i an input value, and o an output value.

In either case, refusals arise from particular operations not being applicable. In the angelic model, these are the only refusals, thus sets of refusals E in a particular state *State* are characterised by

$$Op.i.o \in E \implies \neg \exists State' \bullet State \xrightarrow{Op.i.o} State'$$

In the demonic case, the process is, in addition, allowed to refuse all but one of the possible outputs. Thus $Op.i.o$ will be in a refusal set E if there is another possible output o_2 $(\neq o)$ which is not in E. Hence the refusals in the demonic model are characterised by:

$$Op.i.o \in E \implies \neg \exists State' \bullet State \xrightarrow{Op.i.o} State'$$
$$\lor$$
$$(\exists State'' \bullet State \xrightarrow{Op.i.o} State'' \land$$
$$(\exists o_2 \neq o;\ State' \bullet State \xrightarrow{Op.i.o_2} State' \land Op.i.o_2 \notin E))$$

Note that there are, again, no divergences.

10.3.1 Defining the Extended Finalisation

The finalisation now has to take into account input and output information so it will take the following shape, for sets E whose elements are of the form $Op.i.o$:

$$\{State;\ is : \text{seq } Input;\ os : \text{seq } Output \bullet (is, os, \theta State) \mapsto (\langle\rangle, os, E)\}$$

The modified embedding of the Z ADT into the relational model is as follows.

Definition 10.2 (*Angelic and Demonic Embeddings*)

An abstract data type (*State*, *Init*, $\{Op_i\}_{i \in I}$) with inputs of type *Input* and outputs of type *Output* is embedded in the relational model as follows. The global state is defined by

$$Event = I \times Input \times Output$$
$$\mathsf{G} = \text{seq} \, Input \times \text{seq} \, Output \times \mathbb{P} \, Event$$

The embedding of operations is as before; and the initialisation is extended with an input set of events that is ignored. Finalisation is given by

$$\mathsf{Fin} == \{State; \; is : \text{seq} \, Input, os : \text{seq} \, Output; \; E : \mathbb{P} \, Event \mid Fcond \bullet$$
$$(is, os, \theta State) \mapsto (\langle \rangle, os, E)\}$$

where in the angelic model *Fcond* is:

$$E \subseteq \{(i, in, out) \mid \neg \exists State'; \; Input; \; Output \bullet Op_i \wedge \theta?Op_i = in \wedge \theta!Op_i = out\}$$

and in the demonic model *Fcond* is:

$$E \subseteq \{(i, in, out) \mid (\neg \exists State'; \; Input; \; Output \bullet Op_i \wedge \theta?Op_i = in) \vee$$
$$(\exists State'; \; Input; \; Output \bullet Op_i \wedge \theta?Op_i = in \wedge \theta!Op_i \neq out$$
$$\wedge (i, in, \theta!Op_i) \notin E)\} \qquad \square$$

Note that i and in are treated analogously in both models. This is unsurprising: inputs in process algebras are often considered as syntactic sugar for a richer alphabet of operations. Indeed, we could have reflected this by embedding a Z data type with $\{Op_i\}_{i \in I}$ into a relational data type with $\{Op_i\}_{i \in I \times Input}$ instead.

Having defined the corresponding process and the finalisation we are in a position to show the correspondence with failures-divergences refinement. This result is independent of the model of outputs used, that is, whether demonic or angelic, since these are just coded up in the refusals, and refusal information is preserved across the failures-divergences model and the finalisation.

Theorem 10.3 *In the blocking model, relational refinement with extended finalisations corresponds to failures-divergences refinement.*

Proof Analogous to the proof of Theorem 10.1; however, the events in traces now consist of three parts: operation, input, and output. These are reconstructed, respectively, from the ADT program, the input sequence at initialisation, and the output sequence at finalisation. $\qquad \square$

10.3.2 Deriving the New Simulation Rules

We have shown that under the (natural) correspondence, relational refinement with extended finalisations corresponds to failures-divergences refinement. It remains now to extract simulation rules that can be expressed as predicates on the operations, since we do not wish to work with sets of events as currently embedded in the finalisation. Fortunately we can do this.

10.3.2.1 Demonic Model of Outputs (i.e., The Standard Model)

Prior to discussion of the simulation conditions, we consider the nature of *maximal refusal sets* for a particular state in the demonic model.

Maximal refusal sets. A refusal set at a particular state is a set of events that can be refused in that state. Such a refusal set is *maximal* for that state if it is not strictly included in another refusal set of the same state. By definition, the refusal sets of a state are characterised by its maximal refusal sets, and include all their subsets. When there are no outputs, there is always exactly one such maximal refusal set in any given state, which we have denoted as $Ref(State)$ before. Whether a particular operation with a particular input is refused in a state is independent from all other operations and inputs; thus, each maximal refusal set can be partitioned into independent maximal subsets for each particular operation and input. These maximal subsets contain events with a fixed input and operation, and they are either:

- $\{(i, in, out)\}$ for *all* values of *out*, representing the fact that operation i is blocked for input *in* in this state, or
- $\{(i, in, out)\}$ for all values of *out* except $out = out'$ for some specific output value out', representing the fact that operation i is enabled for input *in* in this state, and that it *may* result in output out'.

As a consequence, there is no guarantee that there is a *single* maximal refusal set for any given state. (This could also be concluded from the "negative occurrence" of E, "$(i, in, \theta!Op_i) \notin E$", in its characterisation in Definition 10.2.)

The relevance of maximal refusal sets is in proofs: when we need to prove inclusion of concrete refusal sets in abstract refusal sets, it is sufficient to consider maximal concrete refusal sets only, as downward closedness of abstract refusal sets then guarantees inclusion of all.

Note that this does not imply a maximal refusal semantics: the maximal refusal sets that are observed in finalisation are the unions of all maximal refusal sets in all concrete (linked) states, e.g., returning the full set for a particular i and *in* if it is blocked in *some* final state.

Forward simulations. The situation for a forward simulation is straightforward. We have the following:

Theorem 10.4 *The forward simulation condition imposed by observing refusals in the finalisation (as given in Definition 10.2) is subsumed by the normal applicability and correctness rules.*

Proof Concrete refusals which are due to the availability of an alternative output arise from the same situation in the abstract world, and this follows from the correctness condition. Concrete refusals due to blocking may arise from blocking or from alternative outputs in the abstract world – the former is guaranteed by the applicability condition, the latter by correctness.   □

An essential observation is that forward simulation still allows reduction of non-determinism of outputs. An output that is possible in the abstract system but not in the concrete system could be refused in either system: in the concrete one because it is impossible, in the abstract one because an alternative output exists.

Backward simulations. In a similar fashion we can extract the requirements due to backward simulations, applying the standard definition of backward simulation to the relational embedding given in Definition 10.2. In this case, the finalisation condition leads to an extra condition.

The requirement that $\mathsf{CFin} \subseteq \mathsf{T} \,\mathring{\,}\, \mathsf{AFin}$, as before, can be simplified to remove all reference to the input and output streams. What remains is a condition on refusals (where $Fcond_C$ and $Fcond_A$ are concrete and abstract versions of the demonic $Fcond$ condition in Definition 10.2):

$$\forall CState;\ E \bullet Fcond_C \Rightarrow \exists AState \bullet T \wedge Fcond_A \tag{10.1}$$

As $Fcond$ is satisfied for $E = \varnothing$, this implies the usual condition of totality of T on the concrete state.

Now consider a maximal refusal set E in the concrete case, in a particular state. As argued above, this set represents, for each operation i and input in, whether it is blocked (in which case E contains all (i, in, out) tuples), or whether a particular output out' is chosen (in which case E contains all (i, in, out) events for which $out \neq out'$). The quantification is such that for each such maximal refusal set, a *different* linked abstract state may be chosen. That this is necessary is clear from the following example.

Example 10.2 Let $AState \cong [\,a : \{0, 1, 2\}\,]$, and $CState \cong [\,c : \{1, 2\}\,]$. Consider the data types $C = (CState, CInit, \{COp_1\})$ and $A = (AState, AInit, \{AOp_1\})$, where

$$\begin{array}{|l} \hline CInit \underline{\hspace{3cm}} \\ CState' \\ \hline c' = 1 \\ \hline \end{array}$$

$$\begin{array}{|l} \hline AInit \underline{\hspace{3cm}} \\ AState' \\ \hline a' = 1 \lor a' = 0 \\ \hline \end{array}$$

$$\begin{array}{|l} \hline COp_1 \underline{\hspace{3cm}} \\ \Delta CState \\ x! : \{3, 4\} \\ \hline c = 1 \land c' = 2 \\ x! = 3 \lor x! = 4 \\ \hline \end{array}$$

$$\begin{array}{|l} \hline AOp_1 \underline{\hspace{3cm}} \\ \Delta AState \\ x! : \{3, 4\} \\ \hline (a = 0 \lor a = 1) \land a' = 2 \\ (a = 0 \Rightarrow x! = 3) \land (a = 1 \Rightarrow x! = 4) \\ \hline \end{array}$$

The following is a backward simulation in the demonic model (see Fig. 10.2):

$$\begin{array}{|l} \hline T \underline{\hspace{8cm}} \\ AState; \ CState \\ \hline a = 2 \Leftrightarrow c = 2 \\ (a = 0 \lor a = 1) \Leftrightarrow c = 1 \\ \hline \end{array}$$

Observe that this is the traditional example of a backward (but not forward) simulation, postponement of non-determinism, here transferred to non-determinism of outputs. The finalisation condition is only of interest for the empty program, i.e., for the initial states. State $a = 0$ contributes refusals $\{\varnothing, \{(1, *, 4)\}\}$, state $a = 1$ contributes refusals $\{\varnothing, \{(1, *, 3)\}\}$; the refusals in $c = 1$ are $\{\varnothing, \{(1, *, 4)\}, \{(1, *, 3)\}\}$.

Fig. 10.2 A backward simulation with outputs

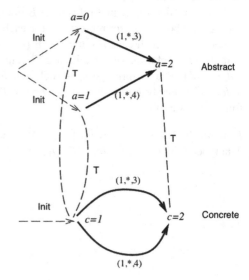

Here a refusal $(1, *, 4)$ means that the event corresponding to operation with index 1 (i.e., AOp_1 or COp_1), output 4 (and no inputs) was refused.

The concrete state $c = 1$ thus has no *single* maximal refusal set. In checking the finalisation condition

$$\forall\, CState;\ E \bullet Fcond_C \Rightarrow \exists\, AState \bullet T \wedge Fcond_A$$

one needs to consider different linked abstract states for different maximal concrete refusal sets. For example, in state $c = 1$, possible refusals satisfying $Fcond_C$ are $E = \varnothing$, $E = \{(1, *, 3)\}$ and $E = \{(1, *, 4)\}$. For $E = \varnothing$, we can check either of the linked abstract states, as $E = \varnothing$ will always satisfy $Fcond_A$. For $E = \{(1, *, 3)\}$, note that $Fcond_C$ is satisfied because of the second disjunct (an output *different* from 3 is *possible*); as a linked abstract state we can only choose $a = 1$ where $(1, *, 3)$ is refused because of it being *impossible* (the first disjunct of $Fcond_A$).   □

Thus, even in the context of a data type with just a *single* operation, we may need to look at different linked states for different output values. This seems somewhat at odds with the backward simulation condition for finalisations which we had before, which insisted on choosing *the same* linked abstract state for every set of enabled operations. In fact, the consideration of maximal refusal sets represents exactly the combination of these two conditions, as we will see below.

Another illustrative example, which highlights the difference between sequential and concurrent refinement in the context of outputs, is the following.

Example 10.3 Visitors are booked into downtown guest houses. En-suite bathrooms and TVs in the room are not considered essential facilities, so only after a booking is made is it known whether these facilities are available, and no visitor is expected to enquire after both facilities after the booking has been made. This is abstractly represented by the following specification.

```
┌─ GuestHouse ──────────────        ┌─ HasEnSuite ──────────────
│ booked, tv, ensuite : 𝔹           │ ΔGuestHouse
├───────────────────────            │ ensuite! : 𝔹
│ ┌─ Init ──────────────            ├──────────────────────────
│ │ GuestHouse'                     │ booked ∧ ¬booked'
│ ├──────────                       │ ensuite! = ensuite
│ │ ¬booked'                        └──────────────────────────
```

```
┌─ Book ────────────────            ┌─ HasTV ───────────────────
│ ΔGuestHouse                       │ ΔGuestHouse
├───────────────                    │ tv! : 𝔹
│ ¬booked ∧ booked'                 ├──────────────────────────
└───────────────────────            │ booked ∧ ¬booked'
                                    │ tv! = tv
                                    └──────────────────────────
```

Two guest houses are St. Thomas' and Marge's Guest House. Marge's Guest House has luxury rooms, with TV and en-suite, and simple rooms without either. Rooms in St. Thomas' have either an en-suite bathroom, or a TV, but never both.

<table>
<tr><td>

___Marges_____
room : none | simple | luxury

___Init_____
Marge′

room′ = none

___Book_____
ΔMarges

room = none ∧ room′ ≠ none

___HasEnSuite_____
ΔMarges
ensuite! : 𝔹

room ≠ none ∧ room′ = none
ensuite! = (room = luxury)

___HasTV_____
ΔMarges
tv! : 𝔹

room ≠ none ∧ room′ = none
tv! = (room = luxury)

</td><td>

___StThomas_____
room : no | tv | ensuite

___Init_____
StThomas′

room′ = no

___Book_____
ΔStThomas

room = no ∧ room′ ≠ no

___HasEnSuite_____
ΔStThomas
ensuite! : 𝔹

room ≠ no ∧ room′ = no
ensuite! = (room = ensuite)

___HasTV_____
ΔStThomas
tv! : 𝔹

room ≠ no ∧ room′ = no
tv! = (room = tv)

</td></tr>
</table>

Both are obviously refinements of *GuestHouse*; moreover, according to the relational refinement rules they are also equivalent to each other. Intuitively, in both cases one books a room, and then asks either whether it has a TV or whether it has an en-suite bathroom, and the answer to either question may be positive or negative. See also Fig. 10.3. (For simplicity, the states *no* and *none* are duplicated in the diagram.) The relation linking *none* to *no*, and linking all combinations of the other states, is a backward simulation according to the standard definition (in either direction – the ADTs are symmetric).

However, failures-divergences refinement does *not* hold between these two systems. The backward simulation finalisation condition fails for the states after booking, as all these states have incomparable refusal sets. For example, *simple* has as its refusals $\mathbb{P}\{(HasEnSuite, *, \text{true}), (HasTV, *, \text{true})\}$, whereas *tv* has as its refusals $\mathbb{P}\{(HasEnSuite, *, \text{true}), (HasTV, *, \text{false})\}$ and *ensuite* has $\mathbb{P}\{(HasEnSuite, *, \text{false}), (HasTV, *, \text{true})\}$.

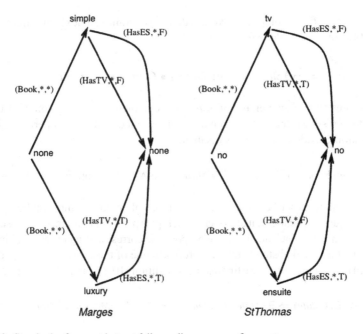

Fig. 10.3 Standard refinement but not failures-divergences refinement

Note also that this example is independent of the output model used, and has the same relevance for both angelic and demonic models: due to absence of output non-determinism the models lead to identical refusals.   □

The example above shows clearly that we cannot reason on the basis of individual refused events, choosing appropriate linked abstract states for each such event. Combining the observations from these two examples, we need to look at *combinations* of different operations, while considering possible output values *individually* (where inputs form part of the "operation").

The simplest way to express the finalisation condition is now via the *complements* of maximal refusal sets, as these are relatively small sets, consisting of at most one event for each operation plus input. This is characterised by the following definition

$$Sim == (I \times Input) \nrightarrow Output$$

Sim (for *sim*ultaneously offered events) is the type of sets of tuples $((i, in), out)$ such that for every pair (i, in) at most one *out* occurs in the set. We also formalise an event being "possible" in a certain state of an ADT, so we define:

$$State \xrightarrow{((i,in),out)} == \exists State'; \; Input; \; Output \bullet COp_i \wedge \theta Input = in \wedge \theta Output = out$$

Similarly, we define a notation to express that an (operation, index) combination may be disabled in a particular state:

$$State \overset{(i,in)}{\nrightarrow} == \neg \exists\, State';\ Input;\ Output \bullet COp_i \wedge \theta Input = in$$

The interpretation of an element of *Sim* as the complement of a maximal refusal set in a particular state is that all the events in it are enabled, and every (operation, index) combination outside its domain is disabled.

$$Maxsim(E, State) == (\forall e : E \bullet State \overset{e}{\longrightarrow}) \wedge (\forall iin : \overline{\mathrm{dom}\,E} \bullet State \overset{iin}{\nrightarrow})$$

The first conjunct describes enabled combinations of operation, input and output; the second conjunct indicates that all (operation, input) pairs *not* contained in the set must be blocked in the given state, i.e. have no possible corresponding output. Taking into account that a linked abstract state may refuse some of the chosen events, and must refuse all the disabled ones, the finalisation condition (10.1) is that $\forall\, CState;\ E : Sim$,

$$Maxsim(E, CState) \Rightarrow \exists\, AState;\ E' : Sim \bullet T \wedge E' \subseteq E \wedge Maxsim(E', AState) \qquad (10.2)$$

This condition is stronger than normal applicability, but it also contains an element of correctness, as can be seen from the similarity to the following consequence of standard backward simulation correctness, $\forall\, CState;\ in : Input;\ out : Output;\ i : I$

$$CState \overset{((i,in),out)}{\longrightarrow} \Rightarrow \exists\, AState \bullet T \wedge AState \overset{((i,in),out)}{\longrightarrow} \qquad (10.3)$$

Bringing this altogether, we have the following definition.

Definition 10.3 (*Backward simulation for demonic outputs*)
Let $A = (AState, AInit, \{AOp_i\}_{i \in I})$ and $C = (CState, CInit, \{COp_i\}_{i \in I})$ be Z data types. Then the relation T on $AState \wedge CState$ is an *backward simulation for demonic outputs* from A to C if

$$\forall\, AState';\ CState' \bullet CInit \wedge T' \Rightarrow AInit$$
$$\forall\, CState;\ E : Sim \bullet \quad Maxsim(E, CState) \Rightarrow$$
$$\exists\, AState;\ E' : Sim \bullet T \wedge E' \subseteq E \wedge Maxsim(E', AState)$$

and for all $i \in I$:

$$\forall\, AState';\ CState;\ CState' \bullet$$
$$(\forall\, AState \bullet T \Rightarrow \mathrm{pre}\, AOp_i) \Rightarrow (COp_i \wedge T' \Rightarrow \exists\, AState \bullet T \wedge AOp_i)$$

> The above rules assume the non-blocking interpretation of ADTs. In the blocking interpretation, the rule for correctness becomes
>
> $$\forall AState'; \; CState; \; CState' \bullet (COp_i \wedge T') \Rightarrow \exists AState \bullet T \wedge AOp_i \qquad \Box$$

Example 10.4 The conditions for backward simulation are fulfilled in Example 10.2. Disregarding output values other than 3 or 4, the only two relevant events are $(1, *, 3)$ and $(1, *, 4)$, as there is only one operation, with no inputs and only those outputs. The abstract states have a single maximal refusal set each: $\{(1, *, 4)\}$ for $a = 0$, $\{(1, *, 3)\}$ for $a = 1$, and the full set $\{(1, *, 3), (1, *, 4)\}$ for $a = 2$. Their complements are $\{(1, *, 3)\}$, $\{(1, *, 4)\}$ and $\varnothing$, respectively. Each of these complements could be viewed as a partial function from the operation index to outputs, i.e. they are elements of *Sim*.

To show that condition (10.2) holds, consider first $c = 1$. There are two sets E satisfying *Maxsim(E, CState)*, namely $E = \{(1, *, 3)\}$ and $E = \{(1, *, 4)\}$. For the first of these, the required abstract state is $a = 0$, with $E' = E$ satisfying *Maxsim(E', AState)*. For the second, the required abstract state is $a = 1$ with $E' = E$ satisfying *Maxsim(E', AState)*. Similarly, for $c = 2$ the only set E satisfying *Maxsim(E, CState)* is the empty set, the required linked state is $a = 2$ where *Maxsim($\varnothing$, AState)* does indeed hold. $\qquad \Box$

Example 10.5 The conditions for backward simulation are *not* fulfilled in Example 10.3. Of course, this by itself, does not prove that it is not a refinement – but recall that this example demonstrated that the traditional backward simulation rule is unsound for failures-divergences refinement.

Apart from the event $(Book, *, *)$, there are four possible events: two operations, no inputs, two possible output values each. Every state following on from the *Book* event in either system has a *single* two-element maximal refusal set, and so their complements have two elements each as well, exactly corresponding to the labels on the arrows in Fig. 10.3. Considering *Marges* as the concrete system, the set of enabled events at state *simple* is $\{(HasEnSuite, *, false), (HasTV, *, false)\}$ – neither *tv* nor *ensuite* has a subset of this as its full set of enabled events. Thus, backward simulation of *StThomas* by *Marges* fails on the finalisation condition as we might have hoped. Analogously, *StThomas* is not a backward simulation of *Marges* either. The standard forward simulation conditions are not satisfied either: the correctness condition prevents the same operation occurring with different outputs in linked states. $\qquad \Box$

10.3.2.2 Angelic Model of Outputs

We now turn to the conditions that arise when we use the angelic model of outputs. The differences between the models in terms of refinement are simple: in the demonic model we can reduce non-determinism in the outputs, but in the angelic version we cannot. This difference can be expressed in the simulation rules by using a different precondition operator.

The change needed is to alter the definition of pre Op to include existential quantification of the after state only (and not the output), since we wish to exclude reduction of non-determinism of the output. Hence for an operation Op defined over state space $State$ we define Pre $Op \mathrel{\widehat{=}} \exists\, State' \bullet Op$, and use Pre in place of pre in some of the simulation conditions. Refinements in this model behave exactly as before, except non-determinism in outputs cannot be resolved. We can then consider the simulations in turn.

Forward simulations. Interestingly now the finalisation condition for a forward simulation is *not* subsumed by the other conditions. Rather, it now adds the constraint that non-deterministic outputs cannot be reduced in a refinement. In addition, the condition *Fcond* is expressed in such a way that we *can* define a unique maximal refusal set *Ref (State)*.

$$Ref\,(State) == \{(i, in, out) \mid \neg\, \exists\, State';\; Input;\; Output \bullet$$
$$Op_i \wedge in = \theta Input \wedge out = \theta Output\}$$

With this in place, the finalisation condition (10.1) is:

$$\forall\, R \bullet (Ref\,(CState) \subseteq Ref\,(AState))$$

which becomes

$$\forall\, R;\; i : I;\; Input;\; Output \bullet \mathrm{Pre}\,AOp_i \Rightarrow \mathrm{Pre}\,COp_i$$

This is stronger than the standard applicability condition, as it precludes reduction of non-determinism in the output. An alternative formulation, assuming standard applicability, is:

$$\forall\, AState;\; CState;\; i : I \bullet R \wedge \mathrm{Pre}\,AOp_i \wedge \mathrm{pre}\,COp_i \Rightarrow \mathrm{Pre}\,COp_i$$

Backward simulations. The simplified condition for the finalisation in a backward simulation:

$$\forall\, CState;\; E \bullet Fcond_C \Rightarrow \exists\, AState \bullet T \wedge Fcond_A$$

can be expressed in terms of maximal refusal sets, as

$$\forall\, CState \bullet \exists\, AState \bullet T \wedge \forall\, Input;\; Output;\; i : I \bullet \mathrm{Pre}\,AOp_i \Rightarrow \mathrm{Pre}\,COp_i$$

This is a strengthening of the applicability condition, similar to the situation without outputs: it requires a fixed linked abstract state with compatible behaviour for all combinations of operations, input and output, rather than a variable linked state for each such combination. Unsurprisingly, the simulation conditions for an angelic model of outputs treat inputs and outputs analogously.

10.3.3 An Example

To illustrate the effects of these simulation rules and the constraints they embody, we describe a cinema booking system as follows. The Marlowe box office allows customers to book tickets in advance by telephone. When a customer calls, if there is an available ticket then one is allocated to the caller. They are then given this ticket when they arrive.

The abstract state contains *mpool* which denotes the pool of tickets, and *tkt*, a partial injective function from *Name* to *Ticket* recording which tickets have been allocated to which customers. Initially, no tickets have been allocated. There is a distinguished seat $t_1 \in mpool$. The operations *SpecRes* and *SpecUnRes* determine whether t_1 is still available for reservation. The description in Z is as follows, and a small fragment of the behaviour is pictured in Fig. 10.4.

```
┌─ Marlowe ─────────────────
│ mpool : ℙ Ticket
│ tkt : Name ⤖ Ticket
└───────────────────────────
```

```
┌─ Init ────────────────────
│ Marlowe'
├───────────────────────────
│ tkt' = ∅
└───────────────────────────
```

```
┌─ Book ────────────────────
│ ΔMarlowe
│ name? : Name
├───────────────────────────
│ name? ∉ dom tkt
│ mpool ≠ ∅
│ ∃ t : mpool •
│   mpool' = mpool \ {t} ∧
│   tkt' = tkt ∪ {name? ↦ t}
└───────────────────────────
```

```
┌─ Arrive ──────────────────
│ ΔMarlowe
│ name? : Name
│ t! : Ticket
├───────────────────────────
│ name? ∈ dom tkt
│ t! = tkt(name?)
│ tkt' = {name?} ⩤ tkt
│ mpool' = mpool
└───────────────────────────
```

```
┌─ SpecRes ─────────────────
│ ΞMarlowe
│ r! : Report
├───────────────────────────
│ t₁ ∉ mpool
│ r! = special seat reserved
└───────────────────────────
```

```
┌─ SpecUnRes ───────────────
│ ΞMarlowe
│ r! : Report
├───────────────────────────
│ t₁ ∈ mpool
│ r! = special seat unreserved
└───────────────────────────
```

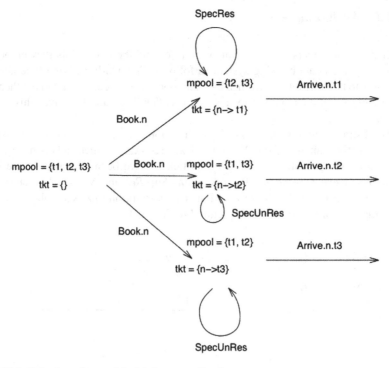

Fig. 10.4 Behaviour of part of the Marlowe specification

We now consider a data refinement where, instead of allocating a ticket when the customer books, their name is simply recorded in a set *bkd*. Only when a customer actually arrives is the ticket used non-deterministically chosen for allocation. This is specified as follows (note the operations *SpecRes* and *SpecUnRes* both have predicate *false*). A fragment of behaviour of this specification is given in Fig. 10.5.

$\_Kurbel_____$
$kpool : \mathbb{P}\ Ticket$
$bkd : \mathbb{P}\ Name$

$\_Init_____$
$Kurbel'$
$_____$
$bkd = \varnothing$

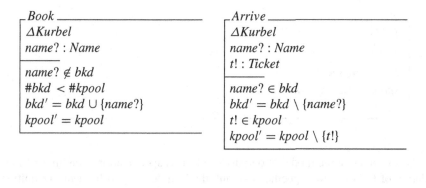

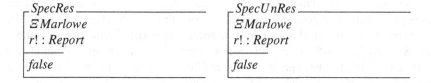

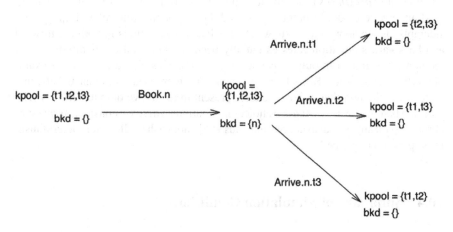

Fig. 10.5 Behaviour of part of the Kurbel specification

If we consider just the book and arrive operations, then the Kurbel specification is a failures-divergences refinement of the Marlowe specification. This can be verified by direct calculation of the failures of both specifications. However, we can also verify this by using simulation rules if we use the following retrieve relation:

```
┌─ Ret ──────────────────────────────────────────────────
│ Kurbel
│ Marlowe
├────────────────
│ bkd = dom tkt
│ kpool = mpool ∪ ran tkt
│ mpool ∩ ran tkt = ∅
└────────────────────────────────────────────────────────
```

Using the demonic model of outputs, the Kurbel specification is an upward simulation of the Marlowe specification, and this can be verified by using Definition 10.3.

As we have seen the simulation rules needed to derive failures-divergences refinement place additional constraints over and above those in the standard definitions. For example, if we consider the complete specification (i.e., include the operations *SpecRes* and *SpecUnRes*), then the Kurbel specification is an upward simulation of the complete Marlowe specification according to the standard backward simulation definition. However, this violates the failures inclusion of failures-divergences refinement, and indeed this is ruled out by Definitions 10.1 and 10.3 (the behaviour of *SpecRes* and *SpecUnRes* is not about outputs, hence Definition 10.1 is also violated).

If an angelic model of outputs was used then the simulation rules simplify considerably, as the above tables show. The finalisation conditions in both the forward and backward simulation rules essentially become applicability conditions where the non-determinism in outputs cannot be reduced. This would prevent, for example, refinements of the Kurbel *Arrive* operation which used particular tickets, that is, resolved the non-deterministic choice present in the above output selection. The intuition behind the use of angelic choices is situations where we consider *Arrive* synchronising on any output available, and thus we do not wish to allow non-determinism in outputs to be reduced.

10.4   Summary of Simulation Conditions

We have derived a number of different possible simulation rules for both forward and backward simulation covering the cases of blocking vs. non-blocking precondition interpretation and demonic vs. angelic model of outputs. In each case, due to the extended finalisation, the simulation rules are sound and jointly complete with respect to failures-divergences refinement.

We can now provide a complete characterisation of all the possibilities: no outputs; angelic outputs; demonic outputs, all in either backward or forward simulation.

For a forward simulation, the various conditions are:

FS.Init:
$\forall CState' \bullet CInit \Rightarrow \exists AState' \bullet AInit \wedge R'$
FS.App:
$\forall CState;\ AState;\ i : I;\ Input \bullet R \wedge \mathrm{pre}\, AOp_i \Rightarrow \mathrm{pre}\, COp_i$
FS.CorrNonBlock
$\forall i : I;\ Output;\ CState';\ CState;\ AState \bullet \mathrm{pre}\, AOp_i \wedge R \wedge COp_i \Rightarrow$
$$\exists AState' \bullet R' \wedge AOp_i$$
FS.CorrBlock:
$\forall i : I;\ Input;\ Output;\ CState';\ CState;\ AState \bullet R \wedge COp_i \Rightarrow$
$$\exists AState' \bullet R' \wedge AOp_i$$
FS.FinAng:
$\forall CState;\ AState;\ i : I;\ Input;\ Output \bullet R \wedge \mathrm{Pre}\, AOp_i \Rightarrow \mathrm{Pre}\, COp_i$

Standard non-blocking data refinement (i.e., the model discussed in Chap. 4) requires: **FS.Init**, **FS.App** and **FS.CorrNonBlock**.

Similarly, the standard blocking data refinement model requires: **FS.Init**, **FS.App** and **FS.CorrBlock**.

Strengthening the standard model to include a refusals embedding then requires additional rules. So for a refusals embedding in the blocking model the following rules are required in the various situations. Each column represents a particular model for (inputs and) outputs; a missing entry indicates a condition dominated by the other conditions in the same column.

Outputs:	none	demonic	angelic
Init		FS.Init	
App		FS.App	-
Corr		FS.CorrBlock	
Fin		-	FS.FinAng

For example, using the demonic interpretation of outputs in the blocking model we would check the conditions **FS.Init**, **FS.App**, and **FS.CorrBlock**, whereas for the angelic model we would use **FS.Init**, **FS.CorrBlock**, and **FS.FinAng**.

For backward simulation, the various possible conditions are:

BS.Init:
$\forall CState';\ AState' \bullet T' \wedge CInit \Rightarrow AInit$
BS.AppBlock
$\forall i : I;\ Output \bullet \forall CState \bullet \exists AState \bullet T \wedge \mathrm{pre}\, AOp_i \Rightarrow \mathrm{pre}\, COp_i$
BS.CorrNonBlock
$\forall i : I;\ Output;\ AState';\ CState';\ CState \bullet T' \wedge COp_i \Rightarrow$
$$\exists AState \bullet T \wedge (\mathrm{pre}\, AOp_i \Rightarrow AOp_i)$$
BS.CorrBlock:
$\forall i : I;\ Input;\ Output;\ AState';\ CState';\ CState \bullet T' \wedge COp_i \Rightarrow$
$$\exists AState \bullet T \wedge AOp_i$$

BS.FinRef:

$\forall\,CState \bullet \exists\,AState \bullet T \wedge \forall\,i : I;\ Input \bullet \operatorname{pre} AOp_i \Rightarrow \operatorname{pre} COp_i$

BS.FinDem:

$\forall\,CState;\ E : Sim \bullet Maxsim(E, CState) \Rightarrow$
$\exists\,AState;\ E' : Sim \bullet T \wedge E' \subseteq E \wedge Maxsim(E', AState)$

BS.FinAng:

$\forall\,CState \bullet \exists\,AState \bullet T \wedge \forall\,i : I;\ Input;\ Output \bullet \operatorname{Pre} AOp_i \Rightarrow \operatorname{Pre} COp_i$

Standard non-blocking data refinement (i.e., the model discussed in Chap. 4) requires: **BS.Init**, **BS.App** and **BS.CorrNonBlock**.

Similarly, the standard blocking data refinement model requires: **BS.Init**, **BS.App** and **BS.CorrBlock**.

For a refusals embedding in the blocking model the following rules are required in the various situations.

Outputs:	none	demonic	angelic
Init	**BS.Init**		
App	-		
Corr	**BS.CorrBlock**		
Fin	**BS.FinRef**	**BS.FinDem**	**BS.FinAng**

In conclusion, forward simulation is unaffected by the move from standard relational refinement to failures-divergences refinement, except in the angelic model for outputs. For backward simulation, the observation of refusals leads to a strengthening of the applicability condition in every case.

10.4.1 Discussion

We have seen that in both the non-blocking and blocking models it has been necessary to place additional restrictions (i.e., observations) on the standard definition of data refinement in order that failures-divergences refinement is achieved in a process semantics. Why this is, is perhaps best illustrated via a few examples.

Without input/output - non-blocking. We have seen that without input/output non-blocking data refinement is equivalent to traces-divergences refinement (see Sect. 9.4). However, it is worth noting that this does not mean that data refinement suffers from the weakness of the CSP traces model. Specifically, although traces refinement is normally considered too weak since the deadlocked behaviour *stop* refines all processes, such a behaviour is not a feasible translation of an ADT. That is, no ADT will have corresponding process *stop*, since the non-blocking model allows all traces due to no operation being refused. In addition, unlike in trace refinement there is no bottom of the refinement ordering since all ADTs with all operations deterministic and fully defined have no strict refinements in this framework.

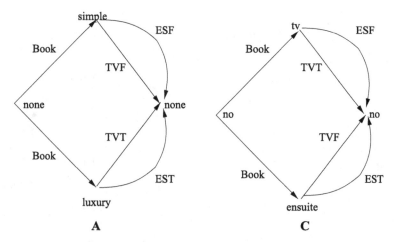

Fig. 10.6 Non-blocking, no input/output = traces-divergences and failures-divergences

Without input/output, non-blocking data refinement is, in fact, also equivalent to failures-divergences refinement. To see this, note that without input/output (specifically without output) the process semantics obtained identifies traces-divergences refinement and failures-divergences refinement, that is, $process(A) \sqsubseteq_{td} process(C)$ iff $process(A) \sqsubseteq_{fd} process(C)$, where $process$ defines the corresponding process to an ADT - again see Sect. 9.4. This is simply because there are no refusals (beyond those after a divergence) in the process semantics, since refusals only arise due to the presence of outputs.

Consider Fig. 10.6 (a modification of Example 10.3), where in this and subsequent examples we define simple LTS to represent the ADTs' partial relations before totalisation.

These two specifications have the same traces and divergences, and are thus data refinement equivalent. There are no refusals in the non-blocking model, thus they are also failures-divergences equivalent. However, note that the stronger applicability condition needed for the blocking model does not hold here – for example for state *ensuite* it is not the case that any abstract state has

$$\forall i : I \bullet T \wedge (\text{pre } AOp_i \Rightarrow \text{pre } COp_i)$$

The difference (i.e., why this does not matter in a traces-divergences model) is that with failures the refusals are tied to the traces, whereas for divergences we simply require their inclusion.

Without input/output - blocking. However, when considered under a blocking totalisation A and C are *not* failures-divergences equivalent. In fact, in a blocking scenario these are singleton failures equivalent and hence a blocking data refinement. To see this note that in a blocking model there are no divergences, the traces are the same in each. Now, although A has failure $(\langle B \rangle, \{TVF, ESF\})$ which is not

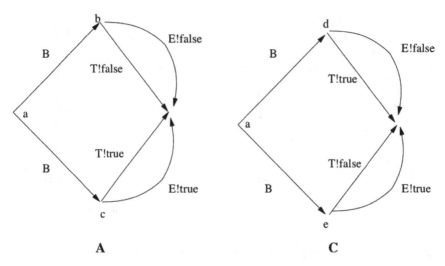

Fig. 10.7 Non-blocking with input/output = traces-divergences but not failures-divergences

present in C, under a singleton failures model in A we just obtain singleton failures $(\langle B \rangle, \{TVF\})$, $(\langle B \rangle, \{ESF\})$, ... thus the difference is not observable. To recover failures-divergences refinement in the blocking model one needs to add the strengthened applicability condition. That is, it is precisely the condition

$$\forall \, CState \bullet \exists \, AState \bullet \forall \, i : I \bullet T \wedge (\mathrm{pre}\, AOp_i \Rightarrow \mathrm{pre}\, COp_i)$$

that fails in this example.

With input/output - non-blocking. When we extend to consider input/output, the presence and modelling of outputs forces a different condition (i.e., different, but related, to the strengthened applicability condition **BS.FinRef**) to be required to recover failures-divergences equivalent.

To see why non-blocking data refinement is not failures-divergences refinement consider Fig. 10.7, where different operations above have been replaced by an operation outputting a different value. Again, in the non-blocking model we have the same traces and same divergences in each specification. The presence of outputs, and non-determinism, causes failures in both specifications. For example, *simple* has as its refusals $\mathbb{P}\{HasES!\,\mathrm{true}, HasTV!\,\mathrm{true}\}$, whereas *tv* has as its refusals $\mathbb{P}\{HasES!\,\mathrm{true}, HasTV!\,\mathrm{false}\}$ and *ensuite* has $\mathbb{P}\{HasES!\,\mathrm{false}, HasTV!\,\mathrm{true}\}$.

This difference is not visible in the traces-divergences model, and consequently not in program observations made in the relational model. Moving some of the observable information (operation names here) from the first example into the outputs has kept that information observable but not under control of the environment, and it is this information that is captured in the failures.

With input/output - blocking. Considering the blocking model we already know we need an additional strengthening of applicability (even without input/output) to regain failures-divergences. This example shows that we need the condition **BS.FinDem** on refusal sets due to outputs as well. Now the strengthened applicability condition holds - each state *simple*, *luxury*, *tv* and *ensuite* has operations *HasES* and *HasTV* enabled - so this does not pick up the different refusal information due to the outputs. Thus we need to impose **BS.FinDem** to ensure this.

Note that in the case of the blocking model, **BS.FinDem** implies **BS.FinRef**. To see this, given a concrete state CS and maximal refusal set E in that state, then events are in E if the associated operation is blocked or there exists an alternate output for that operation. For this E we can find an abstract state AS such that $Fcond_A$ holds for E. Now for this AS consider any operation Op, if pre AOp holds in AS but pre COp does not hold in CS, then we have violated **BS.FinDem**. Hence **BS.FinRef** holds.

10.5 Bibliographical Notes

Work relating concurrent and state-based refinement includes work on semantic aspects due to Josephs [1], He [2] and Woodcock and Morgan [3], as well as work by Bolton and Davies [4, 5]. Relevant also is the work on integrated formal notations, see for example [6–13], as well as that on related questions such as subtyping [14–16].

The aim of the work of Josephs, He, and Woodcock and Morgan [1–3] was, like here, to derive simulation techniques suitable for verifying concurrent refinement relations. However, they did not use a relational model, and the simulation conditions were presented in a different format which has consequences for the translation of the conditions for use within particular specification notations (e.g., Z or Object-Z). In addition, the rôle of input and output was not considered.

In terms of semantic models used, Josephs [1] uses a labelled transition system framework and derives forward and backward simulation conditions for CSP failures refinement (considering only divergence-free processes). The conditions he derives are essentially the same as those we have derived above for systems without input and output. The work of Woodcock and Morgan [3] is similar in essence to [1] but uses a weakest precondition semantics instead of a labelled transition system framework as its semantic model.

Integrations of state-based languages and process algebras led to work on simulation rules for failures-divergences refinement. In particular, combinations of Object-Z and CSP required the use of simulation rules in Object-Z which were compatible with CSP failures-divergences refinement.

Initial application of the work in [1] looked at the articulation of the simulation rules within a schema calculus setting [17–19]. However, the correct use of the strengthened applicability rule was mistranslated. The error was pointed out by Bolton and Davies [5], who showed that data refinement *does not* correspond to failures-divergences refinement, but to a slightly different semantic model which they termed singleton failures.

The work in [5] also did not consider failures-divergences refinement, but in [4] they extended [5] by presenting a translation of the Josephs rules from [1] to the Object-Z schema calculus.

The use of different models of outputs, demonic and angelic, goes back to work on combining Object-Z and CSP, and different approaches to integrated languages have chosen differing models of outputs. For example, [6] adopts an angelic output model, however, the majority of work on integrating Object-Z and CSP have used the demonic model of outputs. The latter includes [7, 9, 10]. A discussion of the merits of both approaches is contained in [20].

Additional work mentioned includes that which deals with standard Z simulation rules (or, in fact, variants for Object-Z) [7, 8, 17] and that which widens the discussion to subtyping [14, 15] which considers additional operations to those present in the initial specification.

References

1. Josephs MB (1988) A state-based approach to communicating processes. Distrib Comput 3:9–18
2. He Jifeng (1989) Process refinement. In: McDermid J (ed) The theory and practice of refinement. Butterworths, Boston
3. Woodcock JCP, Morgan CC (1990) Refinement of state-based concurrent systems. In: Bjorner D, Hoare CAR, Langmaack H (eds) VDM'90: VDM and Z!- formal methods in software development. Lecture notes in computer science, vol 428. Springer, Berlin, pp 340–351
4. Bolton C, Davies J (2002) Refinement in Object-Z and CSP. In: Butler M, Petre L, Sere K (eds) Integrated formal methods (IFM 2002). Lecture notes in computer science, vol 2335. Springer, Berlin, pp 225–244
5. Bolton C, Davies J (2006) A singleton failures semantics for communicating sequential processes. Formal Aspects Comput 18(2):181–210
6. Smith G (1997) A semantic integration of Object-Z and CSP for the specification of concurrent systems. In: Fitzgerald J, Jones CB, Lucas P (eds) FME'97: industrial application and strengthened foundations of formal methods. Lecture notes in computer science, vol 1313. Springer, Berlin, pp 62–81
7. Smith G, Derrick J (2001) Specification, refinement and verification of concurrent systems - an integration of Object-Z and CSP. Formal Methods Syst Design 18:249–284
8. Derrick J, Smith G (2000) Structural refinement in Object-Z/CSP. In: Grieskamp W, Santen T, Stoddart B (eds) International conference on integrated formal methods 2000 (IFM'00). Lecture notes in computer science, vol 1945. Springer, Berlin, pp 194–213
9. Fischer C (1997) CSP-OZ - A combination of CSP and Object-Z. In: Bowman H, Derrick J (eds) Second IFIP international conference on formal methods for open object-based distributed systems. Chapman & Hall, New York, pp 423–438
10. Mahony BP, Dong JS (1998) Blending Object-Z and timed CSP: an introduction to TCOZ. In: Futatsugi K, Kemmerer R, Torii K (eds) 20th international conference on software engineering (ICSE'98). IEEE Press, New Jercy
11. Galloway A, Stoddart W, An operational semantics for ZCCS. In: Hinchey and Liu [23], pp 272–282
12. Treharne H, Schneider S, Using a process algebra to control B operations. In: Araki et al [21], pp 437–456
13. Fischer C, How to combine Z with a process algebra. In: Bowen et al [22], pp 5–23

14. Fischer C, Wehrheim H (2000) Behavioural subtyping relations for object-oriented formalisms. In: Rus T (ed) Algebraic methodology and software technology. Lecture notes in computer science, vol 1816. Springer, Berlin, pp 469–483
15. Wehrheim H (2000) Behavioural subtyping and property preservation. In: Smith SF, Talcott CL (eds) Formal methods for open object-based distributed systems (FMOODS 2000). Kluwer, The Netherlands, pp 213–231
16. Liskov B, Wing JM (1994) A behavioural notion of subtyping. ACM Trans Program Lang Syst 16(6):1811–1841
17. Smith G, Derrick J, Refinement and verification of concurrent systems specified in Object-Z and CSP. In: Hinchey and Liu [101], pp 293–302
18. Bolton C, Davies J, Woodcock JCP, On the refinement and simulation of data types and processes. In: Araki et al [21], pp 273–292
19. Fischer C (2000) Combination and implementation of processes and data: from CSP-OZ to Java. PhD thesis, University of Oldenburg
20. Smith G, Derrick J (2002) Abstract specification in Object-Z and CSP. In: George C, Miao H (eds) Formal methods and software engineering. Lecture notes in computer science, vol 2495. Springer, Berlin, pp 108–119
21. Araki K, Galloway A, Taguchi K (eds) (1999) International conference on integrated formal methods 1999 (IFM'99). Springer, New York
22. Bowen JP, Fett A, Hinchey MG (eds) (1998) ZUM'98: The Z formal specification notation. Lecture notes in computer science, vol 1493. Springer, Berlin
23. Hinchey MG, Liu S (eds) (1997) First international conference on formal engineering methods (ICFEM'97). IEEE Computer Society Press, Hiroshima, Japan

Chapter 11
Process Data Types - A Fully General Model of Concurrent Refinement

11.1 Introduction

Chapter 9 introduced the general approach to relating process refinement and relational refinement by developing a relational framework general enough that we could embed some of the concurrent refinement relations into it. Chapter 10 built on this by looking in depth at the relationship between failures-divergences refinement and data refinement. In this chapter we now generalise the framework defined in Chap. 10 by providing a general flexible scheme for incorporating the two main "erroneous" concurrent behaviours: deadlock and divergence, into a single relational refinement relation. This is a proper generalisation in that it subsumes previous characterisations as well as allowing combinations of these.

The framework allows one to derive forward and backward simulation conditions for specifications containing both internal operations and outputs, such that the simulations correspond to failures-divergences refinement. We highlight the role of divergence due to unbounded internal evolution and the relation between outputs and refusals, and discuss their effect on the simulation conditions.

First of all we introduce the notion of a program controlled ADT. This is an ADT where the global state before initialisation is irrelevant. This ensures that the output of an ADT run is fully determined by the program, not by any other global state information. This does not mean that initialisation is irrelevant: it still describes in which local state the ADT might start, but this choice is not influenced by outside information.

Definition 11.1 (*Program controlled ADT*)
A basic ADT with initialisation Init and global state G is *program controlled* if the initial global state is irrelevant for initialisation, i.e., $\mathsf{Init} = \mathsf{G} \times \mathrm{ran}\,\mathsf{Init}$. □

The restriction to program controlled ADTs makes some of the accounting simpler and does not place any restrictions on the theory that we introduce. The standard construction used in Z embedded a sequences of inputs and outputs into the local and global states. Here, however, without any loss of generality, we can do away with

© Springer International Publishing AG, part of Springer Nature 2018
J. Derrick and E. Boiten, *Refinement*, https://doi.org/10.1007/978-3-319-92711-4_11

the input sequence since any quantification over inputs comes hand in hand with the same quantification over the index set I. That is, it would make no difference for inputs in operations to appear as a shorthand for an increased alphabet of the ADT – as is commonly the interpretation of inputs in process algebras. From this point on we avoid mentioning inputs. In Z versions of the rules, wherever it says $\forall i : I$ we may mentally insert $\forall$ *Input* as well. We do not rely on the conventional assumption that I is finite, and so are not requiring inputs to be from a finite domain either.

The outputs, however, do need an explicit representation in the relational embedding, so we now define an output embedding. This is an axiomatic characterisation of the results of embeddings (such as in Sect. 7.2.1) where the outputs are part of the global state, and initialisation and finalisation perform copying of them between global and local state; the final two conditions state that every operation adds a single output to the output sequence and copies the rest, and that the previous outputs have no influence on the effect of this operation in general, including the new output value.

Definition 11.2 (*Output embedding*)
A basic ADT (State, Init, $\{\mathsf{Op}_i\}_{i \in I}$, Fin) with global state G is said to be an *output embedding* iff types GB, *Output*, StateB exist such that

> $\mathsf{G} = \mathsf{GB} \times \mathrm{seq}\, \mathit{Output}$
> $\mathsf{State} = \mathsf{StateB} \times \mathrm{seq}\, \mathit{Output}$
> $\forall\, \mathsf{i}, \mathsf{gs}, \mathsf{ls}, \mathsf{ls2}, \mathsf{os}, \mathsf{os2}, \mathsf{out} \bullet$
> $\quad ((\mathsf{gs}, \mathsf{os}), (\mathsf{ls}, \mathsf{os2})) \in \mathsf{Init} \Rightarrow \mathsf{os2} = \langle\rangle$
> $\quad ((\mathsf{ls}, \mathsf{os}), (\mathsf{gs}, \mathsf{os2})) \in \mathsf{Fin} \Rightarrow \mathsf{os2} = \mathsf{os}$
> $\quad ((\mathsf{ls}, \mathsf{os}), (\mathsf{ls2}, \mathsf{os2})) \in \mathsf{Op}_i \Rightarrow \exists\, \mathsf{out} \bullet \mathsf{os2} = \mathsf{os} \,\frown\, \langle\mathsf{out}\rangle$
> $\quad ((\mathsf{ls}, \mathsf{os}), (\mathsf{ls2}, \mathsf{os} \,\frown\, \langle\mathsf{out}\rangle)) \in \mathsf{Op}_i \Rightarrow ((\mathsf{ls}, \mathsf{os2}), (\mathsf{ls2}, \mathsf{os2} \,\frown\, \langle\mathsf{out}\rangle)) \in \mathsf{Op}_i$ $\qquad\square$

As in the previous chapter, we wish to observe traces and refusals. The traces are contained in the standard relational semantics, viz. through the notion of programs. As we have seen, the refusals are not present in the standard embedding. Thus to fully encode failures it is necessary to enhance the standard relational theory by adding the observation of refusals at the end of every program. This involves a change only to the global state and the finalisation, as characterised axiomatically in the following definition.

Definition 11.3 (*Refusal embedding*)
Consider a basic ADT (State, Init, $\{\mathsf{Op}_i\}_{i \in I}$, Fin) with global state G, a type of events E, and a refusal relation Ref : State $\leftrightarrow$ $\mathbb{P}$ E. The ADT is said to be an *refusal embedding* (for Ref) iff it is program controlled, and a type GB exists such that

> $\mathsf{G} = \mathbb{P}\,\mathsf{E} \times \mathsf{GB}$
> $\forall\, \mathsf{ls}, \mathsf{r} \bullet (\exists\, \mathsf{gs} \bullet (\mathsf{ls}, (\mathsf{r}, \mathsf{gs})) \in \mathsf{Fin}) \equiv (\mathsf{ls}, \mathsf{r}) \in \mathsf{Ref}$ $\qquad\square$

Note that a basic ADT can be both an output embedding and a refusal embedding, for example, having as the global state $\mathbb{P}\,\mathsf{E} \times \mathrm{seq}\, \mathit{Output}$.

11.2   A Relational ADT with Divergence and Blocking

We have already seen how partial relations can be interpreted in a model of total relations, and the refinement theory then depending on whether the blocking or non-blocking approach was chosen. However, we should note that the two approaches are not exclusive – and indeed, formalisms such as B have both preconditions and guards. Indeed, in general, specification formalisms may include both situations that lead to *divergence* and situations that lead to *deadlock*.

An obvious solution to such a scenario is to apply two totalisations in sequence: one to account for deadlock, and another to account for livelock. What follows here is a generalised reconstruction of that solution, which allows us to derive simulation rules directly for any relational formalism which gives rise to both kinds of errors once the areas of divergence and blocking have been made explicit. In fact, it covers *any* relational formalism modelling at most two kinds of errors, one of which is chaotic, and whose combination satisfies the constraints discussed next.

An important consideration in this is the relative ordering of the two kinds of erroneous behaviours. In particular, we need to decide what observations should be possible when the semantics leads to a non-deterministic choice between any combination of the three behaviours: *normal*, *divergent* and *blocking*.

First, *divergent* behaviour is usually viewed as *anything might happen* (cf. Chap. 5), which means that a choice between divergent and normal behaviour should appear as divergence. Consistent with the CSP chaotic interpretation of divergence (e.g., after divergence any refusal is possible), the choice between divergence and blocking should also result in divergence. All in all, this means that there is no observable difference between possible and certain divergence, and that divergence is a zero of non-deterministic choice.

The remaining issue is the choice between normal and blocking behaviour. It would be possible, using a model of partial relations to take deadlock as a unit of choice, and therefore to not observe possible blocking. Consistent with usual semantics for Z and for CSP, we will distinguish possible blocking in our model. These decisions are summarised in the following table, which also informally hints at the set-based model for this which we will introduce formally later. In particular, $\perp$ represents blocking, and ω represents divergence. In the model, set union acts as the choice operator.

Choice	normal	divergence	deadlock	poss deadlock	model
normal	normal	divergence	poss deadlock	poss deadlock	sets not containing $\perp$, ω
divergence	divergence	divergence	divergence	divergence	State $\cup$ $\{\omega\}$, possibly also $\perp$
deadlock	poss deadlock	divergence	deadlock	poss deadlock	$\{\perp\}$
poss deadlock	poss deadlock	divergence	poss deadlock	poss deadlock	sets containing $\perp$ but not ω

With these considerations in mind, we now define a relational data type with partial operations allowing for both divergence and blocking. Its reduction is the basic data type obtained by removing all blocking and divergence information.

Definition 11.4 (*Process data type; Reduction*)

A *process data type* is a quadruple (State, Inits, $\{Op_i\}_{i\in I}$, Fin), where Inits is a subset of State; every operation $\{Op_i\}$ is a triple (N, B, D) such that dom N, D and B form a partition of State; Fin is a relation from State to G.

Its *reduction* is the basic data type (State, G × Inits, $\{N_i\}_{i\in I}$, Fin). □

In an operation Op = (N, B, D) the relation N represents the operation's normal effect; the sets B and D represent states where the operation would lead to blocking and divergence, respectively. The three sets forming a partition excludes certain situations, such as miracles and possible (as opposed to certain) deadlock from a given state, and ensures that it can be represented by a *total* data type. Possible deadlock still occurs, however, whenever one program (trace) leads to multiple states, some but not all of which are deadlocked.

The blocking and non-blocking approaches to operations are, of course, special cases of process data types, in particular:

- the blocking operation Op is represented by (Op, $\overline{\text{dom Op}}$, ∅), i.e., it never diverges, and blocks in the complement of the operation's domain;
- the non-blocking operation Op is represented by (Op, ∅, $\overline{\text{dom Op}}$), i.e., it diverges in the complement of the operation's domain, but never blocks.

The definition of a process data type is not intended as a new independent relational specification mechanism. It is solely an intermediate formalism that most partial relation frameworks can be embedded into. In turn, it is embedded into the total relations framework in order to define its simulation rules once and for all. The embedding is given below. In effect, it fixes the semantics of a process data type.

In the embeddings we will use state spaces enhanced with special values defined below. For simplicity, we assume in the rest of this chapter that ⊥ (representing blocking), ω (representing divergence), and no are different values not already contained in any local or global state space of interest. The impossibility of making an observation in a final state is encoded in no, and this is added to the global state only. The embedding (and semantics) of a process data type is then defined as follows.

Definition 11.5 (*Enhanced state; Embedding of a process data type*)

For any set State, let

$$\text{State}_{\perp,\omega,\text{no}} == \text{State} \cup \{\perp, \omega, \text{no}\}$$

and similarly for sets subscripted with subsets of these special values.

A process data type (State, Inits, $\{(N_i, B_i, D_i)\}_{i\in I}$, Fin) with global state G is embedded into the total data type (State$_{\perp,\omega}$, Init, $\{[\![Op]\!]_i\}_{i\in I}$, $[\![Fin]\!]$) with global state $G_{\perp,\omega,\text{no}}$ where

$$\text{Init} == G_{\perp,\omega,\text{no}} \times \text{Inits}$$
$$[\![(N, B, D)]\!] == N \cup (B_{\perp,\omega} \times \{\perp\}) \cup (D_\omega \times \text{State}_\omega)$$
$$[\![\text{Fin}]\!] == \text{Fin} \cup (\overline{\text{dom Fin}} \times \{\text{no}\}) \cup \{(\perp, \perp)\} \cup \{\omega\} \times G_{\omega,\text{no}} \qquad □$$

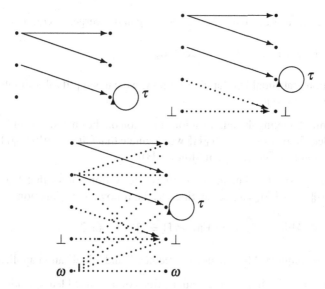

Fig. 11.1 The original Op, and a divergent after-state; with $B_\perp \times \{\perp\}$ added; finally also with $D_\omega \times State_\omega \cup \{(\omega, \perp)\}$

As a process data type has a set of initial states rather than an initialisation relation, the embedding's initialisation relates every global state to all such states. The normal effect of an operation is part of the embedded one. In addition, every blocking state including $\perp$ is related to $\perp$, every state where the operation diverges to every state including ω, and divergent state ω is linked to all states even including $\perp$. Finalisation makes both blocking and divergence visible globally. Figure 11.1 illustrates this operation embedding.

Refinement (i.e., forward and backward simulation) of process data types is derived by embedding them into total data types, applying the simulation rules for total data types, and then eliminating $\perp$, ω, and no from the resulting rules – i.e., expressing them in terms of the process data types only.

Note that the embedding of the initialisation is unusual, in the sense that it is non-strict in the erroneous behaviours $\perp$, ω, and no. This choice was made to ensure the ADT is program controlled; if we were to consider sequential composition of ADTs, strictness would be required.

11.2.1   Forward Simulation for Process Data Types

Let (AState, AInits, $\{AOp_i\}_{i \in I}$, AFin) and (CState, CInits, $\{COp_i\}_{i \in I}$, CFin) be process data types, both with global state G, and R a candidate forward simulation relation between AState and CState. We also embed the simulation relation, in order to relate abstract and concrete blocking and divergence correctly:

$$[\![R]\!] == R \cup \{(\bot, \bot)\} \cup \{\omega\} \times \mathsf{CState}_\omega$$

In a fashion that should be familiar by now, we can simplify the simulation conditions, and we do so now.

Initialisation: Applying the initialisation condition on the embedded data types with the embedded simulation relation $[\![R]\!]$ we calculate that $\mathsf{CInit} \subseteq \mathsf{AInit}\,\mathring{,}\,[\![R]\!]$ reduces to the condition that $\mathsf{CInits} \subseteq \mathrm{ran}(\mathsf{AInits} \lhd R)$.

Finalisation: A similar (but more complex) derivation shows that the condition $[\![R]\!]\,\mathring{,}\,[\![\mathsf{CFin}]\!] \subseteq [\![\mathsf{AFin}]\!]$ can be rewritten as the following conjunction

$$R\,\mathring{,}\,\mathsf{CFin} \subseteq \mathsf{AFin} \;\wedge\; (\mathrm{dom}\,\mathsf{AFin}) \lhd R = R \rhd (\mathrm{dom}\,\mathsf{CFin})$$

We call these conjuncts "finalisation correctness" and "finalisation applicability".

Operations: We first simplify the compositions of an embedded operation $\mathsf{Op} = (\mathsf{N}, \mathsf{B}, \mathsf{D})$ with an embedded simulation, leading to:

$$[\![R]\!]\,\mathring{,}\,[\![\mathsf{Op}]\!] = R\,\mathring{,}\,\mathsf{N} \;\cup\; R\,\mathring{,}\,(\mathsf{B} \times \{\bot\}) \;\cup$$
$$R\,\mathring{,}\,(\mathsf{D} \times \mathsf{State}_\omega) \;\cup\; \{(\bot, \bot)\} \;\cup\; \{\omega\} \times \mathsf{State}_{\bot,\omega}$$

$$[\![\mathsf{Op}]\!]\,\mathring{,}\,[\![R]\!] = \mathsf{N}\,\mathring{,}\,R \;\cup\; (\mathsf{B}_{\bot,\omega} \times \{\bot\}) \;\cup\; \mathsf{D}_\omega \times \mathsf{S}_\omega$$

For corresponding operations $\mathsf{AOp} = (\mathsf{AN}, \mathsf{AB}, \mathsf{AD})$ and $\mathsf{COp} = (\mathsf{CN}, \mathsf{CB}, \mathsf{CD})$, we have that

$[\![R]\!]\,\mathring{,}\,[\![\mathsf{COp}]\!] \subseteq [\![\mathsf{AOp}]\!]\,\mathring{,}\,[\![R]\!]$

$\equiv \{$ above; simplications $\}$

$R\,\mathring{,}\,\mathsf{CN} \;\cup\; R\,\mathring{,}\,(\mathsf{CB} \times \{\bot\}) \;\cup\; R\,\mathring{,}\,(\mathsf{CD} \times \mathsf{CState}_\omega)$

$\subseteq$

$\mathsf{AN}\,\mathring{,}\,R \;\cup\; (\mathsf{AB} \times \{\bot\}) \;\cup\; \mathsf{AD} \times \mathsf{CState}_\omega$

$\equiv \{$ inclusion of set union $\}$

$R\,\mathring{,}\,\mathsf{CN} \subseteq \mathsf{AN}\,\mathring{,}\,R \;\cup\; (\mathsf{AB} \times \{\bot\}) \;\cup\; \mathsf{AD} \times \mathsf{CState}_\omega$

$\wedge\, R\,\mathring{,}\,(\mathsf{CB} \times \{\bot\}) \subseteq \mathsf{AN}\,\mathring{,}\,R \;\cup\; (\mathsf{AB} \times \{\bot\}) \;\cup\; \mathsf{AD} \times \mathsf{CState}_\omega$

$\wedge\, R\,\mathring{,}\,(\mathsf{CD} \times \mathsf{CState}_\omega) \subseteq \mathsf{AN}\,\mathring{,}\,R \;\cup\; (\mathsf{AB} \times \{\bot\}) \;\cup\; \mathsf{AD} \times \mathsf{CState}_\omega$

$\equiv \{$ simplification: domains $\}$

$R\,\mathring{,}\,\mathsf{CN} \subseteq \mathsf{AN}\,\mathring{,}\,R \;\cup\; \mathsf{AD} \times \mathsf{CState}$

$\wedge\, R\,\mathring{,}\,(\mathsf{CB} \times \{\bot\}) \subseteq (\mathsf{AB} \times \{\bot\}) \;\wedge\; R\,\mathring{,}\,(\mathsf{CD} \times \mathsf{CState}_\omega) \subseteq \mathsf{AD} \times \mathsf{CState}_\omega$

$$\equiv \{ \text{ relational calculus } \}$$
$$AD \lhd R \,{}_9^\circ\, CN \subseteq AN \,{}_9^\circ\, R \;\land\; \text{dom}(R \rhd CB) \subseteq AB \;\land\; \text{dom}(R \rhd CD) \subseteq AD$$

These derivations establish the following.

Theorem 11.1 (Forward simulation for process data types)
The relation R *between* AState *and* CState *is a forward simulation between the process data types* (AState, AInits, $\{AOp_i\}_{i \in I}$, AFin) *and* (CState, CInits, $\{COp_i\}_{i \in I}$, CFin), *iff*

$$CInits \subseteq \text{ran}(AInits \lhd R)$$
$$R \,{}_9^\circ\, CFin \subseteq AFin$$
$$(\text{dom } AFin) \lhd R = R \rhd (\text{dom } CFin)$$

and $\forall i : I$, *for* $AOp_i = (AN, AB, AD)$, $COp_i = (CN, CB, CD)$

$$AD \lhd R \,{}_9^\circ\, CN \subseteq AN \,{}_9^\circ\, R$$
$$\text{dom}(R \rhd CB) \subseteq AB$$
$$\text{dom}(R \rhd CD) \subseteq AD \qquad\qquad \square$$

The rules for initialisation and finalisation are identical to the usual rules. The three rules for operations are the expected generalisations. The first is "correctness", ensuring correct after-states, provided the abstract system does not diverge; in the blocking approach, this proviso is immaterial.

The second and third rules both relate to what is normally known as "applicability". When $(B, D) = (\varnothing, \overline{\text{dom } Op_i})$ (i.e., the non-blocking interpretation) the second is vacuously true and the third reduces to the usual $\text{ran}(\text{dom } AOp_i \lhd R) \subseteq \text{dom } COp_i$; in the opposite (blocking) case, the second reduces to the same familiar condition and the third is trivially true.

11.2.2 Backward Simulation for Process Data Types

Let (AState, AInits, $\{AOp_i\}_{i \in I}$, AFin) and (CState, CInits, $\{COp_i\}_{i \in I}$, CFin) be process data types, both with global state G, and T a candidate backward simulation relation between CState and AState, embedded as follows:

$$[\![T]\!] == T \cup \{(\bot, \bot)\} \cup \{\omega\} \times AState_\omega$$

Initialisation: A simple calculation shows that:

$$CInit \,{}_9^\circ\, [\![T]\!] \subseteq AInit \equiv \text{ran}(CInits \lhd T) \subseteq AInits$$

Finalisation: Similarly we find that:

$$[\![\mathsf{CFin}]\!] \subseteq [\![\mathsf{T}]\!] \,\mathbin{\S}\, [\![\mathsf{AFin}]\!]$$
$$\equiv \mathsf{CFin} \subseteq \mathsf{T} \,\mathbin{\S}\, \mathsf{AFin} \;\wedge\; \overline{\mathrm{dom}\,\mathsf{CFin}} \subseteq \mathrm{dom}(\mathsf{T} \mathbin{\rhd} \mathrm{dom}\,\mathsf{AFin})$$

This cannot be further simplified: the first conjunct implies that every finalisable concrete state is linked to *some* finalisable abstract state, and the second similarly links non-finalisable states. However, neither excludes a concrete state being linked to both finalisable and non-finalisable abstract states. Together they do imply totality of T on CState as usual.

Operations: For corresponding operations $\mathsf{AOp} = (\mathsf{AN}, \mathsf{AB}, \mathsf{AD})$ and $\mathsf{COp} = (\mathsf{CN}, \mathsf{CB}, \mathsf{CD})$, we have that

$$[\![\mathsf{COp}]\!] \,\mathbin{\S}\, [\![\mathsf{T}]\!] \subseteq [\![\mathsf{T}]\!] \,\mathbin{\S}\, [\![\mathsf{AOp}]\!]$$
$$\equiv \{\text{ calculus }\}$$
$$\mathrm{dom}(\mathsf{T} \mathbin{\rhd} \mathsf{AD}) \mathbin{\lhd} \mathsf{CN} \,\mathbin{\S}\, \mathsf{T} \subseteq \mathsf{T} \,\mathbin{\S}\, \mathsf{AN} \;\wedge\;$$
$$\mathsf{CB} \subseteq \mathrm{dom}(\mathsf{T} \mathbin{\rhd} \mathsf{AB}) \;\wedge\; \mathsf{CD} \subseteq \mathrm{dom}(\mathsf{T} \mathbin{\rhd} \mathsf{AD})$$

These derivations establish the following.

Theorem 11.2 (Backward simulation for process data types)
The relation T *between* CState *and* AState *is a backward simulation between the process data types* $(\mathsf{AState}, \mathsf{AInits}, \{\mathsf{AOp}_i\}_{i \in \mathsf{I}}, \mathsf{AFin})$ *and* $(\mathsf{CState}, \mathsf{CInits}, \{\mathsf{COp}_i\}_{i \in \mathsf{I}}, \mathsf{CFin})$, *iff*

$$\mathrm{ran}(\mathsf{CInits} \mathbin{\lhd} \mathsf{T}) \subseteq \mathsf{AInits}$$
$$\mathsf{CFin} \subseteq \mathsf{T} \,\mathbin{\S}\, \mathsf{AFin}$$
$$\overline{\mathrm{dom}\,\mathsf{CFin}} \subseteq \mathrm{dom}(\mathsf{T} \mathbin{\rhd} \mathrm{dom}\,\mathsf{AFin})$$

and $\forall\, i : \mathsf{I}$, *for* $\mathsf{AOp}_i = (\mathsf{AN}, \mathsf{AB}, \mathsf{AD})$, $\mathsf{COp}_i = (\mathsf{CN}, \mathsf{CB}, \mathsf{CD})$

$$\mathrm{dom}(\mathsf{T} \mathbin{\rhd} \mathsf{AD}) \mathbin{\lhd} \mathsf{CN} \,\mathbin{\S}\, \mathsf{T} \subseteq \mathsf{T} \,\mathbin{\S}\, \mathsf{AN}$$
$$\mathsf{CB} \subseteq \mathrm{dom}(\mathsf{T} \mathbin{\rhd} \mathsf{AB})$$
$$\mathsf{CD} \subseteq \mathrm{dom}(\mathsf{T} \mathbin{\rhd} \mathsf{AD}) \qquad\qquad\qquad\qquad\qquad \square$$

11.2.3 Simulations on Process Data Types and Basic Data Types

In order to transfer results derived for basic data types, in particular those whose reductions contain an embedding of outputs or refusals, one can compare the rules derived above for process data types with the usual definitions of simulations on total data types.

As the essential information added in constructing a process data type is attached to the operations only, we would expect the conditions on initialisation and finalisation to be identical, and indeed they are (modulo the differences introduced by process data types using initialisation sets rather than relations, and possible partiality of finalisation).

An important consequence of this is in adopting a refusal embedding: this only affects the correctness of finalisation, and so incurs the same extra simulation requirements on process data types as on total ones.

Of course this does require the refusal notion to be expressed in terms of triples (N, B, D), and the resulting requirement may still end up dominating some of the other conditions on operations.

11.3 Using Process Data Types – Failures-Divergences Refinement with Internal Operations and Divergence

We are now in a position to show how we can use process data types to derive simulation conditions for failures-divergences refinement with internal operations and the consequent presence of potential divergence. As expected there will be two versions of the simulation rules: the blocking and the non-blocking approaches, both deriving from the same process data type simulation rules. Having done this, we will then revisit these two approaches, adding outputs to the data types.

11.3.1 Embedding a Basic Data Type with Internal Operations into a Process Data Type

We assume that the basic data type is a refusal embedding – in the first instance in the blocking approach for the basic refusal relation characterised by

$$\forall s : State, E : \mathbb{P} I \bullet (s, E) \in Ref_{State} \equiv (\forall i : E \bullet s \notin dom Op_i)$$

As we are aiming to model also internal operations, we move towards τ-data types (Definition 5.5), i.e. ADTs which have an additional component τ which is the internal operations.

The presence of an internal operation in the τ-data type introduces a number of issues, some of which were briefly discussed in Chap. 5 already:

(a) a finite number of internal operations may take place before and after every operation;
(b) in some states, unbounded internal evolution may be enabled (livelock), making those states and the operations leading into those states divergent;
(c) initial states may also be divergent; if just one initial state is, all traces of the ADT are divergent;
(d) the CSP failures-divergences semantics (see Chap. 6) only observes refusals in stable states, i.e., where no internal evolution is possible. However, from the fact that traces involving unstable states are observable, enabledness of operations in such states may be observable; blocking in unstable states is more subtle, however. It also means that observing refusals at finalisation needs to be treated with care, in case the final state is not stable;
(e) although refusal of operations in unstable states is immaterial, the opposite, i.e., enabled operations in unstable states is *not*: we need to ensure that traces arising from operations being "momentarily" available in unstable states are included.

Notation We define the following auxiliary notations in order to deal with internal evolution. This includes notations for (maximal) finite internal evolution which are used to enhance the operations.

State$\downarrow$ denotes the set of stable states, i.e. those from which it is not possible to do an internal evolution. That is, $v \in$ State$\downarrow$ iff $v \notin \operatorname{dom} \tau$.

τ^* denotes finite internal evolution, defined as the least fixed point of $\lambda R \bullet$ $\operatorname{id}_{\text{State}} \cup \tau \,_9^o\, R$.

$\tau^{*|} == \tau^* \rhd (\operatorname{dom} \tau)$ denotes maximal finite internal evolution, leading to a stable state. Note that all unstable states either are divergent, or are linked by finite internal evolution to a non-empty set of stable states.

$\overset{\leftrightarrow}{\text{Op}} == \tau^* \,_9^o\, \text{Op} \,_9^o\, \tau^*$ represents an operation with internal evolution beforehand and afterwards. Note that $\operatorname{dom} \overset{\leftrightarrow}{\text{Op}} = \operatorname{dom}(\tau^* \,_9^o\, \text{Op})$ as $\operatorname{dom} \tau^* = $ State.

State$\uparrow$ denotes the set of "divergent" states from which unbounded internal evolution is possible. It is defined as the largest fixed point of $\lambda S. \operatorname{dom}(\tau \rhd S)$. If any initial states are in State$\uparrow$, the ADT as a whole is divergent.

$\underline{\tau} == (\text{State}\uparrow) \lhd \tau$ denotes "relevant" internal transitions, excluding those from states which are already divergent. As everything is possible after divergence, the presence of finite internal behaviour from such states is semantically insignificant. Note that $\underline{\tau}^* = \operatorname{id}_{\text{State}\uparrow} \cup (\text{State}\uparrow) \lhd \tau^*$.

liv Op   characterises all the states where the application of Op might be followed by unbounded internal evolution, and is defined by

$$\operatorname{liv} \text{Op} = \operatorname{dom}(\text{Op} \rhd \text{State}\uparrow)$$

Note that these are not generally states which are *themselves* divergent, but states from where Op might lead to divergent states.   □

Using these notations, we can construct embeddings of basic data types with an internal operation into process data types for the blocking and non-blocking approaches. This gives a semantics for these types, and we will later validate that, in combination with the right refusal embedding, this correctly encodes failures-divergences semantics.

Definition 11.6 (*Embeddings of internal operations into process data type*)
A basic data type with internal operation $(\mathsf{State}, \mathsf{Init}, \{\mathsf{Op}_i\}_{i \in I}, \tau, \mathsf{Fin})$ is embedded into the process data type $(\mathsf{State}, \widetilde{\mathsf{Init}}, \{\widetilde{\mathsf{Op}}_i\}_{i \in I}, \widetilde{\mathsf{Fin}})$ with

$$
\begin{aligned}
&\widetilde{\mathsf{Init}} == \mathrm{ran}(\mathsf{Init} \,\fatsemi\, \tau^*) \\
&\widetilde{\mathsf{Fin}} == \mathsf{State} \!\uparrow \lhd \tau^{*|} \,\fatsemi\, \mathsf{Fin} \\
&\widetilde{\mathsf{Op}}_i == (\mathrm{liv}\,\overset{\leftrightarrow}{\mathsf{Op}}_i \lhd \overset{\leftrightarrow}{\mathsf{Op}}_i, B_i, D_i)
\end{aligned}
$$

where in the blocking approach

$$
B_i == \overline{\mathrm{dom}\,\overset{\leftrightarrow}{\mathsf{Op}}_i} \qquad\qquad D_i == \mathrm{liv}\,\overset{\leftrightarrow}{\mathsf{Op}}_i
$$

and in the non-blocking approach

$$
B_i == \varnothing \qquad\qquad D_i == \mathrm{liv}\,\overset{\leftrightarrow}{\mathsf{Op}}_i \cup \overline{\mathrm{dom}\,\overset{\leftrightarrow}{\mathsf{Op}}_i} \qquad\qquad □
$$

This embedding solves most of the issues highlighted above in the following ways:

(a) Using $\overset{\leftrightarrow}{\mathsf{Op}}$ ensures finite internal evolution before and after every operation.
(b) By including $\mathrm{liv}\,\overset{\leftrightarrow}{\mathsf{Op}}$ in the divergence domain of an operation, we ensure that livelock becomes divergence.
(c) This encoding does *not* deal with divergent initial states. The process data type could be enhanced with a Boolean to represent initial divergence (and include ω in Inits whenever it is set), however, this pathological situation can more easily be singled out in the definition of refinement.
(d) There is an initial temptation to consider an embedding that includes internal operations after each operation and initialisation only – the need to include internal operations *before* derives from observing refusals and blocking (in the blocking approach) and divergence outside the precondition (in the non-blocking approach) in stable states only.
  In general, in the context of *stable* failures, treating an operation that is not enabled as one that has an artificial result ($\perp$) does not work across the board – it depends on whether τ is enabled in the same state or not.

The finalisation, additionally, is preceded by maximal finite internal evolution in order to avoid observing refusals in unstable states, and restricted to non-divergent states. Alternatively, we could restrict finalisation to stable states only. Note that a finalisation which observes refusals in the non-blocking case is quite different from the blocking case, as there are no refusals in the non-blocking approach unless outputs are taken into account.

(e) This is addressed by including finite, but *not* necessarily maximal internal behaviour after every operation (and initialisation) – i.e., not considering only the stable after-states.

The definition of refinement for basic data types with internal operations is given in terms of the embedding into process data types, with a small proviso to deal with divergent initial states.

Definition 11.7 (*Refinement with internal operations*)
Let $A = (\text{AState}, \text{AInit}, \{\text{AOp}_i\}_{i \in I}, \tau_A, \text{AFin})$ and $C = (\text{CState}, \text{CInit}, \{\text{COp}_i\}_{i \in I}, \tau_C, \text{CFin})$ be program controlled basic data types with internal operations. Then A is refined by C iff

- One of A's initial states is divergent: $(\text{ran AInit}) \cap \text{AState}{\uparrow} \neq \varnothing$, or
- None of C's initial states are divergent, i.e., $(\text{ran CInit}) \cap \text{CState}{\uparrow} = \varnothing$, and: refinement holds between the embeddings of A and C in their embeddings into process data types.   □

By separating out divergent initial states in this way, we can restrict our discussion of simulations to those cases where the process data type embedding correctly reflects the original specification in all respects.

11.3.2   Correctness of the Embedding: Blocking Approach

The correctness of the embedding becomes more complex with the increasing complexity of the embedding. So in general one has to prove that the embedding of internal operations into process data types, and through that into total data types, correctly reflects the failures-divergences semantics in the blocking approach.

In order to do so, we have to characterise formally the failures-divergences semantics of a τ-data type (ignoring its finalisation). We use the standard LTS notation to facilitate that (see also Chap. 1) with the additional convention that an omitted first state indicates an initial one:

$$\stackrel{s}{\Longrightarrow} x \ == \ \exists x' : \text{Inits} \bullet x' \stackrel{s}{\Longrightarrow} x$$

Failures and divergences are then defined in the usual way. Note that they would be different in the non-blocking approach, producing no refusals but divergences instead.

Definition 11.8 (*Failures-divergences semantics of τ-data type*)
For a τ-data types $\mathsf{T} = (\mathsf{State}, \mathsf{G} \times \mathsf{Inits}, \{\mathsf{Op_i}\}_{i \in I}, \tau, \mathsf{Fin})$ its divergences are

$$div(\mathsf{T}) == \{s : \mathsf{seq}\,\mathsf{I} \mid \exists s' : \mathsf{seq}\,\mathsf{I};\ x : \mathsf{State} \uparrow\ \bullet\ s' \leq s \wedge \overset{s'}{\Longrightarrow} x\}$$

and its failures $f(\mathsf{T})$ are

$$\{s : \mathsf{seq}\,\mathsf{I};\ E : \mathbb{P}\,\mathsf{I} \mid s \in div(\mathsf{T}) \vee (\exists x : \mathsf{State} \downarrow\ \bullet \overset{s}{\Longrightarrow} x \wedge \forall e : E \bullet x \overset{e}{\not\longmapsto}) \bullet (s, E)\} \qquad \square$$

The correctness of the embedding will be proved using the following two lemmas. Recall that we are working in a context where:

- T is defined as in Definition 11.8; and is program controlled, so $\mathsf{Init} \equiv \mathsf{G} \times \mathsf{ran}\,\mathsf{Init}$;
- we use the blocking interpretation of T;
- T observes refusals at finalisation;
- T is not initially divergent.

We have not defined failures and divergences at the level of process data types, and therefore we will have to prove the equivalence of refinement accounting for *two* levels of embedding. Recall that $\widetilde{x}$ is the embedding of x into process data types, and $[\![x]\!]$ is the embedding of x from process data types into basic data types.

Lemma 11.1 *For all programs* $p : \mathsf{seq}\,\mathsf{I}$, *we have that* $p \in div(\mathsf{T}) \equiv \omega \in \mathsf{ran}\,p_{[\![\widetilde{\mathsf{T}}]\!]}$. $\qquad \square$

Lemma 11.2 *For all programs* $p : \mathsf{seq}\,\mathsf{I}$ *and sets of events* $E : \mathbb{P}\,\mathsf{I}$ *such that* $p \notin div(\mathsf{T})$, *we have that* $(p, E) \in f(\mathsf{T}) \equiv E \in \mathsf{ran}\,p_{[\![\widetilde{\mathsf{T}}]\!]}$. $\qquad \square$

These two lemmas are sufficient to prove the following correctness theorem for the embedding.

Theorem 11.3 (Equivalence of failures-divergences and data refinement)
For two τ-data types A *and* C, *failures-divergences refinement holds iff data refinement holds between their embeddings.*

Proof By mutual implication. The proof that relational refinement implies failures-divergences refinement uses Lemma 11.1 for divergences, and Lemma 11.2 for failures. The reverse direction has as its demonstrandum

$$x \in \mathsf{ran}\,p_{[\![\widetilde{\mathsf{C}}]\!]} \Rightarrow x \in \mathsf{ran}\,p_{[\![\widetilde{\mathsf{A}}]\!]}$$

which is proved by case distinction on x ($\bot$, ω, no or a refusal E), assuming failures-divergences refinement and using the lemmas. $\qquad \square$

11.3.3   Simulations in the Blocking Approach

As failures-divergences refinement is correctly represented by relational refinement, we can instantiate simulation rules from Theorems 11.1 and 11.2 into simulation rules for τ-data types.

11.3.3.1   Forward Simulation

Instantiating Theorem 11.1 with the embedding of Definition 11.6 initially gives the following conditions.

$$\mathsf{CInit} \mathbin{\raise0.3ex\hbox{$\scriptstyle\circ$}\kern-0.2em\raise-0.3ex\hbox{$\scriptstyle\circ$}} \tau_C^* \subseteq \mathsf{AInit} \mathbin{\raise0.3ex\hbox{$\scriptstyle\circ$}\kern-0.2em\raise-0.3ex\hbox{$\scriptstyle\circ$}} \tau_A^* \mathbin{\raise0.3ex\hbox{$\scriptstyle\circ$}\kern-0.2em\raise-0.3ex\hbox{$\scriptstyle\circ$}} \mathsf{R} \tag{11.1}$$

$$\mathsf{R} \mathbin{\raise0.3ex\hbox{$\scriptstyle\circ$}\kern-0.2em\raise-0.3ex\hbox{$\scriptstyle\circ$}} \mathsf{CState}{\uparrow} \; \lhd \tau_C^{*|} \mathbin{\raise0.3ex\hbox{$\scriptstyle\circ$}\kern-0.2em\raise-0.3ex\hbox{$\scriptstyle\circ$}} \mathsf{CFin} \subseteq \mathsf{AState}{\uparrow} \; \lhd \tau_A^{*|} \mathbin{\raise0.3ex\hbox{$\scriptstyle\circ$}\kern-0.2em\raise-0.3ex\hbox{$\scriptstyle\circ$}} \mathsf{AFin} \tag{11.2}$$

$$(\mathsf{AState}{\uparrow} \; \lhd \mathsf{R}) = (\mathsf{R} \rhd \mathsf{CState}{\uparrow}) \tag{11.3}$$

and for matching operations AOp and COp:

$$(\mathrm{liv}\,\overset{\leftrightarrow}{\mathsf{AOp}} \lhd \mathsf{R} \rhd \mathrm{liv}\,\overset{\leftrightarrow}{\mathsf{COp}}) \mathbin{\raise0.3ex\hbox{$\scriptstyle\circ$}\kern-0.2em\raise-0.3ex\hbox{$\scriptstyle\circ$}} \overset{\leftrightarrow}{\mathsf{COp}} \subseteq \overset{\leftrightarrow}{\mathsf{AOp}} \mathbin{\raise0.3ex\hbox{$\scriptstyle\circ$}\kern-0.2em\raise-0.3ex\hbox{$\scriptstyle\circ$}} \mathsf{R} \tag{11.4}$$

$$\mathrm{dom}(\mathsf{R} \rhd \mathrm{liv}\,\overset{\leftrightarrow}{\mathsf{COp}}) \subseteq \mathrm{liv}\,\overset{\leftrightarrow}{\mathsf{AOp}} \tag{11.5}$$

$$\mathrm{ran}(\mathrm{dom}\,\overset{\leftrightarrow}{\mathsf{AOp}} \lhd \mathsf{R}) \subseteq \mathrm{dom}\,\overset{\leftrightarrow}{\mathsf{COp}} \tag{11.6}$$

In order to simplify these, in particular to take into account the particular nature of finalisation (observing refusals), we use the following theorem.

Theorem 11.4   (Forward simulation closed under $\underline{\tau}_C^*$)
If the relation $\mathsf{R} \subseteq \mathsf{AState} \times \mathsf{CState}$ *is a forward simulation between program controlled* τ-*data types* $\mathsf{A} = (\mathsf{AState}, \mathsf{AInit}, \{\mathsf{AOp}_i\}_{i\in I}, \tau_A, \mathsf{AFin})$ *and* $\mathsf{C} = (\mathsf{CState},$ $\mathsf{CInit}, \{\mathsf{COp}_i\}_{i\in I}, \tau_C, \mathsf{CFin})$ *then* $\mathsf{R} \mathbin{\raise0.3ex\hbox{$\scriptstyle\circ$}\kern-0.2em\raise-0.3ex\hbox{$\scriptstyle\circ$}} \underline{\tau}_C^*$ *is also a forward simulation between* A *and* C.   □

The relevance of the theorem is that we can, without loss of generality, restrict ourselves to retrieve relations R which satisfy $\mathsf{R} = \mathsf{R} \mathbin{\raise0.3ex\hbox{$\scriptstyle\circ$}\kern-0.2em\raise-0.3ex\hbox{$\scriptstyle\circ$}} \underline{\tau}_C^*$.

The initialisation condition (11.1) can then be simplified to $\mathsf{CInit} \subseteq \mathsf{AInit} \mathbin{\raise0.3ex\hbox{$\scriptstyle\circ$}\kern-0.2em\raise-0.3ex\hbox{$\scriptstyle\circ$}} \tau_A^* \mathbin{\raise0.3ex\hbox{$\scriptstyle\circ$}\kern-0.2em\raise-0.3ex\hbox{$\scriptstyle\circ$}} \mathsf{R}$. The "correctness" condition (11.4) can be simplified using the divergence condition (11.5) to

$$(\mathrm{liv}\,\overset{\leftrightarrow}{\mathsf{AOp}} \lhd \mathsf{R}) \mathbin{\raise0.3ex\hbox{$\scriptstyle\circ$}\kern-0.2em\raise-0.3ex\hbox{$\scriptstyle\circ$}} \overset{\leftrightarrow}{\mathsf{COp}} \subseteq \overset{\leftrightarrow}{\mathsf{AOp}} \mathbin{\raise0.3ex\hbox{$\scriptstyle\circ$}\kern-0.2em\raise-0.3ex\hbox{$\scriptstyle\circ$}} \mathsf{R}$$

The "finalisation" condition (11.2) is implied by the "blocking" condition (11.6) and finalisation applicability (11.3):

$$R \mathbin{\S} \text{CState} \uparrow \,\vartriangleleft\, \tau_C^{*|} \mathbin{\S} \text{CFin} \subseteq \text{AState} \uparrow \,\vartriangleleft\, \tau_A^{*|} \mathbin{\S} \text{AFin}$$

$\equiv \{ \text{ predicate calculus } \}$

$\forall a : \text{AState}; \ E : \mathbb{P}I; \ c, c' : \text{CState} \bullet$

$(a, c) \in R \wedge c \notin \text{CState} \uparrow \wedge (c, c') \in \tau_C^{*|} \wedge (c', E) \in \text{Ref}$

$\Rightarrow a \notin \text{AState} \uparrow \wedge \exists a' : \text{AState} \bullet (a, a') \in \tau_A^{*|} \wedge (a', E) \in \text{Ref}$

The simplifications are summarised in the following theorem.

Theorem 11.5 (Forward simulation for τ-data types)
The relation $R' \subseteq \text{AState} \times \text{CState}$ *is a forward simulation between program controlled τ-data types* $A = (\text{AState}, \text{AInit}, \{\text{AOp}_i\}_{i \in I}, \tau_A, \text{AFin})$ *and* $C = (\text{CState}, \text{CInit}, \{\text{COp}_i\}_{i \in I}, \tau_C, \text{CFin})$ *iff the following conditions hold for* $R == R' \mathbin{\S} \tau_C^*$:

$$\text{CInit} \subseteq \text{AInit} \mathbin{\S} \tau_A^* \mathbin{\S} R \tag{11.7}$$

$$(\text{AState} \uparrow \,\vartriangleleft\, R) = (R \,\vartriangleright\, \text{CState} \uparrow) \tag{11.8}$$

and for matching operations AOp *and* COp:

$$(\text{liv} \overset{\leftrightarrow}{\text{AOp}} \,\vartriangleleft\, R) \mathbin{\S} \overset{\leftrightarrow}{\text{COp}} \subseteq \overset{\leftrightarrow}{\text{AOp}} \mathbin{\S} R \tag{11.9}$$

$$\text{dom}(R \,\vartriangleright\, \text{liv} \overset{\leftrightarrow}{\text{COp}}) \subseteq \text{liv} \overset{\leftrightarrow}{\text{AOp}} \tag{11.10}$$

$$\text{ran}(\text{dom} \overset{\leftrightarrow}{\text{AOp}} \,\vartriangleleft\, R) \subseteq \text{dom} \overset{\leftrightarrow}{\text{COp}} \tag{11.11}$$

$\square$

For specifications in Z, embedded into relations in the usual way, this leads to the following conditions:

FS.Init.τ: $\forall CState' \bullet CInit \Rightarrow \exists AState' \bullet AInit \mathbin{\S} \tau_A^* \wedge R'$

FS.App.τ: $\forall CState; \ AState; \ i : I \bullet R \wedge \text{pre} \overset{\leftrightarrow}{AOp_i} \Rightarrow \text{pre} \overset{\leftrightarrow}{COp_i}$

FS.CorrBlock.τ:

$\forall i : I; \ AState; \ CState; \ CState' \bullet \neg \text{liv} \overset{\leftrightarrow}{AOp_i} \wedge R \wedge \overset{\leftrightarrow}{COp_i} \Rightarrow \exists AState' \bullet R' \wedge \overset{\leftrightarrow}{AOp_i}$

FS.DivStates: $\forall R \bullet AState \uparrow \Leftrightarrow CState \uparrow$

FS.DivOp: $\forall CState; \ AState; \ i : I \bullet R \wedge \text{liv} \overset{\leftrightarrow}{COp_i} \Rightarrow \text{liv} \overset{\leftrightarrow}{AOp_i}$

using the obvious Z versions of notions such as $\overset{\leftrightarrow}{Op}$ and liv Op, and assuming $R = R \mathbin{\S} \underline{\tau_C^*}$. Note, that in the absence of internal operations the first three conditions collapse to the corresponding conditions given in Sect. 10.4 above.

11.3.3.2   Backward Simulation

Instantiating Theorem 11.2 with the embedding of Definition 11.6 initially gives the following conditions.

$$\text{CInit} \, \S \, \tau_C^* \, \S \, T \subseteq \text{AInit} \, \S \, \tau_A^* \tag{11.12}$$

$$\text{CState} \uparrow \; \lhd \; \tau_C^{*|} \, \S \, \text{CFin} \subseteq T \, \S \, \text{AState} \uparrow \; \lhd \; \tau_A^{*|} \, \S \, \text{AFin} \tag{11.13}$$

$$\text{CState} \uparrow \; \subseteq \text{dom}(T \rhd \text{AState} \uparrow) \tag{11.14}$$

and for matching operations AOp and COp:

$$\text{dom}(T \rhd \text{liv} \overset{\leftrightarrow}{\text{AOp}}) \lhd (\text{liv} \overset{\leftrightarrow}{\text{COp}} \lhd \overset{\leftrightarrow}{\text{COp}}) \, \S \, T \subseteq T \, \S \, (\text{liv} \overset{\leftrightarrow}{\text{AOp}} \lhd \overset{\leftrightarrow}{\text{AOp}}) \tag{11.15}$$

$$\text{liv} \overset{\leftrightarrow}{\text{COp}} \subseteq \text{dom}(T \rhd \text{liv} \overset{\leftrightarrow}{\text{AOp}}) \tag{11.16}$$

$$\overline{\text{dom} \overset{\leftrightarrow}{\text{COp}}} \subseteq \text{dom}(T \rhd \text{dom} \overset{\leftrightarrow}{\text{AOp}}) \tag{11.17}$$

We can prove a stronger theorem about closure of simulation under internal evolution in this case:

Theorem 11.6 (Backward simulation closed under internal evolution)
If the relation $T \subseteq \text{CState} \times \text{AState}$ *is a backward simulation between program controlled τ-data types* $A = (\text{AState}, \text{AInit}, \{\text{AOp}_i\}_{i \in I}, \tau_A, \text{AFin})$ *and* $C = (\text{CState}, \text{CInit}, \{\text{COp}_i\}_{i \in I}, \tau_C, \text{CFin})$ *then* $\tau_C^* \, \S \, T \, \S \, \tau_A^*$ *is also a backward simulation between* A *and* C. □

The initialisation condition can be simplified using Theorem 11.6, clearly $\tau_C^* \, \S \, T = T$. Using totality of T and the blocking condition, the correctness condition can be simplified to remove two anti-restrictions.

In general, the conditions are not as clear-cut concerning divergent states as the forward simulation ones, where finalisation applicability ensures that the simulation links divergent states to divergent states only.

Here, the finalisation conditions merely ensure that every abstract divergent state is linked to a concrete one, and vice versa. The blocking condition (11.17) also requires divergent concrete states to be linked to abstract states allowing the same operations. This is clearly a requirement inherited from the relational refinement theory that is redundant and irrelevant due to the chaotic interpretation of divergence represented in our semantics. Thus, using a general semantic theorem we restrict condition (11.17) to non-divergent states only; however, in those states it is dominated by the finalisation correctness condition (11.13).

This is summarised, with some simplifications, in the following theorem.

Theorem 11.7 (Backward simulation for τ-data types)
The relation $T' \subseteq \text{CState} \times \text{AState}$ *is a backward simulation between program controlled τ-data types* $A = (\text{AState}, \text{AInit}, \{\text{AOp}_i\}_{i \in I}, \tau_A, \text{AFin})$ *and* $C = (\text{CState}, \text{CInit}, \{\text{COp}_i\}_{i \in I}, \tau_C, \text{CFin})$ *iff the following conditions hold for* $T == \tau_C^* \, \S \, T' \, \S \, \tau_A^*$:

$$\text{CInit} \, \S \, T \subseteq \text{AInit} \, \S \, \tau_A^* \tag{11.18}$$

$$\mathsf{CState}\!\uparrow\; \lhd\, \tau_C^{*|}\, \stackrel{\circ}{,}\mathsf{Ref}_C \subseteq (\mathsf{T} \lhd \mathsf{AState}\!\downarrow) \stackrel{\circ}{,}\mathsf{Ref}_A \tag{11.19}$$

$$\mathsf{CState}\!\uparrow\; \subseteq \mathrm{dom}(\mathsf{T} \rhd \mathsf{AState}\!\uparrow) \tag{11.20}$$

and for matching operations AOp *and* COp:

$$\mathrm{dom}(\mathsf{T} \rhd \mathrm{liv}\, \overset{\leftrightarrow}{\mathsf{AOp}}) \lhd \tau_C^*\, \stackrel{\circ}{,}\mathsf{COp}\, \stackrel{\circ}{,}\mathsf{T} \subseteq \mathsf{T}\, \stackrel{\circ}{,}\mathsf{AOp}\, \stackrel{\circ}{,}\tau_A^* \tag{11.21}$$

$$\mathrm{liv}\, \overset{\leftrightarrow}{\mathsf{COp}} \subseteq \mathrm{dom}(\mathsf{T} \rhd \mathrm{liv}\, \mathsf{AOp}) \tag{11.22}$$

$$\square$$

For specifications in Z, this leads to the following conditions.

BS.Init.τ: $\forall\, CState'$; $AState' \bullet T' \wedge CInit \Rightarrow AInit\, \stackrel{\circ}{,}\tau_A^*$

BS.CorrBlock.τ: $\forall\, i : I$; $CState$; $CState'$; $AState' \bullet$
$(\forall\, AState \bullet T \Rightarrow \neg \mathrm{liv}\, \overset{\leftrightarrow}{AOp_i}) \wedge COp_i \wedge T' \Rightarrow \exists\, AState \bullet T \wedge AOp_i\, \stackrel{\circ}{,}\tau_A^*$

BS.FinRef.τ: $\forall\, CState$; $CState' \mid \neg CState\!\uparrow\; \wedge\, \tau_C^* \wedge CState'\!\downarrow \bullet$
$\exists\, AState \bullet T \wedge AState\!\downarrow\; \wedge\, \forall\, i : I \bullet \mathrm{pre}\, AOp_i \Rightarrow (\mathrm{pre}\, COp_i)'$

BS.DivStates: $\forall\, CState \bullet CState\!\uparrow\; \Rightarrow \exists\, AState \bullet T \wedge AState\!\uparrow$

BS.DivOp: $\forall\, i : I$; $CState \bullet \mathrm{liv}\, \overset{\leftrightarrow}{COp_i} \Rightarrow \exists\, AState \bullet T \wedge \mathrm{liv}\, AOp_i$

Again note that in the absence of internal operations, these conditions collapse to those we derived earlier.

11.3.4 The Non-blocking Approach

Having considered refinement and simulation for data types with internal operations in the blocking approach, we now turn to the non-blocking approach, where, as before we are not yet considering outputs.

In that context, the semantics is considerably simpler: there are no refusals beyond those after divergence (the basic finalisation maps to a single global value representing a non-divergent run; its totalisation adds a representation of divergence). The embedding into process data types was already given above in Definition 11.6, the only difference being that an operation Op is embedded by $(\mathsf{B}, \mathsf{N}, \mathsf{D})$ where

$$\mathsf{B} == \varnothing \qquad\qquad \mathsf{D} == \mathrm{liv}\, \overset{\leftrightarrow}{\mathsf{Op}} \cup \overline{\mathrm{dom}\, \overset{\leftrightarrow}{\mathsf{Op}}}$$

As discussed above in this context failures-divergences refinement is equivalent to traces-divergences refinement. Moreover, the trace sets for all ADTs with the same alphabet are identical. We thus need to look at divergences only. For a definition of (non-blocking) failures-divergences semantics analogous to Definition 11.8, Lemma 11.1 holds and forms the essence of the correctness proof of this embedding.

11.3.4.1   Forward Simulation

We now extract the simulation rules for the non-blocking approach in a way similar to that in Sects. 11.3.3.1 and 11.3.3.2. Instantiating Theorem 11.1 with the embedding of Definition 11.6 initially gives:

$$\text{CInit} \,\mathbin{\raise0.4ex\hbox{$\scriptstyle\circ$}\kern-0.3em\lower0.4ex\hbox{$\scriptstyle\circ$}}\, \tau_C^* \subseteq \text{AInit} \,\mathbin{\raise0.4ex\hbox{$\scriptstyle\circ$}\kern-0.3em\lower0.4ex\hbox{$\scriptstyle\circ$}}\, \tau_A^* \,\mathbin{\raise0.4ex\hbox{$\scriptstyle\circ$}\kern-0.3em\lower0.4ex\hbox{$\scriptstyle\circ$}}\, R \tag{11.23}$$

$$R \,\mathbin{;}\, \text{CState} \uparrow \;\lhd\; \tau_C^{*|} \,\mathbin{;}\, \text{CFin} \subseteq \text{AState} \uparrow \;\lhd\; \tau_A^{*|} \,\mathbin{;}\, \text{AFin} \tag{11.24}$$

$$(\text{AState} \uparrow \;\lhd\; R) = (R \rhd \text{CState} \uparrow) \tag{11.25}$$

and for matching operations AOp and COp:

$$(\text{liv}\,\overleftrightarrow{\text{AOp}} \cup \overline{\text{dom}\,\overleftrightarrow{\text{AOp}}}) \lhd R \,\mathbin{;}\, (\text{liv}\,\overleftrightarrow{\text{COp}}) \lhd \overleftrightarrow{\text{COp}} \subseteq (\text{liv}\,\overleftrightarrow{\text{AOp}} \lhd \overleftrightarrow{\text{AOp}}) \,\mathbin{;}\, R \tag{11.26}$$

$$\text{dom}(R \rhd (\text{liv}\,\overleftrightarrow{\text{COp}} \cup \overline{\text{dom}\,\overleftrightarrow{\text{COp}}})) \subseteq \text{liv}\,\overleftrightarrow{\text{AOp}} \cup \overline{\text{dom}\,\overleftrightarrow{\text{AOp}}} \tag{11.27}$$

$$\text{dom}(R \rhd \varnothing) \subseteq \varnothing \tag{11.28}$$

These can be simplified, although there is no theorem analogous to Theorem 11.4 (simulations closed under τ) – this is due to the fact that properties such as

$$s \in \text{dom}\,\overleftrightarrow{\text{Op}} \wedge (s, s') \in \tau^* \Rightarrow s' \in \text{dom}\,\overleftrightarrow{\text{Op}}$$

do not hold in general. The finalisation condition (11.24) is implied by finalisation applicability (11.25) for the trivial finalisation. The blocking condition (11.28) is obviously satisfied. Two domain restrictions in (11.26) can be removed, one due to preservation of divergence in (11.27).

Taken altogether this establishes the following.

Theorem 11.8 (Forward simulation for τ-data types (non-blocking))
The relation $R \subseteq \text{AState} \times \text{CState}$ *is a forward simulation between program controlled τ-data types* $A = (\text{AState}, \text{AInit}, \{\text{AOp}_i\}_{i \in I}, \tau_A, \text{AFin})$ *and* $C = (\text{CState}, \text{CInit}, \{\text{COp}_i\}_{i \in I}, \tau_C, \text{CFin})$ *iff the following conditions hold:*

$$\text{CInit} \,\mathbin{;}\, \tau_C^* \subseteq \text{AInit} \,\mathbin{;}\, \tau_A^* \,\mathbin{;}\, R \tag{11.29}$$

$$(\text{AState} \uparrow \;\lhd\; R) = (R \rhd \text{CState} \uparrow) \tag{11.30}$$

and for matching operations AOp *and* COp:

$$(\text{liv}\,\overleftrightarrow{\text{AOp}} \cup \overline{\text{dom}\,\overleftrightarrow{\text{AOp}}}) \lhd R \,\mathbin{;}\, \overleftrightarrow{\text{COp}} \subseteq \overleftrightarrow{\text{AOp}} \,\mathbin{;}\, R \tag{11.31}$$

$$\text{dom}(R \rhd (\text{liv}\,\overleftrightarrow{\text{COp}} \cup \overline{\text{dom}\,\overleftrightarrow{\text{COp}}})) \subseteq \text{liv}\,\overleftrightarrow{\text{AOp}} \cup \overline{\text{dom}\,\overleftrightarrow{\text{AOp}}} \tag{11.32}$$

$\square$

For specifications in Z this leads to the following conditions:

FS.Init.$\tau\tau$: $\forall\, CState' \bullet CInit \,{}_9^\circ\, \tau_C^* \Rightarrow \exists\, AState' \bullet AInit \,{}_9^\circ\, \tau_A^* \wedge R'$

FS.AppDivOp:

$\forall\, CState;\ AState;\ i : I \bullet R \wedge \mathrm{pre}\, A\overset{\leftrightarrow}{Op}_i \wedge \neg\, \mathrm{liv}\, A\overset{\leftrightarrow}{Op}_i \Rightarrow \mathrm{pre}\, C\overset{\leftrightarrow}{Op}_i \wedge \neg\, \mathrm{liv}\, C\overset{\leftrightarrow}{Op}_i$

FS.CorrNonBlock.τ:

$\forall\, i : I;\ AState;\ \Delta CState \bullet \neg\, \mathrm{liv}\, A\overset{\leftrightarrow}{Op}_i \wedge \mathrm{pre}\, A\overset{\leftrightarrow}{Op}_i \wedge R \wedge C\overset{\leftrightarrow}{Op}_i \Rightarrow$

$$\exists\, AState' \bullet A\overset{\leftrightarrow}{Op}_i \wedge R'$$

FS.DivStates: $\forall\, AState;\ CState \mid R \bullet AState \uparrow\ \Leftrightarrow\ CState \uparrow$

11.3.4.2 Backward Simulation

Again instantiating the backward simulation theorem for process data types with the non-blocking embedding into process data types, we obtain the following, after some small simplifications.

Theorem 11.9 (Backward simulation for τ-data types (non-blocking))
The relation $\mathsf{T} \subseteq \mathsf{CState} \times \mathsf{AState}$ *is a backward simulation between program controlled τ-data types* $\mathsf{A} = (\mathsf{AState}, \mathsf{AInit}, \{\mathsf{AOp}_i\}_{i\in I}, \tau_A, \mathsf{AFin})$ *and* $\mathsf{C} = (\mathsf{CState},$ $\mathsf{CInit}, \{\mathsf{COp}_i\}_{i\in I}, \tau_C, \mathsf{CFin})$ *iff the following conditions hold:*

$$\mathsf{CInit} \,{}_9^\circ\, \tau_C^* \,{}_9^\circ\, \mathsf{T} \subseteq \mathsf{AInit} \,{}_9^\circ\, \tau_A^* \tag{11.33}$$

$$\overline{\mathsf{CState}\uparrow} \subseteq \mathrm{dom}(\mathsf{T} \rhd \mathsf{AState}\uparrow) \tag{11.34}$$

$$\mathsf{CState}\uparrow \subseteq \mathrm{dom}(\mathsf{T} \rhd \mathsf{AState}\uparrow) \tag{11.35}$$

and for matching operations AOp *and* COp, *using* $\mathrm{divOp} == \mathrm{liv}\,\overset{\leftrightarrow}{\mathsf{Op}} \cup \mathrm{dom}\,\overset{\leftrightarrow}{\mathsf{Op}}$:

$$\mathrm{dom}(\mathsf{T} \rhd \mathrm{divAOp}) \lhd \overset{\leftrightarrow}{\mathsf{COp}} \,{}_9^\circ\, \mathsf{T} \subseteq \mathsf{T} \,{}_9^\circ\, \overline{\overset{\leftrightarrow}{\mathsf{AOp}}} \tag{11.36}$$

$$\mathrm{divCOp} \subseteq \mathrm{dom}(\mathsf{T} \rhd \mathrm{divAOp}) \tag{11.37}$$

$$\square$$

For specifications in Z, this leads to the following conditions:

BS.Init.$\tau\tau$: $\forall\, CState';\ AState' \bullet CInit \,{}_9^\circ\, \tau_C^* \wedge T' \Rightarrow AInit \,{}_9^\circ\, \tau_A^*$
BS.AppDivOp: $\forall\, i : I;\ CState \bullet \mathrm{div} COp_i \Rightarrow \exists\, AState \bullet T \wedge \mathrm{div} AOp_i$
BS.CorrNonBlock.τ: $\forall\, i : I;\ \Delta CState;\ AState' \bullet$
$(\forall\, AState \bullet T \Rightarrow \neg\, \mathrm{div}\, AOp_i) \wedge C\overset{\leftrightarrow}{Op}_i \wedge T' \Rightarrow \exists\, AState \bullet T \wedge A\overset{\leftrightarrow}{Op}_i$
BS.DivStates: $\forall\, CState \mid CState\uparrow\ \bullet \exists\, AState \bullet T \wedge AState\uparrow$
BS.NonDivStates: $\forall\, CState \mid \neg CState\uparrow\ \bullet \exists\, AState \bullet T \wedge \neg AState\uparrow$

using the analogous definition of $\mathrm{div}Op$, etc.

The forward and backward simulation conditions derived in this section extend those discussed above by adding internal evolution. No additional conditions are necessary in order to achieve equivalence with failures-divergences refinement – that only becomes necessary when we add outputs to the model, which we do now for both blocking and non-blocking models.

11.4   Adding in a Consideration of Outputs

So far we have considered a simple model with no outputs, although even in this 'simple' model there is considerable complexity due to potential divergence. We now enhance these results by considering data types with outputs. There are two initial points to note about what follows:

- The addition of outputs as characterised in data types with output embeddings has a very localised effect on the refinement conditions. We discuss this in Sect. 11.4.1.
- The addition of outputs leads to refusals, even in the non-blocking approach, and even when outputs are deterministic; as a consequence more stringent simulation conditions derive from the finalisation observing refusals. This is discussed in Sects. 11.4.2 and 11.4.3.

11.4.1   Refinement Conditions for Output Embeddings

Embedding, for example, a Z state-and-operations specification with state *State* and output type *Output* into a relational framework normally involves the creation of what we have called an output embedding, where the global and local state contain an output sequence as well as the "real" state, see Definition 11.2.

Starting from the standard derivation of Z refinement rules it should be clear that the properties contained in Definition 11.2 suffice to derive refinement conditions which vary only in small details from those without outputs:

- the initialisation and finalisation applicability conditions are unaffected;
- all quantifications over after-states in the operation conditions, including in the definition of the precondition pre, are extended with the same quantification over the operation's output *Output*.

This result is obtained using a retrieve relation that is the identity on the output sequence – this is enforced by the particular finalisation which prevents change of output (type) in refinement.

Consider a process data type D, its reduction D_r and its embedding in total data types D_e, where D_r is an output embedding. First, clearly D_e is *not* an output embedding: Consider a process data typeits global state will be $(GB \times seq\ Output)_{\perp,\omega}$ when D_r has $GB \times seq\ Output$. However, the construction of D_e still guarantees (in both the blocking and non-blocking case) the crucial property: an operation's result is independent of previously produced outputs. A state (ls, os) being in the domain of an operation only depends on ls, due to the last condition of Definition 11.2, and thus ls alone determines whether an operation will block or diverge for that reason.

Some obvious restrictions on the internal operation τ are also required to ensure this. First, τ cannot produce outputs (as this would make its occurrence visible), and second, it must be independent of previous outputs just like normal operations (cf.

the last condition of Definition 11.2). So in the context of data types with outputs, we will also require:

$$((\mathsf{ls}, \mathsf{os}), (\mathsf{ls2}, \mathsf{os2})) \in \tau \Rightarrow \mathsf{os2} = \mathsf{os} \tag{11.38}$$

$$((\mathsf{ls}, \mathsf{os}), (\mathsf{ls2}, \mathsf{os})) \in \tau \Rightarrow ((\mathsf{ls}, \mathsf{os2}), (\mathsf{ls2}, \mathsf{os2})) \in \tau \tag{11.39}$$

This guarantees that the occurrence of livelock is independent of previous outputs, and thus the previous output sequence does not affect outcomes of operations in *any* of the three parts $(\mathsf{N}, \mathsf{B}, \mathsf{D})$ of an operation. Consequently, the derivations in the previous section can be adapted with minor modifications as previously.

From this point on, we will concentrate on deriving the Z rules (which are explicit about outputs) rather than the relational ones, taking the rules derived in the previous section as our basis. Note that the embedding of Z operations into relational ones ensures that conditions in Definition 11.2 and properties (11.38) and (11.39) are satisfied. Additional consequences from output refusals in finalisations will be outlined in the next subsections.

11.4.2 Outputs in the Blocking Approach

Recall that the inclusion of outputs changes the notion of an event – rather than just an index $i : I$, it now also includes an output value. Traces (including divergences) and refusal sets will have these events as their elements. Definition 10.2 provides two possible refusal finalisations in the blocking approach; here we only consider the *demonic* view of output, where the system is in charge of selecting an output value and consequently output values may be refused if alternative output values are possible. This is characterised by the predicate $Fcond(s, E)$ which is defined to be:

$$\forall (i, out) : E \bullet (\neg \exists Op_i \bullet \theta State = s \wedge \theta Output = out) \vee$$
$$(\exists Op_i \bullet \theta State = s \wedge \theta Output \neq out \wedge (i, \theta Output) \notin E)$$

The proof that the relational embedding using this finalisation correctly represent the failures-divergences semantics characterised by demonic output refusals proceeds similarly to the proof of Theorem 11.3.

For a forward simulation the initialisation conditions and conditions for operations remain unchanged from Sect. 11.3.3.1. Finalisation applicability is unchanged: we still finalise only in non-divergent states. What is also unchanged is that in any such state, we observe all possible refusals in all stable states reachable from it by (necessarily finite) internal evolution. Moreover, we can assume that the retrieve relation is closed under composition with $\underline{\tau}_C^*$ (Theorem 11.4). Using similar reasoning as for the corresponding condition in Sect. 11.3.3.1, we end up with the proof obligation:

$$\forall a : AState; \; c' : CState; \; E \bullet (a, c') \in R \land c' \in CState{\downarrow} \; \land Fcond(c', E)$$
$$\Rightarrow \exists a' : AState \bullet (a, a') \in \tau_A^{*|} \land Fcond(a', E)$$

Unlike in Sect. 11.3.3.1, this is *not* implied by the other conditions. This is clear from the following (counter) example.

Example 11.1 Consider the following two specifications, here written in Z:

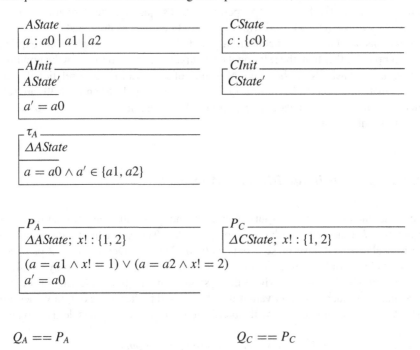

$$Q_A == P_A \qquad\qquad\qquad Q_C == P_C$$

The concrete data type can refuse $\{P!1, Q!2\}$ after the empty trace; this is not possible in the abstract data type. Thus, it is not a refinement, however, it satisfies all downward simulation conditions except the finalisation condition. $\square$

The link to a process algebraic semantics should be obvious when we realise that we can rewrite such an example in CSP as: $(p!1 \Box q!1) \sqcap (p!2 \Box q!2) \not\sqsubseteq (p!1 \sqcap p!2) \Box (q!1 \sqcap q!2)$.

The remaining finalisation condition looks cumbersome to check (quantifying over all sets of events that a concrete state might refuse); however two further simplifications are possible:

- only sets E that are maximal in the concrete state need to be considered; downward closedness of refusals in the linked abstract state then ensures that the property is also satisfied for subsets;

- only events refused because of the availability of alternative outputs need to be considered; operations whose precondition does not hold in the concrete state must be refused in any linked abstract state, due to the blocking condition.

Maximal refusals are most easily characterised by their complements, which select a single output value for each enabled operation (and refuse all other output values, whether possible or impossible), i.e., they are partial functions from I to $Output$. $Maxsim$ is a schema operation, in this case effectively a predicate on states, parameterised by such a partial function (and implicitly by the state schema).

$$Sim == I \nrightarrow Output$$
$$Maxsim(E) ==$$
$$\forall i : I \setminus \mathrm{dom}\, E \bullet \neg\, \mathrm{pre}\, Op_i$$
$$\wedge\, \forall i : \mathrm{dom}\, E \bullet \exists\, State';\; Output \bullet Op_i \wedge \theta Output = E(i)$$

Thus, in addition to the conditions from Sect. 11.3.3.1, we require here

FS.FinDemBlock.τ:

$$\forall AState;\; CState;\; E \mid R \wedge CState \downarrow \wedge Maxsim(E) \bullet$$
$$\exists AState' \bullet \tau_A^* \wedge AState' \downarrow \wedge \forall i : \mathrm{dom}\, E \bullet$$
$$(\exists (AOp_i)' \bullet \theta Output' = E(i)) \vee \neg\, \exists (AOp_i)'$$

where the consequent ensures that for each operation that is enabled in the concrete state, some stable abstract state connected by $R \,{}_9^\circ\, \tau_A^*$ either selects the same output, or disables the operation (leading to a superset of refusals in either case).

In Example 11.1, this condition fails on the maximal refusal set $\{P!1, Q!2\}$ represented by its complement $\{P!2, Q!1\}$. There is no abstract state which, for each of these events, either allows it or completely disallows the operation (P or Q).

In Sect. 10.4.1 we discussed how, in the blocking model with input/output, we needed the condition **BS.FinDem** to correctly link up refusal sets due to outputs. The example above has shown that, in the presence of internal operations, a similar extra condition is needed for downward simulations, and this we have called **FS.FinDemBlock.τ**.

For a backward simulation the reasoning here is similar to the corresponding case without outputs, and we get the following. Again, for a concrete non-divergent state c, we need to find a linked abstract state for each stable state c' reachable from c by internal evolution. However, as in this model such a state c' does not necessarily have a single maximal refusal set, we need to find a (possibly different) linked abstract state for each maximal refusal set in each such c'.

BS.FinDemBlock.τ:

$$\forall E : Sim;\; \Delta CState \mid \neg CState \uparrow \wedge \tau_C^* \wedge CState' \downarrow \wedge (Maxsim(E))' \bullet$$
$$\exists AState, F : Sim \bullet T \wedge AState \downarrow \wedge F \subseteq E \wedge Maxsim(F)$$

In the absence of internal operations this, of course, collapses to **BS.FinDem**.

11.4.3   Outputs in the Non-blocking Approach

In the non-blocking approach with demonic outputs, it may at first seem surprising that there are refusals (other than those after divergence), even in states where operations are not enabled.

However, we still expect output values to be determined "by the system", and thus output values will still be refused if other values are possible. Moreover, consider an operation that is not enabled (in a particular state), and thus leads to divergence. If none of the possible output values of that operation is refused, it also means that defining the operation to be enabled and have a particular output (or any choice of outputs) will not be a valid refinement, as it introduces new refusals.

Thus, where an operation is not enabled in a particular state, we will allow any set of output values to be refused, except for the full set. In particular, this means that an operation whose output is from a singleton set will produce no refusals. This is consistent with the view that having no output, or having an output from a singleton set are isomorphic.

The resulting definition of refusals is then given by modifying the predicate *Fcond* in Definition 10.2 as follows.

$$\mathsf{Fin} == \{State;\ os : \mathrm{seq}\ Output;\ E : \mathbb{P}(I \times Output) \mid Fcond \bullet$$
$$(os, \theta State) \mapsto (os, E)\}$$

where *Fcond* is

$$E \subseteq \{(i, out) \mid (\exists\, State';\ Output \bullet (\mathrm{pre}\ Op_i \Rightarrow Op_i) \wedge \theta Output \neq out \wedge (i, \theta Output) \notin E)\}$$

$$\tag{11.40}$$

Thus, the first disjunct from Definition 10.2 defining refusals when the operation is not applicable is dropped. The operation Op_i is replaced by (effectively a totalisation) $(\mathrm{pre}\ Op_i \Rightarrow Op_i)$ which allows an arbitrary result outside the precondition.

For a forward simulation, the example above also shows why the rules from Theorem 11.8 do not suffice in the case of demonic output refusals. It is not a refinement, but it satisfies all the conditions of Theorem 11.8. However, the finalisation condition fails.

Assuming the other conditions, the finalisation condition in this case reduces to

$$\forall\, a : AState;\ c, c' : CState;\ E \bullet$$
$$(a, c) \in R \wedge (c, c') \in \tau_C^* \wedge c \notin CState \uparrow\ \wedge c' \in CState \downarrow\ \wedge Fcond_{c'}$$
$$\Rightarrow \exists\, a' : AState \bullet (a, a') \in \tau_A^* \wedge a' \in AState \downarrow\ \wedge Fcond_{a'}$$

As usual, it suffices to consider only maximal refusal sets in particular states, and these can be represented by their complements. These now select an output for *every*

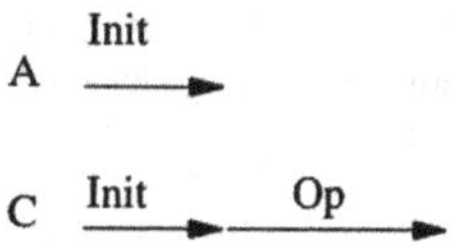

Fig. 11.2 Refusals in the
non-blocking model

operation (enabled or not), and thus they are *total* functions. This is characterised by:

$$Maxsimtot(E) \;==\; \operatorname{dom} E = I \wedge$$
$$\forall i : I \bullet \operatorname{pre} Op_i \Rightarrow \exists State';\; Output \bullet Op_i \wedge \theta Output = E(i)$$

This leads to the following refinement condition.

FS.FinDemNonBlock.τ:

$$\forall AState;\; E;\; CState;\; CState' \mid$$
$$R \wedge \neg CState \uparrow \wedge \tau_C^* \wedge CState' \downarrow \wedge (Maxsimtot(E))' \bullet$$
$$\exists AState' \bullet \tau_A^* \wedge AState' \downarrow \wedge (Maxsimtot(E))'$$

As E is a total function from I to $Output$, it necessarily also represents a maximal set of simultaneously enabled events in A.

For backward simulations we require the conditions given in Sect. 11.3.4.2 and, additionally, the conditions represented by the finalisation $CFin \subseteq T \,\fatsemi\, AFin$. This leads to the requirement that

$$\forall c, c' : CState;\; E \bullet c \notin CState \uparrow \wedge (c, c') \in \tau_C^* \wedge c' \in CState \downarrow \wedge Fcond_{c'}$$
$$\Rightarrow \exists a, a' : AState \bullet (c, a) \in T \wedge (a, a') \in \tau_A^* \wedge a' \in AState \downarrow \wedge Fcond_{a'}$$

where $Fcond$ is the predicate in (11.40) above. This can be rewritten as:

BS.FinDemNonBlock.τ:

$$\forall \Delta CState;\; E : Sim \mid \neg CState \uparrow \wedge \tau_C^* \wedge CState' \downarrow \wedge (Maxsimtot(E))' \bullet$$
$$\exists \Delta AState \bullet TAState' \downarrow \wedge \tau_S^* \wedge (Maxsimtot(E))'$$

In this non-blocking model, refusals arise solely from the presence of outputs, since the internal choice of an observable aspect means refusals can occur if the environment was only prepared to accept a different value. To understand the requirement, consider the following scenario, in a simpler context without any internal operations.

In the first there is just one operation in C without input or output, and none in A (see Fig. 11.2.). The non-blocking totalisation of A (given as a CSP process) is

$$Op \to \operatorname{div}$$

Fig. 11.3 Refusals in the
non-blocking model - with
outputs

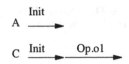

In the initial state, the refusals of A and C are thus the same (i.e., none). This is consistent with the construction of E and $Fcond$, since in both A and C we cannot find different output values occurring, thus $E = \varnothing$. The finalisation condition thus does not impose any further constraint on upward simulations in a model without input or output, since there are no refusals.

However, now consider a model with input and output. Consider A and C with one operation that can potentially output o_1 or o_2. Adapting the above example, we derive that in Fig. 11.3. The non-blocking totalisation of A now has an internal choice of possible output values

$$(Op.o_1 \rightarrow \text{div}) \sqcap (Op.o_2 \rightarrow \text{div})$$

Thus refusals of A after the empty trace are $\{Op.o_1\}$ and $\{Op.o_2\}$, whereas those of C are just $\{Op.o_2\}$.

The presence of non-determinism in the specification, together with refusals due to outputs complicates the finalisation requirement. In particular, if an operation has a non-deterministic output at a given state, this can, in a refinement, be transfered to non-determinism prior to the operation invocation. This means the subsetting of refusals can be split across different states. For example, in Fig. 11.4 the refusals initially in C are $\{Op.o_1\}$ and $\{Op.o_2\}$ but not $\{Op.o_1, Op.o_2\}$. The condition $\forall CState; E \bullet Fcond_C \Rightarrow \exists AState \bullet T \wedge Fcond_A$ allows the chosen $AState$ for $E = \{Op.o_1\}$ to be $s = 2$ but that for $E = \{Op.o_2\}$ to be $s = 1$.

Fig. 11.4 Non-determinism
and refusals inclusion

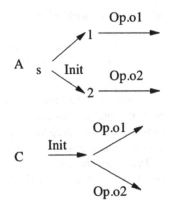

11.5 Summary

From simple beginnings we have ended up with quite considerable complexity. Some of this was due to dealing with internal actions, and the consequent possibility of divergence. But perhaps the surprise is the complexity added by consideration of outputs from a relational model, and how those played out in terms of divergence and refusals. Although the full-blown theory has all of this complexity, we should add that in the majority of cases one won't be dealing with both internal evolution and its divergence and subtle issues to do with outputs refusals at the same time, and that in many instances the rules outlined in Sect. 10.4 will suffice.

11.6 Bibliographical Notes

The work in this chapter presents the culmination of a succession of papers introducing the relational concurrent framework with increasing complexity. Reference [1] presented the basic relational model, which was followed by [2] which introduced process data types. Our coauthor on [2], Gerhard Schellhorn, formalised and checked the essential proofs in that paper, which are also the core of this chapter, in the KIV system [3]. The material in Chap. 9 was first discussed in [4]. Consideration of divergence was added in [5].

References

1. Derrick J, Boiten EA (2003) Relational concurrent refinement. Form Asp Comput 15(1):182–214
2. Boiten EA, Derrick J, Schellhorn G (2009) Relational concurrent refinement II: internal operations and outputs. Form Asp Comput 21(1–2):65–102
3. Schellhorn G (2006) Web presentation of the KIV proofs of 'Relational concurrent refinement Part II: internal operations and output'. http://www.informatik.uni-augsburg.de/swt/projects/Refinement/Web/CSPRef/. Accessed 15 June 2018
4. Derrick J, Boiten EA (2012) Relational concurrent refinement part III: traces, partial relations and automata. Formal aspects of computing 26:407–432
5. Boiten EA, Derrick J (2009) Modelling divergence in relational concurrent refinement. In Leuschel M, Wehrheim H (eds) IFM 2009: integrated formal methods. Lecture notes in computer science, vol 5423. Springer. pp 183–199

Chapter 12
Conclusions

The purpose of this book has been to explain the foundations for refinement in a variety of semantic models, and then see how these foundations are realised in some example specification languages. This has taken us on a tour through some different ways of looking at computation. So in Chap. 1 we discussed how labelled transition systems offer a convenient formalism to explore different refinement relations based upon different notions of observation. This was followed up by the introduction of Automata in Chap. 2, a model of computation closely related to labelled transition systems. One difference we introduced here was the presence of an internal event in automata that we didn't consider in Chap. 1.

Chapter 1 defined a number of different refinement relations. Chapter 2 built on the material from Chap. 1 by introducing a technique by which refinements can be verified, namely that of simulations, which play a central role in this book. We also introduced bisimulations, an important refinement relation from the literature, which although isn't central to the work in this book has an important place in some specific languages, e.g., such as CSP. Chapter 3 paved the way for looking at systems from the perspective of changing state, rather than concentrating on behavioural steps, and introduced a basic concrete relational semantics. Chapter 4 introduced a very different way of looking at computation, specifically using a relational model of abstract data types, and showing how refinement is derived in that model. Both an LTS model with internal events, and a relational model have the possibility to describe systems that can diverge - and how refinement relations treat divergence is an important factor in understanding them. Chapter 5 discusses these issues.

Part II of this book then looked at how these different facets are realised in different formal notations. This included process algebras in Chap. 6 where we introduced CSP, LOTOS and CCS. Chapter 7 introduced state-based notations Z and B, and then we subsequently discussed refinement in Event-B and ASM.

Part III of the book then attempts to draw some of these strands together. In particular, it is structured around answering the question: what is the relationship between the refinement relations introduced in Chaps. 1 and 2 and those in a relational or state-based model, as in Chap. 4. It does this under the heading of *relational concurrent refinement*, which broadly speaking means a relational model whereby

© Springer International Publishing AG, part of Springer Nature 2018
J. Derrick and E. Boiten, *Refinement*, https://doi.org/10.1007/978-3-319-92711-4_12

LTS models of refinement can be embedded. This allows a comparison to be made between the differing models. Chapter 9 sketched out the general landscape, followed by a more in depth look at data refinement and failures-divergences refinement in the subsequent chapter. The part ended with the introduction of a general model - process data types - capable of coding up divergence and blocking in a relational framework by which one could extract simulation rules for concurrent refinement relations.

There is, however, a wealth of material that we have not touched upon. This includes **semantic models** as well as specific formal notations. In terms of semantic models there is an extensive literature covering some of the models we have already introduced. For example, the monograph by de Roever and Engelhardt [1] covers the relational theory in more depth than we have had the opportunity here to.

An alternative semantic basis to the relational framework that underpins Z and other state-based notations is that of the **weakest precondition semantics**. Indeed, many of the results found in the relational setting have direct counterparts in the weakest precondition framework. This semantic basis has been used for a number of notations such as action systems [2–5]. In general predicate transformer semantics define the meaning of an imperative programming paradigm by assigning to each statement in the language a corresponding predicate transformer: a total function between two predicates on the state space of the statement. In fact we met a small portion of the weakest precondition semantics in the context of B in Chap. 7.

B and Z, etc are all examples of state-based languages. Additional state-based notations with well-defined theories of refinement include **VDM** and **Object-Z**. The Vienna Development Method (VDM) [6] is similar in many respects to Z (for a discussion of the differences see [7]), and was developed around the same time. Being a methodology, as opposed to a notation, there is a well-defined notion of refinement, which for VDM is the use of forward simulations restricted to total surjective functions (from concrete to abstract). The use of total surjective functions, along with the omission of backward simulations, of course, makes the method incomplete.

Examples of refinement in VDM are given in Jones and Shaw [8], Jones [6, 9], and Bicarregui [10]. Clement discusses the VDM approach to refinement in [11] and extensions to refinement in VDM are considered in [12].

Object-Z [13, 14] is an object-oriented extension to Z. Its semantics is described in [15, 16], and it is equipped with a refinement methodology based upon a relational semantics as discussed in Part I of this book. Refinement in Object-Z is discussed in [17, 18]. Integrations, and the associated theory of refinement, of Object-Z and process algebras are described in [18–23].

Another formal notation that is an integration of several methods is the **RAISE** notation [24]. RAISE stands for a *Rigorous Approach to Industrial Software Engineering*, and was developed as part of the European ESPRIT II LaCoS project in the 1990s. It consists of a set of tools designed for a specification language (*RSL*) for software development. RSL was inspired by and unifies features of several specification languages including VDM, CSP and ACT-ONE. RSL is often called a wide-spectrum language in the sense that it may be used to express high-level, abstract specifications, as well as low-level designs (e.g., using explicit imperative constructs such as loops). In addition to the specification notation, there is a RAISE method [25, 26] which includes stepwise development in a fashion similar to the use of simulations in this book.

Alloy [27] is another notation with well-developed tool support. It was influenced by Z, however, the syntax of Alloy owes more to languages such as Object Constraint Language. Tool support is provided by the *Alloy Analyser*, details are given at http://alloytools.org.

The particular specification notations we looked at in Part II of the book all provided methods by which to specify systems abstractly and then refine the abstract model. One aspect which we have not touched upon is the refinement of abstract models into code, and this is dealt with by the **refinement calculus**.

The refinement calculus [28, 29] is a notation that allows incremental refinement of specification statements into code. The semantics of the refinement calculus is based upon a weakest precondition semantics.

In the refinement calculus a specification statement is an abstract program which consists of a precondition, postcondition and a list of variables known as a frame. This is interpreted as describing an operation which begins in a state satisfying the precondition, ends in a state satisfying the postcondition, and which only changes variables in the frame.

The refinement calculus provides laws to introduce programming constructs into specification statements, allowing computational detail to be included in the description of the operation. There is an extensive literature on the refinement calculus and its use, see for example [30, 31].

Work that discusses how Z specifications can be integrated with the refinement calculus includes [32, 33]. Cavalcanti and Woodcock have defined the **ZRC** [34], a refinement calculus for Z. With Sampaio, they defined a language called **Circus** which includes the main elements of Z, CSP, and refinement calculus [35], grounded in Hoare and He's Unifying Theories of Programming [36].

There is also a relevant strand of work based upon temporal logic. This includes **TLA+** [37] (TLA standing for Temporal Logic of Actions). For example, Merz [38] discusses the refinement concepts underlying TLA+, and Hesselink [39] has studied the foundations of refinement in the TLA context.

In addition to approaches to refinement in different languages, there is a spectrum of different types of refinement. In this book we have largely considered conformal refinement of one action or operation by another, in a basic model that includes simple evolution of state.

However, as we have touched upon already, the assumption of conformality can be dropped and one can consider *action* or *non-atomic* refinement. Action refinement as defined in [40] allows the refinement of one operation (or action) into a complex process. It is usual for action refinement to be defined via an *operator* in the process algebra as opposed to a *relation* between specifications. As a consequence the majority of work has been into considering whether a semantic equivalence which is a congruence with respect to action refinement can be found [41–44].

There has also been limited work on non-atomic refinement in the state-based context [45]. In that approach an abstract operation AOp is always refined into a sequence of concrete operations, say $COp_1 \, {}^\circ_9 \, COp_2$. The simplest technique for treating such non-atomic refinements is to require that, apart from one, every concrete operation in the sequence refines $skip$ and that the remaining operation refines AOp. The use of coupled simulations, as described in [46], generalises that idea to allow arbitrary refinements even when the individual concrete operations do not refine $skip$. To do so they use a generalisation of data refinement called IO-refinement whereby the inputs and outputs of the abstract operation can be distributed across the concrete decomposition.

In [47] the relationship between notions of non-atomic refinement as defined in [46] with that in a behavioural setting is discussed. In particular, it is shown that the definition of non-atomic coupled downward simulation as defined in [46] is sound with respect to an action refinement definition of CSP failures refinement (the precise definition is given in [47]).

The models of computation we have considered in this book, and the associated refinement relations have not had an explicit representation of *time*. There is, of course, significant work on timed semantic models, and some work on timed refinement arising out of those models.

For example, in [48] the relational model we have used in this book is extended to include an explicit modelling of time. Using this simulations for relational embeddings of a number of refinement preorders found in timed process algebras are derived. Specifically, it considers the timed failure preorder defined in [48], which determines the refusals at the end of a trace, in a fashion similar to the definition of refusal sets for an untimed automata or the failures preorder in CSP.

In fact, this is in contrast to a number of failures models given for timed CSP, where refusals are determined throughout the trace rather than simply at the end. Thus these models are closer to a timed failure trace semantics as opposed to a timed failure semantics. The need to do this arises largely due to the treatment of internal events and, specifically, their urgency due to maximal progress under hiding. There are a number of variants of these models, perhaps reflecting the fact that the presence of time has some subtle interactions with the underlying process algebra. They include the infinite timed failures model discussed in [49, 50], which as the name suggests includes infinite traces in its semantics, as well as the timed failures-stability model of Reed and Roscoe [51]. A number of different models are developed in [51–53], and a hierarchy described in [54].

A final important generalisation of state-based and behavioural formalisms is to include a notion of *probability*, often but not always as a generalisation of non-determinism. Early work in this area included that by Jonsson and Larsen [55], where transitions are labeled by sets of allowed probabilities. Formal verification research for probabilistic formalisms in recent years has concentrated more on model checking (e.g. PRISM [56]). A comprehensive calculus for refinement, abstraction and proof that includes non-determinism alongside probability is given by McIver and Morgan [57].

References

1. de Roever W-P, Engelhardt K (1998) Data refinement: model-oriented proof methods and their comparison. CUP
2. Back RJR, Kurki-Suonio R (1988) Distributed cooperation with action systems. ACM Trans Program Lang Syst 10(4):513–554
3. Back RJR, von Wright J (1994) Trace refinement of action systems. In: Jonsson B, Parrow J (eds) CONCUR'94: concurrency theory. Lecture notes in computer science, vol 836. Springer, Sweden, pp 367–384
4. Back RJR, Sere K. From action systems to modular systems. In: Naftalin et al. [58], pp 1–25
5. Bonsangue M, Kok J, Sere K (1998) An approach to object-orientation in action systems. In: Jeuring J (ed) Mathematics of program construction (MPC'98). Lecture notes in computer science, vol 1422. Springer, Berlin, pp 68–95
6. Jones CB (1989) Systematic software development using VDM. Prentice Hall
7. Hayes IJ (1992) VDM and Z: a comparative case study. Form Asp Comput 4(1):76–99
8. Jones CB, Shaw RCF (eds) (1990) Case studies in systematic software development. Prentice Hall
9. Jones CB (1980) Software development: a rigorous approach. Prentice Hall
10. Bicarregui JC (ed) (1998) Proof in VDM: case studies. Springer, FACIT
11. Clement T. Comparing approaches to data reification. In: Naftalin et al. [58], pp 118–133
12. Elvang-Goransson M, Fields RE. An extended VDM refinement relation. In: Naftalin et al. [58], pp 175–189
13. Smith G (2000) The Object-Z specification language. Kluwer Academic Publishers
14. Duke R, Rose GA (2000) Formal object-oriented specification using Object-Z. Cornerstones of computing. Macmillan
15. Duke DJ, Duke R (1990) Towards a semantics for Object-Z. In: Bjorner D, Hoare CAR, Langmaack H (eds) VDM'90: VDM and Z! - formal methods in software development. Lecture notes in computer science, vol 428. Springer, Kiel, FRG, pp 244–261
16. Smith G (1995) A fully abstract semantics of classes for Object-Z. Form Asp Comput 7(3):289–313
17. Derrick J, Boiten EA (2014) Refinement in Z and Object-Z, 2nd edn. Springer, Berlin
18. Smith G, Derrick J (2001) Specification, refinement and verification of concurrent systems - an integration of Object-Z and CSP. Form Methods Syst Des 18:249–284
19. Smith G (1997) A semantic integration of Object-Z and CSP for the specification of concurrent systems. In: Fitzgerald J, Jones CB, Lucas P (eds) FME'97: Industrial Application and Strengthened Foundations of Formal Methods. Lecture notes in computer science, vol 1313. Springer, Berlin, pp 62–81
20. Mahony BP, Dong JS (1998) Blending Object-Z and timed CSP: an introduction to TCOZ. In: Futatsugi K, Kemmerer R, Torii K (eds) 20th international conference on software engineering (ICSE'98). IEEE Press
21. Smith G, Derrick J (2002) Abstract specification in Object-Z and CSP. In: George C, Miao H (eds) Formal methods and software engineering. Lecture notes in computer science, vol 2495. Springer, Berlin, pp 108–119
22. Derrick J, Smith G (2003) Structural refinement of systems specified in Object-Z and CSP. Form Asp Comput 15(1):1–27
23. Bolton C, Davies J (2002) Refinement in Object-Z and CSP. In: Butler M, Petre L, Sere K (eds) Integrated formal methods (IFM 2002). Lecture notes in computer science, vol 2335. Springer, Berlin, pp 225–244
24. The RAISE Language Group (1993) The RAISE specification language. Prentice-Hall Inc., USA
25. Nielsen M, Havelund K, Wagner KR, George C (1989) The RAISE language, method and tools. Form Asp Comput 1(1):85–114
26. The RAISE Development Method (1995) The RAISE specification language. Prentice-Hall Inc., USA

27. Jackson D (2016) Software abstractions: logic, language, and analysis. The MIT Press
28. Back RJR, Wright J (1998) Refinement calculus - a systematic introduction. Texts in computer science. Springer, Berlin
29. Morgan CC (1994) Programming from specifications, 2nd edn. Prentice hall international series in computer science
30. Back RJR (1989) A method for refining atomicity in parallel algorithms. PARLE'89 parallel architectures and languages europe. Lecture notes in computer science, vol 366. Springer, Berlin, pp 199–216
31. Back RJR (1990) Refinement calculus, part II: parallel and reactive programs. In: de Bakker JW, de Roever W-P, Rozenberg G (eds) Stepwise refinement of distributed systems. Lecture notes in computer science, vol 430. Springer, Berlin
32. Potter B, Sinclair J, Till D (1991) An introduction to formal specification and Z, 2nd edn. International series in computer science. Prentice Hall 1996
33. Woodcock JCP, Davies J (1996) Using Z: specification, refinement, and proof. Prentice Hall
34. Cavalcanti A, Woodcock JCP (1998) ZRC - a refinement calculus for Z. Form Asp Comput 10(3):267–289
35. Sampaio A, Woodcock JCP, Cavalcanti A (2002) Refinement in circus. In: Eriksson L-H, Lindsay PA (eds) FME. Lecture notes in computer science, vol 2391. Springer, Berlin, pp 451–470
36. Hoare CAR, He Jifeng (1998) Unifying theories of programming. Prentice Hall
37. Lamport L (2002) Specifying systems. Addison-Wesley, Boston
38. Merz S (2008) The specification language TLA$^+$. In: Bjørner D, Henson MC (eds) Logics of specification languages. Monographs in theoretical computer science. Springer, Berlin, pp 401–451
39. Hesselink WH (2005) Eternity variables to prove simulation of specifications. ACM Trans Comput Log 6(1):175–201
40. Aceto L (1992) Action refinement in process algebras. CUP, London
41. Aceto L, Hennessy M (1993) Towards action-refinement in process algebras. Inf Comput 103:204–269
42. Vogler W (1991) Failure semantics based on interval semiwords is a congruence for refinement. Distrib Comput 4:139–162
43. van Glabbeek R, Goltz U (1989) Equivalence notions for concurrent systems and refinement of actions. In: Kreczmar A, Mirkowska G (eds) Mathematical foundations of computer science 1989. LNCS, vol 379. Springer, Berlin, pp 237–248
44. Rensink A, Gorrieri R (1997) Action refinement as an implementation relation. In: Bidoit M, Dauchet M (eds) TAPSOFT '97: theory and practice of software development. Lecture notes in computer science, vol 1214, pp 772–786
45. Derrick J, Boiten EA (1999) Non-atomic refinement in Z. In: Woodcock J, Wing J (eds) FM'99, world congress on formal methods. Lecture notes in computer science, vol 1709. Springer, Berlin, pp 1477–1496
46. Derrick J, Wehrheim H. Using coupled simulations in non-atomic refinement. In: Bert et al. [59], pp 127–147
47. Derrick J, Wehrheim H. Non-atomic refinement in Z and CSP. In: Treharne et al. [60], pp 24–44
48. Derrick J, Boiten EA (2011) Relational concurrent refinement: timed refinement. In: Bruni R, Dingel J (eds) Formal techniques for distributed systems. Lecture notes in computer science, vol 6722. Springer, Heidelberg, pp 121–137
49. Schneider S (1999) Concurrent and real time systems: the CSP approach. Wiley, New York
50. Mislove MW, Roscoe AW, Schneider SA (1995) Fixed points without completeness. Theor Comput Sci 138(2):273–314
51. Reed GM, Roscoe AW (1999) The timed failures-stability model for CSP. Theor Comput Sci 211(1–2):85–127
52. Reed GM, Roscoe AW (1986) A timed model for communicating sequential processes. In: Kott L (ed) ICALP. Lecture notes in computer science, vol 226. Springer, Berlin, pp 314–323

53. Reed GM, Roscoe AW (1988) A timed model for communicating sequential processes. Theor Comput Sci 58(1–3):249–261
54. Reed GM (1988) A uniform mathematical theory for real-time distributed computing. Ph.D. thesis, Oxford University
55. Jonsson B, Larsen KG (1991) Specification and refinement of probabilistic processes. Proceedings of the sixth annual IEEE symposium on logic in computer science, pp 266–277
56. Kwiatkowska M, Norman G, Parker D (2011) PRISM 4.0: verification of probabilistic real-time systems. In: Gopalakrishnan G, Qadeer S (eds) Proceedings of the 23rd international conference on computer aided verification (CAV'11). Lecture notes in computer science. Springer, Berlin, vol 6806, pp 585–591
57. McIver A, Morgan CC (2005) Abstraction, refinement and proof for probabilistic systems. Springer, Berlin
58. Naftalin M, Denvir T, Bertran M (eds) (1994) Second international symposium of formal methods europe. FME'94: industrial benefit of formal methods. Lecture notes in computer science, vol 873. Springer, Berlin
59. Bert D, Bowen JP, King S, Waldén MA (eds) (2003) Third international conference of B and Z users. ZB 2003: formal specification and development in Z and B. Lecture notes in computer science, vol 2651. Springer, Berlin
60. Treharne H, King S, Henson MC, Schneider SA (eds) (2005) Proceedings of the 4th international conference of B and Z users. ZB 2005: formal specification and development in Z and B. Lecture notes in computer science, vol 3455. Springer, UK

Printed in the United States
By Bookmasters